The Air Pilot's **Manual**

Volume 3
Air Navigation

Trevor Thom

Revised & edited by
Peter D. Godwin

Airlife England

Copyright © 1987, 2001 Aviation Theory Centre

ISBN 1 84037 140 4

First edition published 1987
Second revised edition 1987
Reprinted 1988
Reprinted with amendments 1989, 1991, 1993 and 1994
Reprinted 1995
This third revised edition published 1997
Reprinted with amendments 1998
Fourth edition 1999
Reprinted with amendments 2000
Reprinted with amendments 2001
Reprinted with amendments 2002

Origination by Bookworks Ltd, Ireland.

Printed in England by Livesey Ltd, Shrewsbury, England.

A Technical Aviation Publications Ltd title
under licence by

Airlife Publishing Ltd

101 Longden Road, Shrewsbury SY3 9EB, Shropshire, England
Website: www.airlifebooks.com E-mail: airlife@airlifebooks.com

The Air Pilot's **Manual**

Volume 3

Contents

Section Four – En Route Navigation with Radio Navaids

Section Four covers the en route navigation requirements of the JAR-FCL syllabus. Refer to the notes on page 304. Section Four will not apply to the UK PPL training syllabus.

Appendix 1

Appendix 2

Exercises and Answers

Index

Editorial Team

Trevor Thom
A former Boeing 757 and 767 Captain with a European airline, Trevor has also flown the Airbus A320, Boeing 727, McDonnell Douglas DC-9 and Fokker F-27. He has been active in the International Federation of Airline Pilots' Associations (IFALPA), based in London, and was a member of the IFALPA Aeroplane Design and Operations Group. He also served as IFALPA representative to the Society of Automotive Engineers (SAE) S7 Flight-Deck Design Committee, a body which makes recommendations to the aviation industry, especially the manufacturers. Prior to his airline career Trevor was a Lecturer in Mathematics and Physics, and an Aviation Ground Instructor and Flying Instructor. He is a double degree graduate from the University of Melbourne and also holds a Diploma of Education.

Peter Godwin
Head of Training at Bonus Aviation, Cranfield (formerly Leavesden Flight Centre), Peter has amassed over 14,000 instructional flying hours as a fixed-wing and helicopter instructor. He has edited this series since 1995 and recently updated it to cover the JAR-FCL. As a member of the CAA Panel of Examiners, he is a CAA Flight Examiner for the Private Pilot's Licence (FEPPL[A]), Commercial Pilot's Licence (FECPL[A]), Flight Instructor Examiner (FIE[A]), as well as an Instrument Rating and Class Rating Examiner. A Fellow of the Royal Institute of Navigation (FRIN), Peter is currently training flying instructors and applicants for the Commercial Pilot's Licence and Instrument Rating. He has been Vice Chairman and subsequently Chairman of the Flight Training Committee on behalf of the General Aviation Manufacturers' and Traders' Association (GAMTA) since 1992 and is a regular lecturer at AOPA Flight Instructor seminars. In 1999 Peter was awarded the Pike Trophy by The Guild of Air Pilots and Air Navigators for his contribution to the maintenance of high standards of flying instruction and flight safety. Previously he was Chief Pilot for an air charter company and Chief Instructor for the Cabair group of companies based at Denham and Elstree.

Warren Yeates
Warren has been involved with editing, indexing, desktop publishing and printing Trevor Thom manuals since 1988 for UK, US and Australian markets. He currently runs a publishing services company in Ireland.

Graeme Carne
Graeme is a BAe 146 Captain with a dynamic and growing UK regional airline. He has been a Training Captain on the Shorts 360 and flew a King Air 200 for a private company. He learned to fly in Australia and has an extensive background as a flying instructor in the UK. He has also been involved in the introduction of JAR OPS procedures to his airline.

Robert Johnson

Bob produced the first two editions of this manual. His aviation experience includes flying a Cessna Citation II-SP executive jet, a DC-3 (Dakota) and light aircraft as Chief Pilot for an international university based in Switzerland, and seven years on Fokker F27, Lockheed Electra and McDonnell Douglas DC-9 airliners. Prior to this he was an Air Taxi Pilot and also gained technical experience as a Draughtsman on airborne mineral survey work in Australia.

Acknowledgements

The Civil Aviation Authority; ICAO; Cessna, Piper, and Gulfstream American for technical material; Airtour International Ltd, John Fenton, Brian Harbit, Jim Hitchcock, Edward Pape, Ron Smith, Capt. R. W. K. Snell (CAA Flight Examiner [ret.]), Martin Watts; and the many other instructors and students whose comments have helped to improve this manual.

Introduction

Volume 3 of *The Air Pilot's Manual – Air Navigation* – presents this important area of training for the Private Pilot's Licence in a logical sequence of theory, preparation and performance.

The Cockpit is a Difficult Environment in which to Learn

As with the other volumes of *The Air Pilot's Manual,* in *Air Navigation* we have avoided the presentation of 'facts only'. A thorough understanding of the principles will enable you to gain maximum benefit from your actual navigation exercise flights.

This approach will enable you to become a competent pilot/navigator and will also help to minimise your flight training hours. (It does, however, mean that our book is a little longer than it could be if the aim was only to cram in facts without a reasonable understanding.)

In determining the order in which the information is presented, care has been taken to keep things as logical and practical as possible. Consequently, in the first section – *Basic Navigation Theory* – the simpler, more practical topics of *Speed, Direction* and *Using the Navigation Computer* come first to give you the feel of practical operations, before some more involved subjects: *Vertical Navigation, The Earth,* and *Aeronautical Charts.*

Understanding makes for remembering.

Operational Decisions

Navigation of an aeroplane consists mainly of making common sense operational decisions. These decisions are based on knowledge and experience. Very few are difficult to make – most being logical and simple – but occasionally there are difficult decisions (both on the ground and in flight) to be made. These are the ones we must prepare for.

We have adopted a professional approach right from the start, whether your ultimate aim is to be a private pilot or to go on and make aviation your career.

Operational decisions will often have to be taken well away from your home base, and to a large extent you will be on your own. They fall into two categories:

■ **those made on the ground** during pre-flight planning; and

■ **in-flight operational decisions.**

Many decisions are so simple and 'second nature' that you don't realise you are making them. Others require a calm, cool but quick assessment, followed by a decision and action. Proceeding into an area of poor visibility could fall into this category.

The aeroplane will not stand still while you decide what to do in difficult in-flight situations. You cannot just pull over to the side of the road and study your maps. Good pre-flight planning, with many operational decisions taken on the ground – and alternative courses of action considered in the event of in-flight problems occurring – takes a lot of pressure off the pilot/navigator.

The Navigation Computer

As a pilot/navigator you will become adept at estimating angles, distances, time intervals, fuel consumption, and so on. The art of estimating is an important skill to develop. It is also important that you can calculate these various quantities easily and accurately. To achieve this you will use a navigation computer. It is a simple device (looks complicated but isn't) that allows us to carry out almost every navigation calculation with speed and accuracy.

Electronic navigation computers are available but we suggest you steer away from them, at least initially, because they do not encourage the pilot/navigator to visualise each situation – an important ability to develop. Once you are adept at the various computing problems involved in air navigation you might decide to 'go electronic'.

The basic concept of the slide navigation computer dates back to early navigation days. The modern version is an essential piece of equipment for a pilot/navigator.

The slide navigation computer has two sides:
- **a wind side,** which enables solution of *triangle of velocities* problems for flight-planning and en route navigation; and
- **a calculator side** (the main component of which is a circular slide-rule on the outer scales), used to perform the simple arithmetical calculations involved in flight operations, e.g. distance, speed and time; conversion of units; fuel quantities and consumption; true airspeed.

Two chapters in the first section describe using the navigation computer – one chapter for each side. Although it may appear a little complicated at first, working through the examples and illustrations we have set out will make using the computer logical and simple.

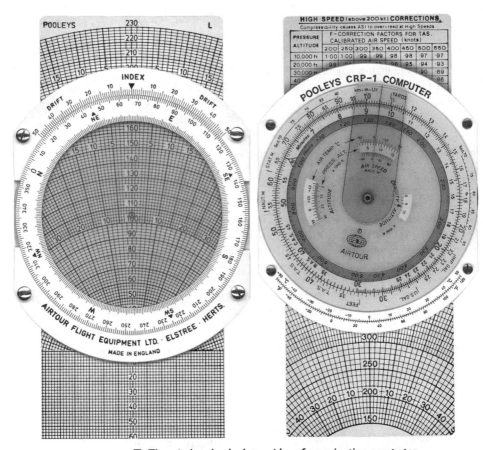

■ *The wind and calculator sides of a navigation computer*

The Theory Examination

Navigation is part of one of the theory examinations for the UK Private Pilot's Licence (PPL), which you will sit at your flying school. Prior to this you should be achieving considerable success in completing the **Exercises** at the back of the book. They are mentioned at the relevant places in each chapter, and in this volume some chapters have exercises interspersed through the text to give you practice on a particular aspect of the chapter before moving on.

The Exercises form an important part of the course and we recommend that you work through them carefully.

This manual is more than just a text to allow you to pass the examination, though this is one of its aims. It is designed to remain as a reference text on your shelf for as long as you fly.

In places we have included more information than is required for the Air Navigation examination section. For example,

Appendix 2 shows you how to plan a climb – something which, although not required of you in the PPL examination, will enable you to plan longer, higher altitude flights in the future.

The Enroute Navigation Section (PPL(A) Skill Test)

This is the province of your flying instructor. The test is carried out at the completion of your flying training and is part of the PPL(A) Skill Test (although with the agreement of your examiner it may be flown as a separate section.) It is designed to assess your ability as a pilot/navigator. This manual, and your navigation cross-country training, will prepare you fully for the Navigation element of the PPL(A) Skill Test.

The JAR-FCL (Joint Aviation Regulations Flight Crew Licence)

Note that while this edition covers the new European JAR-FCL, it still covers the existing UK PPL training syllabus. Students who began their training before 30 June 1999 under the UK syllabus have until 30 June 2002 to complete it under that syllabus. Students beginning their training after 30 June 1999 must follow the new JAR-FCL syllabus. Section Four of this manual applies only to the JAR-FCL. Refer also to the notes on page 304.

Operational Information

For safe flight operations it is essential that all pilots refer to current operational information. This basically involves using latest issues of aeronautical charts, and amended flight information publications, circulars and NOTAMs (Notices to Airmen).

In the UK, the primary source of operational information is the UK Aeronautical Information Publication (AIP), a large, frequently amended manual produced to an international standard by the Civil Aviation Authority. Your flying school and Air Traffic Services (ATS) units should have amended copies of the UK AIP available for reference.

As the AIP is a formidable and bulky set of documents for a PPL holder (because the majority covers airline-type instrument flight procedures), there is also available a conveniently sized publication known as *Pooley's Flight Guide,* which is revised regularly.

You will find references to both *Pooley's Flight Guide* and the UK AIP throughout *The Air Pilot's Manual.* Note that these references are no substitute for referring to current, amended documents.

If you are ever in any doubt about operational information, in *Pooley's Flight Guide* or the UK AIP, refer to an amended copy of the AIP and current air legislation documents; and **always** check the latest AIRACs (which detail AIP updates), AIP Supplements and Aeronautical Information Circulars (AICs) and NOTAMs prior to flight.

Section **One**

Basic Navigation Theory

The Pilot/Navigator

Air Navigation

All air navigation involves basic principles that apply to all aeroplanes, from the simplest trainer to the most sophisticated passenger jets. These basic principles are discussed in this manual.

Since *The Air Pilot's Manual* is a training programme for the Private Pilot's Licence (PPL), we will concentrate on accurate navigation of a light aircraft, flown by a single pilot, in visual conditions.

PPL holders, when flying cross-country, act as pilot, navigator and radio operator. They must:

☐ **primarily fly the aeroplane** safely and accurately;
☐ **navigate correctly;**
☐ **operate the radio** and attend to other duties in the cockpit.

In short, they must 'aviate, navigate and communicate'.

To conduct a cross-country flight efficiently, navigation tasks must be coordinated with (and not interfere with) the smooth flying of the aeroplane. It is most important that the pilot/navigator clearly understands the basic principles underlying navigation so that correct techniques and practices can be applied quickly and accurately without causing distraction or apprehension.

Prepare Soundly

Sound preparation is the basis for a confident navigation exercise.

Being properly prepared prior to a cross-country flight is essential if it is to be successful. Always flight plan meticulously. This establishes an accurate base against which you can measure your in-flight navigation performance.

Pre-flight consideration should be given to navigation items such as:

☐ the **serviceability** of your watch or aircraft clock – time is vital to accurate navigation;
☐ the **contents** of your 'nav bag' – pencils, navigation computer, protractor and scale (or a plotter), suitable maps and charts, and relevant flight information publications;
☐ the **preparation** of the appropriate maps and charts;
☐ the **desired route;**
☐ the **terrain en route;**
☐ the **airspace en route** (uncontrolled, controlled, special rules, advisory etc.);
☐ the **suitability** of the destination and any alternate aerodromes;
☐ the **forecast weather en route** and at the destination and alternate aerodromes (plus any actual reports that are available);

▢ **the calculation** of accurate headings and groundspeeds;
▢ **consideration** of fuel consumption, and accurate fuel planning.

It sounds like a lot, but each item considered individually is simple to understand. After considering them one by one in separate chapters, we will put them all together and see how they fit into a normal cross-country flight.

In Flight, Fly Accurate Headings

Once the aeroplane is in flight, flying a reasonably accurate heading (which involves reference to both the heading indicator and outside cues) is essential if the aeroplane is to track towards the desired destination. Maintaining cruise airspeed, and comparing your progress and times of arrival at various fixes with those estimated at the flight-planning stage, will normally ensure a pleasant and drama-free journey.

Navigation Tasks are Additional to Flying the Aeroplane

Our objective in this volume of *The Air Pilot's Manual* is to show you navigation techniques that will not increase your workload in the cockpit to an unacceptable degree, but will still allow time to fix your position and navigate the aeroplane safely to your desired destination.

We make the assumption that you already know how to fly the aeroplane; the idea here is to add to these flying skills the basic principles of air navigation. Other aspects that have a bearing on the conduct of a cross-country flight are covered in their own sections (for instance, airspace, radio procedures and meteorology in Vol. 2).

The Earth

All navigation is done with reference to the surface of the earth – starting from the elementary exercise of 'navigating' the aeroplane around the circuit during your initial training (which requires visual reference to ground features such as the runway and points ahead of the aeroplane for tracking) and progressing to the large passenger jets using sophisticated instrument navigation techniques to cover vast distances around the earth.

Direction on Earth

Direction is the angular position of one point to another without reference to the distance between them. It is expressed as the angular difference from a specified reference direction. In air navigation this reference direction is either:
▢ **north** (for *true* or *magnetic* bearings); or
▢ **the heading** (or the nose) of the aircraft (for *relative bearings*).

The simplest means of describing direction is to consider a circle laid flat and then divided into 360 units, called degrees (°). These units are numbered clockwise from 000 in the reference direction all the way around the circle to 360.

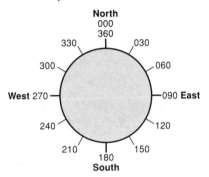

■ *Figure 1-1* **To measure direction, a circle is divided into 360 degrees (°)**

It is usual to refer to direction as a three-figure group to prevent any misunderstanding in the transmission of messages. For example, north is referred to as 360. East is referred to as 090, southwest as 225.

Position on Earth

The main method of specifying the position of a place on the surface of the earth is the *latitude* and *longitude* system. This involves covering the surface of a reduced earth with an evenly spaced *graticule* of lines – north–south lines joining the North and South Poles, and east–west lines parallel with the equator. The north–south lines are known as **meridians of longitude** and the east–west lines are called **parallels of latitude**.

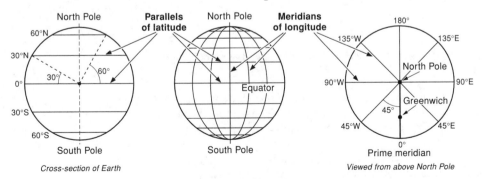

■ *Figure 1-2* **Position on earth is usually specified with reference to meridians of longitude and parallels of latitude**

The position of any place on the surface of the earth can be then specified with reference to the equator and a *datum* (or prime) meridian of longitude. The universal base longitude used throughout the world – **longitude 0°** – is the meridian drawn (north–south) through Greenwich, near London, known as the **prime meridian.**

Distance on Earth

The separation of two points on earth is called **distance** and is expressed as the length of the shortest line joining them.

> The standard unit of distance in navigation is the **nautical mile (nm).**
> 1 nm = 1,852 metres (1.852 km).

The nautical mile is related to the size of the earth in that it is the length of 1 minute of latitude. It is slightly longer than the familiar statute mile; 1 nautical mile (nm) measures 6,076 ft compared to 5,280 ft in the statute mile (sm).

> 1 nautical mile equals
> 1 minute of latitude.

One minute of latitude is measured down the side of a chart, i.e. along a meridian of longitude, which is a **great circle.** A great circle is one whose centre lies at the centre of the earth. All meridians of longitude and the equator are great circles. Thus 1 minute of arc of any great circle will be 1 nautical mile. This is explained in more detail in Chapter 8, *The Earth.*

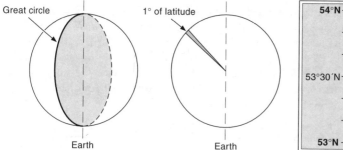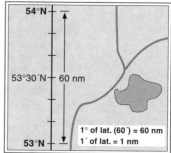

■ *Figure 1-3* **A great circle, and 1° of latitude on the earth and on a chart**

There are 360 degrees in a circle and each degree has 60 minutes, i.e. a circle has (360 × 60) = 21,600 minutes – which makes the circumference of the earth approximately 21,600 nautical miles.

If an aeroplane travels 1 nautical mile through an air mass, we refer to this as 1 **air nautical mile (anm).** As well as the aeroplane moving through the air mass, the air mass will be moving across the ground (in the form of a 'blowing' wind) and will carry the aeroplane along with it. The wind velocity adds an extra effect to the passage of the aeroplane over the ground. If an aeroplane travels 1 nautical mile over ground or water, we refer to this as 1 **ground nautical mile (gnm)**.

NOTE While navigation distances are measured in nautical miles, other shorter horizontal distances, such as runway length or horizontal distance from cloud, may be referred to in metres.

In air navigation we are concerned not only with *horizontal navigation* but also with *vertical navigation* (see Chapter 6). The traditional and standard unit for vertical distance, or height, is the foot (ft).

Speed

Speed is the rate at which distance is covered; in other words, speed is distance per unit time.

> The standard unit for speed is the **knot (kt)**.
> 1 knot =1 nautical mile per hour.

Direction and Speed Combined

An aeroplane flies in the medium of air. Its motion relative to the air mass is specified by its:

☐ direction (known as **heading**); and
☐ speed through the air mass (**true airspeed**).

HEADING (HDG). When flown in balance (as it normally is) the aeroplane will travel *through* the air in the direction in which it is heading. If the aeroplane is headed east (090), then its passage relative to the air mass will be easterly (090) also.

TRUE AIRSPEED (TAS). This is the actual speed of the aeroplane *relative* to the air mass. True airspeed is normally abbreviated to TAS, but occasionally to V when used in aerodynamic formulae. (See *Principles of Flight* in Vol. 4 of *The Air Pilot's Manual*.)

When considered together, HDG/TAS constitute a **vector** quantity, which requires both *magnitude* (in this case TAS) and *direction* (here HDG) to be completely specified. HDG/TAS is the velocity (direction and speed) of the aeroplane through the air.

> The **HDG/TAS** vector fully describes the motion of the aeroplane relative to the air mass.

HDG/TAS is symbolised by a single-headed arrow ——————▷———— ; the direction of the arrow indicates the direction of movement along the vector line.

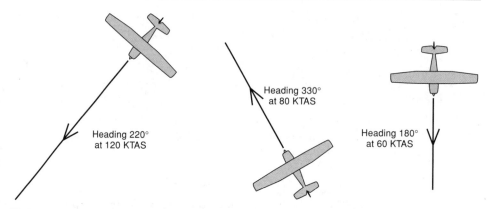

■ Figure 1-4 **Examples of the HDG/TAS vector**

An Air Mass can Move Relative to the Ground (a Wind can 'Blow')

The general movement of air relative to the ground is called **wind velocity** and is abbreviated to **W/V**. Like HDG/TAS, W/V is a vector quantity because both direction and magnitude are specified.

By convention, the wind direction is expressed as the direction *from* which it is blowing. For example, a northerly wind blows from the north towards the south. W/V is symbolised by a triple-headed arrow ──≫── .

> The **W/V** vector fully describes the horizontal motion of the air mass relative to the earth's surface.

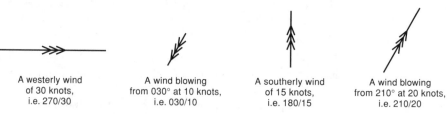

■ Figure 1-5 **Examples of the wind vector**

With a W/V of 230/20, the air mass will be moving relative to the earth's surface from a direction of 230° at a rate of 20 nautical miles per hour.

In a 6 minute period, for example, the air mass will have moved 2 nm (6 minute = ¹⁄₁₀ hour; ¹⁄₁₀ of 20 nm = 2 nm) from a direction of 230°, and therefore towards (230 − 180) = 050°.

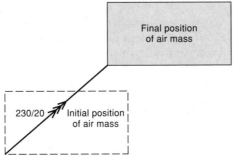

■ Figure 1-6 **A wind of 230/20**

The motion of the aeroplane relative to the surface of the earth is made up of two velocities:

- **the aeroplane** moving relative to the air mass (HDG/TAS); and
- **the air mass** moving relative to the surface of the earth (W/V).

Adding these two together gives the resultant vector of:

- **the aeroplane** moving relative to the surface of the earth. This is the track and groundspeed (TR/GS), which is symbolised by a double-headed arrow ———⟩⟩— .

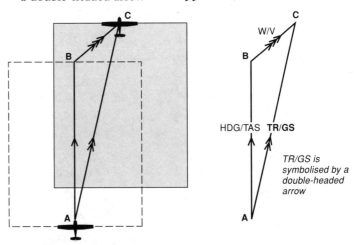

■ Figure 1-7 **HDG/TAS + W/V = TR/GS**

An aeroplane flying through an air mass is in a similar situation to you swimming across a fast flowing river. If you dive in at A and head off through the water in the direction of B, the current will carry you downstream towards C. To an observer sitting overhead in the branch of a tree, you will appear to be swimming a little bit 'sideways' as you get swept downstream, even though in fact you are swimming straight through the water.

In the same way, it is common to look up and see an aeroplane flying somewhat 'sideways' in strong wind situations. Of course the aeroplane is not actually flying sideways through the air, rather it is flying straight ahead relative to the air mass (HDG/TAS). It is wind velocity (W/V) which, when added to the aeroplane's motion through the air (HDG/TAS), gives it the resultant motion over the ground (track/groundspeed).

To fly from A to C in the above situation, the pilot must fly on a HDG of A–B through the air, i.e. maintain the nose of the aeroplane in a direction parallel to A–B. The wind will have the effect of B–C. The combined effect of these, known as the resultant, will give the aeroplane a track over the ground of A–C.

> The **TR/GS** vector fully describes the motion of the aeroplane relative to the earth's surface.

The Triangle of Velocities

The two velocities:

☐ **HDG/TAS:** the aeroplane moving through the air mass; and

☐ **W/V:** the air mass moving over the ground;

when added together as vectors, give the resultant:

☐ **TR/GS (track/groundspeed)** – the aeroplane moving over the ground.

These three vectors form the **triangle of velocities.** It is a pictorial representation of the vector addition:

HDG/TAS + W/V = TR/GS

i.e. the combined effect of HDG/TAS plus W/V will give the resultant TR/GS (Figure 1-8).

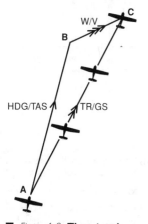

■ Figure 1-8 **The triangle of velocities**

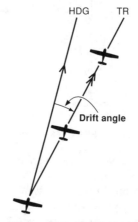

■ Figure 1-9 **Drift is the angle between heading and track**

We add the two vectors for HDG/TAS and W/V 'head to tail', i.e. starting from A, the head of the HDG/TAS vector at B is the starting point for the tail of the W/V vector which then ends up at C.

The resultant effect of the two combined is the TR/GS vector starting at A and finishing at C. This is the path that the aeroplane would fly over the ground. The angle between the HDG and the track (TR) is called the **drift angle** (Figure 1-9).

You may have already seen this triangle of velocities illustrated on a navigation computer, as in Figure 1-10.

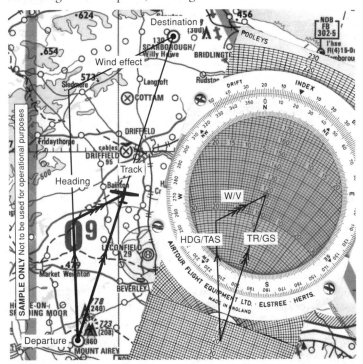

■ *Figure 1-10* **The triangle of velocities laid on the wind side of a navigation computer**

Do not be put off by the apparently complicated appearance of the navigation computer. It is a marvellous device designed to make navigation tasks easier. Chapter 4 describes using the wind side of the computer in detail, so it will become quite clear.

At the flight planning stage:
- ☐ **you will know the desired track** (track required); and
- ☐ **will obtain a forecast wind velocity.**

Using the known true airspeed, you will be able to calculate:

☐ **the heading required** to 'make good' the desired track; and
☐ **the expected groundspeed.**

Later on during the flight you may find that, even though you have flown the HDG/TAS accurately, your actual **track made good (TMG)** over the ground differs from your desired track; in other words there is a **track error.** It is most likely to be caused by the actual wind being different from the forecast wind that you used at the flight planning stage. You will then have to make some adjustments to the HDG to carry out the navigation task of rejoining your desired track and continuing to the destination.

This is what air navigation is all about. The essential principles are simple and have now been covered. All we have to do is expand on them in the following chapters and combine them into practical navigation operations.

Summary of Terminology

HDG/TAS: Heading (HDG) is the actual heading of the aeroplane in degrees steered by the pilot. It may be related to true north, magnetic north or compass north.

True airspeed (TAS) is the actual speed of the aeroplane through the air. It will differ significantly from the airspeed indicated on the airspeed indicator (the indicated airspeed) due to the air being less dense the higher the aeroplane flies. The pilot will need to complete a small calculation to convert indicated airspeed (IAS) to true airspeed (TAS) when flying at altitude.

The normal unit for airspeed is the knot. IAS is useful for aerodynamics, but TAS is necessary for navigation. The normal unit of distance for navigation is the nautical mile (nm) and if it is distance relative to the air, we call it an air nautical mile (anm).

TR/GS: Track (TR) is the path of the aeroplane over the surface of the earth, and is usually expressed in degrees true or magnetic.

Groundspeed (GS) is the actual speed of the aeroplane over the ground and is measured in knots. A GS of 120 kt means that 120 ground nautical miles would be covered in 1 hour at that GS.

DRIFT is the difference between the HDG steered by the pilot and the track of the aeroplane over the ground. The wind blows the aeroplane from its HDG/TAS through the air onto its TR/GS over the earth's surface.

Drift is measured from the HDG (the nose of the aeroplane) to the TR, and is specified in degrees left (port) of HDG or right (starboard) of HDG.

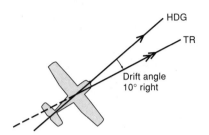

■ *Figure 1-11* **Drift is the angle between heading and track**

W/V: **Wind direction** is expressed in degrees *true* or *magnetic* and is the direction *from* which the wind is blowing. **Wind speed** is measured in knots (kt). 1 kt = 1 nm per hour.

TRACK ERROR: The actual **track made good** (TMG) over the ground will often differ from the *desired track*. The angular difference between the desired track and the TMG is called **track error** and is specified in degrees left (port) or right (starboard) of the desired track.

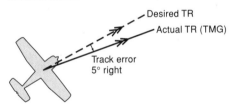

■ *Figure 1-12* **Track error is the angle between desired track and the track made good (TMG)**

NOTE Track error is a totally different thing to *drift*.

LATITUDE: The distance of a place north or south from the equator, measured in degrees.

LONGITUDE: The distance of a place from the prime meridian (0°), through Greenwich, also measured in degrees.

NAUTICAL MILE: The length of 1 minute of latitude measured along a meridian, i.e. down the side of a chart.

KNOT: Unit of speed equal to 1 nautical mile per hour.

GREAT CIRCLE: Intersection of the earth's surface and a plane passing through the earth's centre.

Now complete **Exercises 1 – The Pilot/Navigator.**

Exercises and Answers are at the back of the book.

Speed

Airspeed

A sound understanding of the factors involved in *airspeed* is important if you are to become a competent pilot/navigator. The **true airspeed (TAS)** of an aircraft is its rate of progress or speed through the air mass in which it is flying. Whether the air mass is moving over the ground or is stationary is irrelevant to the true airspeed. TAS is simply the speed of the aircraft through the air.

In contrast, a hot-air balloon or a cloud has no horizontal driving force of its own and so just hangs in the air. This means the TAS of a balloon or a cloud is zero because it is not moving *relative* to the air mass.

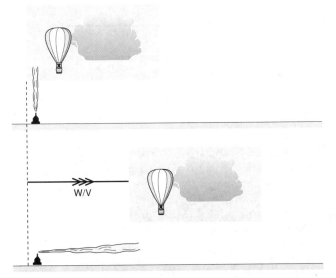

■ *Figure 2-1* **An air mass can be stationary or move as wind**

If the air mass is moving relative to the ground (i.e. the wind velocity is other than zero), then the balloon or cloud will be carried by the air mass across the ground. Being static in the air mass, the balloon or the cloud could theoretically be used as a point against which to measure the true airspeed (TAS) of an aircraft. In other words, an aircraft will fly past a balloon, or a cloud, at its true airspeed.

The actual speed of an aircraft relative to the ground is called the **groundspeed (GS)**. The resultant groundspeed is a combination of:

☐ **the true airspeed** (TAS – the movement of the aircraft relative to the air mass); and

☐ **the wind velocity** (W/V – the movement of the air mass relative to the ground).

This is familiar from the 'triangle of velocities' in Chapter 1.

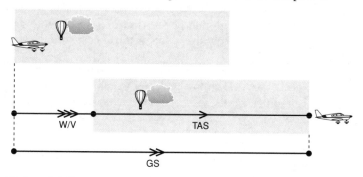

■ *Figure 2-2* **The groundspeed is the resultant of the true airspeed (TAS) and the wind velocity (W/V)**

At this stage we are only interested in airspeed – the speed of the aircraft through the air. (Groundspeed comes later in the book.)

The International Standard Atmosphere (ISA)

A *standard atmosphere* has been defined as a 'measuring stick' against which we can compare the actual atmosphere that exists at a given place on a given day. The standard atmosphere has:

☐ **A standard mean sea level (MSL) pressure** of 1013.25 millibars (mb), which decreases by about 1 mb for each 30 ft of altitude gained. For practical purposes, we use 1013 mb.

☐ **A standard MSL temperature** of + 15°C, which decreases by about 2°C for each 1,000 ft of altitude gained.

☐ **The ISA MSL air density** is 1,225 gm/cubic metre, and this also decreases as altitude is gained.

NOTE The **hectopascal (hPa),** a new standard unit of pressure for aviation, equivalent to millibars, has been adopted in many countries. Because 1 mb = 1 hPa, only the name change is significant. The UK plans to use *millibars* for the foreseeable future, but you will see hPa in the Republic of Ireland and on the Continent. To remind you, we will occasionally show pressure as mb (hPa).

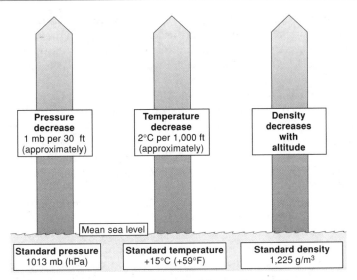

■ Figure 2-3 **The International Standard Atmosphere (ISA)**

Speed Measurement

To measure the speed of an aircraft is a little more complicated than you might expect. The basic instrument used is the **airspeed indicator (ASI)** which is a pressure-operated instrument. The air-speed displayed is given the logical name **indicated airspeed (IAS).**

Due to the nature of the atmosphere – in which air pressure and air density decrease with altitude – and the design of the air-speed indicator, the indicated airspeed (IAS) is usually *less* than the true airspeed (TAS).

■ Figure 2-4 **Airspeed indicator with a TAS correction scale**

The indicated airspeed shown on the airspeed indicator in the cockpit and the true airspeed of the aeroplane through the air will only be the same value when International Standard Atmosphere mean sea level (ISA MSL) conditions exist. Such conditions are usually not experienced.

In conditions other than ISA MSL, pilots must make simple calculations (either mentally or by navigation computer) to convert the IAS they read on the airspeed indicator to the TAS needed for navigation.

The fact that the word *airspeed* has a number of meanings in aviation may be confusing at first but you must understand the differences.

☐ **Performance** of the aeroplane is related to **indicated airspeed (IAS)** (i.e. whether the plane will stall or not, its rate of climb performance, lift/drag ratio etc.), and is a function of IAS. Indicated airspeed is related to dynamic pressure.

☐ **Navigation and flight planning** depend on **true airspeed (TAS), wind velocity (W/V)** and **groundspeed (GS)**. True airspeed is the actual speed of the aeroplane through the air.

To understand the difference between the two basic airspeeds: indicated airspeed (IAS), and true airspeed (TAS), we need to consider briefly certain properties of the atmosphere and the principles of fluid flow.

Static Pressure

Static pressure at any point in the atmosphere is exerted equally in all directions. It is a result of the weight of all the molecules composing the air above that point. At this very moment, static pressure of the atmosphere is being exerted at all points on the skin of your hand.

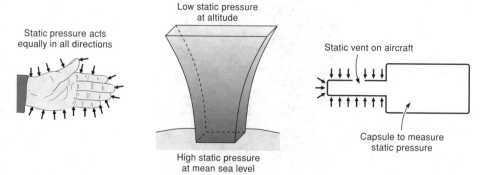

Low static pressure at altitude

Static pressure acts equally in all directions

Static vent on aircraft

Capsule to measure static pressure

High static pressure at mean sea level

■ Figure 2-5 **Static pressure**

As its name implies, static pressure does not involve any motion of the body relative to the air.

Dynamic Pressure

If you hold your hand up in a strong wind or out of the window of a moving car, then an extra wind pressure, or 'moving pressure', is felt due to the air striking your hand.

This extra pressure, over and above the static pressure which is always present, is called **dynamic pressure,** or pressure due to relative movement. It is felt by a body that is moving relative to the air, i.e. it could be moving through the air, or the air could be flowing past it.

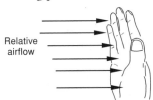

■ Figure 2-6 **Dynamic pressure**

Just how strong dynamic pressure is depends on a number of things, the two main ones being:

1. **The speed of the body relative to the air.** The faster the car drives or the faster the wind blows, then the stronger the extra dynamic pressure that you feel on your hand. This is because of the greater number of air molecules that strike it per second.

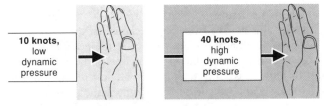

■ Figure 2-7 **Dynamic pressure increases with airspeed**

2. **The density of the air.** In outer space, no matter how fast you travelled, you would not feel any dynamic pressure because there are practically no molecules to strike you. In contrast, at sea level, where the atmosphere is densest, your hand would be struck by many molecules per second – certainly many more than in the upper regions of the atmosphere. Even though you might be travelling at the same speed, you will feel a much lower dynamic pressure in the higher levels of the atmosphere, where the air is less dense, than in the lower levels.

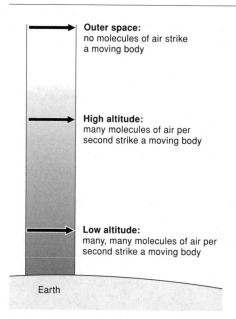

Outer space:
no molecules of air strike
a moving body

High altitude:
many molecules of air per
second strike a moving body

Low altitude:
many, many molecules of air per
second strike a moving body

Earth

■ Figure 2-8 **Air density decreases with altitude**

So, for an aircraft moving at a constant true airspeed, less dynamic pressure is experienced the higher the altitude. The actual measure of dynamic pressure is written:

Dynamic pressure $= \frac{1}{2} \times$ *rho* $\times$ *V-squared*

☐ *rho* represents air density, which decreases with altitude.
☐ V represents the speed of the body relative to the air, i.e. the true airspeed. (It does not matter whether the body is moving through the air, or the air blowing past the body, or a combination of both – as long as they are moving relative to one another there will be an airspeed and a dynamic pressure.)

Total Pressure

In the atmosphere some static pressure is always exerted, but only if there is motion of the body relative to the air will any dynamic pressure (due to relative motion) be felt by the surface exposed to the airflow. Thus:

Total pressure consists of static pressure plus dynamic pressure.

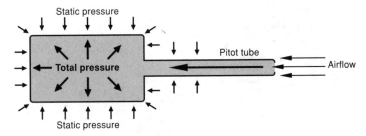

Static pressure

Pitot tube

Airflow

Total pressure

Static pressure

■ Figure 2-9 **Total pressure is measured by a pitot tube**

Much of this theory about pressure was developed by the Swiss scientist Daniel Bernoulli, and is expressed in Bernoulli's equation, which, in simplified form, is:

Static pressure	+	**Dynamic pressure**	=	**Total pressure**
measured by static line		$\frac{1}{2}$ rho × V-squared		measured by
(barometer or altimeter)				pitot tube

An expression for dynamic pressure can be obtained by subtracting the term static pressure from both sides of this equation:

Dynamic pressure = total pressure − static pressure

Indicated Airspeed (IAS)

A measure of dynamic pressure can be found by starting with the total (pitot) pressure, and subtracting the static pressure from it. This is done using a diaphragm with total pressure from the pitot tube fed onto one side, and static pressure from the static line fed onto the other side.

The diaphragm in the airspeed indicator (ASI) system positions itself according to the difference between the total pressure and the static pressure, i.e. according to the dynamic pressure. A pointer connected to the diaphragm through a gearing mechanism then moves around the ASI scale as the diaphragm responds to these pressure variations.

If we assume that the density of air (*rho*) remains constant at its mean sea level value (which it does not), the scale around which the pointer moves can be graduated in units of speed. This results in an airspeed indicator that displays the airspeed accurately only under ISA MSL conditions, i.e. when the air density is 1,225 grams per cubic metre (the same as at + 15°C, pressure altitude zero).

If the air density (*rho*) is precisely 1,225 gm/cubic metre, then the airspeed indicator will show an indicated airspeed that is the same as the true airspeed of the aeroplane through the air.

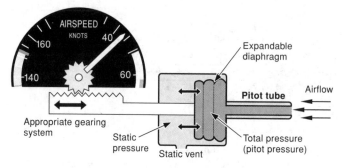

■ *Figure 2-10* **The flexible diaphragm in the airspeed indicator drives the pointer to display indicated airspeed (IAS)**

NOTE Airspeed indicators are usually calibrated in knots but you may see indicators graduated in statute miles per hour, the familiar mph.

> *Indicated airspeed (IAS) is what we read on the airspeed indicator (ASI).*

Rectified Airspeed (RAS)

A particular pitot-static system and its cockpit airspeed indicator (ASI) will experience some small errors. The main two are:

1. **Instrument error** – resulting from poor design and construction of the ASI itself, or from friction within it.

2. **Position error** – resulting from sensing errors inherent in the position on the aircraft of the static vent and the pitot tube. Their position with respect to the airflow is critical and may lead to somewhat incorrect readings when the airflow pattern is disturbed at certain airspeeds, angles of attack, or wing flap settings.

The pilot can correct the reading of indicated airspeed shown on the ASI by using a calibration table (found in the Pilot's Operating Handbook for the aeroplane) to obtain a value known as **rectified airspeed (RAS)** or **calibrated airspeed (CAS)**.

NOTE Rectified airspeed is the term commonly used in the United Kingdom, whereas calibrated airspeed is used in the United States of America, many European countries, Australia and New Zealand. Navigation computers may be labelled with either RAS or CAS, or both.

The calculated RAS figure is what the ASI would read if the particular airspeed indicator system was perfect. RAS is therefore more accurate than IAS and, if you have taken the trouble to calculate RAS, it should be used in preference to IAS in navigation calculations.

The instrument and position errors of an airspeed indicator system are usually no more than a few knots and, for our purposes at PPL level, we can generally assume that indicated airspeed (IAS) and rectified airspeed (RAS) are equal. To remind you we will occasionally write IAS (RAS).

Now complete **Exercises 2, Speed – 1.**

Relating True Airspeed to Indicated Airspeed

The aeroplane will rarely be flying in an air mass that has the same density as that under ISA MSL conditions (1,225 gm/cubic metre), the basis of the calibration of the airspeed indicator. Generally an aeroplane flying at altitude will be experiencing an air density significantly less than this, because air density *(rho)* decreases with altitude. This will also be the case when there is an increase in temperature.

The indicated airspeed (even if it has been corrected for instrument and position errors to give rectified airspeed) will need to be further corrected for **density error** if the pilot is to know the exact speed at which the aeroplane is moving through the air – the true airspeed.

Whereas the position and instrument error (if any) will be different for each ASI system, the density error applies equally to all systems because it is a function of the atmospheric conditions at that time and place.

Air density varies for two main reasons:

1. Temperature. Cold air is dense, warm air is less dense, so on a warm day an aircraft must travel faster through the air for the same number of molecules per second to strike it, and for the same IAS to be indicated. TAS varying with temperature (for a constant IAS) is one reason why, on a warm day, an aeroplane requires longer take-off and landing distances. The TAS is higher to give you the same IAS, and the IAS is what you 'fly by'.

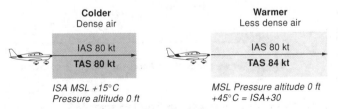

■ *Figure 2-11* **Constant IAS (RAS): TAS varies with air temperature**

2. Pressure. The greater the pressure altitude (i.e. the lower the air pressure), the fewer the molecules per unit volume. For two aircraft with the same true airspeed (TAS), the higher aircraft will have a lower indicated airspeed (IAS) because it will strike fewer molecules of air per second than the lower aircraft.

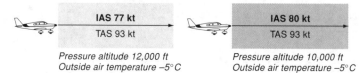

Pressure altitude 12,000 ft   Pressure altitude 10,000 ft
Outside air temperature –5°C   Outside air temperature –5°C

■ *Figure 2-12* **Same TAS: the aircraft in less dense air has a lower IAS (RAS)**

Remember that IAS (RAS) is only equal to TAS under ISA MSL (International Standard Atmosphere mean sea level) conditions. At higher altitudes the IAS (or RAS) will be less than the TAS because the aircraft will be flying through the thinner air with an airspeed well in excess of that indicated on the ASI.

What Happens When We Climb at a Constant IAS?

As an aeroplane gains altitude, the air density (*rho*) decreases. If we adopt the usual climb technique of maintaining a constant IAS (a constant dynamic pressure '½ × *rho* × V-squared'), the decrease in *rho* is made up by an increase in *V* (the true airspeed).

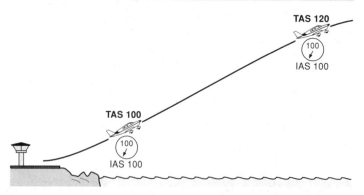

The higher we climb, when flying at a constant IAS, the greater the TAS.

■ *Figure 2-13* **The higher we climb, the greater the TAS for a constant IAS (RAS)**

Using the Navigation Computer to Find TAS from IAS

Finding TAS from IAS is simple with a navigation computer. The principles illustrated here apply to most types available.

On the calculator side of most navigation computers is an **air-speed correction window,** which allows us to:

☐ **match up** the *pressure altitude* and the *air temperature* (the main factors determining density); and then

☐ **from IAS** (or RAS/CAS) on the inner scale, read off TAS on the outer scale.

NOTE On many navigation computers the inner scale is labelled RAS or CAS (or IAS) and the outer scale TAS. Check your own computer.

Ensure that you use the Celsius temperature scale, as all temperatures in UK meteorology forecasts (and those for most other countries) are given in degrees Celsius (formerly centigrade).

EXAMPLE 1

1. Temperature is −10°C at pressure altitude 8,000 ft.

2. RAS (CAS) 115 kt gives TAS 127 kt.

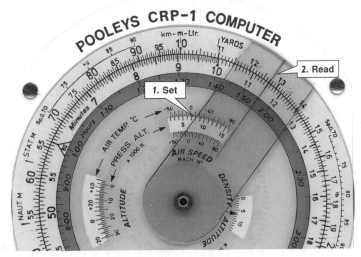

■ *Figure 2-14* **Example 1, finding TAS from IAS (RAS) and air temperature on the navigation computer**

As a further example, line up the ISA MSL conditions of +15°C and pressure altitude 0. The computer will then show that under these conditions IAS (inner scale) and TAS (outer scale) are the same.

Variation of TAS with Altitude

Assume that the recommended climb speed for your aeroplane is 100 kt IAS. Using your navigation computer, see if you can come up with similar answers for the TAS as we have in Figure 2-15, for a climb at IAS 100 kt from MSL to 20,000 ft. (Assume standard atmosphere conditions, where temperature decreases by 2°C for each 1,000 ft climbed.)

Pressure altitude	Temp.	IAS/RAS	TAS
20,000 ft	−25°C	100 kt	137 kt
15,000 ft	−15°C	100 kt	126 kt
10,000 ft	−5°C	100 kt	117 kt
5,000 ft	+5°C	100 kt	108 kt
ISA MSL	+15°C	100 kt	100 kt

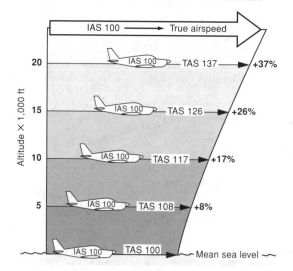

■ *Figure 2-15* **IAS 100 kt: TAS increases with altitude**

NOTE At 5,000 ft, TAS exceeds IAS by about 8%. At 10,000 ft, TAS exceeds IAS by about 17%.

These are handy figures to remember for rough mental calculations and also for when experienced pilots are talking about the speeds at which their aeroplanes 'true-out'. If you are cruising at 5,000 ft with IAS 180 kt showing on the airspeed indicator, then your TAS will be approximately 8% greater (8% of 180 = 14), i.e. 194 kt TAS.

Now complete **Exercises 2 – Speed 2.**

For a Constant TAS, What IAS is Required?
It is interesting to compare what indicated airspeed will be shown in the cockpit if a constant true airspeed is required at various

levels. See if you can obtain the same answers as us for IAS with a constant true airspeed of 200 kt at various pressure altitudes. Once again, assume a standard atmosphere to be present.

Pressure Altitude	Temp.	TAS	IAS/RAS
· 20,000 ft	–25°C	200 kt	146 kt
15,000 ft	–15°C	200 kt	159 kt
10,000 ft	–5°C	200 kt	172 kt
5,000 ft	+5°C	200 kt	185 kt
ISA MSL	+15°C	200 kt	200 kt

To fly same TAS, IAS will decrease with higher altitudes as the air density decreases.

So, for the same TAS, the greater the pressure altitude, the lower the IAS.

The higher an aircraft flies, the more the TAS exceeds the IAS.

Variation of TAS with Outside Air Temperature (OAT)

Temperature at the one level in the atmosphere will vary from place to place and from time to time. Since temperature affects air density, it will also affect the relationship between IAS and TAS.

1. The mean sea level situation if temperature varies:

	Temp.	IAS/RAS	TAS	
	ISA+20 = +35°C	100 kt	104 kt	(less dense air)
Pressure altitude 0 ft	ISA+10 = +25°C	100 kt	102 kt	
	ISA = +15°C	100 kt	100 kt	
	ISA–10 = +5°C	100 kt	98 kt	
	ISA–20 = –5°C	100 kt	96 kt	(more dense air)

The less dense the air, the greater the TAS, compared to IAS (RAS).

2. The situation at pressure altitude 10,000 ft, if temperature varies:

	Temp.	IAS/RAS	TAS	
	ISA+20 = +15°C	100 kt	121 kt	(less dense air)
Pressure altitude 10,000 ft	ISA+10 = +5°C	100 kt	119 kt	
	ISA = –5°C	100 kt	117 kt	
	ISA–10 = –15°C	100 kt	115 kt	
	ISA–20 = –25°C	100 kt	113 kt	(more dense air)

True airspeed is important for navigation and flight planning because TAS is the actual speed of the aeroplane through the air mass.

More IAS to TAS Computer Calculations

EXAMPLE 2 At FL70, OAT –5°C, IAS (RAS) 105 kt. Find the TAS.

Working:

Set the pressure altitude 7,000 ft against –5°C OAT in the true airspeed (TAS) window.

Then, against RAS 105 kt on the inner scale, read off TAS 115 kt on the outermost scale.

TAS is 115 kt.

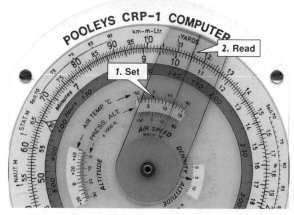

■ *Figure 2-16* **Example 2**

In some situations the required pieces of information are not always given directly, but have to be first derived from other information which is provided. We will take an example from a high flight level to illustrate the widening gap between IAS (RAS) and TAS as an aeroplane climbs.

EXAMPLE 3 A turboprop plans on flying at flight level 280 (FL280), where the temperature is forecast to be ISA+10°C. If its rectified airspeed (RAS) will be 150 kt, what TAS can be expected?

Working:

FL280 is pressure altitude 28,000 ft.

$$\text{At FL280, ISA} = +15 - (2 \times 28)$$
$$= +15 - 56$$
$$= -41°C$$
$$\text{so ISA}+10 = -41 + 10$$
$$= -31°C$$

In the computer *airspeed* window, set *pressure altitude* 28,000 against OAT –31.

Against RAS 150 kt, read off TAS 240 kt on the outer scale.

Finding the Required IAS to Achieve a Particular TAS

The usual in-flight problem is to determine the TAS from the indicated airspeed read off the ASI. Sometimes, however, you need to be able to work these problems in reverse, say to achieve a certain desired TAS or GS for flight planning purposes, when you will start with these and work back to find the IAS (RAS/CAS) necessary to achieve this.

EXAMPLE 4 Cruising at FL100 and temperature ISA–10, what is the required RAS (CAS) to give you a true airspeed of 200 kt?

Working:

Pressure altitude is 10,000 ft,

$$\text{where ISA} = +15 - (2 \times 10)$$
$$= +15 - 20$$
$$= -5°C$$
$$\text{so ISA–10} = -5 - 10$$
$$= -15°C$$

In the computer *airspeed* window, set *pressure altitude* 10,000 against OAT –15°C.

Against TAS 200 on the outer scale, read off RAS 175 kt on the inner scale.

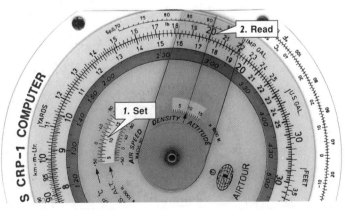

■ *Figure 2-17* **Example 4**

Airspeed Terminology

IAS: Indicated airspeed.

RAS OR CAS: Rectified airspeed or calibrated airspeed. Generally approximately equal to indicated airspeed.

TAS: True Airspeed. At higher altitudes, TAS is usually greater than IAS/RAS/CAS).

Now complete **Exercises 2 – Speed-3.**

Direction

D irection is obviously of prime importance to accurate navigation. As aircraft navigate with reference to the earth's surface, we will begin with a brief look at the earth itself.

There is a geographical axis passing through two physical points on the surface of the earth about which the planet rotates. These points are the *geographic* North and South Poles. Any 'straight' line drawn around the earth's surface joining these two points is aligned in a true north–south direction.

By convention, the basic reference direction is **north**, and other directions are measured clockwise from this reference in degrees (°). Since there are 360° in a circle, **east** is described as 090°, **south** as 180°, **west** as 270°, and **north** as 000° or 360°. Any direction (be it the desired track of an aeroplane, or the direction from which the wind is blowing) can be defined in this way.

True Direction

If direction is described with reference to **true north** (the direction to the geographic North Pole), it is called the **true direction,** symbolised by 'T'. East is therefore written as 090°T or 090T. The track between town A and town B illustrated below is 327°T.

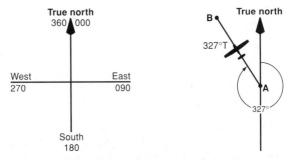

■ *Figure 3-1* ***True direction***

A more approximate means of describing direction is using the **cardinal points,** which are the four chief directions of north, south, east and west – further divided by the **quadrantal points** north-east, south-east, south-west and north-west. If necessary, these can be even further divided to give, for instance, NNW (nor-nor-west). Obviously, the 360° method is superior for aeronautical navigation.

True direction, however, is a problem for pilots, because most aeroplanes do not have an instrument that can determine the direction of true north. The magnetic compass, the prime source of directional information in the cockpit, aligns itself with **magnetic north,** rather than with true north.

NOTE As you will see, this statement does not hold true if there are extraneous magnetic fields, say due to radios or nearby magnetic materials, that are strong enough to affect the magnet within the compass. At this stage, we will assume that the magnet is influenced only by the earth's magnetic field and none other.

Magnetic Direction

Near to the true (geographic) North Pole is an area from which the earth's magnetic field emanates, known as the **north magnetic pole** to avoid confusion with the geographic pole. Similarly, there is a **south magnetic pole** located near the true South Pole.

A small magnet that is suspended and free to move will seek to align itself with these roughly north–south lines of magnetic force. This is the basis of the **magnetic compass.** If a compass card is attached to a magnetic 'needle', then the magnetic heading of an aeroplane can be read-off against a **lubber line,** or index, on the compass face.

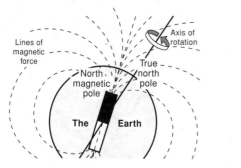
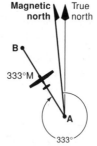

■ *Figure 3-2* ***Magnetic direction***

A direction defined by reference to the north-seeking end of a magnetic compass is known as a **magnetic direction.** In Figure 3-2, the direction between the same two towns, A and B, is now described as 333°M.

The actual direction between the two towns of course has not changed, only our description of it has, because of the two different reference directions, TN and MN. In the above case, 327°T and 333°M are the same physical direction described differently.

Direction Related to Magnetic North

Why introduce the complication of degrees related to magnetic north? Because the simple magnetic compass is the most reliable source of directional information. Instruments that display direction relative to true north are both complicated and expensive, and subject to certain operational limitations not associated with the conventional magnetic compass. Even in the most sophisticated aircraft flying today, such as the Boeing 767, Airbus A320 and BAe 146, a simple magnetic compass is installed.

In most light aircraft, the magnetic compass is the primary source of directional information, to which other heading or heading indicators (often gyroscopic) are aligned.

■ *Figure 3-3* **The magnetic compass**

To obtain accurate directional information from the magnetic compass, you must understand how it operates, and also its inaccuracies while the aeroplane is turning or changing speed. This is covered fully in the *Flight Instruments* section of Vol. 4 of this series. A summary follows here.

A bar magnet that is freely suspended horizontally will swing so that its axis points roughly north–south. The end of the magnet that points towards the earth's north magnetic pole is called the **north-seeking pole** of the magnet.

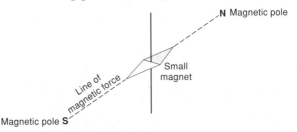

■ *Figure 3-4* **Simple bar magnet**

The Earth's Magnetic Field (Terrestrial Magnetism)
The earth acts like a very large and weak magnet. Its surface is covered by a weak magnetic field – lines of magnetic force that begin deep within the earth near Hudson Bay in Canada and flow towards a point deep within the earth near South Victoria Land in Antarctica. Because of their proximity to the *geographic* North and South Poles, the magnetic poles are referred to as the **north magnetic pole** and the **south magnetic pole**.

Variation

The latitude-longitude grid shown on charts is based on the geographic poles at either extremity of the earth's axis of rotation, so the **meridians of longitude** run true north and true south, and the **parallels of latitude** run true east and true west.

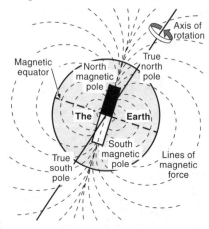

■ *Figure 3-5* **The earth has a magnetic field**

Our small compass magnet, however, does not point exactly at true north and true south. A magnetic compass, if it is working perfectly and is influenced only by the earth's magnetic field, will point at the north *magnetic* pole, near Hudson Bay in Canada. At most points on the earth this is a different direction to true north. The angular difference between true north and magnetic north at any particular point on the earth is called the **magnetic variation** at that point.

If the magnet points slightly east of true north, the variation is *east*. If the magnet points to the west of true north, the variation is *west*. West variation is experienced over the entire UK.

Variation at any point on the earth is measured from true north to magnetic north. For example, a magnetic compass in London will point 3½° west of true north, i.e. the magnetic variation is 3½°W, since magnetic north lies 3½° west of true north. In Liverpool the magnetic variation is 5°W. In the area of the two towns A and B illustrated in Figure 3-2 it is 6°W; 327°T and 333°M are one and the same direction when the magnetic variation is 6°W.

> **Variation** *is the angular difference from true north to magnetic north.*

NOTE Because the earth's magnetic poles are not stationary, variation changes over time. In the British Isles variation reduces by 7–8 minutes annually (about 1° every 8 years).

Isogonals

As well as the lines forming the latitude-longitude grids, maps have other lines joining places that have the same magnetic variation. These lines are known as **isogonals** or **isogonic lines**. On the UK 1:500,000 aeronautical chart, the isogonals are shown as dashed lines coloured blue.

The 4½° west isogonal joins all the places having a variation of 4½° west (e.g. Sunderland, Bradford, Stoke, Newport, Torquay). If you are anywhere on this line, then the message that your compass is giving you about magnetic north can be related to true north; your compass will point at magnetic north, which will be 4½° west of true north.

> **Isogonals** *are lines on a chart joining places of equal magnetic variation.*

To assist you in choosing the magnetic variation in your area, CAA 1:500,000 UK aeronautical charts show half-degree isogonals. Between these lines you use the appropriate whole number of variation, as shown in Figure 3-6.

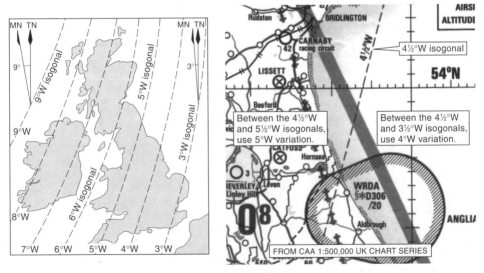

■ *Figure 3-6* **Variation is the angle between true and magnetic**

If magnetic north is to the west of true north (west variation), then °M will exceed °T. Conversely, if magnetic north is to the east of true north (east variation), then °M will be less than °T. An easy way to remember the relationship between true and magnetic is:

> *Variation west, magnetic best.   Variation east, magnetic least.*

EXAMPLE 1 While flying on the Continent, you are steering your aeroplane on a heading of 300°M with reference to the magnetic compass. From an aeronautical chart you determine that magnetic variation in the vicinity is 4°W. What is the aeroplane's heading in °true?

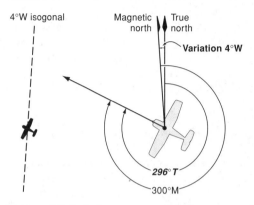

■ *Figure 3-7* **Variation west, magnetic best; answer 296°T**

EXAMPLE 2 Convert 100°T to a magnetic direction in an area where variation is 10°E.

100°T
−10°E (Variation east, magnetic least)
090°M *(Answer)*

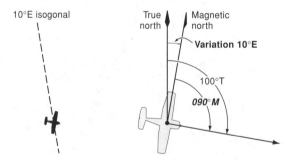

■ *Figure 3-8* **Variation east, magnetic least; answer 090°M**

The Agonic Line
The isogonal that joins places that have zero variation (i.e. magnetic north and true north coincide) is called the **agonic line.** It passes through Europe.

Compass Deviation
Unfortunately, the magnet in the magnetic compass is affected not only by the magnetic field of the earth, but by any magnetic field that exists in its vicinity, such as the magnetic fields surrounding

the metal structure of the aeroplane, rotating parts in the engine, the radios, etc. The effect of these additional magnetic fields in a particular aeroplane is to deviate or deflect the compass from indicating magnetic north precisely. This imprecision is known as **compass deviation.**

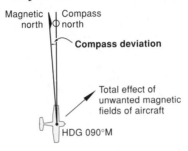

■ Figure 3-9 **Compass deviation**

Deviation varies according to the heading that the aeroplane is on, since these unwanted extra magnetic fields are related to the aeroplane itself. If their resultant is diagonal to the longitudinal axis of the aeroplane (Figure 3-10) then, when the aeroplane is steering 045°, or its reciprocal 225°, it will be aligned with the earth's magnetic field and will not cause the compass needle to deviate. In other words, on these headings, compass deviation is zero.

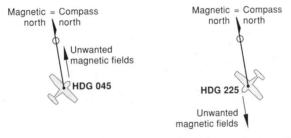

■ Figure 3-10 **Compass deviation nil in this aeroplane on these headings**

If, on the other hand, the aeroplane is headed east, the alignment of the unwanted magnetic fields will deviate the compass as shown by the deviation card in Figure 3-13. The compass needle will then point towards a *compass north* that is slightly to the east of magnetic north in this case (by 1°). Even though the magnetic heading might be 090°M, the compass will indicate 089°.

An easy way to remember the relationship between magnetic and compass directions is:

Deviation east, compass least.   Deviation west, compass best.

EXAMPLE 3 An aeroplane is flying with a heading of 257° indicated on the magnetic compass in the cockpit. If, on that heading, deviation is 3°W, what is the aeroplane's magnetic heading?

257°C (compass)
<u> −3 </u> (Deviation west, compass best)
254°M *(Answer)*

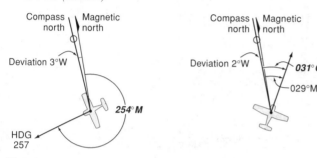

■ *Figure 3-11* **Example 3**   ■ *Figure 3-12* **Example 4**

EXAMPLE 4 What compass direction must be steered to achieve a magnetic heading of 029°M, if the compass deviation is 2° west?

Deviation west, compass best: 029°M + 2 = 031°C *(Answer)*

The Compass Deviation Card

Rather than continually having to carry out deviation corrections to the compass headings, a simpler approach is for each aircraft to have a small placard known as the deviation card displayed near the compass. This card shows the pilot what corrections need to be made to the actual magnetic compass reading (described as °C, for compass) in order to obtain the desired magnetic direction in °M. This correction usually involves no more than a few degrees (and in fact, the correction may be so small that the pilot does not apply it).

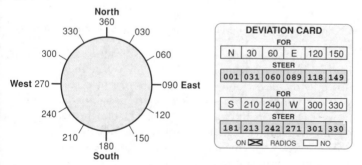

■ *Figure 3-13* **A compass rose and compass deviation card. To achieve a magnetic heading of 270° using this compass, steer 271°C.**

> **Deviation** is the angular distance from magnetic north to compass north for that particular compass, with the aircraft on that particular heading.

Precautions When Carrying Magnetic or Metal Goods

The compass deviation card is filled out by an engineer who has checked the compass in that particular aeroplane with it headed in different directions. It may be done with electrical services off, or with them on (which is the normal in-flight situation). Electrical services, such as radios, often generate their own magnetic fields and may affect the compass indication.

The compass deviation correction card allows only for the magnetic influences in the aeroplane that were present when the engineer calibrated the compass in a procedure known as *swinging the compass.*

Any other magnetic influences introduced into the aeroplane at a time following the swinging of the compass will not be allowed for, even though they can significantly affect the compass. Therefore, as pilot, ensure that no metal or magnetic materials, such as metal pens, clipboards, books with metal binders, key rings, headsets, electronic calculators, transistor radios, or other devices that generate magnetic fields are placed anywhere near the compass.

Such magnetic or metal materials placed near the compass may introduce large and unpredictable errors. Many pilots have been lost or 'temporarily uncertain of their position' as a result of random deviations in the compass readings caused by these extraneous magnetic fields.

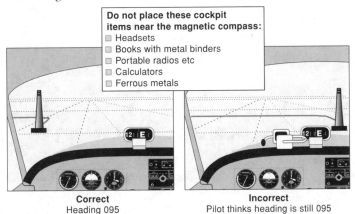

Do not place these cockpit items near the magnetic compass:
☐ Headsets
☐ Books with metal binders
☐ Portable radios etc
☐ Calculators
☐ Ferrous metals

Correct
Heading 095

Incorrect
Pilot thinks heading is still 095
but in reality it is now 040

■ *Figure 3-14* **Keep foreign objects away from the magnetic compass**

Relating True, Magnetic and Compass Headings

1. **HDG(C) is the actual heading** that you observe on the magnetic compass in the cockpit. It relates to compass north for that particular compass in that particular aeroplane on that particular heading.

2. **Either refer to the deviation card,** or apply 'Deviation east, compass least; deviation west, compass best,' to convert HDG(C) to HDG(M). The aeroplane has not changed its direction in space, but its heading is now related to *magnetic north* rather than *compass north* (since the peculiarities of that particular compass have been accounted for and corrected). Usually this correction for deviation is insignificant and is often disregarded.

3. **Apply variation** (found on a chart) to HDG(M) to convert it to HDT(T), which is the heading of the aeroplane related to the geographic poles, known as the North and South Poles or the *true poles.* The correction for variation can be large and should always be applied (and in the right sense – applying 6°W variation as if it were 6°E variation will give you a 12° error). Remember: 'Variation east, magnetic least; variation west, magnetic best.'

The above process takes you from *degrees compass* to *degrees magnetic* to *degrees true*. It is just as easy to carry out the reverse process to go from °T to °M to °C.

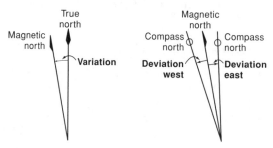

■ Figure 3-15 **Variation and deviation**

EXAMPLE 5

Aircraft heading	020°T
Variation	7°W
Aircraft heading	027°M
Deviation	2°E
Aircraft heading	025°C *(Answer)*

EXAMPLE 6

Aircraft heading 025°C
Deviation 2°E
Aircraft heading 027°M
Variation 7°W
Aircraft heading 020°T *(Answer)*

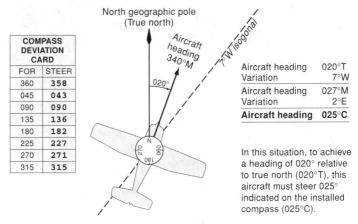

North geographic pole
(True north)

COMPASS DEVIATION CARD	
FOR	STEER
360	358
045	043
090	090
135	136
180	182
225	227
270	271
315	315

Aircraft heading 020°T
Variation 7°W
Aircraft heading 027°M
Variation 2°E
Aircraft heading 025°C

In this situation, to achieve a heading of 020° relative to true north (020°T), this aircraft must steer 025° indicated on the installed compass (025°C).

■ *Figure 3-16* **The relationship of compass heading, magnetic heading and true heading with variation and deviation**

The maximum accuracy we consider practical in navigation is 1°, hence there is no need for us to consider the further subdivision of 1° into 60 minutes and each of these minutes into 60 seconds. Only apply a variation or deviation correction accurate to the nearest degree.

Pilot Serviceability Checks on the Magnetic Compass

☐ **Pre-flight,** check that the compass is securely installed and can be read easily. The liquid in which the magnet is suspended should be free of bubbles and should not be discoloured. The glass should not be broken, cracked or discoloured, and it should be secure.

☐ **Check the position** of the compass deviation card.

☐ **Check that the compass indication** is at least approximately correct. Runways are named according to their magnetic direction (e.g. a runway pointing 243°M is called Runway 24), so when pointing in the same direction as this runway, your compass should indicate this, at least approximately.

☐ **When taxiing out** prior to take-off, turn the aircraft left and right and check that the response of the magnetic compass is correct. Remember that the magnet should remain in the same north–south direction, and the aeroplane turn around it.

■ *Figure 3-17* **Always cross-check compass direction**

Magnetic Dip and Compass Errors

The earth's magnetic field is weak, and varies in strength and direction over the entire surface of the earth. The strength of the magnetic field can be resolved into two components:

☐ **a horizontal component** parallel to the surface of the earth, which is used to align the compass needle with magnetic north; and

☐ **a vertical component,** which causes the magnetic needle to dip down.

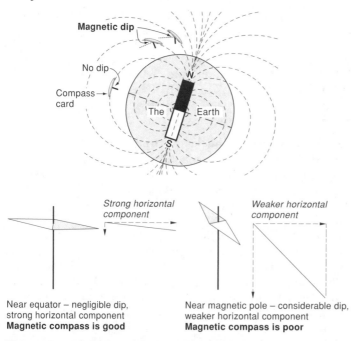

■ *Figure 3-18* **The horizontal component of the earth's magnetic field is strong near the equator and weak near the poles**

A magnetic compass indicates direction more accurately at middle and low latitudes than near the poles.

At the so-called 'magnetic equator' (roughly mid-way between the magnetic poles), the lines of magnetic force are parallel with the earth's surface (i.e. they are horizontal). Consequently, the horizontal component of the earth's magnetic field is at its strongest here and so the magnetic compass is stable and accurate in these areas.

At the higher latitudes near the magnetic poles, where the lines of magnetic force run in through the earth's surface, the vertical component of the earth's magnetic field causing dip is stronger, and the horizontal component parallel to the surface of the earth is weaker. This makes the compass less effective as an indicator of horizontal direction in the polar regions compared with its performance at the lower latitudes.

At latitudes higher than 60 degrees north or south (i.e. closer to the poles than 60°N or S), the magnetic compass is not very reliable at all.

As a means of avoiding the compass needle *dipping* down in line with the magnetic force, it is suspended in a manner that displaces its centre of gravity (CG) from the pivot point at which it is suspended (and indirectly attached to the aeroplane structure).

The greater the dip, the more the needle dips down towards the nearer magnetic pole, and the more its CG is displaced. This causes the weight force to *balance* the dip force and at least keep the needle approximately horizontal.

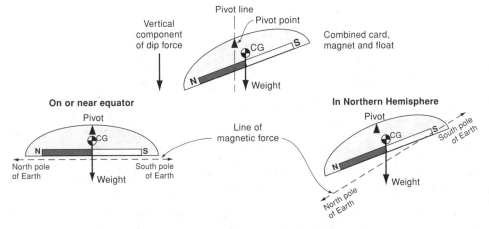

■ *Figure 3-19* **To minimise the effect of magnetic dip, the needle's CG is displaced**

Turning and Acceleration Errors

Any acceleration of the aeroplane will be transmitted to the compass needle via its pivot. The needle's CG will tend to continue at its previous velocity and so will be left behind in an acceleration, and will move ahead in a deceleration. In a turn, the aeroplane (and the pivot) is accelerating towards the centre of the turn, with the CG trying to 'fly off at a tangent'.

Indication errors in the magnetic compass and what causes them is covered in detail in Vol. 4 of *The Air Pilot's Manual*. It will suffice here to summarise the effect of these errors on the magnetic compass indications (which you should know for the examination in this subject):

TURNING ERRORS are greatest when turning through headings of magnetic north or south (and zero when turning through headings of east or west).

When heading towards the nearer magnetic pole, the magnetic compass is 'sluggish' and will under-indicate the amount of turn (for both left and right turns). You should stop the turn before the magnetic compass indicates your desired heading. Once settled into steady straight and level flight, the compass will settle down and (hopefully) indicate your desired heading. If not, make minor adjustments to your heading.

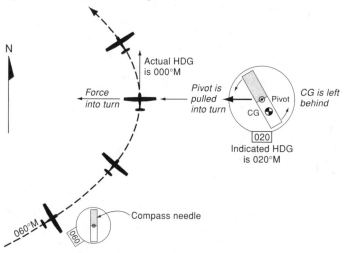

■ *Figure 3-20* **The compass is sluggish and lags behind when turning through north (in the Northern Hemisphere)**

In the case illustrated in Figure 3-20, an aeroplane flying initially on a heading of 060°M is turning left through north. The CG tends to fly off at a tangent and so the compass card rotates anticlockwise, thereby under-indicating the amount of turn. For example, when the aeroplane is turning through 000°M (magnetic north), the compass is only indicating 020°M.

When heading towards the more distant magnetic pole, the magnetic compass is 'lively' and will over-indicate the amount of turn. You should continue the turn through your desired heading as indicated on the magnetic compass during the turn. Once settled into steady straight and level flight, the compass will settle down and (hopefully) indicate your desired heading. If not, make minor adjustments to your heading.

ACCELERATION ERRORS are maximum on east and west magnetic headings (and zero on north and south headings).

Acceleration produces a false indication of turning towards the nearer magnetic pole (i.e. towards north in the Northern Hemisphere). Increasing speed (accelerating) towards the east will cause the compass needle and its attached card to rotate clockwise, causing a false indication of say 080° (instead of 090°). Another way of looking at this is that, on accelerating in an easterly direction, the centre of gravity is left behind, causing the compass card to rotate to the right. This gives a *false* indication of a turn towards north.

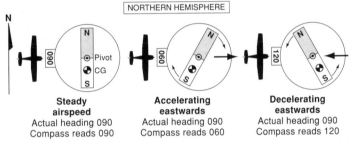

■ *Figure 3-21* **Acceleration east produces a false indication of a turn towards the north**

Considering an acceleration on a westerly heading, again the centre of gravity is left behind, the compass card in this case turning anticlockwise and indicating (incorrectly) a turn towards north.

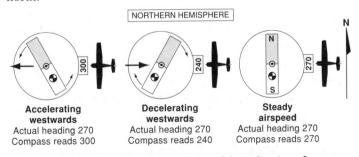

■ *Figure 3-22* **Acceleration west produces a false indication of a turn towards north**

Conversely, deceleration on an easterly or westerly heading produces a false indication of turning towards the further magnetic pole (i.e. towards south in the northern hemisphere).

If the aeroplane is heading north or south, the pivot supporting the compass needle and the needle's centre of gravity are in line, and so the needle will not be displaced by accelerations or decelerations in the north–south directions.

On intermediate headings, the acceleration error will increase with the proximity of the aeroplane's heading to east or west.

EXAMPLE 7 You are flying in the UK. When turning from 150°M through south onto a heading of 220° using the magnetic compass, because it will over-indicate the amount of turn, you should continue the turn beyond a compass indication of 220 (say by 10°) and then level the wings and allow the compass to settle down.

EXAMPLE 8 You are flying in Scotland and accelerating from 80 kt to 150 kt on an easterly heading. Even though, by reference to a point on the horizon, you are still heading east, the needle of the magnetic compass will swing in a clockwise direction and indicate an apparent turn to the north. Once you attain a steady speed and allow the compass to settle down, it should indicate the correct heading again.

The Direction or Heading Indicator

Most light aircraft instrument panels include a gyroscopic **direction indicator (DI)**. This instrument is also known as the **heading indicator (HI)** or **directional gyro (DG)**.

Being a gyro-based instrument, its indication is steady compared to that of the magnetic compass but, due to the fact that the earth is rotating (at 15° per hour) and the direction indicator's axis is fixed in space by the gyroscope, the direction indicator has to be re-aligned with a known reference direction at regular intervals.

■ *Figure 3-23*
Direction indicator (DI)

The magnetic compass is used as the reference for the direction indicator and so, when aligned with the compass, the DI will indicate the heading of the aircraft in degrees magnetic.

NOTE Do not align the direction indicator (DI) with the magnetic compass if you are changing speed or direction, as the magnetic compass will be experiencing acceleration or turning errors, i.e. keep the wings level and maintain a constant speed when aligning the DI with the compass.

One of the advantages of a direction indicator is that it is not subject to turning or acceleration errors. Its accuracy depends on it being correctly aligned with magnetic north, so this must be done when the magnetic compass is indicating correctly.

Relative Bearings

It is usual to define the direction of an object from an aeroplane in terms of its **relative bearing,** or its direction relative to the nose (or heading) of the aeroplane.

A relative bearing of an object from an aeroplane is its angular distance from the aircraft's heading measured clockwise from the nose of the aeroplane from 000°REL through to 360°REL.

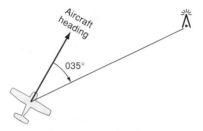

■ *Figure 3-24* **The radio mast bears 035°** **relative from the aeroplane**

Converting Relative Bearings to Magnetic Bearings

To convert a relative bearing to a magnetic bearing (and vice versa), simply add the relative bearing of the object to the magnetic heading of the aircraft to obtain the magnetic bearing of the object from the aeroplane.

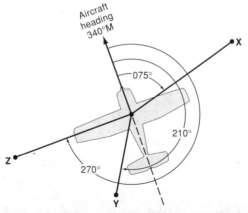

	AIRCRAFT HEADING		RELATIVE BEARING		MAGNETIC BEARING
Point X	340°M	+	075°	=	055°M
Point Y	340°M	+	210°	=	190°M
Point Z	340°M	+	270°	=	250°M

■ *Figure 3-25* **Relative bearings and magnetic bearings**

Aircraft magnetic heading	±	Relative bearing of object from aircraft	=	Magnetic bearing of object from aircraft

If the answer works out to be in excess of 360°, then this means you have gone more than once around the complete circle. To achieve a usable answer simply deduct 360°, e.g. 372° is the same direction as 012°.

These are two different ways of describing the position of an object seen from the aeroplane:

☐ **the relative bearing** is related to the nose (HDG) of the aeroplane; and
☐ **the magnetic bearing** is related to magnetic north.

You will come across relative bearings later in your flying training when you study radio navigation aids in preparation for obtaining an Instrument Meteorological Conditions (IMC) Rating. In radio navigation:

☐ **a fixed-card radio compass** uses relative bearings;
☐ **a radio magnetic indicator** (which has a radio compass needle superimposed on a compass card that indicates directions relative to magnetic north) uses magnetic bearings.

Now complete **Exercise 3 – Direction.**

Wind Side of the Navigation Computer

The slide navigation computer is a wonderful invention that allows you to handle navigation problems involving the **triangle of velocities** quickly and accurately. The three vectors in the triangle can be marked on the plotting disc so that they appear in the same relationship, one to the other, as in flight, making it easier to visualise the situation and check that the vectors have been applied correctly.

Components of the **wind side** of a navigation computer are:

☐ **A circular, rotatable compass rose** (or azimuth) set in a fixed frame which is marked with an **index** at the top.

☐ **A transparent plastic plotting disc** attached to the rotatable compass rose, marked with a **centre-dot.**

☐ **A slide plate** printed with concentric *speed arcs* and radial *drift lines.* This plate slides through the frame and compass rose assembly, hence the name 'slide' navigation computer.

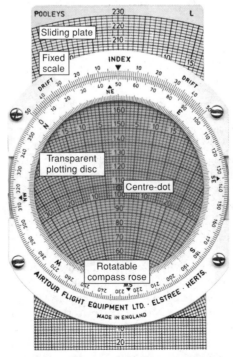

■ *Figure 4-1* **Wind side of a slide navigation computer**

The Triangle of Velocities

Before you can use the navigation computer effectively, you must understand the triangle of velocities which, of course, has three sides. The first two are:

1. The motion of the aeroplane through the air – heading/true airspeed.

2. The motion of the air over the ground – wind velocity (direction and speed).

When these two are added together, the third side of the triangle, which is their resultant effect, is:

3. The motion of the aeroplane over the ground – track/ground-speed.

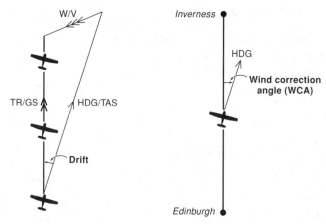

■ Figure 4-2 *The triangle of velocities and wind correction angle*

Note that the wind always blows the aeroplane from its heading to its track. In other words, the wind vector must start at the HDG/TAS vector and end at the TR/GS vector. If you have this firmly fixed in your mind, then computer solutions will follow easily and correctly.

A wind from the right will carry an aeroplane onto a track that is to the left of its heading. This is known as left drift or port drift. The drift angle is measured from HDG to TR. In Figure 4-2, 10° left drift is shown.

To achieve a particular track, say between two towns, the aeroplane must be steered into-wind on a heading that allows for the drift. In the above illustration, to achieve the track shown, the aeroplane is being steered on a steady heading 10° to the right of track. This can be described as a wind correction angle of 10° right. The wind correction angle is measured from TR to HDG and is, of course, equal and opposite to the drift angle.

Each of the three vectors in the triangle of velocities has two aspects: magnitude (size) and direction. This means that in the triangle of velocities there are six components:

VECTOR	MAGNITUDE	DIRECTION
HDG/TAS	TAS	HDG
W/V	Wind speed	Wind direction (from)
TR/GS	GS	TR

Typical navigation problems involve knowing four of these six elements and finding the other two. It is as simple as that!

Marking the Vector on the Plotting Disc

If you can sketch a triangle of velocities with the three vectors placed properly, then the wind side of the computer will create no difficulties at all.

While you are still learning how to use the computer, it is a good idea to mark each of the vectors with their arrowheads on the plotting disc to ensure that the triangle of velocities is portrayed correctly. Marks on the plotting disc can be removed quite easily at the end of each problem with a moist finger.

Once you become familiar with the use of the computer, however, the actual drawing in of each vector becomes unnecessary, and just one single mark (known as the wind-mark) to illustrate the extent of the wind velocity is all that is needed.

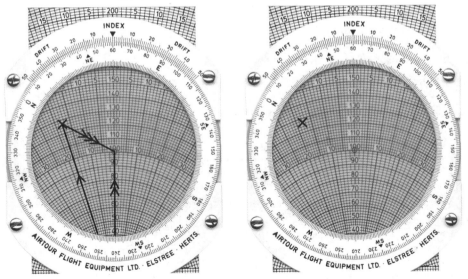

■ Figure 4-3 **Initially show the vectors (left); with practice you need only show the wind-mark**

Work Totally in Degrees True (or Totally in Degrees M)

It is most important that, when working out the vector triangle, the directions are all related to the one datum. In the UK, it is traditional for PPL pilots to work in degrees true. You may work in degrees magnetic; the eventual results are identical but, whatever you do with the wind side of your computer, ensure that you stay either totally in degrees true or totally in degrees magnetic. Do not mix °T and °M in the one triangle of velocities! Our initial examples are worked in °T.

Choice of Method

The navigation computer is such that each problem can be solved in a number of ways, each method producing the correct results. You will find a variety of methods in common use – choose the method that suits you best.

We recommend that you first learn your instructor's preferred method and disregard the others. Later in your training you may like to consider the other methods but, in the early stages, use one method only.

Most use of the navigation computer is made at the flight planning stage on the ground prior to flight, when the pilot already knows:

- the **track** in °T, measured on an aeronautical chart;
- the **wind velocity** in °T/kt, found on the weather forecast; and
- the **true airspeed** that the aeroplane will achieve.

The wind side of the computer can then be used to calculate:

- the **heading** to steer; and
- the **groundspeed** that will be achieved.

The flight planning problem can be summarised as:

KNOWN:	FIND:
TR, W/V and TAS	*HDG and GS*

Our preferred method for wind side calculations finds HDG and GS very efficiently. We consider it first as Method A, beginning on page 53.

Method B is another commonly used approach to solving the triangle of velocities, and is known as the 'wind-mark-down' method. It is considered second, beginning on page 65.

Now proceed to the method recommended by your instructor.

Wind Side Method A

Determining HDG and GS When Flight Planning

Example 1. Find HDG and GS

KNOWN:		FIND:
Required track (TR) measured off chart	**150°**	**HDG and GS**
True airspeed (TAS) known, or calculated from expected RAS/CAS	**100 kt**	
Wind velocity (W/V) stated on forecast	**360°T/30**	
Magnetic variation shown on chart	**5°W**	

An efficient way to record navigation data is to use a flight log, like that in Figure 4-4. The known information can be entered first as shown, with the results of your calculations following at a later stage.

From/To	Safety ALT	ALT Temp	RAS	TAS	W/V	TR °T	Drift	HDG °T	Var	HDG °M	GS	Dist	Time	ETA	HDG °C
				100	360/30	150			5°W						

■ Figure 4-4 **Typical flight log**

STEP 1. PLACE THE W/V ON THE PLOTTING DISC.

Wind direction and wind speed are known, i.e. both aspects of the W/V vector are known.

Rotate the compass rose until the wind direction 360 (north) is under the index. Mark the start of the W/V vector 30 kt above the centre-dot.

Since the track is known, show the W/V blowing towards the centre-dot, i.e. the wind vector will come from direction 360° and end at the centre-dot. Marking the starting point of the wind 30 kt above the centre-dot is most easily achieved by first setting one of the labelled wind arcs under the centre-dot, and then placing the wind-mark 30 kt above it.

At this early stage in your training, mark in the full W/V, showing the three arrowheads of the W/V vector pointing down towards the centre-dot. This will give you a clear picture as the whole triangle of velocities is developed.

STEP 2. PLACE THE TR/GS VECTOR ON THE PLOTTING DISC.

Track is known (having been measured on the chart); ground-speed is not known. In this case, only one aspect of the TR/GS vector is known – its direction, but not its magnitude.

Rotate the compass rose until the required TR of 150°T is under the index. (We cannot position the appropriate ground-speed arc under the centre-dot because we do not yet know its value.)

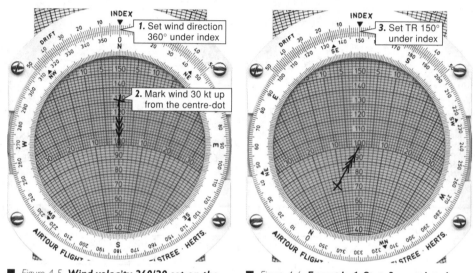

■ Figure 4-5 **Wind velocity 360/30 set on the computer at the flight planning stage: Example 1, Step 1**

■ Figure 4-6 **Example 1, Step 2 completed**

STEP 3. PLACE THE HDG/TAS VECTOR ON THE PLOTTING DISC.

True airspeed is known, but the heading is not. In this case, only one aspect of the HDG/TAS vector is known – its magnitude.

Move the slide and place the TAS 100 kt speed arc under the wind-mark (which is the starting point of the W/V vector). This is where a clear understanding of the triangle of velocities is most important! The end of the HDG/TAS vector is where the W/V begins.

STEP 4. READ OFF THE ANSWERS FOR HDG AND GS.

The GS of 125 kt appears under the centre-dot. From the drift lines, the wind correction angle is 9° to the left of the track. This means to achieve TR 150°T, the aeroplane must be pointed 9° into-wind and flown on a HDG of 141°T to allow for the 9° of right (starboard) drift.

The arithmetic (for determining HDG 141 from TR 150 and a wind correction angle of 9° into-wind) can be checked on the scale near the index mark.

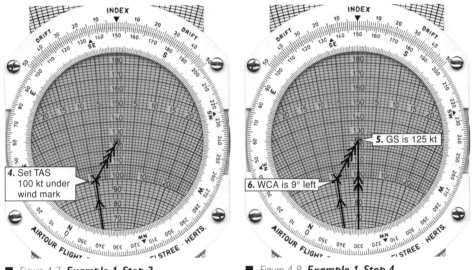

4. Set TAS 100 kt under wind mark	**5.** GS is 125 kt
	6. WCA is 9° left

■ Figure 4-7 **Example 1, Step 3**   ■ Figure 4-8 **Example 1, Step 4**

ANSWER HDG 141°T, GS 125 kt

NOTE If magnetic heading is required, it is simply a matter of applying variation. If variation is 5°W, then 141°T is 146°M (variation west, magnetic best).

From/To	Safety ALT	ALT Temp	RAS	TAS	W/V	TR °T	Drift	HDG °T	Var	HDG °M	GS	Dist	Time	ETA	HDG °C
			100	360/30	150	9°R	141	5°W	146	125					

■ Figure 4-9 **Example 1**

Example 2. Find HDG and GS

Given a true airspeed of 174 kt, a forecast W/V of 240°T/40 kt, and a desired track of 290°T, calculate the true heading required and the groundspeed that will be achieved. What is the magnetic heading if variation in the vicinity of the flight is 6°W?

KNOWN:		FIND:
TAS.	174 kt	HDG and GS
Required TR	290°T	
W/V	240°T/40	

From/To	Safety ALT	ALT Temp	RAS	TAS	W/V	TR °T	Drift	HDG °T	Var	HDG °M	GS	Dist	Time	ETA	HDG °C
				174	240/40	290			6°W						

■ *Figure 4-10* **Example 2**

STEP 1. PLACE THE W/V ON THE PLOTTING DISC.

Both wind speed and wind direction are known. Since the required TR is known, we show the W/V blowing down from the index towards the centre-dot.

Set wind direction 240 under the index. Mark in the wind strength 40 kt above the centre-dot.

STEP 2. PLACE THE TR/GS VECTOR ON THE PLOTTING DISC.

TR is known. GS is not known. Rotate the compass rose until the required TR 290°T is under the index. (We cannot position the appropriate speed arc under the centre-dot because we do not yet know the GS.)

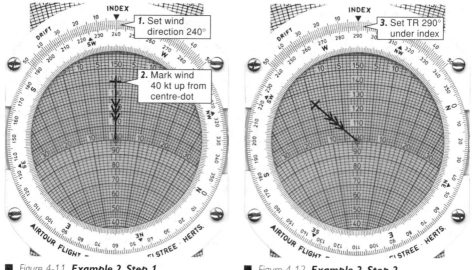

■ *Figure 4-11* **Example 2, Step 1**   ■ *Figure 4-12* **Example 2, Step 2**

STEP 3. PLACE THE HDG/TAS VECTOR ON THE PLOTTING DISC.

TAS is known. HDG is not known. Move the slide to place the TAS 174 kt under the wind-mark, which is starting point of the W/V vector (since the W/V vector begins where the TAS/HDG vector ends).

STEP 4. READ OFF THE ANSWERS FOR HDG AND GS.

The wind correction angle of 10° left can now be read off the drift lines, i.e. the aeroplane must be steered 10° into wind (i.e. left of the desired track to allow for the 10° right, or starboard, drift). In this case, to achieve the desired track of 290°T, the aeroplane must be steered on a heading of 280°T.

The groundspeed 145 kt lies under the centre-dot.

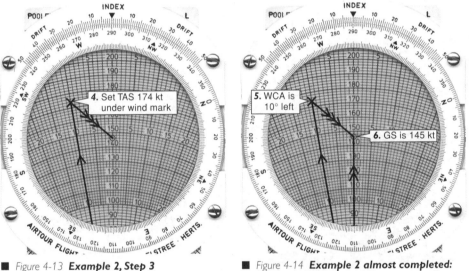

■ Figure 4-13 **Example 2, Step 3**

■ Figure 4-14 **Example 2 almost completed: HDG 280°T, GS 145 kt**

Magnetic variation in the area is 6°W, so HDG 280°T is 286°M.

ANSWER HDG 280°T, variation 6°W, HDG 286M; GS 145 kt

From/To	Safety ALT	ALT Temp	RAS	TAS	W/V	TR °T	Drift	HDG °T	Var	HDG °M	GS	Dist	Time	ETA	HDG °C
				174	240/40	290	10°R	280	6°W	286	145				

■ Figure 4-15 **Example 2**

Example 3. Finding HDG/TAS to Achieve a Particular TR/GS

Occasionally you may want to achieve a particular groundspeed, for instance to arrive overhead the destination at a particular time. This example is a variation on the previous one.

We want to know what true airspeed is required to achieve a groundspeed of 120 kt in Example 2.

KNOWN:	FIND:
TR 290°T	**TAS and HDG**
W/V 240°/40 kt	
GS 120 kt	

From/To	Safety ALT	ALT / Temp	RAS	TAS	W/V	TR °T	Drift	HDG °T	Var	HDG °M	GS	Dist	Time	ETA	HDG °C
					240/40	290			6°W		120				

■ Figure 4-16 **Example 3**

STEP 1. PLACE W/V ON THE PLOTTING DISC.

Set wind direction 240° under the index. Place wind-mark 40 kt above the centre-dot, wind blowing down.

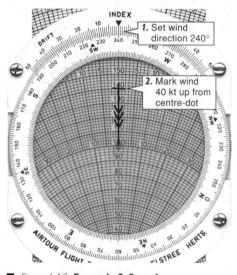

■ Figure 4-17 **Example 3, Step 1**

STEP 2. PLACE THE TR/GS VECTOR ON THE PLOTTING DISC.

In this case both TR 290°T and GS 120 kt are known. Rotate the compass rose and set TR 290°T under the index. Set GS 120 kt under the centre-dot.

STEP 3. READ OFF TAS, AND DETERMINE HDG FROM DRIFT.

Read off TAS 150 kt under the wind-mark. Read off drift of 12°, therefore HDG is 12° left of TR. HDG is 278°T.

NOTE The wind is from the left, so the wind correction angle is 12° left of the desired track to allow for the expected 12° right (starboard) drift. You can check your arithmetic against the small scale near the index mark.

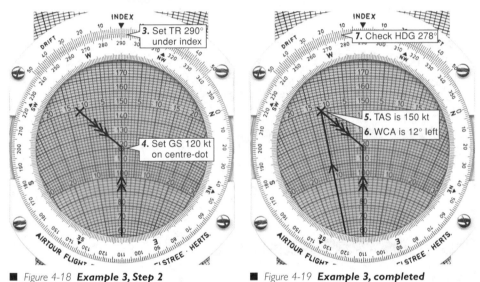

■ Figure 4-18 **Example 3, Step 2**   ■ Figure 4-19 **Example 3, completed**

ANSWER TAS 150 kt, HDG 278°T

From/To	Safety ALT	ALT		RAS	TAS	W/V	TR °T	Drift	HDG °T	Var	HDG °M	GS	Dist	Time	ETA	HDG °C
		Temp			150	240/40	290	12°R	278	6°W	284	120				

■ Figure 4-18 **Example 3**

Now complete **Exercises 4 – Wind Side –1.**

Calculating the Wind Velocity In Flight

After obtaining two position fixes en route, it is possible to determine the actual W/V, which can then be used in further calculations rather than the less-accurate forecast wind.

The two position fixes enable you to determine the track made good (TMG) and the groundspeed achieved during the time you have maintained a reasonably steady heading and true airspeed.

When in-flight, the pilot knows:
- the **heading maintained** from the compass or heading indicator;
- **true airspeed;**
- the **track made good** (TMG) by observation of the ground and map;
- the **groundspeed** by comparing distance covered with the time it takes.

These are four of the six items in the triangle of velocities and, using them, you can find the other two – wind direction and wind speed (i.e. wind velocity). This problem can be summarised as:

KNOWN:	FIND:
HDG/TAS and TR/GS	W/V

> Remember that in the UK it is usual for PPL pilots to work in degrees true.

Example 4. Finding the W/V In Flight

KNOWN:		FIND:
HDG	143°M	W/V
Variation	5°W, (HDG 138°T)	
TAS	120 kt	
TR	146°T	
GS	144 kt	

NOTE Another way of asking the same question is to give HDG 138°T and right drift 8° (rather than TR 146°T).

From/To	Safety ALT	ALT	Temp	RAS	TAS	W/V	TR °T	Drift	HDG °T	Var	HDG °M	GS	Dist	Time	ETA	HDG °C
					120		146		138	5°W	143	144				

■ Figure 4-19 **Example 4**

STEP 1. PLACE THE TR/GS VECTOR UNDER THE CENTRE-DOT.

Rotate the compass rose and set track 146°T under the index. Set GS 144 kt under the centre-dot.

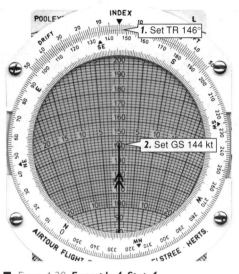

■ *Figure 4-20* **Example 4, Step 1**

STEP 2. PLACE THE HDG/TAS VECTOR ON THE PLOTTING DISC.

From HDG 138°T and TR 146°T, the drift is 8° to the right; the HDG is 8° to the left of TR (i.e. the wind correction angle is 8° left).

Mark in the HDG direction as the 8° drift line to the left of track. Mark the TAS where the 120 kt speed arc intersects the drift line; this indicates the HDG/TAS vector.

The W/V blows the aircraft from HDG to TR.

STEP 3. DETERMINE THE W/V.

Rotate the compass rose until the wind-mark is on the index line with the arrows pointing down towards the centre-dot. The direction the wind is blowing from, 360°T, is now indicated under the index.

Read off the wind strength of 30 kt. (Setting a definite speed arc under the centre-dot, 100 kt in this case, makes the wind strength easier to read.)

ANSWER W/V 360°T/30 kt

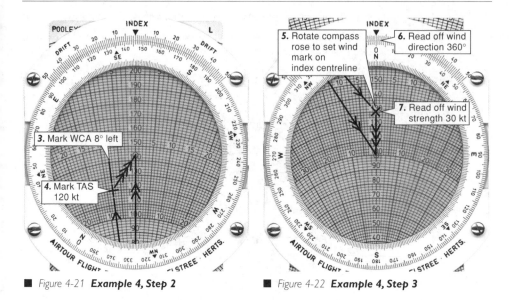

■ Figure 4-21 **Example 4, Step 2**   ■ Figure 4-22 **Example 4, Step 3**

From/To	Safety ALT	ALT Temp	RAS	TAS	W/V	TR °T	Drift	HDG °T	Var	HDG °M	GS	Dist	Time	ETA	HDG °C
				120	360/30	146	8°R	138	5°W	143	144				

■ Figure 4-23 **Example 4**

Now complete **Exercises 4 – Wind Side-2.**

Finding TMG and GS In Flight

The usual means of determining track made good and ground-speed is by visually fixing your position over ground features. On a flight over water or featureless terrain or in poor visibility, however, where you are unable to fix your position, it is possible to estimate a 'dead reckoning' track and groundspeed using:

- ☐ **heading** from the compass (corrected to HDG in degrees true, using variation if required);
- ☐ **TAS** (calculated from the rectified/calibrated airspeed if necessary);
- ☐ **W/V** (speed and direction, known from the forecast or previous calculations).

Example 5. Find TR and GS

KNOWN:		FIND:
HDG	057°M	**TR/GS**
TAS	120 kt	
W/V	115°T/40	
VAR	7°W	

From/To	Safety ALT	ALT Temp	RAS	TAS	W/V	TR °T	Drift	HDG °T	Var	HDG °M	GS	Dist	Time	ETA	HDG °C
				120	115/40			050	7°W	057					

■ Figure 4-24 **Example 5**

Since the HDG is known, but the TR is not, the HDG/TAS vector will be set under the centre-dot and the W/V will emanate from there. In this case, with the wind direction set under the index, the wind will start at the centre-dot and blow down the slide, hence the wind-mark will be shown down from the centre-dot.

STEP 1. PLACE THE W\V VECTOR ON THE PLOTTING DISC.

Rotate the compass rose until the wind direction 115°T is under the index. Mark the end of the W/V vector 40 kt below the centre-dot.

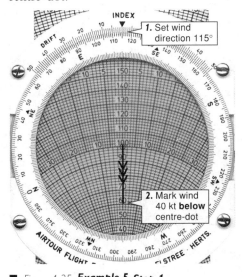

■ Figure 4-25 **Example 5, Step 1**

STEP 2. PLACE THE HDG/TAS VECTOR UNDER THE CENTRE-DOT.

Set HDG 050°T under the index. Move the slide so that TAS
120 kt is under the centre-dot.

STEP 3. READ OFF THE GS AND DRIFT.

The HDG/TAS vector is now set under the centre-dot and the
W/V vector acts out from the centre-dot. The wind-mark on the
outer end of the W/V vector lies over the TR/GS vector.

The GS of 108 kt appears under the wind dot. The drift lines
indicate 19° of drift left of HDG 050°, giving a TMG of 031°T.
(You can check your arithmetic against the small scale near the
index mark.)

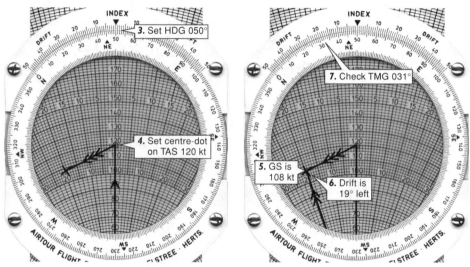

■ *Figure 4-26* **Example 5, Step 2**   ■ *Figure 4-27* **Example 5, completed**

From/To	Safety ALT	ALT	Temp	RAS	TAS	W/V	TR °T	Drift	HDG °T	Var	HDG °M	GS	Dist	Time	ETA	HDG °C
					120	115/40	031	19L	050	7°W	057	108				

■ *Figure 4-28* **Example 5**

ANSWER Drift 19° left (port), TR 031°T; GS 108 kt.

Now complete **Exercises 4 – Wind Side-3.**

If you are satisfied with the above method of using the wind side of your computer, then it is not necessary to work through the next part (Method B), as the calculations are a repeat of what you have just completed.

You should, however, complete the final part of this chapter, beginning on page 76, which shows how to work out wind components. This is important information for take-off and landing operations on runways where the wind is not blowing directly along the runway (often the case).

Wind Side *Method B*

Use Method B if your flying instructor recommends it. It is called the 'wind-mark-down' method because:

☐ **the wind direction** (from which it blows) is placed under the index;

☐ **the centre-dot** is used as the starting point of the W/V vector; and

☐ **the wind-mark,** in this case representing the end of the W/V vector, is drawn beneath the centre-dot ('down' from the centre-dot).

Since the W/V blows the aeroplane from its heading to its track, and the heading vector ends where the W/V vector starts, the heading/TAS vector should be placed up the centre of the slide so that it ends at the centre-dot.

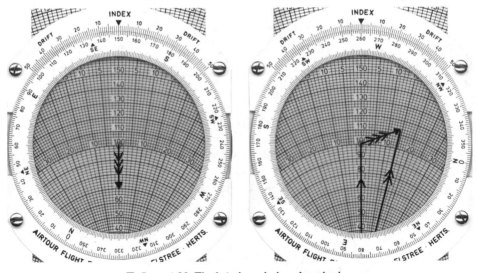

■ *Figure 4-29* **The 'wind-mark-down' method**

The simplest type of problem to solve using the wind-mark-down method is the in-flight situation of knowing the HDG, TAS and W/V, and then having to find the TR and GS. This situation could arise on an over-water flight, or a flight over barren terrain or in poor visibility, where it is difficult to obtain two position fixes to determine TR and GS. HDG is found from the compass, TAS is calculated from the indicated airspeed, and forecast W/V (in °T) is used.

Remember that all calculations on the computer must be totally in °T, or totally in °M. Do not mix them! In the UK, it is usual for PPL pilots to work in °T, so this will mean converting the compass reading into °T, using magnetic variation (and deviation if required).

Finding Track and Groundspeed In Flight

Example 1. Find TR and GS

KNOWN:		FIND:
HDG	050°T	**TR and GS**
TAS	120 kt	
W/V	140°T/30 kt	

In practice, you would probably enter this data on a flight log to keep it neat and orderly.

From/To	Safety ALT	ALT / Temp	RAS	TAS	W/V	TR °T	Drift	HDG °T	Var	HDG °M	GS	Dist	Time	ETA	HDG °C
				120	140/30			050							

■ Figure 4-30 **Example 1**

STEP 1. PLACE THE W/V ON THE PLOTTING DISC.

Rotate the compass rose until the wind direction 140°T is under the index. Set the centre-dot (in transparent window) on an easily noted value (100 in the illustration) and mark the end of the W/V vector 30 knots down from the centre-dot.

STEP 2. PLACE THE HDG/TAS VECTOR UNDER THE CENTRE-DOT.

Rotate the compass rose until the HDG 050°T is under the index. Move the slide so that the TAS 120 kt is under the centre-dot.

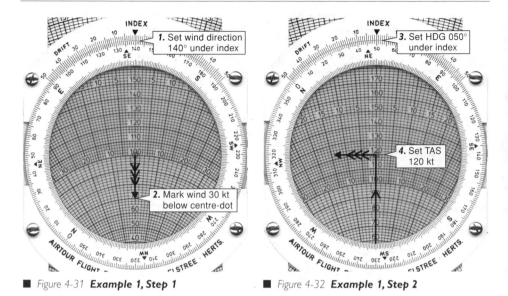

■ Figure 4-31 **Example 1, Step 1**   ■ Figure 4-32 **Example 1, Step 2**

STEP 3. READ OFF GS AND DRIFT, THEN CALCULATE TRACK.

The wind-mark now lies over the groundspeed 123 kt. The wind-mark lies over the 14° drift line, which means the wind blowing from the right will cause a HDG of 050°T to result in a track of (050 – 14) = 036°T. (You can check your arithmetic against the small scale near the index mark.)

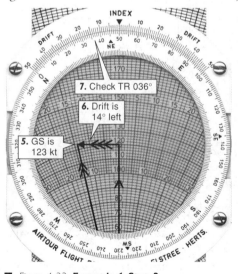

■ Figure 4-33 **Example 1, Step 3**

ANSWER GS 123 kt, TMG 036°T added to the flight log.

From/To	Safety ALT	ALT		RAS	TAS	W/V	TR °T	Drift	HDG °T	Var	HDG °M	GS	Dist	Time	ETA	HDG °C
		Temp														
				120	140/30		036		050			123				

■ Figure 4-34 **Example 1**

Now complete **Exercises 4 – Wind Side-3.**
(Wind Side-2 and Wind Side-1 follow)

Finding the Wind Velocity In Flight

Example 2. Find W/V

This is a typical in-flight situation, where HDG and TAS are known, and two position fixes allow you to determine the track made good and the groundspeed.

KNOWN:		FIND:
HDG	160°T	**W/V** (direction
TAS	145 kt	and strength)
TMG	168°T	
GS	157 kt	

From/To	Safety ALT	ALT		RAS	TAS	W/V	TR °T	Drift	HDG °T	Var	HDG °M	GS	Dist	Time	ETA	HDG °C
		Temp														
				145			168		160			157				

■ Figure 4-35 **Example 2**

NOTE The same question could have been asked differently, with HDG 160°T and drift 8° right given, rather than TR 168°T.

STEP 1. PLACE THE HDG/TAS VECTOR UNDER THE CENTRE-DOT.
Rotate the compass rose until the HDG 160°T appears under the index. Move the slide until TAS 145 kt is under the centre-dot.

STEP 2. PLACE THE TMG/GS ON THE PLOTTING DISC.
Mark in the 8° right drift line, since the drift is 8° to the right, calculated from the HDG 160°T and the TMG 168°T. Mark the point along this line where the GS is 157 kt. This point is the end of the TR/GS vector. (The wind has blown the aeroplane from the centre-dot to this point marked on the plotting disc.)

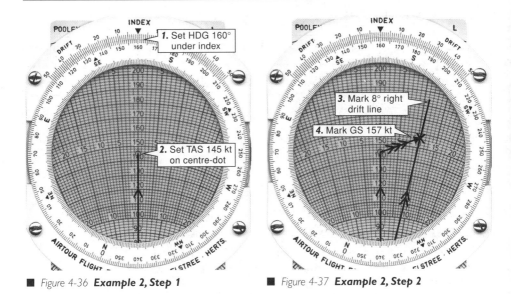

■ Figure 4-36 **Example 2, Step 1**　　■ Figure 4-37 **Example 2, Step 2**

STEP 3. READ OFF THE W/V.

Rotate the compass rose until the wind dot appears directly down from the centre-dot. The direction from which the wind is blowing appears under the index, i.e. 045°T.

The wind strength of 26 kt can be read from the distance beneath the centre-dot. (You can adjust the slide to make reading this easier.)

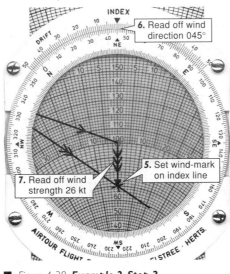

■ Figure 4-38 **Example 2, Step 3**

ANSWER W/V is 045°T/26 kt

From/To	Safety ALT	ALT		RAS	TAS	W/V	TR °T	Drift	HDG °T	Var	HDG °M	GS	Dist	Time	ETA	HDG °C
		Temp														
				145		045/26	168		160			157				

■ *Figure 4-39* **Example 2**

Now complete **Exercises 4 – Wind Side-2.**

The Flight-Planning Situation

Example 3. Find HDG and GS, Knowing TR, TAS and W/V

This is the typical situation prior to flight. Since it is at the flight-planning stage when the navigation computer is used most, you must become adept at this sort of problem.

From the aeronautical chart, you can measure the desired track (and distance). The wind is known from the forecast. The aeroplane's performance in terms of true airspeed is known, or can be found from the Flight Manual or Pilot's Operating Handbook.

KNOWN:		FIND:
Desired track	295°T	**HDG and GS**
TAS	97 kt	
Forecast W/V	320°T/25	

From/To	Safety ALT	ALT		RAS	TAS	W/V	TR °T	Drift	HDG °T	Var	HDG °M	GS	Dist	Time	ETA	HDG °C
		Temp														
					97	320/25	295									

■ *Figure 4-40* **Example 3**

STEP 1. PLACE THE W/V ON THE PLOTTING DISC.
Rotate the compass rose until the direction from which the wind is blowing is under the index, i.e. 320°T. Put a wind-mark 25 kt down from the centre-dot.

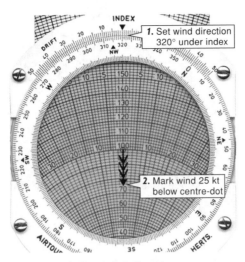

■ Figure 4-41 **Example 3, Step 1**

STEP 2. PLACE THE HDG/TAS UNDER THE CENTRE-DOT.

Since the W/V starts at the centre-dot and blows away from it, place the end of the HDG/TAS vector under the centre-dot.

Move the slide until TAS 97 kt appears under the centre-dot. Set approximate HDG 295°T under the index.

When we come to set the HDG under the index, we are faced with a problem – we do not know the HDG! To get started, use the desired track as an approximate HDG; i.e. assume that the HDG is approximately 295°T and rotate the compass rose until 295°T appears under the index.

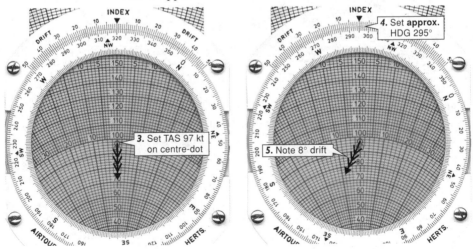

■ Figure 4-42 **Example 3, Step 2a**   ■ Figure 4-43 **Example 3, Step 2b**

STEP 3. ADJUST THE APPROXIMATE HDG TO ALLOW FOR DRIFT.

The W/V dot lies over the 8° left drift line, so, on a HDG of 295°T, the aeroplane should achieve a track 8° to the left of this.

Since the desired track is 295°, the aeroplane should be headed approximately 8° to the right of this to allow for the left drift, i.e. on a HDG of 303°T, with a wind correction angle of 8° right.

Rotate the compass rose until 303°T appears under the index, and check the drift (and calculate the track). The drift is now indicated to be only 6° (not the original 8°), so adjust the HDG to allow for only 6°, i.e. an adjusted HDG is 301°T.

Set the adjusted HDG 301°T under the index. By checking the position of the wind-mark, we see that this minor 'jiggle' of the compass rose has not appreciably altered the 6° drift. (In other words, the adjusted HDG and the expected 6° left (port) drift will allow us to achieve the desired track of 295°T.)

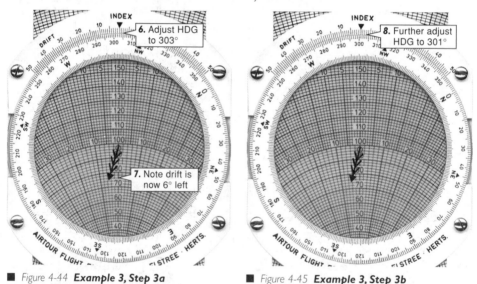

■ Figure 4-44 **Example 3, Step 3a**   ■ Figure 4-45 **Example 3, Step 3b**

STEP 4. READ OFF THE HDG AND GS.

The HDG 301°T appears under the index. The GS 73 kt appears under the wind-mark.

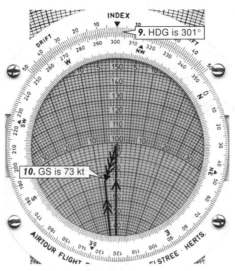

■ *Figure 4-46* **Example 3, Step 4**

ANSWER HDG 301°T, GS 73 kt

From/To	Safety ALT	ALT Temp	RAS	TAS	W/V	TR °T	Drift	HDG °T	Var	HDG °M	GS	Dist	Time	ETA	HDG °C
			97	320/25	295			301			73				

■ *Figure 4-47* **Example 3**

NOTE Because there have to be some adjustments to the initial HDG by rotating the compass rose a few degrees this way and that, the above method is sometimes also known as the 'jiggle' method, as well as the 'wind-mark-down' method. It still gives accurate answers.

To solve a slightly unusual flight-planning problem such as "What TAS is required to achieve a groundspeed of 80 kt?" the same procedure as above can be used, except that the wind-mark is placed over the appropriate GS arc, and then the TAS and HDG can be read off under the centre-dot.

Now complete **Exercises 4 – Wind Side-1.**

Example 4. Find HDG and GS, Knowing TR, TAS and W/V

This variation on the 'wind-mark-down' method avoids having to jiggle the compass rose when calculating HDG and GS at the flight-planning stage. It repeats the previous example. Check if your instructor recommends this method.

KNOWN:		FIND:
TR	295°T	**HDG and GS**
TAS	97 kt	
W/V	320°T/25 kt	

From/To	Safety ALT	ALT / Temp	RAS	TAS	W/V	TR °T	Drift	HDG °T	Var	HDG °M	GS	Dist	Time	ETA	HDG °C
				97	320/25	295									

■ *Figure 4-48* **Example 4**

STEP 1. SET W/V ON THE PLOTTING DISC USING THE SQUARE GRID.

Rotate the compass rose until the wind direction 320°T appears under the index.

Set the zero point of the square grid under the centre-dot. Put a wind-mark 25 kt down from the centre-dot.

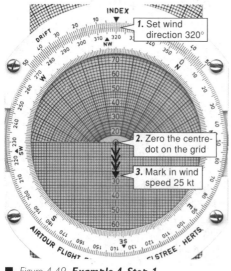

■ *Figure 4-49* **Example 4, Step 1**

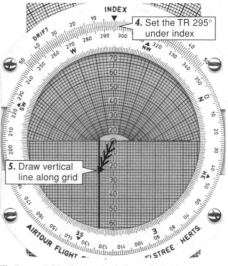

■ *Figure 4-50* **Example 4, Step 2**

STEP 2. SET TRACK, AND MARK IN CROSSWIND LINE.

Rotate the compass rose until the TR 295°T appears under the index. Run a vertical line down through the wind-mark, which is a 10 kt crosswind component. It is this crosswind component from the right that causes the left drift.

STEP 3. SET HDG/TAS ON THE PLOTTING DISC.

Move the slide and place TAS 97 kt under the centre-dot. Note that the crosswind effect line does not parallel the drift lines at this stage.

Rotate the compass rose until the crosswind effect line is parallel with one of the drift lines.

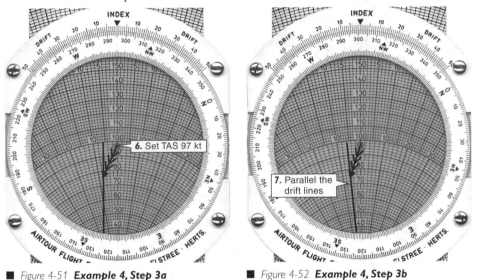

■ *Figure 4-51* **Example 4, Step 3a**   ■ *Figure 4-52* **Example 4, Step 3b**

STEP 4. READ OFF HDG AND GS.

HDG/TAS lies under the centre-dot. The TR/GS vector ends where the W/V vector ends.

Read off HDG 301°T under the index. Read off GS 73 kt under the wind-mark.

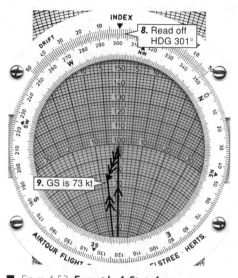

Figure 4-53 **Example 4, Step 4**

ANSWER HDG 301°T, GS 73 kt

From/To	Safety ALT	ALT	Temp	RAS	TAS	W/V	TR °T	Drift	HDG °T	Var	HDG °M	GS	Dist	Time	ETA	HDG °C
				97	320/25	295			301			73				

Figure 4-54 **Example 4**

Now complete **Exercises 4 – Wind Side-1** *using this method.*

Wind Components

Often a wind needs to be broken down into its two components:
☐ the **headwind or tailwind** component; and
☐ the **crosswind** component.

This is especially the case when taking off and landing, because:

1. **For performance reasons,** you often need to know the head-wind or tailwind component to determine the take-off or landing distance required.

2. **For safe aeroplane handling,** you always need to know (at least approximately) the crosswind component on the runway that you intend using. The crosswind component is very

important and every aeroplane has a maximum crosswind limit specified in its Flight Manual. This crosswind limit should never be exceeded.

Winds found on forecasts, which are most likely to be used for flight-planning purposes, are given in degrees true, whereas the wind in take-off and landing reports broadcast by Air Traffic Control are given in degrees magnetic, so that they can be easily related to runway direction, which is always in °M. This applies to the direction of the wind given to you by the Tower, or as broadcast on the Automatic Terminal Information Service (ATIS).

A runway whose centreline lies in the direction 074°M will be designated Runway 07. A runway whose centreline lies in the direction 357°M will be designated Runway 36. A wind of 350°M/25 kt would favour RWY 36, which is almost directly into-wind. RWY 07 would experience a strong crosswind from the left; the pilot should determine just how strong before using this particular runway.

Since both wind direction and runway direction are measured from the same datum (magnetic north), there is no need to convert into degrees true for your computer manipulations. When using your computer, work either totally in °T or totally in °M.

In Vol. 4 of *The Air Pilot's Manual,* when discussing take-off and landing performance, we illustrate a simple way of determining wind components mentally. Here we show you how to do it using the **square grid** on your navigation computer.

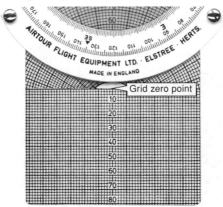

■ *Figure 4-55* **The square grid on the computer slide**

Finding Wind Components

What crosswind and headwind components exist on Runway 18 if the wind broadcast by the Tower is 120°M/30? (Runway 18 means that the runway direction is approx 180°M.)

STEP 1. SET UP THE W/V ON THE SQUARE GRID.

Set the zero point of the square grid under the centre-dot. Rotate the compass rose and set wind direction 120° under the index. Put a wind-mark 30 kt down from the centre-dot.

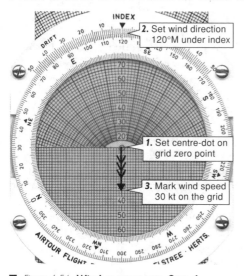

■ *Figure 4-56* **Wind components, Step 1**

STEP 2. SET RUNWAY DIRECTION.

Rotate the compass rose until the runway direction 180°M is under the index.

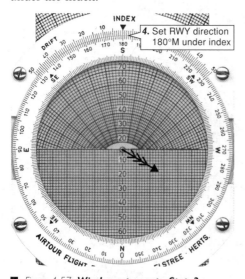

■ *Figure 4-57* **Wind components, Step 2**

STEP 3. READ OFF HEADWIND AND CROSSWIND COMPONENTS.
Drop a vertical line to the wind-mark. The length of this line is the headwind component, 15 kt.

The horizontal distance of this line from the centre-dot is the crosswind component, 26 kt.

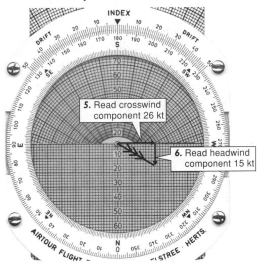

■ *Figure 4-58* ***Wind components, Step 3***

ANSWER Headwind (H/W) 15 kt, crosswind (X/W) 26 kt

NOTE If, when the runway direction is set under the index, the end of the wind vector is above the horizontal line through the centre-dot, then there is a tailwind component and it is advisable to consider changing runways. The precise strength of the down-wind component can be found by placing the reciprocal to the runway direction under the index (360 in the above case), which allows you to find what is a headwind component for a take-off in that direction.

Now complete ***Exercises 4 – Wind Side-4.***

Calculator Side of the Navigation Computer

The calculator side of the navigation computer looks complicated at first, but once you become familiar with it you will find its use straightforward. A little work now learning how to use it will be repaid many times over, as it simplifies your calculations and saves lots of time. The calculator side is useful for solving quickly and accurately the numerous small calculations involved in air navigation.

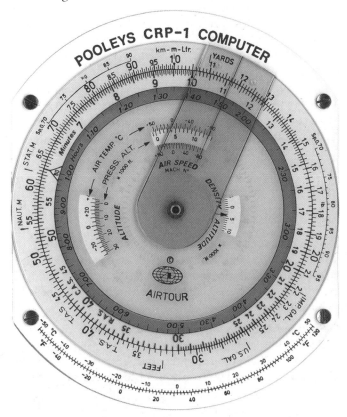

■ *Figure 5-1* **Calculator side of a navigation computer**

Various computer types differ in minor ways on the calculator side but the way they are used is the same. As you go through this chapter we suggest that you have your computer close by and follow our examples with it.

Use of the computer for solving the altitude and airspeed problems on the small scales in the mid-area of the calculator side is covered in Chapter 2, Speed and Chapter 7, Time. In this chapter we cover what can be done with the two outside scales, which form a circular slide rule.

The Circular Slide Rule

Simple multiplication and division can be done mentally, or, if more complicated, with electronic calculators, or with *logarithms*. A logarithm is one of a series of numbers, set out in tables, that make it possible to work out problems by adding and subtracting numbers, instead of multiplying and dividing. A slide rule is just a pictorial means of using logarithms.

To avoid the need for pilots to carry long, straight slide rules, a circular slide rule has been devised. It is fast, never has flat batteries, and is accurate enough for our purposes. The circular slide rule has two scales:

☐ **an inner** rotary scale; and
☐ **an outer** fixed scale.

Both scales are marked with logarithmic graduations, making it possible to multiply and divide simply by the physical addition or subtraction of lengths of the graduated scales. The numbers on the scales are marked in order from 10 all the way around the scale to 100, but the larger the number the closer it is to its neighbour.

■ *Figure 5-2* **A simple logarithmic scale**

If you look at your circular slide rule you will see that the numbers 1, 10, 100, 1,000, 0.1, 0.001, etc., are completely interchangeable and are all labelled at the same point as 10. Similarly, 5, 50, 500, 0.5, 0.005 are interchangeable and are all labelled at the same point as 50.

Slide Rules are Accurate to Three Significant Figures

Slide rules and navigation computers are fairly small in size, so the accuracy to which you can read them depends on your eyesight. Most slide rule scales allow you to read to an accuracy of three digits.

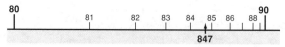

■ *Figure 5-3* **This scale reads 847**

Unfortunately the scale does not tell us where the decimal point belongs in relation to the three significant figures. For example, 847 could be written any of the following ways:

847.0
84.7
8.47
0.847
8,470.0

To know where to place the decimal point you must estimate the approximate answer to the question by quick mental arithmetic. The mental calculations give an approximate answer (allowing us to place the decimal point correctly); the slide rule manipulations give us that answer accurate to three signifcant figures.

Calculations

When using the slide rule part of the navigation computer, always follow this procedure:

1. Rough mental calculation.

2. Slide rule manipulation to obtain three significant figures.

3. Place the decimal point (from rough mental calculation).

As well as telling you where to place the decimal point, the rough mental calculation is a check that your computer manipulations were at least approximately correct and your answer not grossly in error. First doing the mental check results in fewer errors, and is good practice for the many times in flight and on the ground when mental calculations are necessary.

Multiplication

EXAMPLE 1 Multiply 3.25 × 4.29

Step 1. Rough mental calculation
3 × 5 = 15

Step 2. Computer manipulation
Treat 10 on the outer scale as the starting point and find 3.25. Set 10 on the inner scale below 3.25 on the outer (or 32.5 of 325 or 3,250). Find 4.29 on the inner scale and mark directly above it, i.e. 139.

Step 3. Place the decimal point
Determine position of decimal point by referring back to the rough calculation 3 × 5 = 15, so the answer is 13.9. It is obviously not 1.39 or 139.0.

ANSWER 3.25 × 4.29 = 13.9

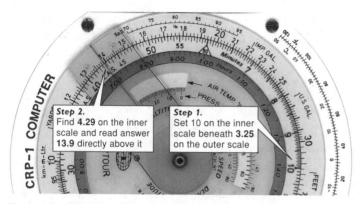

■ *Figure 5-4* **The multiplication 3.25 × 4.29 = ? on the circular slide rule**

Division

EXAMPLE 2 The division 36 divided by 12 (36 ÷ 12) is an easy one to begin with. We simply need to subtract the logarithm of 12 from the logarithm of 36.

■ *Figure 5-5* **The division 36 ÷ 12 on the circular slide rule**

Step 1. Rough calculation
36 ÷ 12 = 3

Step 2. Computer manipulation
Treat 10 on the outer scale as the starting point; the logarithm of 36 is the distance from 10 to 36 on the outer scale. Beneath 36 place 12 (the logarithm of 12 is the distance from 10 to 12 on the inner scale).

Then locate 10 on the inner scale and above it find the answer, 30. (Do not confuse 10 with 1:00 which symbolises *1 hour = 60 minutes* on some navigation computers.) The log of 12 has thus been subtracted from the log of 36.

Step 3. Place the decimal point
To determine the position of the decimal point is easy in this case, because we know that 36 ÷ 12 = 3, and so the answer is not 30 or 300 but 3.0.

ANSWER 36 ÷ 12 = 3.0

Combined Multiplication and Division

Occasionally calculations involve both multiplication and division, and the circular slide rule is ideal for this. The best approach is to begin with a division and follow with the multiplication. This process can be repeated as many times as necessary.

EXAMPLE 3 Calculate 25 times 15, divided by 5. (Another simple one that can be done mentally, but a good example to begin with.)

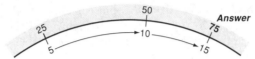

■ *Figure 5-6* **The calculation** $\dfrac{25 \times 15}{5}$ **on the circular slide rule**

Step 1. Rough check
$25 \div 5 = 5$ which, multiplied by 15, gives $5 \times 15 = 75$.

Step 2. Computer manipulation
Do the division $25 \div 5$ by placing 5 on the inner scale under 25 on the outer scale. (The answer to this appears on the outer scale above the 10 on the inner scale, and the setting does not have to be altered to do the multiplication of this answer by 15.)

Do the multiplication by finding 15 on the inner scale and marking the answer above it on the outer scale, i.e. 75. (You will determine the position of the decimal point by doing a quick mental check $25 \div 5 = 5$, which is multiplied by 15 to give 75.0.)

Step 3. Place the decimal point
Reference to our rough check confirms that the decimal point is placed to give 75.0.

ANSWER 75.0

EXAMPLE 4 Calculate $\dfrac{25.7 \times 3.96}{5.12}$

Step 1. Rough calculation

$$\frac{25 \times 4}{5} = 20$$

Step 2. Computer manipulation
Set 25.7 on the outer scale against 5.12 on the inner scale. Against 3.96 on the inner scale read off on the outer scale the result 199.

■ *Figure 5-7* **Calculation of** $\dfrac{25.7 \times 3.96}{5.12}$

Step 3. Place the decimal point
From our mental calculation, the decimal point should be placed thus: 19.9.

ANSWER 19.9

Ratios

$$D = \frac{25 \times 4}{5}$$ may be expressed slightly differently as a ratio:

$$\frac{D}{4} = \frac{25}{5}$$ and find D.

A rough mental check indicates that D is approximately 20. The set-up on the circular slide rule is shown in Figure 5-8. The answer is of course 20.0. This could be the answer to a number of navigation questions:

EXAMPLE 5 If an aeroplane travels 25 nautical miles (nm) in 5 minutes, how far would it travel in a further 4 minutes?

ANSWER 20 nm

■ Figure 5-8 **Finding ratios on the circular slide rule**

EXAMPLE 6 If an aeroplane burns 25 litres of fuel in 5 minutes, how many litres would the aeroplane have burned at the same rate in 4 minutes?

ANSWER 20 litres

EXAMPLE 7 If an aeroplane travels 25 nm in 5 minutes, how far would it travel in 40 minutes?

ANSWER 200 nm

EXAMPLE 8 If you descend 2,500 feet in 5 minutes, how far would you expect to descend in the next 4 minutes? What is your rate of descent?

ANSWER 2,000 ft, and 500 ft/min (1 minute is 10 on the inner scale)

These are all common navigation calculations and you must be able to perform them with speed and accuracy.

Solving Speed, Distance, Time and Ratio Problems

Speed is the ratio of distance/time. As there are 60 minutes in 1 hour, a speed of 140 knots is the same as travelling a distance of 140 nautical miles over the ground in 60 minutes. We can set this up on the circular slide rule by placing the 60 minutes (sometimes written as 1:00 hour) on the inner TIME scale against the 140 on the outer DISTANCE scale.

On most computers the **inner scale** is marked TIME and the **outer scale** DISTANCE (usually somewhere near the 60 mark). This is important to keep in mind – that TIME is always on the inner scale and DISTANCE/SPEED on the outer.

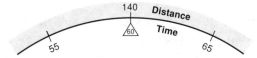

■ Figure 5-9 *A typical distance-time problem*

The circular slide rule is now set up to answer many questions, such as:

EXAMPLE 9 At a groundspeed (GS) of 140 kt, how far will you travel in 30 minutes?

Step 1. Rough Check
30 minutes is half an hour which, at 140 kt, is 70 nm.

Step 2.
Find 30 minutes on the inner TIME scale and read off the answer 70 nm on the outer DISTANCE scale.

ANSWER 70 nm

EXAMPLE 10 At a groundspeed (GS) of 140 kt, how far will you travel in 15 minutes?

Step 1. Rough Check
15 minutes is ¼ hour which, at 140 kt, gives 140 ÷ 4 = 35 nm.

Step 2.
Find 15 minutes on the inner TIME scale and then read off the answer 35 nm on the outer DISTANCE scale.

ANSWER 35 nm

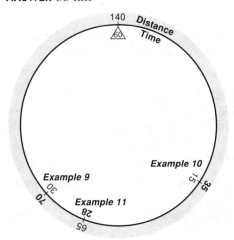

■ Figure 5-10 *Speed, time and distance problems on the circular slide rule*

EXAMPLE 11 At a GS of 140 kt, how long will it take you to travel 65 nm?

Step 1. Rough Check
65 nm is slightly less than ½ of 140 nm which, at 140 kt, will take slightly less than 30 minutes to cover.

Step 2.
Find 65 nm on the outer DISTANCE scale and read off the answer 28 minutes (approximately) on the inner TIME scale.

ANSWER 28 minutes (approximately)

Now complete **Exercises 5 – Calculator-1.**

Further Problems
The computer can be used to help us solve many different types of problem involving multiplication, division or ratios. Another sort of calculation we can make is:

EXAMPLE 12 If we cover 16 nm over the ground in 10 minutes, what is our groundspeed?

Step 1. Rough check
10 minutes is ⅙ hour. We cover 16 nm in 10 minutes, so we will cover six times this distance in an hour, i.e. 6 × 16 = 96 nm. The speed is therefore 96 kt.

Step 2.
Set up 16 nm on the outer DISTANCE scale against 10 minutes on the inner TIME scale.

Step 3.
Against 60 minutes (1:00 hour) on the inner TIME scale read off on the outer DISTANCE scale the distance you would travel in that time, which of course is 96 nm; that is, the GS is 96 kt.

ANSWER 96 kt

■ *Figure 5-11* **Finding groundspeed**

The computer is now set up to answer other questions relevant to this situation, such as:

EXAMPLE 13 How far will the aeroplane then travel in a further 5 minutes?

ANSWER 8 nm

EXAMPLE 14 How long will it take to travel 24 nm?

ANSWER 15 minutes

In each case, a rough mental check will confirm that the answers are 8 nm (and not 80 or 0.8) and 15 minutes (and not 150 or 1.5).

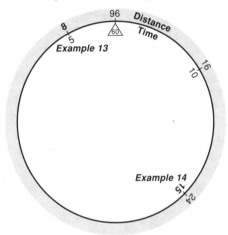

■ *Figure 5-12* **Time-speed-distance set-up**

Now complete **Exercises 5 – Calculator-2.**

Fuel Consumption Problems

EXAMPLE 15 If an aeroplane is burning fuel at the rate of 30 litres per hour, what fuel burn-off can you expect in 8 minutes?

Step 1. Rough check
30 litres per hour is ½ litre per minute which, for 8 minutes, will give a burn-off of 4 litres.

Step 2.
Set 60 minutes (1:00 hour) on the inner TIME scale against 30 (litres) on the outer scale.

Step 3.
Against 8 minutes on the inner TIME scale read off 4 (litres) on the outer scale. (Our rough mental calculation indicates that the answer is 4 and not 40 or 400 or 0.4).

ANSWER 4 litres

■ *Figure 5-13* **Example 15, a typical fuel consumption problem**

EXAMPLE 16 If we have burned 4 litres in 10 minutes, how much will we burn in the next 25 minutes?

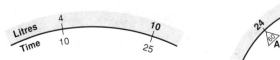 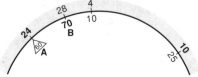

■ *Figure 5-14* **Example 16**

Step 1. Rough check
25 = 2.5 × 10, so expect to use 2.5 × 4 = 10 litres.

Step 2.
Set up 10 minutes on the inner TIME scale against 4 litres on the outer scale.

Step 3.
Against 25 minutes on the inner TIME scale read off 10 litres on the outer scale.

ANSWER 10 litres (not 1 or 100 or 1,000)

The circular slide rule is now set up to answer other problems relevant to this situation, such as:

1. What is the rate of fuel consumption in litres/hour?
Answer: 24 litres/hour

2. How long would it take to burn 28 litres?
Answer: 70 minutes

EXAMPLE 17 If your aeroplane has 26 US gallons of usable fuel in the tanks, and the average consumption rate is 5.5 USG/hour, what is the safe flight endurance if you wish to land with 1 hour's reserve unused?

Step 1. Rough check
Subtracting the reserve (5.5 USG in this case) leaves 20.5 USG as flight fuel. A rough mental check (20 USG at 6 USG/hour) = 3⅓ hours.

Step 2.
By computer, with 60 minutes on the inner scale set against 5.5 USG on the outer, read against 20.5 USG on the outer scale the answer of 224 minutes on the inner.

ANSWER 3 hours 44 minutes (224 minutes)

Remember the Rough Mental Check

The rough mental check will avoid gross errors being made. For example, an answer of 22.4 minutes to the above question may not seem in error to a pilot who does not back up his computer manipulations with mental checks, yet it is in error by a factor of 10. As well as allowing you to place the decimal point correctly, a mental check also allows an approximate check of the numbers involved.

Do not neglect the mental check in order to save time or energy. What is the point of calculating the fuel to be 139 and ordering 1.39 litres or 13.9 litres rather than 139 litres?

It seems ridiculous, but rough estimates to back up computer calculations could have prevented a number of accidents, including some involving large jets. Learn the value of mental checks early in your flying career; professional pilots make mental checks all the time.

Now complete **Exercises 5 – Calculator-3.**

'Off-Track' Problems

EXAMPLE 18 If an aeroplane is 5 nm off-track after travelling 20 nm, how far off-track will it be after travelling 45 nm?

Step 1. Rough check

This is a simple ratio problem of $\dfrac{5}{20} = \dfrac{?}{45}$

$\dfrac{5}{20} = \dfrac{10}{40}$ Answer will be slightly greater than 10.

Step 2.

1. Set up 5 against 20.

2. Find the answer 11.2 against 45.

■ *Figure 5-15*

ANSWER 11.2 nm off-track

The computer is now set up to find answers to problems such as:

1. If you are 5 nm off-track after travelling 20 nm, how far off-track will you be after travelling a total of 60 nm?
Answer: 15 nm

■ *Figure 5-16* **An off-track problem**

These numbers are particularly significant as they relate to the *1-in-60 rule.* If you measure it out you will find that:

☐ **1 nm** off-track in 60 nm is a track error of 1°.

☐ **15 nm** off-track in 60 nm is a track error of 15°.

☐ **5 nm** off-track in 20 nm is a track error of 15°, because 5 nm off-track in 20 nm is the same as 15 nm off-track in 60 nm.

EXAMPLE 19 If an aeroplane is 3 nm off-track after travelling 20 nm, what is its track error?

■ *Figure 5-17* **Example 19**

ANSWER 3 nm off-track in 20 nm is 9° track error using the 1-in-60 rule.

NOTE The 1-in-60 method of calculating angles is sufficiently accurate up to about 20°. It is explained fully in Section 3, *En Route Navigation Techniques.*

Now complete **Exercises 5 – Calculator-4.**

Conversions

You will often have to convert from one unit to another. Some of the common conversions are labelled on the scales of the circular slide rule, but they vary from computer to computer so check your own computer handbook.

Temperatures

The standard unit for temperature is the degree Celsius (°C), except in the USA and a few other places where they still use degrees Fahrenheit (°F). Both systems are based on the freezing and boiling points of water.

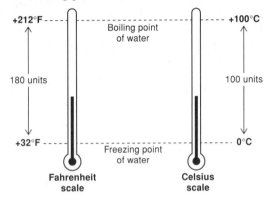

■ *Figure 5-18* **Temperature scales are based on the freezing and boiling points of water**

Some computers have a separate F/C scale that allow simple conversions from one to the other. The reason for this separate scale is that we cannot convert from Fahrenheit to Celsius, or vice versa, by a simple arithmetical conversion, because the zero on one scale is not zero on the other. 0°C = +32°F.

EXAMPLE 20 Convert +15°C to °F.

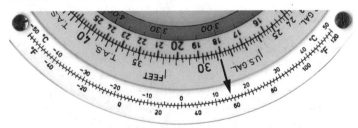

■ *Figure 5-19* **+15°C = +60°F**

NOTE There are formulae that convert °C to °F and vice versa, but the computer conversion is much easier.

°F = (⅗ × °C) +32   °C = ⅝ × (°F – 32)

Now complete **Exercises 5 – Calculator-5.**

Distances

Nautical Miles, Statute Miles and Kilometres

It is an unfortunate fact of life that we have to deal with the same physical distance being measured in different units. For most navigation purposes we use the **nautical mile**. Nautical miles are important because of their relationship to the *angular* measurement of latitude on the earth.

In the UK long distances are measured in **statute miles,** which are shorter than nautical miles. A statute mile is an arbitrary distance laid down by Royal Statute during the reign of Elizabeth I.

In the metric system, which is based on the number 1,000, the unit of distance is the **metre.** Kilometres (1,000 metres) are used for long distances; centimetres ($\frac{1}{100}$ metre) and millimetres ($\frac{1}{1,000}$ metre) for short distances.

A metre is $\frac{1}{10,000,000}$ (one ten millionth) of the distance from the equator to a pole, which makes a kilometre $\frac{1}{10,000}$ of the distance from the equator to a pole, so the average distance from the equator to a pole is 10,000 km.

The kilometre is much shorter than the nautical mile. It is the standard unit for distance in most of Europe and many other parts of the world. The UK is in the process of changing over from imperial and statute standards to metric standards, so, eventually, the kilometre may officially replace the statute mile.

Pilots need to understand the relationship between these units of distance and be able to convert from one to the other. The relationship between navigation, statute and metric units is:

1 nautical mile = 1.15 statue miles = 1.852 kilometres (1,852 metres).

FOR QUICK MENTAL CHECKS, REMEMBER:				
1 nm	=	*1.2 sm*	=	*2 km*
0.9 nm	=	*1 sm*	=	*1.5 km*
0.5 nm	=	*0.6 sm*	=	*1 km*

The navigation computer can provide accurate and straightforward unit conversions. It has indices for nautical miles, statute miles and kilometres marked on the outer scale.

How to Convert from One Unit to Another

1. As with all computer calculations, do a rough mental check.

2. Set the known quantity on the inner scale of the computer against its index on the outer scale.

3. Against the index of the required unit on the outer scale, read off the answer on the inner scale.

EXAMPLE 21 Convert 10 nm to sm and km.

Step 1. Rough check:

1 nm = approx. 1.2 sm = approx. 2 km

10 nm = approx. 12 sm = approx. 20 km

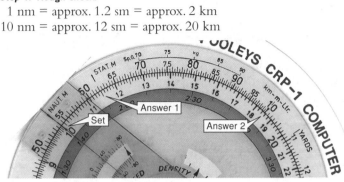

Figure 5-20 **Example 21**

ANSWER 10 nm = 11.5 sm = 18.5 km

This method may also be used to convert speeds:

EXAMPLE 22 Convert 231 kph to mph and kt.

Step 1. Rough check

approx. 0.5 nm = approx. 0.6 sm = 1 km

231 kph = approx. 0.6 × 231 mph = approx. 138 mph

231 kph = approx. 0.5 × 231 kt = approx. 115 kt

ANSWER 231 kph = 144 mph = 125 kt

Now complete **Exercises 5 – Calculator-6.**

Converting Feet to Metres and Vice Versa

The standard unit for altitude is the **foot** in most countries, but many Eastern countries use metres. Pilots flying in both these areas need to be able to convert quickly from one system to the other (although the aeroplanes are usually fitted with separate altimeters – one showing feet and the other showing metres).

UK pilots visiting European countries will find topographical charts with the elevation of high ground marked in metres. Some of these charts cover parts of the UK, but the elevations are still shown in metres. A hill with a spot height marked as 1,000 on a metric chart will be 3,280 feet high. Beware!

If you use a chart with heights *above mean sea level* marked in metres, but you are flying an altitude in feet, then you must be able to convert confidently between these two units. For approximate checks, use 1 metre = 3.3 feet.

Also, many older pilots (as well as American pilots) may be used to thinking of runway lengths in feet rather than metres. If you are contemplating flying in the USA or even if you read American aviation books, conversion of feet to metres and vice versa is necessary. It is also in the syllabus for the navigation examination.

> 1 metre = 3.28 feet approximately.

The conversion is very simple using the red indices for feet and metres on the outer scale of the computer.

EXAMPLE 23 Convert 1,000 metres to feet on the computer.

Step 1. Rough check
   1 m = approx. 3.3 ft
   1,000 m = approx. 3,300 ft

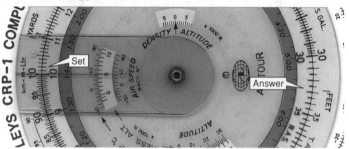

■ *Figure 5-21* **Example 23**

ANSWER 1,000 m = 3,280 ft

EXAMPLE 24 Convert 2,000 feet to metres.

Step 1. Rough check

$$1 \text{ ft} = \text{approx. } \frac{1}{3.3} \text{ m}$$

$$2,000 \text{ ft} = \text{approx. } 2,000 \times \frac{1}{3.3} \text{ m}$$

$$= \frac{2,000}{3.3} \text{ m} = \text{approx. } 600 \text{ m}$$

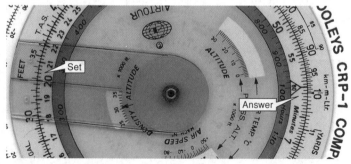

■ *Figure 5-22* **Example 24**

ANSWER 2,000 ft = 610 metres

SUMMARY OF LENGTH UNITS	
1 nm = 1.15 sm	*1 sm = 5,280 ft*
1 nm = 6,076 ft	*1 km = 3,281 ft*
1 nm = 1,852 metres	*1 metre = 3.28 ft*

Now complete **Exercises 5 – Calculator-7.**

Volume and Weight

In aviation we are faced with three different units for volume: the **imperial gallon,** the **US gallon** and the **litre.** In most general aviation aircraft the fuel gauges are marked in US gallons, yet you order fuel from the fuel agent in litres. There is great potential for confusion here, so you must become proficient in converting fuel quantities from one unit to another.

The weight of the fuel on board, as well as its volume, concerns the pilot for two main reasons:

☐ **weight and balance** (loading of the aircraft); and
☐ **energy content** of the fuel (which depends on weight, rather than volume).

So you must be able to convert fuel from a volume to a weight with accuracy.

100 octane (or higher) Avgas weighs only about 0.71 or 0.72 times the weight of an equal volume of water. We can describe this by saying that the **specific gravity (SG)** of Avgas = 0.71 or 0.72. The precise value depends to some extent on temperature and you should consult your instructor as to which value to use in your usual flying conditions.

Relative density is the modern term and it clearly describes its purpose, which is to compare the density of a particular fluid to the density of water. Most navigation computers, however, are marked with *Sp. G,* so we will continue to use the term *specific gravity.* It means the same thing.

The conversion from one unit of volume to another (imperial gallons, US gallons or litres), or to a weight (kg or lb) is easy on the *CRP-1* computer.

Weight Conversions

FOR QUICK MENTAL CHECKS, REMEMBER:		
1 kilogram (kg)	**=**	**2.2 pounds (lb)**

EXAMPLE 25 Convert 83 pounds (lb) to kilograms (kg).

Step 1. Rough calculation

1 kg = approx. 2.2 lb

83 lb = approx. 83 ÷ 2.2 kg = approx. 40 kg

Step 2.

Set 83 on the inner scale against *lb* on the outer scale. Against *kg* on the outer scale read off 38 on the inner scale.

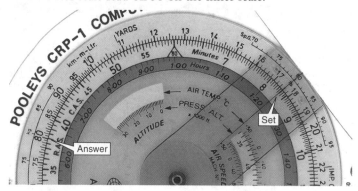

■ *Figure 5-23* **Example 25 answer: 36. Use the rotating arm to help align the numbers with the index.**

ANSWER 36 kg

EXAMPLE 26 Convert 293 kg to lb.

Step 1. Rough check

1 kg = approx. 2.2 lb

293 kg = approx. 2.2 × 300 lb = 660 lb

Step 2.

Set 293 on the inner scale against *kg* on the outer scale. Against *lb* on the outer scale, read off 648.

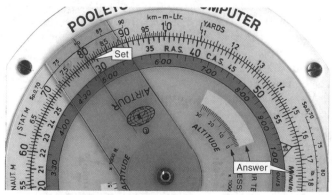

■ *Figure 5-24* **Example 26 answer: 648**

ANSWER 648 lb

Now complete **Exercises 5 – Calculator-8.**

Volume Conversions

FOR QUICK MENTAL CHECKS, REMEMBER:				
1 imperial gallon	**=**	*1.2 US gallons*	**=**	*4.5 litres*
0.8 imperial gallon	**=**	*1 US gallon*	**=**	*4 litres*
0.2 imperial gallon	**=**	*0.25 US gallon*	**=**	*1 litre*

For volume conversions, use the indices marked on the outer scale for *US gal, Imp gal* and *ltr.*

1. Set the known quantity on the inner scale against its index on the outer scale.

2. Read off the answer on the inner scale against the desired index on the outer scale.

EXAMPLE 27 Convert 24 US gallons to imperial gallons and litres.

Step 1. Rough check
1 US gal = 0.8 imp gal
24 US gal = 0.8 × 24 = approx. 20 imperial gal
1 US gal = 4 litres
24 US gal = 4 × 24 = approx. 96 litres

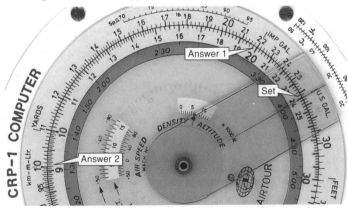

Figure 5-25 **Example 27, Step 2**

ANSWER 24 USG = 20 IG = 91 litres

Volume to Weight Conversions

We need to remember:

> Specific gravity (SG) of Avgas = 0.71 or 0.72.

It is useful to know the relationship of volume to weight for water, since water is the standard for relative density (specific gravity). At normal temperatures and pressure:

☐ **1 litre** of water weighs 1 kg;
☐ **1 imperial gallon** of water weighs 10 lb;
☐ **1 US gallon** of water weighs 8.33 lb.

For a rough check on the volume/weight relationship for Avgas, use:

AVGAS: VOLUME/WEIGHT (APPROX.)	
Quantity	Weight
1 litre	1 × SG kg
1 imperial gallon	10 × SG lb
US gallons	first convert to imperial gallons (1 IG = 1.2 USG), then use 10 × SG to find weight in lb

Our navigation computer has two scales (one graduated in *kg* and one in *lb*) to cater for fluids of different specific gravity (SG). This is useful as the SG for Avgas (used in piston engines) is usually about 0.71 or 0.72, and the SG for Avtur (used in turbine engines) is usually about 0.79.

TO CONVERT A VOLUME TO WEIGHT:

1. Set the volume on the inner scale against its index on the outer scale.

2. Against the given SG (on the *kg* or *lb* scale) read off the weight on the inner scale.

EXAMPLE 28 What does 37 USG of Avgas (SG 0.71) weigh in lb and kg?

Step 1. Rough check

$$37 \text{ US gal} = 0.8 \times 37$$
$$= \text{approx. } 30 \text{ IG}$$
$$= 30 \times 10 \times 0.7 \text{ lb}$$
$$= 210 \text{ lb}$$
$$= \frac{210}{2.2}$$
$$= \text{approx. } 100 \text{ kg}$$

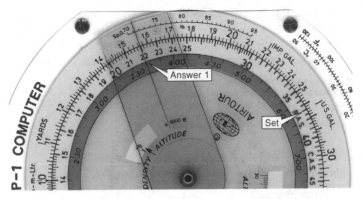

Figure 5-26 **Example 28, Step 2**

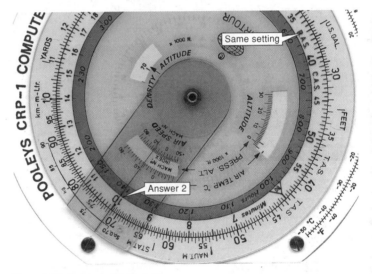

Figure 5-27 **Example 28, Step 3**

ANSWER 37 USG (SG 0.71) = 220 lb or 99.5 kg

Now complete **Exercises 5 – Calculator-9.**

Standard Specific Gravity Values

The density of a fluid will vary with temperature; however, for our purposes in light aircraft where only relatively small quantities will be used, we can assume standard SG values for fuel and oil.

Remember:
Specific gravity of Avgas
is 0.71 or 0.72.

AVGAS SPECIFIC GRAVITIES	
Avgas 100 octane & higher	SG = 0.71 or 0.72
Avgas less than 100 octane	SG = 0.72

In round figures:

AVGAS WEIGHTS	
QUANTITY OF AVGAS	WEIGHT
1 litre	0.7 kg
1 imperial gallon	7 lb
1 US gallon	2.69 kg

You do not need to know the following specific gravity values at PPL level but they may be of interest. Jet engines burn Avtur (kerosene), which has a higher specific gravity than Avgas. Some aircraft load sheets require oil to be considered, so you need to know its specific gravity.

OTHER SPECIFIC GRAVITIES	
Avtur (for turbine engines)	SG = 0.79
Mineral oil	SG = 0.90
Synthetic oil	SG = 0.96

Vertical Navigation

Navigating a car or a ship is a two-dimensional activity – horizontal navigation – concerned with speed and direction in the horizontal plane. Navigating an aeroplane requires three-dimensional awareness, and we must also consider height. Vertical navigation is important to pilots for three basic reasons:

1. **For terrain clearance,** to ensure that the aircraft will not collide with terrain or fixed obstacles on the ground.

2. **For traffic separation,** to allow pilots to cruise at an altitude different to that of nearby aircraft, to ensure safe vertical separation.

3. **To calculate the performance capabilities** of the aircraft and its engine, so as to operate safely and efficiently.

Vertical navigation is the guidance of flight in the vertical plane, and includes the science of measuring vertical distances in the atmosphere, known as *altimetry*.

Measuring vertical distance in the atmosphere is not as simple as it sounds. There are errors in the measuring instrument (the altimeter) and compromises in the principle on which it is built, with the result that the altimeter presents the pilot with approximate vertical information of the aircraft's position.

Altitude

Altitude is the vertical distance of a level, point, or object, measured from *mean sea level* (MSL). This definition appears in the UK Aeronautical Information Publication (AIP). The abbreviation for altitude is *alt* or ALT.

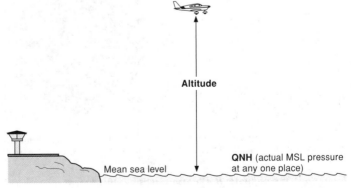

Altitude

Mean sea level

QNH (actual MSL pressure at any one place)

■ *Figure 6-1* **Altitude is the vertical distance above mean sea level (amsl)**

In the UK and the Western world the standard unit of height for aviation purposes is the *foot*. In many Eastern countries it is the *metre*.

The Altimeter

The basic instrument used to measure altitude is the pressure altimeter. This is simply a **barometer** – a device that measures atmospheric pressure. Barometers work on the principle that, in the atmosphere, air pressure decreases as height increases. This means that the higher you are in the earth's atmosphere, the lower the pressure – hence the need for most people to wear oxygen masks when they climb Mount Everest or when they fly above 10,000 ft in unpressurised aeroplanes.

There are various types of pressure altimeter. The most compact and robust type suitable for installation in an aircraft is the **aneroid barometer,** which is similar to those seen in many homes. As the aeroplane goes higher, the atmospheric pressure of the air in which it is flying decreases, and the aneroid, which is an expandable and compressible metal capsule containing a fixed amount of air, is able to expand.

Through a system of linkages, a pointer is driven around a scale. This scale does not read directly in units of pressure, such as *millibars* (or the equivalent SI unit *hectopascals*), but rather in *feet*. Calculations by the designer have been made to relate the pressure to the altitude, and the scale reads in units of altitude, which is what pilots need. The altitude indication is known as **indicated altitude.**

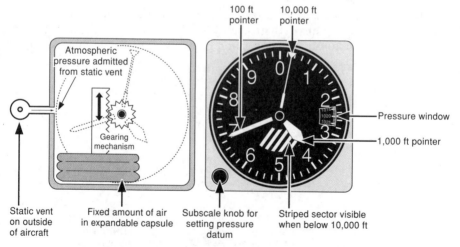

■ Figure 6-2 *The altimeter is a pressure-sensitive instrument*

As the aeroplane climbs, the aneroid expands, driving the pointer to indicate a higher altitude. As the aeroplane descends, the static air pressure in the surrounding atmosphere increases, forcing the aneroid to contract and drive the pointer to indicate a lower altitude.

A number of errors are evident in altimeters, and these may be broken into two main types:

1. Errors in the particular altimeter.

2. Errors in the principle on which altimetry is based, i.e. by how much the pressure in the atmosphere decreases with height.

Errors in the Altimetry Principle

The rate at which air pressure decreases with height varies from time to time and from place to place. The simple barometric altimeter cannot cope with this because it has been calibrated according to a **standard atmosphere** in which a particular height **above mean sea level (amsl)** always corresponds with a particular pressure. Any variation of the actual atmosphere from the standard atmosphere will cause the altimeter to indicate an altitude different from the actual height amsl of the aeroplane.

The various gases surrounding the earth and forming its atmosphere are bound to it by gravity. A standard atmosphere is something that does not exist permanently, since this mixture of gases (or *air* as we call it) has constantly changing values of:

☐ pressure;
☐ temperature;
☐ density; and
☐ water content (humidity).

Thus it is necessary to have some sort of measuring stick or standard, be it only a theoretical one, against which to compare the actual atmosphere in our vicinity. That measuring stick is the International Standard Atmosphere (ISA).

Lapse Rates

In the International Standard Atmosphere, pressure, temperature and density are defined as decreasing at specified rates with gain in height.

TEMPERATURE. The temperature lapse rate (rate of fall of temperature with increase in height) in the ISA is 1.98°C per 1,000 ft up to 36,090 ft, above which the temperature remains constant at minus 56.6°C (at least in the levels up to which commercial aeroplanes fly). For our purposes, in the ISA:

☐ **temperature falls** by 2°C per 1,000 ft up to 36,000 ft; and
☐ **above 36,000 ft,** remains constant at −57°C.

PRESSURE. The rate at which pressure in the ISA decreases with height varies, but is approximately 1 mb per 30 ft up to about 5,000 ft. (This rate drops to about 1 mb per 70 ft at high levels of the atmosphere, but this need not concern us here.) For our purposes, in the lower levels of the ISA, pressure decreases by 1 mb (hPa) for each 30 ft increases in altitude.

DENSITY. Air density decreases with height, so that at 20,000 ft the air density is about one-half of its MSL value, one-quarter at 40,000 ft, and one-tenth at 60,000 ft.

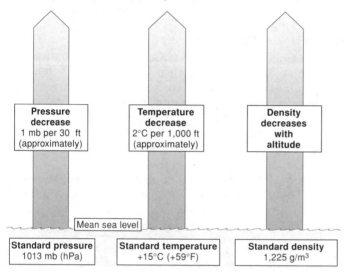

■ *Figure 6-3* **The International Standard Atmosphere (ISA)**

The main use of the International Standard Atmosphere is to calibrate altimeters. This is to provide a mathematical relationship between the air pressure measured by the aneroid barometer and the altitude calibrations placed on the scale around which the pointer is driven, so that all aircraft convert pressure to altitude by a standard method.

Pressure Altitude

Pressure altitude (called *pressure height* in some countries), is the height in the ISA above the 1013 mb pressure datum at which the pressure equals that of the level under consideration. For example, the ISA pressure at a point 600 ft higher than the 1013 pressure level is approximately 993 mb. If your aeroplane is flying in air whose pressure is 993 mb, then its pressure altitude is 600 ft.

NOTE 1013.25 mb(hPa) is the precise value of standard or ISA MSL pressure. For our purposes, 1013 is sufficiently accurate. There is a Q-code for pressure altitude, QNE, but it is rarely used.

Pressure altitudes are often described in an abbreviated form as **flight levels,** where the final two zeros are omitted. For example, a pressure altitude of 4,500 ft (i.e. 4,500 ft higher than the 1013 pressure level) is also known as flight level 45 (written FL45). Flight levels are used for cruising at higher levels and are usually separated by at least 500 ft, e.g. FL55, FL60, FL65.

> *A flight level is a pressure altitude.*

EXAMPLE 1 35,000 ft in the International Standard Atmosphere above the standard pressure level of 1013 may be referred to as:
☐ **pressure altitude** (or pressure height) of 35,000 ft; or as
☐ **flight level 350,** FL350 (where the last two zeros are dropped).

EXAMPLE 2 3,500 ft in the International Standard Atmosphere above the standard pressure level of 1013 may be referred to as:
☐ **pressure altitude** (or pressure height) of 3,500 ft, or as
☐ **flight level 35,** FL35, (where the last two zeros are dropped).

Air Pressure

The earth's atmosphere consists of countless numbers of molecules all moving at high speed and colliding with any object, be it another molecule or the earth's surface or a person that blocks their path. The force that these molecules exert as they collide gives rise to a *pressure,* or a 'force per unit area'. As these molecules are moving in all directions, the pressure at any point in the atmosphere will be exerted in all directions.

Because of gravity, the ambient pressure at any point in the atmosphere will depend on the weight of air that is above and pressing down. On a 'standard day', the column of air pressing down on the earth's surface exerts a pressure of 1013 millibars at sea level.

Low static pressure at altitude

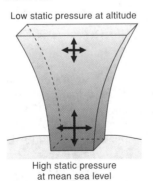

High static pressure
at mean sea level

■ *Figure 6-4* **Pressure decreases with increase of altitude**

At higher levels in the column of air, the weight pressing down is less and so the pressure will be less. In the lower levels of the atmosphere (up to about 5,000 ft amsl), the pressure drops by about 1 mb for each 30 ft climbed.

EXAMPLE 3 If the pressure at MSL is 1013 (to the nearest mb), what is the pressure at 60 ft amsl?

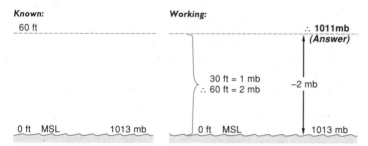

Known:

60 ft

0 ft   MSL   1013 mb

Working:

∴ **1011mb**
↕ *(Answer)*

30 ft = 1 mb
∴ 60 ft = 2 mb   −2 mb

0 ft   MSL   1013 mb

■ *Figure 6-5* **Example 3 answer: 1011 mb. Diagrams make altimetry problems simple.**

EXAMPLE 4 If the MSL pressure is 1013, at what altitude (height amsl) would you expect the pressure to be 1000 mb?

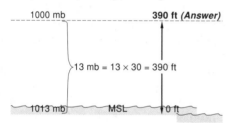

1000 mb   **390 ft** *(Answer)*

13 mb = 13 × 30 = 390 ft

1013 mb   MSL   0 ft

■ *Figure 6-6* **Example 4 answer: 390 ft**

Now complete **Exercises 6 – Vertical Nav-1.**

Air Temperature

The temperature in any one place varies from hour to hour, from day to day, and from season to season. On an 'average day' in a temperate zone, the temperature at MSL (mean sea level) may be +15°C. By convention, +15°C is the standard temperature at sea level in the International Standard Atmosphere. As we climb, the temperature decreases by about 2°C for every 1,000 ft increase in height.

EXAMPLE 5 What temperature exists at 3,000 ft above the 1013 pressure surface (or pressure level) in the International Standard Atmosphere?

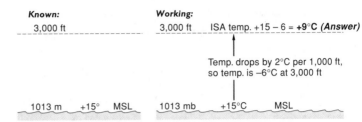

■ *Figure 6-7* **Example 5 answer: +9°C**

EXAMPLE 6 What temperature exists at 4,500 ft in the ISA?

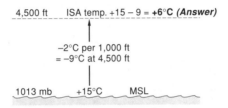

■ *Figure 6-8* **Example 6 answer: +6°C**

EXAMPLE 7 What temperature exists at 45,000 ft in the ISA?

ANSWER –57°C because in the ISA, temperature is constant at –57°C above 36,000 ft.

EXAMPLE 8 What temperature exists at 36,000 ft in the ISA?

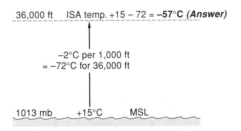

■ *Figure 6-9* **Example 8 answer: –57°C**

EXAMPLE 9 Calculate the ISA values of pressure and temperature for a pressure altitude of 6,000 ft.

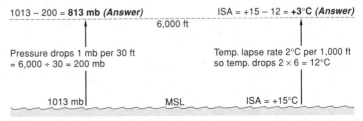

■ *Figure 6-10* **Example 9 answers: 813 mb and +3°C**

EXAMPLE 10 Calculate the ISA values of pressure and temperature for a pressure altitude of −1,500 ft (i.e. 1,500 ft below the 1013 pressure level).

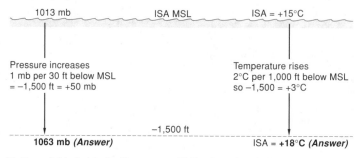

1013 mb	ISA MSL	ISA = +15°C

Pressure increases
1 mb per 30 ft below MSL
= −1,500 ft = +50 mb

Temperature rises
2°C per 1,000 ft below MSL
so −1,500 = +3°C

−1,500 ft

1063 mb (Answer)   ISA = +18°C **(Answer)**

■ Figure 6-11 **Example 10 answers: 1063 mb and +18°C**

NOTE This sort of calculation for below ISA MSL is sometimes required because:

1. There are places on the earth's surface that are below mean sea level (e.g. Rotterdam, the Dead Sea, Lake Eyre in Australia).

2. The actual atmosphere is always different to our so-called standard atmosphere and negative pressure altitudes are not uncommon.

EXAMPLE 11 What is the pressure altitude of the 990 mb pressure surface?

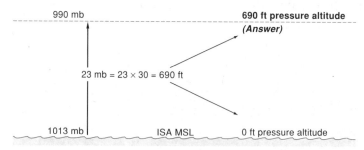

990 mb   **690 ft pressure altitude**
                                       (Answer)

23 mb = 23 × 30 = 690 ft

1013 mb   ISA MSL   0 ft pressure altitude

■ Figure 6-12 **Example 11 answer: 690 ft pressure altitude**

Even though some of these exercises are simple, do not avoid them. A sound understanding of altimetry will stand you in good stead throughout your flying career!

Now complete **Exercises 6 – Vertical Nav-2.**

Variations in Mean Sea Level Pressure – QNH

On maps and charts the height of terrain is given as height **above mean sea level (amsl)**. It is therefore essential that a pilot knows the aircraft's height above mean sea level so that he can relate this to the height of terrain or obstructions and determine if there is sufficient vertical separation.

So far in our discussion the altimeter has only measured height above the ISA MSL datum of 1013 mb (hPa). In reality, mean sea level pressure varies from day to day, and indeed from hour to hour, as the various high- and low-pressure systems move across the surface of the earth. You will notice this on daily weather maps.

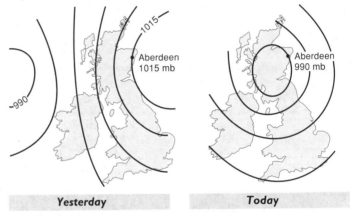

■ *Figure 6-13* **Two different synoptic situations**

Consider the situations illustrated in Figure 6–13. Yesterday, a high-pressure system of 1015 mb was sitting over Aberdeen. In 24 hours, the pressure system has moved on, and today Aberdeen is experiencing a lower pressure of 990 mb. A profile of the atmosphere over Aberdeen on each of these days is shown in Figure 6–14.

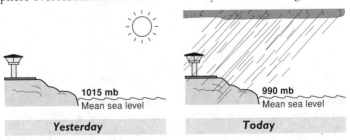

■ *Figure 6-14* **Profile of MSL pressure situations – yesterday and today**

Figure 6-15 shows the position of the 1013 mb pressure level in relation to each of these situations.

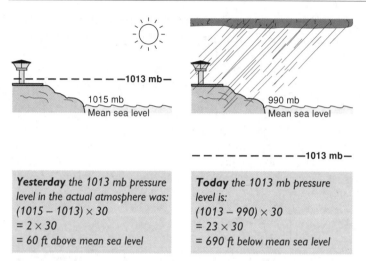

Yesterday the 1013 mb pressure level in the actual atmosphere was:
(1015 – 1013) × 30
= 2 × 30
= 60 ft above mean sea level

Today the 1013 mb pressure level is:
(1013 – 990) × 30
= 23 × 30
= 690 ft below mean sea level

■ Figure 6-15 **The standard pressure level in relation to the MSL pressure**

Since height amsl is vital information to a pilot, instead of this unwieldy calculation being required in the cockpit, the design of the altimeter incorporates a small subscale and knob geared to the altimeter pointer. By rotating the knob, the desired pressure datum from which height will be measured is set in the subscale.

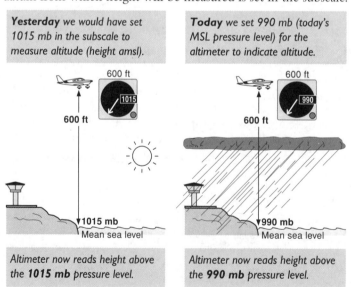

Yesterday we would have set 1015 mb in the subscale to measure altitude (height amsl).

Today we set 990 mb (today's MSL pressure level) for the altimeter to indicate altitude.

Altimeter now reads height above the **1015 mb** pressure level.

Altimeter now reads height above the **990 mb** pressure level.

■ Figure 6-16 **When MSL pressure is set in the altimeter subscale, the altimeter indicates height amsl for that pressure situation**

QNH

The Q-code name for the altimeter subscale setting which gives us this altitude is QNH (i.e. the MSL pressure level in the *actual* atmosphere). The QNH is the atmospheric pressure corresponding to mean sea level pressure at that place and time.

> An altimeter with **QNH** set on its subscale will indicate **altitude**
> – height above mean sea level (amsl).

From the previous example, we can see that yesterday in Aberdeen the QNH was 1015 mb; today in Aberdeen the QNH is 990 mb.

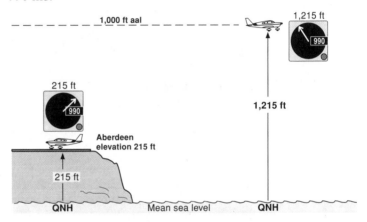

■ *Figure 6-17* **Today in Aberdeen the QNH is 990 mb**

The official elevation of a particular aerodrome is that of the highest point on the landing area. Since most aerodromes are fairly level, it gives the pilot who is taxiing an opportunity to check his altimeter prior to take-off. With QNH set, the altimeter of an aeroplane on the ground should indicate close to aerodrome elevation.

The Altimeter Subscale

The altimeter subscale is controlled by a knob which the pilot can turn. It is connected to the pointer and mechanically geared in the ratio of approximately 1 mb (hPa) to 30 ft, i.e. altering the subscale setting by 1 millibar will alter the indicated height by about 30 ft. Altering the subscale setting by 10 millibars will alter the altimeter indication by about 300 ft.

An easy means of determining pressure altitude is simply to wind 1013 into the subscale. The altimeter will then indicate the height in the ISA above the 1013 mb (hPa) pressure level: pressure altitude.

EXAMPLE 12 Suppose that the MSL pressure is 1030 (i.e. QNH) and the aeroplane is 600 ft amsl. With QNH 1030 set in the subscale, the altimeter will indicate an altitude of 600 ft amsl. The pressure altitude can be found (without any calculation) by winding 1013 into the subscale. In this case the pressure altitude is 90 ft.

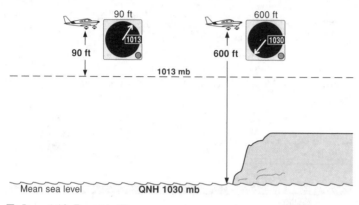

■ *Figure 6-18* **Example 12**

Wind on millibars, wind on height (and vice versa).

The correct QNH can be obtained from a number of sources, including Air Traffic Control, meteorological forecasts (at least approximately) and your own observations. By 'your own observations', we mean that if you are on the ground at an aerodrome whose elevation you know, then, after turning the knob until the altimeter indicates the aerodrome elevation, the reading in the subscale will be the current aerodrome QNH.

To illustrate this, suppose you arrive by car at a country aerodrome, elevation 1,290 ft, to go flying, and find that the altimeter indicates something quite different to 1,290. Simply by turning the knob until the pointers of the altimeter indicate 1,290 ft, which is the altitude (height amsl) of the aircraft, you will have wound the current QNH onto the subscale.

It is obvious that, for the altimeter indication to have any significance, the pilot must be aware of the setting on the subscale.

EXAMPLE 13 You are flying overhead Elstree aerodrome with the current QNH of 1020 set in the subscale, and the altimeter indicating 1,500 ft. What pressure altitude is that?

ANSWER 1,290 ft (Figure 6-19)

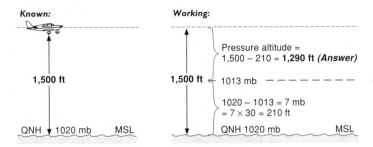

■ *Figure 6-19* **Example 13 answer: 1,290 ft**

EXAMPLE 14 Your aircraft is sitting on the tarmac at Compton Abbas airfield, elevation 810 feet. The altimeter reads 900 ft (i.e. 90 ft too high) with 1015 set on the subscale. What is the airfield QNH (i.e. what is the mean sea level pressure at Compton Abbas at that time, assuming the atmosphere extends down to MSL)?

ANSWER With 1015 set in the subscale, the altimeter over-reads the known elevation by 90 ft. By winding off this 90 ft, we wind off 3 mb, i.e. QNH is 1012.

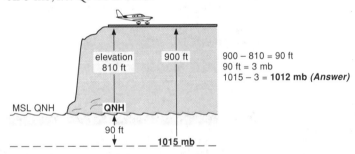

■ *Figure 6-20* **Example 14 answer: QNH 1012 mb**

Now complete **Exercises 6 – Vertical Nav-3.**

Height Above Aerodrome Level – QFE

It is very convenient for circuit operations if the altimeter can be set to indicate height **above aerodrome level (aal)**. This means that a 1,000 ft circuit at, for example, Leicester airfield (elevation 469 ft) can be achieved with the altimeter indicating 1,000 ft, rather than 1,469 ft if QNH was set in the subscale. It is a satisfactory procedure in the UK to set QFE in the subscale when flying in the circuit.

On the aerodrome, the altimeter should indicate within ±50 ft of zero with QFE set in the subscale. QFE is the pressure at aerodrome level. In flight, the altimeter, with QFE set, will indicate height above the runway. (Having departed the circuit area, however, QFE is of little value, since the surrounding terrain will probably be at a different level to the aerodrome.)

> *QFE is the pressure at aerodrome level.*

EXAMPLE 15 You plan to do some circuits at an aerodrome (elevation 749 ft amsl). On the ground you adjust the subscale of your altimeter until the altimeter indicates 0 feet, which it does with, say, 996 set in the subscale.

Calculate the current QFE, QNH and pressure altitude of this aerodrome, and the altimeter readings you would expect with these subscale settings when the aeroplane is on the ground.

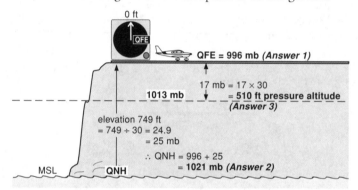

■ *Figure 6-21* **Example 15 answers: QFE 996 mb, QNH 1021 mb, pressure altitude 510 ft**

Remember that the information your altimeter gives you depends on what you have set in the subscale.

> *For terrain clearance, use QNH.*

Now complete **Exercises 6 – Vertical Nav-4.**

Flying With Changing Sea Level Pressures

Consider an aeroplane flying from Land's End to Popham, with the barometric pressure over the south-west of England as shown in Figure 6-22.

We depart Land's End with the Land's End QNH of 995 set on the subscale (i.e. MSL pressure at Land's End), and cruise 3,000 ft above this with our altimeter indicating 3,000 ft.

Tracking towards Popham, we are flying into an area of higher pressure, and so the 995 pressure level will be gradually rising. If we maintain 3,000 ft indicated on the altimeter, with 995 set, we will in fact be climbing with respect to sea level.

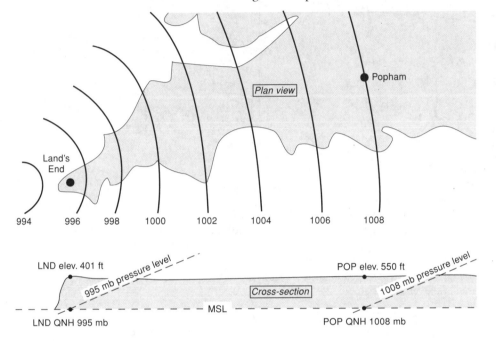

■ *Figure 6-22* **Plan and cross-section views of this synoptic situation**

Conversely, another aircraft flying in the opposite direction with the Popham QNH of 1008 set on its subscale and cruising at 4,000 ft will in fact be gradually descending. Can you spot the two inherent dangers?

Remember that two of the most important tasks for pilots are:
☐ **to avoid hitting the ground unexpectedly; and**
☐ **to avoid colliding with other aircraft.**

The aircraft coming from Popham, flying from a higher-pressure area towards an area of lower pressure, will actually be gradually descending if the altimeter reading 4,000 ft continues to have 1008 mb (hPa) set on the subscale. The aircraft will in fact be lower than 4,000 ft amsl, so terrain clearance could be a problem. When flying 'From *high* to *low,* beware below!' (Danger No. 1)

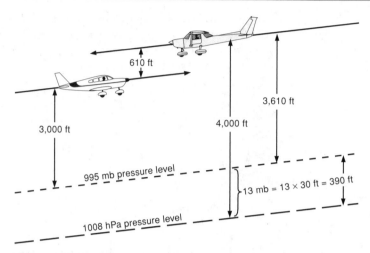

Figure 6-23 Flying from high to low, beware below!

The two pilots may think that they have 1,000 ft vertical separation because the altimeter in one aeroplane indicates 3,000 ft, and the altimeter in the other indicates 4,000 ft. In fact, the vertical separation is only 610 ft, because 4,000 ft above the 1008 mb pressure level is only (4,000 − 390) = 3,610 ft above the 995 mb pressure level. (Danger No. 2)

Regional Pressure Setting (Regional QNH)

The practical solution to both of these problems (terrain clearance and traffic separation) because of changing QNHs is to have all aircraft which are cruising in the same area, below the transition altitude, use the same altimeter subscale setting. For this reason the UK is divided into a number of Altimeter Setting Regions (ASRs) – see Vol. 2 of *The Air Pilot's Manual*.

Regional QNH can be obtained from:
- ☐ all aerodromes with Air Traffic Services;
- ☐ any Air/Ground ATC channel;
- ☐ by land-line (for pre-flight planning);
- ☐ the London and Scottish ATCCs; or
- ☐ the Manchester Sub-Centre.

When cruising en route, the appropriate subscale setting is the **Regional Pressure Setting,** also known as the **Regional QNH** or the **Area QNH,** which is the current QNH for that region at that time. Its value will be updated by ATC at least every hour.

The QNH will in fact vary slightly throughout the Altimeter Setting Region, depending on the pressure pattern. To be on the conservative side, the Regional QNH is the lowest forecast QNH value for that hour, and so will be at sea level or slightly higher.

This ensures that the aircraft will be at or slightly higher than the altitude indicated, and not lower.

For example, with Regional QNH set and the altimeter indicating 2,000 ft, the aeroplane should be 2,000 ft amsl or slightly higher. No Aerodrome QNH in that region will be lower than the value of the Regional QNH.

When cruising cross-country, set Regional QNH, and update it when you fly into another region, or whenever ATC communicates an amended value.

Altimetry Procedures for Cross-Country Flights

In the UK, a typical private cross-country flight in a light aircraft is usually conducted at or below 3,000 ft amsl. We will use a flight from Land's End to Popham as an example.

1. Set Aerodrome QNH or QFE for Take-Off

With Aerodrome QNH set, the altimeter indicates height amsl, which is useful information in the circuit area and during the climb-out, especially over high terrain or if ATC requires you to report altitude. On the ground, the altimeter should indicate aerodrome elevation, which at Land's End is 401 ft amsl.

If you choose to set QFE, the altimeter will indicate height aal, and this reading has little significance away from the vicinity of the aerodrome. On the ground, with QFE set, the altimeter should indicate close to zero (within ±50 ft).

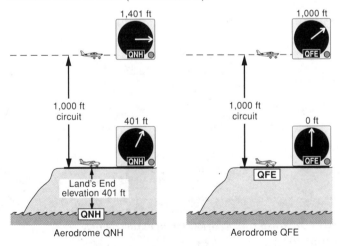

■ *Figure 6-24* **Set Aerodrome QNH, or Aerodrome QFE, for circuit operations**

2. Set Regional QNH if Cruising Below the Transition Altitude

On reaching cruising altitude 3,000 ft, the Scillies Regional QNH should be set. Flying with the altimeter indicating 3,000 ft should ensure that the height above mean sea level is 3,000 ft or slightly more (since the Regional QNH is always the lowest QNH for that area).

The Regional QNH should be updated as you cross each ASR boundary (shown on aeronautical charts) – in this case passing from Scillies ASR to the Wessex ASR to the Portland ASR, or whenever the appropriate regional pressure setting is updated by ATC.

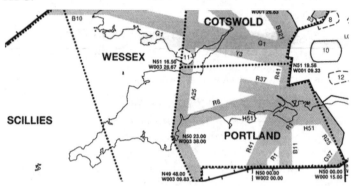

■ *Figure 6-25* **Excerpt from the ASR map**

With Regional QNH set in the subscale, the pilot can evaluate:
- ☐ **terrain clearance** (the height of terrain is found from the aeronautical charts); and
- ☐ **vertical separation** from other aircraft.

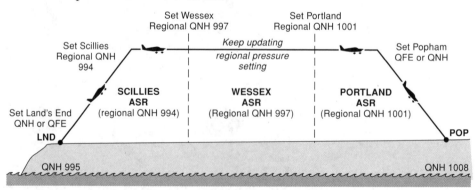

■ *Figure 6-26* **When cruising below the transition altitude, set**
Regional QNH

NOTE It is insufficient to assume that errors in horizontal tracking will safeguard you from other traffic in your vicinity operating at or near the same level. Modern tracking aids, such as VOR, GPS, and inertial navigation systems, have made extremely accurate tracking possible.

En route you may be required, when flying beneath a Terminal Control Area (TMA) or Control Area (CTA), to set the QNH of an aerodrome situated beneath that area, to assist in separation from other aeroplanes or to ensure that you do not inadvertently penetrate the controlled airspace above you. The Aerodrome QNHs will not differ greatly (if at all) from their Regional QNH.

When transiting a Military Aerodrome Traffic Zone (MATZ) where military aircraft may be operating, you may be required to set the MATZ Aerodrome QNH for separation purposes. Once clear of the MATZ, Regional QNH should be reset on the sub-scale.

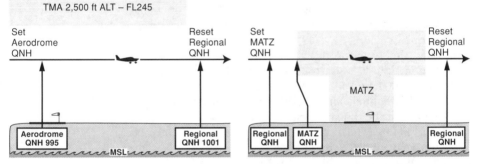

■ *Figure 6-27* **Aerodrome (rather than Regional) QNH, may be required en route**

3. Set QFE or Aerodrome QNH when Approaching for Landing

In preparation for joining the circuit, set the aerodrome QFE (or QNH if preferred) for the destination aerodrome as the circuit area is approached. For instance, approaching Popham, you would set QFE 990, or QNH 1008, on the altimeter subscale. (Note: In some countries only QNH is used.)

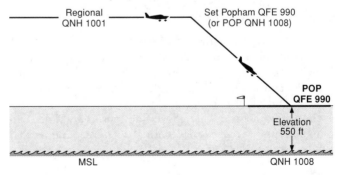

■ *Figure 6-28* **Approaching the circuit, set aerodrome QFE (or QNH if preferred)**

Cruising Above the Transition Altitude

The highest terrain in the UK is 4,406 ft amsl at Ben Nevis in Scotland. Obviously most of the UK is much lower than this. To avoid the need for continually updating the altimeter setting, it is common practice when flying at levels where high terrain is not a problem to set standard pressure 1013 mb on the subscale. All aircraft cruising at these levels, with 1013 set, thereby obtain adequate vertical separation from each other.

The altitude in the climb at which the transition from QNH to 1013 mb is made is called the **transition altitude**. In the UK, the transition altitude is generally 3,000 ft amsl. There are some exceptions to this in the vicinity of some major airports, where the transition altitude may be higher because traffic density is high and where the high rates of climb and descent of jet aircraft is a consideration.

In other parts of the world where the terrain is much higher, the transition altitude is much higher. In the USA the transition altitude is 18,000 ft; in Papua New Guinea (a mountainous country just north of Australia) it is 20,000 ft; in Australia it is 10,000 ft.

Exceptions, at the time of printing, to the usual UK transition altitude of 3,000 ft are noted below. You need not remember them; they are included here for interest.

☐ London Terminal Control Area (TMA): 6,000 ft;
☐ Manchester TMA: 5,000 ft;
☐ Scottish TMA (covering Edinburgh, Glasgow and Prestwick): 6,000 ft;
☐ Aberdeen CTR/TMA: 6,000 ft;
☐ Belfast CTR/TMA: 6,000 ft;
☐ Teesside CTR/CTA: 6,000 ft;
☐ Edinburgh CTR: 6,000 ft;
☐ Glasgow CTR: 6,000 ft;
☐ Leeds Bradford CTR/CTA, 5,000 ft;
☐ Birmingham CTR/CTA: 4,000 ft.

Choice of Altimeter Setting for VFR Flights

Outside controlled airspace and above the transition altitude, VFR flights may cruise with Regional QNH, but it is advisable to use 1013 and cruise on flight levels as aircraft operating on Instrument Flight Rules are required to do.

In controlled airspace and above the transition altitude, aircraft should cruise at flight levels (with 1013 mb set), rather than at altitudes (with QNH set).

The Transition Layer

There would be a possibility of conflict if aircraft cruising above the transition altitude were on Regional QNH and aircraft only slightly above it were on the 1013 reference datum. For this reason there is a layer above the transition altitude in which cruising flight should not occur, to ensure satisfactory vertical separation of at least 500 ft.

In practice, flight levels are nominated in 500-foot steps, e.g. FL35, FL40, FL45, FL50, FL55, etc. Since the 1013 mb reference datum may not be at mean sea level, it is possible (indeed most likely) that the actual vertical spacing between a transition altitude of 3,000 ft and a transition level of FL35 will not be 500 ft, as illustrated in Figure 6-29.

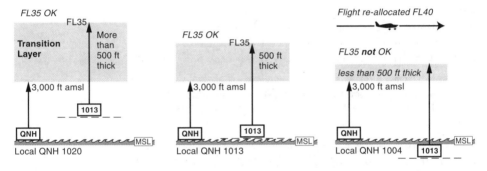

■ *Figure 6-29* **The thickness of the transition layer varies with QNH**

As you can see, the transition altitude remains fixed, but the transition level moves up or down according to the QNH. If the Regional QNH is less than 1013 mb, FL35 is lower than 3,500 ft amsl and there is less than 500 ft vertical separation between a transition altitude of 3,000 ft and FL35. So you would need to cruise at FL40 to retain a 500 ft or better vertical separation from an aircraft cruising at 3,000 ft on Regional QNH.

If needed, a table to convert altitudes to flight levels (and vice versa) is contained in the UK Aeronautical Information Publication (AIP ENR) and is reproduced in Vol. 2 of this series.

To use the table (Figure 6-30):
▢ take a vertical line upwards from the QNH value along the bottom axis until it meets the appropriate (sloping) flight level line; then
▢ read horizontally across to the equivalent altitude.

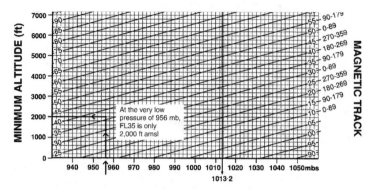

■ Figure 6-30 **Using the altitude/flight level conversion table**

Summary

THE TRANSITION ALTITUDE is the altitude at, or below, which the vertical position of aircraft is controlled by reference to altitudes, i.e. with regional QNH set. In the UK, it is usually 3,000 ft amsl.

THE TRANSITION LEVEL is the flight level at, or above, which the vertical position of aircraft is controlled with reference to flight levels, i.e. with 1013 set. In the UK, it is usually FL35 (or higher if QNH is less than 1013).

THE TRANSITION LAYER is the airspace between the transition altitude and the transition level. It varies in thickness, depending on the regional QNH.

Cruising Level Selection

As a student pilot, or a basic-PPL holder (no IMC or Instrument Rating), you will be restricted to flying under Visual Flight Rules (VFR) and as such should always be clear of cloud, satisfy minimum visibility requirements and be in sight of the ground if below 3,000 ft amsl.

It is not mandatory for VFR flights to cruise at any particular altitude or flight level, but it is recommended (in the UK AIP) that VFR flights adopt the IFR cruising level system, known as the **quadrantal rule,** if cruising above the transition altitude.

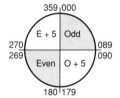

■ *Figure 6-31*

The quadrantal rule (advisable to follow, but not mandatory if VFR and outside controlled airspace)

MAGNETIC TRACK	CRUISING FLIGHT LEVEL
000°M to 089°M	FLs in **odd** thousands of feet; FL30, 50, 70, etc.
090°M to 179°M	FLs in **odd** thousands **plus 500**, FL35, 55, 75, etc.
180°M to 269°M	FLs in **even** thousands; FL40, 60, 80, etc.
270°M to 359°M	FLs in **even** thousands **plus 500**, FL85, etc.

■ *Now complete* **Exercises 6 – Vertical Nav-5.**

Safety Altitude (or Safety Height)

Where possible on cross-country flights, choose a suitable cruising level that will ensure adequate terrain clearance and vertical separation from other aircraft. The best technique is to:

☐ **determine a safety altitude** which will ensure adequate terrain clearance; and then

☐ **select an appropriate cruising level,** (conforming with the quadrantal rule above 3,000 ft amsl, if applicable).

NOTE In certain circumstances it may not always be possible to cruise above the calculated minimum safe altitude; for example, due to over-lying controlled airspace around a major airport. In such cases extra care to avoid terrain and obstructions should be taken, particularly in minimum visibility, until it is possible to climb above the safety altitude.

To determine a safety altitude or safety height:

☐ **determine the highest obstacle** en route to a set distance either side of track, or take the highest maximum elevation figure (MEF) en route; then:

☐ **add a safety clearance** height above this.

There are no hard and fast rules as to how far either side of track you should consider, or how high above obstacles you should fly. Reasonable values are 1,000 ft or 1,500 ft above the highest obstacle within 5 nm or 10 nm either side of track. This allows for navigational errors. On long tracks or over mountainous areas such as North Wales, 15 or 20 nm might be more appropriate, or use the *maximum elevation figures* shown on 1:500,000 UK charts.

To assist you in determining the highest obstacle, it is a good idea to mark in lines 5 nm (or 10 nm) either side of track. Another approach to finding a reasonable extra height to add is to add 10% of the elevation of the highest obstacle plus a further 1,500 ft.

EXAMPLE 16 Elevation of highest obstacle within 5 nm of track is 438 ft amsl, and within 10 nm it is 798 ft.

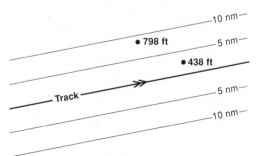

■ *Figure 6-32* ***Example 16***

☐ If you decide to use **1,000 ft clearance within 5 nm** of track, the safety altitude is 1,438 ft, say 1,500 ft.

☐ If you decide to use **1,000 ft clearance within 10 nm** of track, the safety altitude is 1,798 ft, say 1,800 ft.

☐ If you decide to use **1,500 ft clearance within 10 nm** of track, the safety altitude is 2,298 ft, say 2,300 ft.

☐ If you decide to use **10% plus 1,500 ft clearance within 10 nm** of track, the safety altitude is:

Additional height as a safety buffer =
80 (10% of 800) + 1,500 = 1,580 ft, say 1,600 ft

Safety altitude = obstacle 800 ft + safety buffer 1,600 ft
= 2,400 ft.

If you remain above your calculated safety altitude, there should be sufficient buffer to absorb any indication errors in the altimeter (position, instrument and temperature errors) and to stay out of any turbulent areas near the ground, where a downdraft or wind-shear could be dangerous. In certain circumstances (such as in standing waves downwind of mountain ridges), it may be advisable to add rather more than 10% plus 1,500 ft to give sufficient safety margin.

Determining your own safety altitude is a point of airmanship (common sense). Your flying instructor will recommend a technique for calculating safety heights.

EXAMPLE 17 Calculate the lowest cruising level, according to the quadrantal rule, that will ensure a terrain clearance of 1,000 ft within 10 nm of track.

☐ Highest obstacle within area of possible navigation error = 2,117 ft.
☐ Track to be flown 177°T.
☐ VAR 6°W.
☐ Regional QNH 1006 mb.
☐ Transition altitude 3,000 ft.

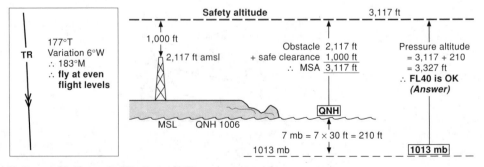

■ *Figure 6-33 **Example 17 answer: FL40***

EXAMPLE 18 Calculate the lowest cruising level, according to the quadrantal rule, that will ensure a terrain clearance of 10% of the highest obstacle plus 1,500 ft in the above case.

ANSWER 183°M, MSA 4,039 ft, FL60

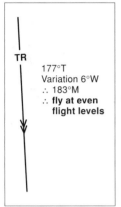

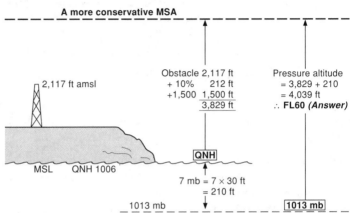

■ *Figure 6-34* **Example 18 answer: FL60**

Now complete **Exercises 6 – Vertical Nav-6.**

The Effect of Temperature Variations

So far we have only considered pressure variations from the International Standard Atmosphere. Temperature variations from ISA play a role not only in vertical navigation and altimetry, but also in aeroplane performance (see Vol. 4 of this series). ISA MSL temperature is +15°C, and the temperature lapse rate is 2°C/1,000 ft (decrease with altitude).

TEMPERATURE STRUCTURE IN THE ISA	
Pressure Altitudes	*ISA Temperatures*
above 36,000 ft	*constant at –57°C*
36,000 ft	*–57°C (ISA = +15 – [2 × 36] = +15 – 72 = –57°C)*
20,000 ft	*–25°C (ISA = +15 – [2 × 20] = +15 – 40 = –25°C)*
3,000 ft	*+9°C (ISA = +15 – [2 × 3] = +15 – 6 = +9°C)*
2,000 ft	*+11°C (ISA = +15 – [2 × 2] = +15 – 4 = +11°C)*
1,000 ft	*+13°C (ISA = +15 – 2 = +13°C)*
MSL 1013 mb	*+15°C*

Temperature Deviation from ISA

Suppose that in the 'real' atmosphere, the temperature at 2,000 ft is not +11°C as in the ISA, but +16°C, i.e. it is 5°C warmer than in the ISA. This can be expressed as +16°C, a straight out temperature, or as a deviation from the ISA, which in this case is ISA+5. In aviation it is common practice to use this ISA deviation means of describing temperature.

EXAMPLE 19 Express −10°C at FL80 as a deviation from the ISA.

At FL80, i.e. pressure altitude 8,000 ft ISA = +15 − (2 × 8)
= +15 − 16
= −1°C

ANSWER Now −10°C is colder than −1°C by 9°C, and this is expressed as ISA−9.

In Cold Air, the Altimeter Over-Reads

The altimeter is essentially a barometer that converts pressure measurements to altitude. It is calibrated according to the International Standard Atmosphere. On a cold day when the air is more dense, various pressure levels at altitude will be lower than on a warm day.

The 913 mb pressure level that equates with a pressure altitude of 3,000 ft in the International Standard Atmosphere may be at only 2,900 ft. The altimeter, however, because it is calibrated according to the ISA, will indicate this as 3,000 ft even though the aeroplane is at 2,900 ft. On a day that is warmer than ISA, when the altimeter indicates 3,000 ft, the aeroplane may in fact be slightly higher.

This is not significant for separation between aircraft, since all altimeters will be affected identically. It is important for terrain separation, however, so when flying from a high to low temperature, beware below because the altimeter will read too high.

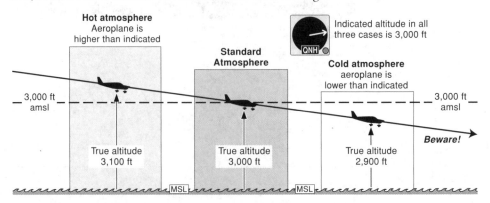

■ Figure 6-35 **When flying from high to low temperature, beware below! (Same rule as for pressure.)**

Density Altitude (or Density Height)

Density is the mass per unit volume, or if you like, the number of molecules in each unit volume, and is affected directly by variations in temperature. Aeroplane performance (the speed at which it can fly, and the height to which it can climb) depends, among a number of factors, mainly on the ambient air density. Consequently it is important to be able to calculate density altitude.

Density altitude is the atmospheric density expressed in terms of altitude in the International Standard Atmosphere which corresponds to that density.

If, for example, at 1,000 ft amsl in the actual atmosphere the density is the same as the density at 2,400 ft in ISA, i.e. our altitude is 1,000 ft amsl but our density altitude is 2,400 ft, the aircraft and engines will perform as if the aeroplane were at 2,400 ft.

How to Calculate Density Altitude

It is impractical for a pilot to have the equipment necessary to measure air density, so we make use of two pieces of information already available and on which density depends: pressure altitude and temperature. Density altitude can be calculated in three ways:

1. By correcting pressure altitude for ISA temperature deviation by 120 ft per 1°C.

2. Graphically, as in most aeroplane performance charts, on which both pressure altitude and temperature are the criteria used in entering the graph. Though density altitude itself may not be specified, it is implied by these other two parameters.

3. By navigation computer.

EXAMPLE 20 Calculate the density altitude at Huddersfield (Crosland Moor), elevation 825 ft, if the current QNH is 999, and the OAT (outside air temperature) +28°C.

ANSWER PA 1,245 ft, DA 3,105 ft

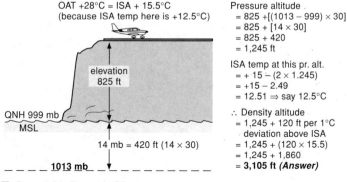

OAT +28°C = ISA + 15.5°C
(because ISA temp here is +12.5°C)

elevation 825 ft

QNH 999 mb
MSL

14 mb = 420 ft (14 × 30)

1013 mb

Pressure altitude
= 825 +[(1013 – 999) × 30]
= 825 + [14 × 30]
= 825 + 420
= 1,245 ft

ISA temp at this pr. alt.
= + 15 – (2 × 1.245)
= +15 – 2.49
= 12.51 ⇒ say 12.5°C

∴ Density altitude
= 1,245 + 120 ft per 1°C
  deviation above ISA
= 1,245 + (120 × 15.5)
= 1,245 + 1,860
= **3,105 ft (Answer)**

■ Figure 6-36 **Example 20**

NOTE Even though the aircraft is at less than 1,000 ft amsl, the engines will perform, and the aircraft will fly, as if it were at about 3,000 ft in the International Standard Atmosphere, i.e. it will have a much poorer performance. As a good pilot you should be aware of poor performance when hot and high.

EXAMPLE 21 Calculate the density altitude of Shoreham, elevation 6 ft, QNH 1031 mb, OAT –2°C.

ANSWER PA – 534 ft, DA – 2,694, i.e. bmsl

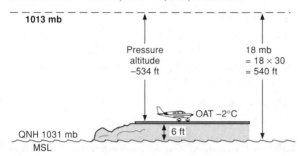

1013 mb

Pressure altitude –534 ft

18 mb = 18 × 30 = 540 ft

OAT –2°C

QNH 1031 mb MSL

6 ft

Pressure altitude
= 6 ft – 540 ft
= –534 ft
i.e. 534 ft bmsl in the ISA,
where ISA temp is +15° +1° = +16°
(temp increases 2°C per 1,000 ft
below MSL in the ISA)

OAT –2°C = ISA – 18°C
∴ Density altitude
= –534 – (120 × 18)
= –534 – 2,160
= **–2,694 ft bmsl** *(Answer)*

■ *Figure 6-37* **Example 21**

NOTE A high QNH (i.e. high air pressure) increases density as does the low temperature, with the temperature usually being the critical factor to watch out for. In this particular case of a low aerodrome elevation and a low temperature at Shoreham, we could expect the engines and the aeroplane to perform very well.

Any graph or table in an Aeroplane Performance or Flight Manual that has both pressure altitude and temperature on it means that density height is being allowed for, and will not have to be calculated directly as above or by computer.

Now complete **Exercises 6 – Vertical Nav-7.**

Time

Time is of great importance to the air navigator, and the clock is one of the basic instruments used in the cockpit. Time enables you to:

☐ **regulate** affairs on board your aeroplane;

☐ **measure** the progress of your flight;

☐ **anticipate** arrival time at certain positions;

☐ **calculate** a safe endurance for flight;

☐ **estimate** when weather conditions at the destination are likely to improve;

☐ **measure** rest periods between flights ... and so on.

Time is also used to measure the earth's rotation. We relate the rotation of our planet Earth to the position of celestial or heavenly bodies, such as the sun and other stars. By using time we can specify the beginning of day, sunrise, noon, sunset, commencement of night, midnight, moonrise, moonset, and so on.

To all navigators – land, sea and air – time is of vital importance, and a subject that must be mastered.

Motion of the Earth

To measure the passage of time, we need to relate it to some repetitive event. For our ancestors, and indeed for us, a suitable recurring event is the apparent passage of the sun across our skies – its highest point in the sky simply indicated when the shadows that it casts are shortest. The sun appears to cross our skies once in every day.

On a longer time scale, we notice the regular passage of the seasons – spring, summer, autumn and winter – a complete cycle of these being called one year.

The sun has been used as a simple clock for thousands of years. Whereas early man thought that it was the sun which moved around the earth, we now know that this is not the case. It is, in fact, the rotation of the earth on its axis that causes the appearance of the sun travelling across our skies each day, hence the term 'apparent passage of the sun'.

As man's knowledge increased it was realised that one day is the approximate time span of one revolution of the earth on its own axis. One year is the approximate time span of one complete orbit of the earth about the sun.

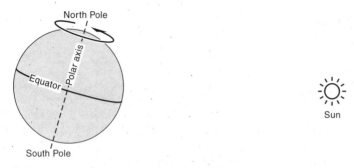

■ *Figure 7-1* **The earth rotates about its own axis once every 24 hours**

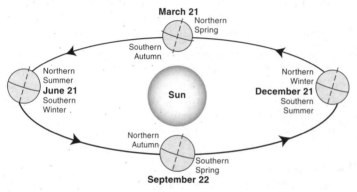

■ *Figure 7-2* **The earth rotates around the sun once a year**

There is a third fundamental type of time apart from the rotation of the earth about its own axis and the orbiting of the earth around the sun. It is **international atomic time (TAI),** where atomic vibrations, such as those occurring at very short time intervals in quartz crystals, are used to define the SI second and calibrate clocks extremely accurately. As this was endorsed internationally as recently as 1971 you can see that the subject of time is still not a closed book. In fact, only in 1985 was the international basis for standard time changed from Greenwich Mean Time (GMT) to Coordinated Universal Time (UTC).

Each day is divided into 24 hours, each hour further divided into 60 equal minutes, and each of these minutes further divided into 60 equal seconds.

To complete one orbit of the sun, the earth takes about 365 and ¼ solar days. It is convenient to have a whole number of days in a year, and so we define the civil year as 365 days. At the end of each 4 years, when the extra ¼ day each year adds up to one whole day, the extra day is added in to give a **leap year** of 366 days. This keeps the calendar reasonably in step with the seasons.

Measurement and Expression of Time

To measure time, use is again made of a repetitive event, such as the swinging of a pendulum, or the atomic vibrations within a quartz crystal, to design clocks that measure hours, minutes and seconds.

Each day is divided into 24 hours, which begins at midnight (00 hours 00 minutes), then proceed through midday (1200) to midnight (2400), at which instant the next day begins (0000).

The hours are numbered from 00 hours to 24 hours (rather than 0 to 12 a.m. and 0 to 12 p.m.), and the 60 minutes of each hour are numbered from 00 min to 59 min. The term a.m. means *ante meridiem,* in the sense that the sun has yet to pass over your meridian of longitude, so the time is before noon; p.m. means *post meridiem,* because the sun has passed overhead and the time is afternoon.

For flight planning and navigation purposes we do not usually refer to the year or the month, but only the **day** of the month as the **date,** followed by the time in **hours** and **minutes.** As most air navigation occurs within a few hours, and only rarely in excess of 30 hours, we can be reasonably confident of which year and month we are talking about, so there is no need to specify them.

Seconds, which are $\frac{1}{60}$ of a minute, are too short a time interval for practical navigation, so date/time is usually expressed as a six figure date/time group.

Six-Figure Date/Time Group

In the six-figure date/time group:
- the date is a two-figure group for the day of the month from 00 to 31, and is followed by:
- the time, written as a four-figure group on a 24 hour clock – the first two figures representing the hours from 00 to 24, and the last two figures representing the minutes from 00 through to 59.

EXAMPLE 1 Express 13th of September, 1986, 10:35 a.m. as a six-figure date/time group.

> *date*   *time*
> 13   10   35
>   *hr*   *min*

ANSWER 131035

EXAMPLE 2 Express 3:21 p.m. on March 17th, 1987, as a six-figure date/time group.

> 3:21 p.m. = 1200 noon
>   + 321
>   ‾‾‾‾‾
>   1521 on the 24 hr clock

ANSWER 171521

Eight-Figure Date/Time Group

To specify the month, the six-figure date/time is preceded by two figures representing the month, and so is expanded into an eight figure time-group. This is often used in NOTAMs (Notices to Airmen).

In the eight-figure date/time group:
☐ **the first two** numbers refer to month;
☐ **the second two** numbers refer to the date; and
☐ **the last four** numbers refer to the time.

EXAMPLE 3 5:45 p.m. on September 30th may be written as:

SEP 30 17 45
or 09 30 17 45
or 09301745

Now complete **Exercises 7 – Time-1.**

The Relationship Between Longitude and Time

In one day, the earth makes one complete rotation of 360° with respect to the chosen celestial body, which is the sun. The time of day is a measure of this rotation and indicates how much of that day has elapsed or, in other words, how much of a rotation has been completed.

As observers on the earth, we do not feel its rotation about its own axis, but rather we see the sun apparently move around the earth. In one mean solar day the sun will appear to have travelled the full 360° of longitude around the earth.

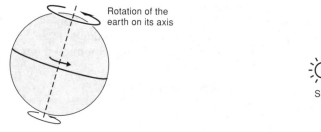

■ *Figure 7-3* **The earth rotates at 15° of longitude per hour**

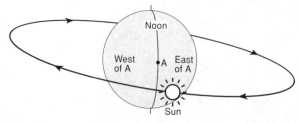

■ *Figure 7-4* **Apparent motion of the sun around the earth**

The angular difference between different longitudes is known as arc of longitude and has a direct relationship with time.

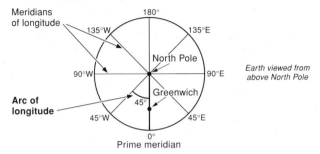

■ Figure 7-5 **Arc of longitude**

The arc of longitude in degrees and minutes of arc is related to the time interval in hours and minutes as shown below.

ARC	TIME	
360°	24 hours	(divide by 24)
15°	1 hour	(divide by 15)
1°	4 minutes	(divide by 4)
15′	1 minute	(divide by 15)
1′	4 seconds	

Time to Arc Conversions

1. Multiply the hours by 15 to obtain degrees (1 hour = 15° arc of longitude).

2. Divide the minutes of time by 4 to obtain degrees (a minute of time = ¼° or 15′ arc) and then multiply the remaining minutes of time by 15 to obtain minutes of arc.

EXAMPLE 4 Convert 9 hr 23 min to arc units.

9 hr × 15 = 135°; as 1 hr = 15°

23 min ÷ 4 = 5°; as 4 min = 1°

and the remaining 3 minutes of time × 15 = 45′ of arc as 1 minute = 15′

ANSWER Adding these, we get 140°45′

There is a table in the *Air Almanac* (a book containing, among many other astronomical items, daylight and darkness data), which allows rapid conversion of arc to time, and vice versa, thereby avoiding the above calculation. PPL pilots do not require the *Air Almanac*.

Arc to Time Conversions

1. Divide the degrees by 15 to obtain hours, and multiply the remaining degrees by 4 to obtain minutes of time.

2. Divide the minutes of arc by 15 to obtain minutes of time, and multiply the remainder by 4 to obtain seconds of time.

EXAMPLE 5 Convert 140°49′ of arc of longitude to time units.

140 ÷ 15 = 9 hr, with 5 left over × 4 = 20 min of time, i.e. 140° of arc = 9 hr 20 min.

49′ ÷ 15 = 3 min of time, with 4 left over × 4 = 16 sec of time.

Adding these: 140°49′ = 9 hr 23 min 16 sec.

ANSWER 9 hr 23 min 16 sec

Now complete **Exercises 7 – Time-2.**

Local Time

Time is a measure of the rotation of the earth, and any given time interval can be represented by a corresponding angle through which the earth turns. Suppose that the sun (the celestial reference point) is directly overhead, i.e. it is noon. For every point along that same meridian of longitude, the sun will be at its highest point in the sky for that day.

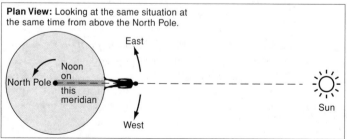

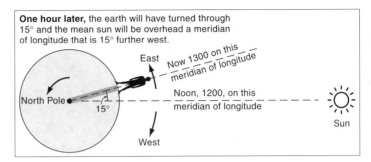

One hour later, the earth will have turned through 15° and the mean sun will be overhead a meridian of longitude that is 15° further west.

East
Now 1300 on this meridian of longitude

North Pole
15°

Noon, 1200, on this meridian of longitude

Sun

West

■ *Figure 7-6* **Noon is when the sun is at its highest point in the sky**

Meridians of longitude further east are ahead in local time.
Meridians of longitude further west are behind in local time.

EXAMPLE 6 Place A is 45° of longitude west of place B. How much earlier or later will noon occur at A compared to B?

45° arc of longitude = 3 hours, and because A is to the west of B, noon will occur three hours later at A.

Local Mean Time (LMT)

LMT uses the sun as its celestial reference point, and the local meridian of longitude as its terrestrial (earthly) reference point. Therefore, all points along the same meridian of longitude will have the same local mean time.

The local mean time along one meridian of longitude will differ from the local mean time along another meridian of longitude, and this difference will equal the difference (or change) in longitude expressed in time units. The further east the place is, the further ahead it is in LMT.

EXAMPLE 7 If it is noon LMT in Kingston upon Hull (00°20′W longitude) with the sun passing over the 00°20′W meridian of longitude, how much earlier or later will it be noon LMT in Blackpool (3°W longitude)?

Kingston upon Hull longitude: 00°20′W
Blackpool longitude: 03°00′W
difference, or change, of longitude = 02°40′

which, in time units, is:
2° = 8 min (as 1° = 4 min of time)
40′ = 2 min 40 sec (as 1′ = 4 sec of time)

Therefore 2°40′ = 10 min 40 sec of time.

ANSWER Because Blackpool is to the west of Kingston upon Hull, noon at Blackpool with the sun passing over its meridian will be 10 minutes 40 seconds later than at Kingston upon Hull.

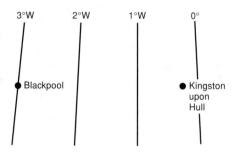

■ *Figure 7-7* **Example 7**

In air navigation, the main use of local mean time (LMT) is in extracting data from tables in the Air Almanac on the rising and setting of celestial bodies such as the sun, moon and stars. We can use these tables to determine sunrise, sunset, twilight and so on.

Coordinated Universal Time (UTC)

UTC is the **local mean time** (LMT) at the meridian of longitude that runs through the observatory at Greenwich, near London. The Greenwich meridian is longitude 0, also known as the **prime meridian.** Until recently the international time standard was Greenwich Mean Time (GMT), but this term has now been replaced by **coordinated universal time** (UTC). UTC has a more academic definition and is slightly more precise than GMT.

UTC is a 'universal time', and all aeronautical communications around the world are expressed in UTC. For this reason, pilots need to be able to convert quickly and accurately from their local time to UTC, and vice versa.

Meridians to the east are ahead in time, thus:

Longitude east, universal least.

Meridians to the west are behind in time:

Longitude west, universal best.

EXAMPLE 8 If it is 231531 LMT on the 150°E meridian of longitude running through Sydney, Australia, what is the time in UTC (i.e. in the UK on the Greenwich meridian)?

150° = 10 hours, as 15° of arc = 1 hour
and *longitude east, universal least.*

23 15 31 LMT at 150°E
<u>– 10 00</u>   arc to time
<u>23 05 31</u> UTC

ANSWER 230531 UTC

NOTE Australian Eastern Standard Time is based on the 150°E longitude, which is 10 hours ahead of UTC. Standard Time in Vancouver, British Columbia, Canada, is based on 120°W longitude and is therefore 8 hours behind UTC.

EXAMPLE 9 If it is 282340 on the 138°15′W meridian of longitude, express this LMT in Coordinated Universal Time (UTC).

Converting arc to time: 138°15′ = 9 hr 13 min
and *longitude west, universal best.*

28 23 40 LMT at 138°15′W
+   9 13   arc to time
<u>28 32 53</u>   32 hr = 1 day + 8 hr
<u>29 08 53</u> UTC

ANSWER 290853 UTC

EXAMPLE 10 Convert 300825 UTC to LMT at the 138°15′W meridian.

138° 15′ = 9 hr 13 min
and *longitude west, universal best.*

30 08 25 UTC
<u>–   9 13</u>   arc to time (9 from 32 (24 + 8), and carry
<u>29 23 12</u> LMT   1 over into *days* column)

ANSWER 292312 LMT at 138° 15′W

*Now complete **Exercises 7 – Time-3.***

Zone Time

Obviously Local Mean Time (LMT) is not practical in day-to-day life, because every different meridian of longitude has its own LMT. Ships at sea set their clocks to the LMT of the nearest meridian divisible by 15 (which means that, as 15° = 1 hour, these times will differ from UTC by a whole number of hours).

Even though the ship may not be precisely on that meridian, it means that its clocks will be set to read the same time as the clocks of all the ships in that area or zone, and they will not be too far out of step with the sun – noon at the ship's actual meridian occurring at, or close to, 1200 zone time.

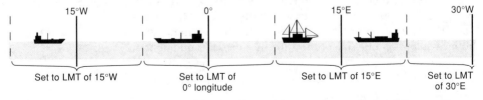

■ *Figure 7-8* **Ships set their clocks according to the local time zone**

For example, a ship at longitude 145°27′E, when considered in proximity to the nearest meridian divisible by 15, is closest to the 150°E meridian of longitude. It would therefore set the LMT at 150°E on its clocks, and as this zone time differs from UTC by (150 ÷ 15) = 10 hours, and (longitude east, universal least) UTC will be 10 hours behind this.

The 150°E zone is called 'zone minus 10' because:

☐ **the zone meridian** is divisible by fifteen 10 times; and

☐ **minus 10,** because you need to subtract 10 from this zone time to obtain UTC (remember that east longitudes are ahead in time).

Zone times are not widely used in aviation.

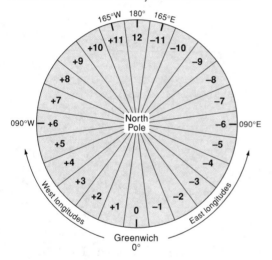

■ *Figure 7-9* **Longitudes as seen from a north polar satellite**

The Date-Line

Suppose that the time at the Greenwich meridian is 261200 LMT (i.e. 261200 UTC). Now, if you instantaneously travel *eastwards* from Greenwich to the 180° East meridian, the Local Mean Time there is 12 hours ahead of the LMT at Greenwich, that is 262400 LMT at 180°E, or midnight on the 26th LMT at 180°E.

If, however, you travel *westwards* from Greenwich to the 180° West meridian, then the time there is 12 hours behind Greenwich, i.e. 260000 or, as it is usually written, 252400 LMT at 180°W, midnight on the 25th. Note that the time is midnight in both cases, but on one side of the 180° meridian it is midnight on the 25th, and on the other side it is midnight on the 26th.

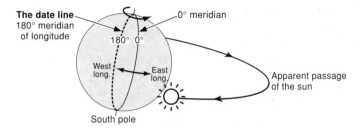

■ Figure 7-10 **The date-line runs basically along the 180° meridian**

The 180°E and 180°W meridians are one and the same meridian – the anti-meridian to Greenwich. We have the situation of it being midnight in its vicinity, but on different dates, depending on which side of the 180° meridian you are on. Making a complete trip around the world, you would lose a day travelling westwards or gain a day travelling eastwards.

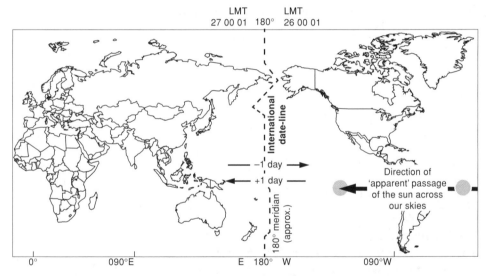

■ Figure 7-11 **Crossing the date-line travelling east, subtract one day; travelling west, add one day**

To prevent the date being in error and to provide a starting point for each day, a date-line has been fixed by international agreement, and it basically follows the 180° meridian of longitude, with minor excursions to keep groups of islands together. Crossing the date-line, you alter the date by one day – in effect changing your time by 24 hours to compensate for the slow change during your journey around the world.

Standard Times or Local Times

Standard times operate in a similar way to zone time in that all clocks in a given geographical area are set to the LMT of a given standard meridian. This is known as **standard time** or **local time** (not to be confused with Local Mean Time) for that area.

Standard time in the UK is based on the Greenwich meridian. In other words, 1545 standard time in the UK is also 1545 UTC. Standard time in Germany is based on the 15°E meridian of longitude, and so is 1 hour ahead of the UK. At 1545 UTC, the time in London is 1545, and in Hamburg it is 1645 German standard time. In Tokyo, which is 9 hours ahead of UTC, it is 2445, i.e. 0045 Japanese standard time the next morning.

When flights involve travel between different time zones, it is easiest to work entirely in UTC and convert the answer to local time at the end.

EXAMPLE 11 You depart Prestwick, Scotland on a flight of 3 hours 40 minutes duration to Bremen in Germany at 0945 UK standard time, i.e. 0945 UTC. At what time should your German friends meet you in Bremen?

Departure Prestwick: 09 45 UTC
Flight Time: 3 40

ETA Bremen: 13 25 UTC
arc to time: +1 00 (to convert British to
                               German time)
                     14 25

ANSWER 1425 MEZ (German standard time)

Now complete **Exercises 7 – Time-4.**

Light from the Sun

The sun's rays strike different parts of the earth at different angles depending on latitude and season.

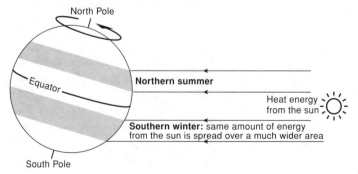

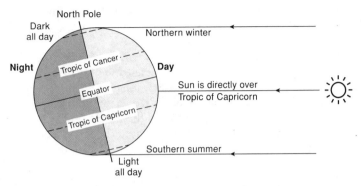

■ *Figure 7-12* **The sun does not shine evenly on the earth**

Sunrise occurs when the upper limb of the sun (the first part visible) is on the visible horizon. **Sunset** occurs when the upper limb of the sun (the last part visible) is just disappearing below the visible horizon. Sunlight occurs between sunrise and sunset.

As we have all observed when waking early, it starts to become light well before the sun actually rises, and it stays light until well after the sun has set. This period of incomplete light, or if you like, incomplete darkness, is called **twilight**, and the period from the start of morning twilight until the end of evening twilight is called **daylight**.

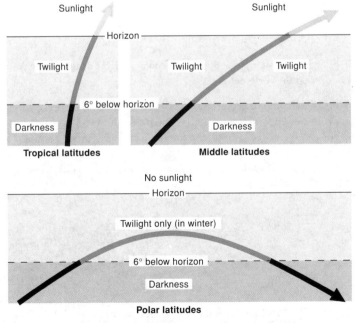

■ *Figure 7-13* **The higher the latitude, the longer the twilight**

In the tropics the sun rises and sets at almost 90° to the horizon, which makes the period of twilight quite short, and the onset of daylight or night dramatically rapid.

In the higher latitudes, towards the North and South Poles, the sun rises and sets at a more oblique angle to the horizon, consequently the period of twilight is much longer and the onset of daylight or darkness far more gradual than in the tropics.

At certain times of the year inside the Arctic and Antarctic Circles, the period of twilight occurs without the sun actually rising above the horizon at all during the day. This is the winter situation.

While to an observer at sea level the sun may appear to have set and the earth is no longer bathed in sunlight, an aeroplane directly overhead may still have the sun shining on it. In other words, the time at which the sun rises or sets will depend on the altitude of the observer.

In fact it is possible to take off after sunset at ground level and climb to an altitude where the sun appears to rise again and shine a little longer on the aeroplane. This is especially noticeable in polar regions when the sun might be just below the horizon, as seen from sea level, for long periods of time (twilight).

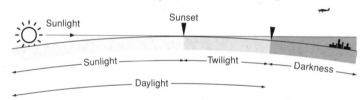

■ *Figure 7-14* **An aeroplane at altitude can be in sight of the sun after it has set on the earth below**

It is easy to be deceived by brightness at altitude only to find a few minutes later after a descent to near ground level, and possibly under some cloud cover, that it has become dark. High ground to the west of the aerodrome will also reduce the amount of light from the sun reaching the vicinity of the aerodrome as night approaches. (An important point to remember when flying!)

■ *Figure 7-15* **Local sunrise and sunset is affected by terrain**

Time of Sunset and Sunrise

The times at which sunrise and sunset occur depend on two things:

☐ **The date:** In summer sunrise is earliest and sunset later, i.e. the daylight hours are longer in summer. The reverse occurs in winter.

☐ **The latitude:** In the northern summer for instance, place B in Figure 7-16 experiences sunrise while place A is already well into the day, and it is still night at place C, yet all are on the same meridian of longitude. Because of this they all have the same Local Mean Time (LMT), but are experiencing quite different conditions of daylight due to being on different latitudes.

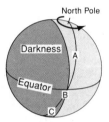

Sun

■ *Figure 7-16* **Places A, B and C, although on the same meridian, experience different sunrise and sunset times because they are on different latitudes**

Effect of Latitude on Sunrise and Sunset

The Local Mean Time of sunrise and sunset on a particular date depends on latitude. The *Air Almanac* (a bi-annual publication of HMSO) contains tables that give Local Mean Time for the occurrence of sunrise and sunset at ground level at different places in the UK. (The *Air Almanac* also contains tables for Morning and Evening Civil Twilight, but these are of no significance to air navigation in the UK.)

Effect of Longitude on Sunrise and Sunset

The Local Mean Time of sunrise and sunset depends further on the longitude of the place. Sunrise at places on a particular latitude occurs at the same Local Mean Time at each place but different places on the same latitude will have a different Local Standard Time for the event, depending on their *longitude*. The same applies to sunset.

Fishguard in Wales and Ipswich in Suffolk are both on the same latitude (52°N) but, because their arc of longitude difference is 6° (5°W to 1°E), the sun will rise ⁹⁄₁₅ of an hour (24 minutes) earlier at Ipswich than Fishguard. It will set the same amount of time later in Fishguard than Ipswich on Local Standard Time – be it UTC or, in summer, British Summer Time (BST). Also, the sun will rise ¹⁄₁₅ of an hour (4 minutes) earlier at Ipswich than Greenwich.

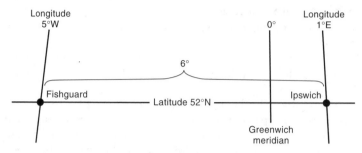

■ Figure 7-17 **Fishguard and Ipswich experience sunset at the same LMT, but at different local standard times (UTC or BST)**

The Local Mean Time for the event (e.g. sunrise or sunset), extracted from the *Air Almanac* tables, is therefore corrected for arc of longitude east or west of the standard meridian – which, in the case of the UK, is (conveniently) the Greenwich (0°) meridian – to give Local Standard Time.

Fortunately you don't need to buy an *Air Almanac* every six months because sunrise and sunset times are available in the UK AIP GEN 2-7-1 and from ATS Units and Met Offices throughout the UK. These times are already corrected from LMT to UTC or BST, as appropriate, so they can be used with no further conversion needed.

For smaller places the precise times may not be available, so interpolation between localities either side may be necessary to give a good estimate within a few minutes. Common sense dictates to err on the conservative side, especially for sunset.

Sunrise/sunset tables are published in *Pooley's Flight Guide*.

SUNRISE – SUNSET TABLES
All times are LOCAL, allowances have been made for British Summer Time — 26 March to 21 October 1995

	Jersey	London	Cardiff	Manchester	Dublin	Newcastle	Glasgow	Inverness	
Jan 1	0803 1626	0806	0818 1619	0824 1605	0840 1621	0831 1554	0848 1559	0856 1546	Jan 1
7	0801		0815 1626	0820 1613	0836 1629	0827 1603	0844 1608	0852 1556	7
13			0811 1636	0816 1623	0832 1639	0821 1614	0837 1619	0844 1608	13
19			0804 1646	0809 1633	0825 1649	0813 1625	0829 1631	0835 1620	19
25		1645	0757 1657	0800 1654	0816 1701	0804 1636	0819 1644	0825 1634	25
31	1711	0735 1655	0747 1707	0750 1657	0806 1713	0753 1650	0808 1657	0812 1648	31
Feb 6	0727 1722	0725 1706	0737 1718	0738 1709	0754 1725	0741 1702	0756 1710	0759 1703	Feb 6
12	0717 1732	0714 1717	0726 1729	0727 1720	0743 1736	0728 1715	0742 1723	0745 1716	12
18	0706 1741	0702 1728	0714 1740	0714 1732	0703 1748	0715 1727	0728 1736	0730 1730	18
24	0655 1750	0650 1739	0702 1751	0700 1744	0716 1800	0702 1739	0713 1749	0714 1744	24
Mar 2	0642 1800	0637 1749	0649 1801	0647 1755	0703 1811	0647 1752	0658 1800	0658 1758	Mar 2
8	0630 1809	0623 1759	0635 1811	0633 1806	0649 1822	0632 1803	0643 1814	0642 1812	8
14	0617 1818	0610 1810	0622 1822	0618 1818	0634 1834	0616 1816	0627 1827	0625 1825	14
20	0606 1826	0559 1818	0610 1830	0605 1827	0622 1843	0603 1825	0614 1836	0610 1835	20
26	0652 1937	0642 1937	0654 1943	0648 1940	0704 1956	0645 1940	0655 1951	0651 1951	26
Apr 1	0639 1945	0628 1940	0640 1952	0634 1951	0650 2007	0600 1951	0640 2003	0635 2004	Apr 1
7	0627 1954	0615 1950	0620 2002	0627 2002	0636 2018	0615 2003	0624 2016	0619 2017	7
13	0615 2003	0602 2000	0614 2012	0606 2013	0622 2029	0601 2015	0609 2028	0602 2030	13
19	0603 2013	0549 2011	0601 2023	0552 2024	0608 2040	0546 2026	0554 2040	0547 2043	19
25	0552 2021	0537 2021	0549 2033	0539 2035	0555 2051	0533 2037	0540 2052	0532 2056	25

SAMPLE ONLY
Not to be used for flight operations or flight planning

■ Figure 7-18 **Sample excerpt of the sunrise/sunset tables in Pooley's Flight Guide**

Flight operations of light aircraft in the UK, especially by pilots without a night rating, are closely geared to the times of sunrise and sunset. The earliest time at which basic PPL holders can legally fly with passengers is sunrise minus 30 minutes, and they must be on the ground again no later than sunset plus 30 minutes, irrespective of the length of twilight time. (This stems from the Air Navigation Order definition of **night,** which commences at sunset plus 30 minutes and ends at sunrise minus 30 minutes, both times being taken at surface level.)

NOTE Good airmanship may dictate to use an earlier time than SS+30 when planning a flight, if, for example, the destination aerodrome has high ground to the west of it, or the weather forecast indicates poor visibility, or cloud cover approaching from the west, as in a cold front.

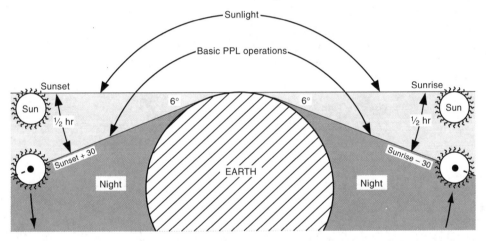

■ *Figure 7-19* **In the UK, official night commences at sunset plus 30 minutes and ends at sunrise minus 30 minutes**

Another important consideration related to sunset is that many smaller airfields in the UK (and throughout Europe) close at sunset. This may also apply to the alternate aerodrome(s) chosen for a flight. UK aerodrome operating hours are given in the AD section of the UK AIP and also in *Pooley's Flight Guide* – the latter contains details on most private airfields also.

Summer Time

To take advantage of the longer daylight hours and better weather in summer, the clocks in many countries are put forward, usually by one hour, to give a new standard time known as **summer time.**

In the UK, summer time is usually between the fourth Sundays in March and October (unless otherwise specified). For example, 1200 UTC becomes 1300 British Summer Time (BST).

British Summer Time = UTC + 1 hour.

A final reminder that daylight can end earlier than the published time for a number of reasons, including:

☐ **significant cloud cover;**
☐ **poor visibility;**
☐ **high ground** to the west of an aerodrome.

Remember also that the closer to the equator you are, the shorter the twilight time.

Make allowances for these when planning a flight that may end near the beginning of 'official night' or SS+30. It is good airmanship to plan on arriving *at least* 30 minutes before this time (sunset). Common sense encourages you to increase this margin on long journeys or on flights where it is difficult to estimate your time of arrival accurately, for reasons such as poor weather that is forecast to occur en route or at the destination.

Now complete **Exercises 7 – Time-5.**

The Earth

To navigate an aeroplane efficiently from one place to another over long distances or in poor visibility, we need to refer to some representation of the earth. This representation must be smaller in size than the earth; in other words, it must be a picture of a 'reduced earth'.

The simplest and most accurate reduced earth is a globe, which retains the spherical shape of the earth and displays the various oceans, continents, cities, and so on. But a cumbersome globe is not the ideal navigation tool to have in a cockpit, especially if detailed information is required, hence the need for maps or charts that can be folded and put away. The task of the cartographer (map-maker) is to project a picture of a reduced earth globe onto a flat surface and make a map or a chart from this.

Maps represent the earth's surface (or parts thereof) on a flat surface; **charts** show further information or special conditions, possibly using only an outline of geographical features such as the coastline. Since most maps that pilots use show specific aeronautical and navigation data, they are referred to as charts.

The Form or Shape of the Earth

The exact shape of the earth's surface is constantly changing. Volcanoes erupt and grow, new islands form and others disappear, landslides and earthquakes cause large land movements, the ocean surface continually changes in height with the tides and, on a very long-term basis, the continents gradually move.

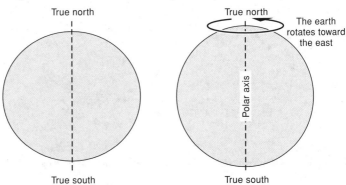

■ *Figure 8-1* **The earth is a slightly flattened (oblate) sphere**

■ *Figure 8-2* **The earth rotates about its axis**

The regular geometric shape which the earth resembles most is a sphere but, even when all the surface bumps are ironed out, the earth is still not a perfect sphere. It is slightly flat at the North and South Poles, forming a flattened (or oblate) spheroid, the polar diameter being approximately 23 nm less than the equatorial diameter (6,865 nm as against 6,888 nm). For the purposes of practical navigation, however, the earth can be treated as a sphere.

As well as moving in an orbit about the sun, the earth rotates on its own axis. The axis of rotation is called the geographic **polar axis,** and the two points where the axis meets the surface of the sphere are called:

- ☐ the **geographic North Pole** or **true north;** and
- ☐ the **geographic South Pole** or **true south.**

If you stand anywhere on earth and face towards the geographic North Pole, then you are facing true north.

Imaginary Lines on the Earth's Surface

A GREAT CIRCLE drawn on the earth's surface is one whose plane passes through the centre of the sphere (earth). Significant properties of great circles are:

- ☐ **A great circle** is the largest circle that can be drawn on the surface of the earth or on any sphere.
- ☐ **The shortest distance** between any two points on the surface of a sphere is the arc of a great circle.
- ☐ **Only one great circle** can be drawn between two points on the surface of a sphere (unless the two points are diametrically opposed, as are the geographic poles).

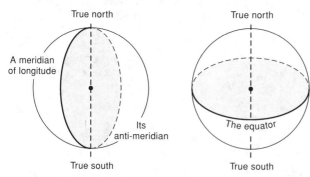 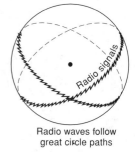

■ *Figure 8-3* ***A great circle has the centre of the earth as its axis***

Some examples of great circles are:

- ☐ meridians of longitude;
- ☐ the equator;
- ☐ the paths that radio waves follow.

A SMALL CIRCLE is any circle on the surface of a sphere that is not a great circle, i.e. the centre of a small circle is not at the centre of the earth. Parallels of latitude (except for the equator) are small circles.

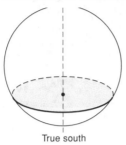

True south

■ *Figure 8-4* **The plane of a small circle does not pass through the centre of a sphere**

Latitude and Longitude

A convenient way of specifying the position of any point on earth is to relate it to the imaginary lines that form the latitude and longitude graticule (or grid) on the surface of the earth.

LATITUDE. The reference for latitude is the plane of the equator, the great circle whose plane is perpendicular (i.e. at right angles, or 90°) to the polar axis.

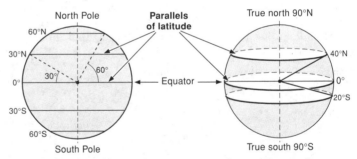

■ *Figure 8-5* **Latitude**

☐ **The latitude of a place** is its angular distance in degrees from the equator, measured at the centre of the earth and designated either north or south. For instance, Nottingham is at 53°N latitude.

☐ **A parallel of latitude** joins all points of the same latitude and (except for the equator) is a small circle. Nottingham, Bremen in Germany, Torun in Poland, Yellowhead Pass in the Canadian Rockies, and Wicklow in Ireland are all about 53° north of the equator, and therefore the line joining them is called the 53°N parallel of latitude.

☐ **Parallels of latitude** are parallel to the equator and to each other.

☐ **The longest parallel** of latitude is the equator (latitude 0°). The other parallels, as you move away from the equator towards the higher latitudes, progressively decrease in size, until the 90° parallels of latitude become just points at the north and south geographic poles.

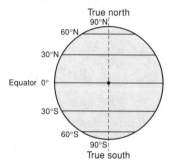

■ *Figure 8-6* **The further from the equator, the smaller the parallel of latitude**

LONGITUDE. The basic reference for longitude is the **Greenwich meridian**, which is also known as the **prime meridian.** It is that half of the great circle which contains the polar axis (about which the earth rotates), and passes through the Greenwich Observatory near London, as well as the north and south geographic poles. The prime meridian is designated as 'longitude 0°'.

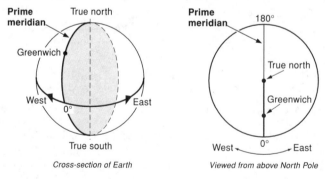

Cross-section of Earth   Viewed from above North Pole

■ *Figure 8-7* **The prime meridian**

The other half of the same great circle that contains the prime meridian runs from the north geographic pole to the south geographic pole, but on the other side of the earth to Greenwich. It passes down the western side of the Pacific Ocean and is known as 'longitude 180°'. It can be reached by travelling either east from the prime meridian or by travelling the same angular distance (180°) west from the prime meridian. Therefore it can be called either '180°E' or '180°W'. It is also called the **anti-meridian** of Greenwich.

- **All of the great circles** containing the polar axis (and therefore passing through the north and south geographic poles) are called meridians of longitude.
- **Meridians of longitude** are specified by their angular difference in degrees east or west from the prime meridian.

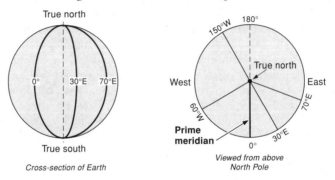

■ *Figure 8-8* **The longitude of a place is the angle between its meridian of longitude and the prime (Greenwich) meridian, measured eastward or westward from the prime meridian**

Specifying Position

The parallels of latitude and meridians of longitude form an imaginary graticule or grid over the surface of the earth. The position of any point on the earth can be specified by its:

- **latitude** – angular position north or south of the plane of the equator; together with:
- **longitude** – angular position east or west of the prime meridian.

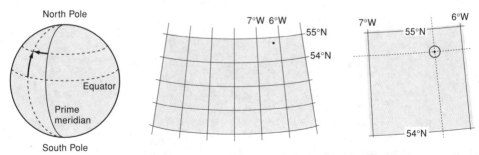

■ *Figure 8-9* **The position of Belfast (Aldergrove) in Northern Ireland is 54°39′N, 06°14′W**

It is usually sufficiently accurate to specify the latitude and longitude of a place in degrees and minutes (one minute equals ⅟₆₀ of one degree). For extreme accuracy, each minute can be divided into 60 seconds of arc. The symbols used are ° (degrees), ′ (minutes) and ″ (seconds).

For example, the position of Belfast (Aldergrove) in Northern Ireland is: 543927N 0061257W (54°39′15″N, 006°13′30″W). For our purposes 54°39′N, 006°14′W is sufficiently accurate.

NOTE With the advent of inertial navigation systems that use latitude/longitude reference, some documents, show the N or S and E or W *prior* to the coordinate, as this is the order in which latitude and longitude are entered on such equipment. Also, instead of seconds (mentioned above), the minutes of the coordinates are decimalised, i.e. N52°16.4′, W002°45.9′; or N5216.4, W00245.9. (The standard is that the N/S coordinate has four digits prior to the decimal point, while that for E/W has five; the reason being that latitude extends to 90° N or S, and longitude extends to 180° E or W.)

Specifying latitude and longitude is the normal method of indicating a particular position on earth, and is the one we most commonly use at the flight-planning stage when preparing maps and flight plans. Once in flight, however, there are other means of specifying the position of the aircraft, such as:

- ☐ **By position over or abeam** a landmark or radio beacon, for instance, "over Shrewsbury", "abeam Prestatyn", "over Lydd VOR".
- ☐ **By range (distance) and bearing** from a landmark or radio beacon, for instance, "10 nm on a bearing of 290°T from Ocean City" (see Figure 8-10).

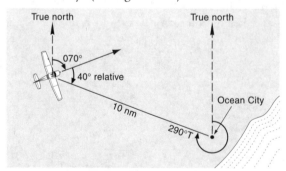

■ *Figure 8-10* **Specifying position by relative bearing**

NOTE The use of place names needs to be confined to places that are likely to be known to the recipient of the message, and that are shown on the commonly used aeronautical charts. In the UK, with its high density of population, place names are frequently duplicated and can be misleading.

Distances

The standard unit of distance in navigation is the **nautical mile (nm),** which is the length of 1 minute of arc of any great circle on earth (assuming the earth to be a perfect sphere).

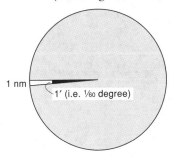

■ *Figure 8-11* **1 nm is the length of 1 minute of arc of a great circle on the earth**

There are 360 degrees in a circle and 60 minutes in a degree, making $60 \times 360 = 21,600$ minutes of arc in a circle. The circumference of the earth is therefore $(60 \times 360) = 21,600$ minutes of arc, which is 21,600 nm.

LATITUDE (the angular distance north or south of the equator) is measured up and down a meridian of longitude (which is a great circle) and therefore:

1 minute of latitude at any point on earth = 1 nautical mile (nm).

This is useful for measuring distance on a chart.

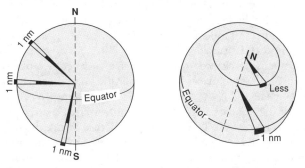

■ *Figure 8-12* **1 minute of latitude = 1 nm; 1 minute of longitude varies in length**

1 degree of latitude at any point on earth = 60 nm.

LONGITUDE is measured around the parallels of latitude (small circles except for the equator), and so 1 minute of longitude varies in length depending on where it is on the earth's surface.

The only place where 1 minute of longitude is equal to 1 nm is around the equator; the higher the latitude, the further away from the equator the place is, and the shorter the length in nm of 1 minute of longitude in that region.

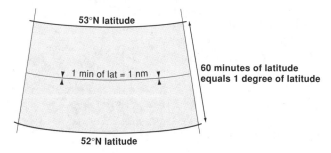

■ *Figure 8-13* ***1 minute of latitude = 1 nautical mile***

When using charts, do not be confused by the fact that we measure 1 minute of latitude (always 1 nm) up or down the side of the chart along a meridian of longitude. It is logical when you think about it.

Angles

The most fundamental reference from which angles are measured is that of true north, from 000°T, through 090°T, 180°T, 270°T, to 360°T. Figure 8-14 shows that if an aeroplane follows a long-range great circle track, the track direction referred to true north will gradually change, i.e. the **great circle (GC) track** will cross successive meridians at a gradually changing angle.

Sometimes it is convenient to fly a track whose direction remains constant when referred to true north, i.e. so that the track crosses all meridians of longitude at the same angle. This is known as a **rhumb line (RL) track.**

The rhumb line track and great circle track between two places coincide only if the two places lie on either the same meridian of longitude (a great circle), the track between them being 180°T or 360°T, or on the equator (which is also a great circle), the track between them being 090°T or 270°T. In practical terms, the GC direction and the RL direction may be considered to be the same over short distances, such as those typically flown within the UK.

You must always be clear as to whether you are referring direction to true north or to magnetic north, the difference between the two being the magnetic variation, as discussed in Chapter 3. In this chapter, we are referring direction to true north.

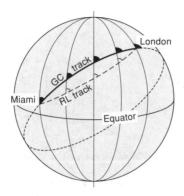

■ *Figure 8-14* **The great circle track and
the rhumb line track**

Representing the Spherical Earth on Flat Charts

The latitude–longitude graticule is translated onto maps and charts by cartographers whose major problem is to represent the spherical surface of the earth on a flat sheet of paper. The process consists of:

☐ **scaling** the earth down to a 'reduced earth'; and then
☐ **projecting** the reduced earth's surface onto a sheet.

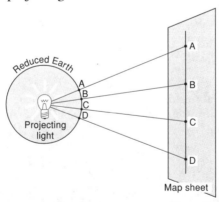

■ *Figure 8-15* **Making a chart**

This process always leads to some distortion, either of areas, distances, angles or shapes. By using certain mathematical techniques when projecting the spherical earth onto a flat chart, the cartographer can preserve some properties, but not all – a spherical orange peel cannot be perfectly flattened out! Some property will always be distorted to a greater or lesser extent depending on how the points on the surface of the reduced spherical earth are transferred onto the flat chart.

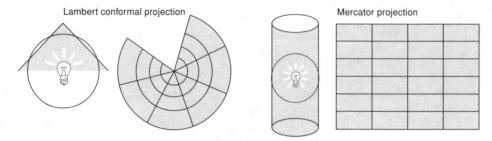

■ *Figure 8-16* **A conical projection and a cylindrical projection**

Unlike a sphere, certain other curved surfaces (such as a cylinder or a cone) can be cut and laid out flat; conversely, a cylinder or a cone can be made out of a flat sheet of paper. This is not possible with a spherical surface – try it with an orange peel! By projecting points on the surface of the reduced earth onto either a conical or cylindrical surface (which can then be flattened out to form a sheet), less distortion occurs and a better chart results, compared with a projection onto an already flat sheet as illustrated in Figure 8-15.

A simple view of map-making is to think of a light projecting the shadows of the latitude–longitude graticule of the reduced sphere onto a cone (Lambert's conical projection) or onto a cylinder (Mercator's cylindrical projection). The cone or cylinder is then laid out flat to form a chart.

Charts based on conic and cylindrical projections are widely used in aviation, mainly because they:

☐ **preserve shape** (of islands, lakes, towns, countries, etc.);
☐ **preserve angular relationships** – (in mathematical terminology, maps exhibiting this vital property are said to be conformal or orthomorphic); and
☐ **have a reasonably constant scale** over the whole chart (for ease of measuring distance).

Topographical Charts

When navigating by visual reference to the ground we refer to land features. A topographical chart showing the surface features of the area in detail is therefore of great value. There are various topographical charts available for visual navigation in the UK, and these include (in order of importance):

☐ **ICAO Aeronautical Charts,** scale 1:500,000 (half-million).
☐ **Topographical Air Charts** of the United Kingdom, scale 1:250,000 (quarter-million).
☐ **Operational Navigational Chart** series (ONC), scale 1:1,000,000 (one million).

The ICAO and ONC series charts are based on the Lambert's conformal *conic* projection. The chart sheet is formed from a secant cone that cuts the sphere representing the reduced earth at two standard parallels of latitude. Just which two parallels of latitude are chosen by the cartographer depends on which part of the earth, and how much of it, he wants to represent on that particular chart.

The standard parallels are usually mentioned at the bottom or on the side of the chart – for example, on the 'one to half-million Southern England and Wales' chart (Map Sheet Number 2171 CD), the standard parallels are 49°20′N and 54°40′N. There is no distortion along the standard parallels, and very little distortion north or south of them in the UK because of the short distance involved.

The projection for the 1:250,000 Topographical Air Charts of the UK is based on a *cylindrical* projection known as the transverse Mercator projection. Whereas the normal Mercator projection starts with a cylinder wrapped around the equator with its sides parallel to the polar axis, the transverse Mercator starts with a cylinder wrapped around a chosen meridian of longitude and its anti-meridian, with the sides of the cylinder at 90° to the polar axis.

The UK 1:250,000 transverse Mercator charts are based on the 2° west meridian of longitude, which passes north–south through the middle of the British Isles. When flattened out, this provides a chart with no distortion down the 2°W meridian and, in fact, very little distortion anywhere east or west of this meridian within the UK.

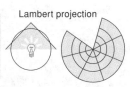

AERONAUTICAL CHART ICAO 1:500 000

Lambert Conformal Conic Projection Standard Parallels 49°20′ and 54°40′
Convergence factor 0·78829§

■ *Figure 8-17* **Most 1:1,000,000 and 1:500,000 aeronautical charts are based on the Lambert conformal conic projection**

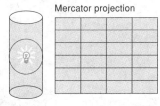

TOPOGRAPHICAL AIR CHART OF THE UNITED KINGDOM

SCALE 1:250 000
TRANSVERSE MERCATOR PROJECTION

■ *Figure 8-18* **The UK 1:250,000 topographical air charts are based on the transverse mercator cylindrical projection**

Both chart types covering the relatively small area of the UK have the following properties:

☐ **conformal** – angles and bearings are accurate (absolutely vital);
☐ **constant scale** over the whole chart in practical terms (i.e. distances are accurate);
☐ **shapes are preserved** in practical terms;
☐ **the track between two places is a straight line** (there is no significant difference between the rhumb line and the great circle track between any two places within the UK).

Scale

Charts represent a scaled-down view of the earth, and there are various ways of describing just how much the earth is scaled down on a particular chart. **Scale** is defined as the ratio of the chart length compared to the earth distance that it represents.

$$Scale = \frac{chart\ length}{earth\ distance} \quad (with\ both\ items\ in\ the\ same\ unit)$$

The greater the chart length for a given earth distance, the larger the scale and the more detail that can be shown. A large-scale chart covers a small area in detail. For example, a UK 1:250,000 Topographical Air Chart has a larger scale and can show more detail than an ICAO 1:500,000 Aeronautical Chart.

One centimetre on a 1:250,000 chart represents 250,000 cm on the earth, whereas, on a 1:500,000 chart, it represents double this earth distance, i.e. 500,000 cm, hence not as much detail can be shown.

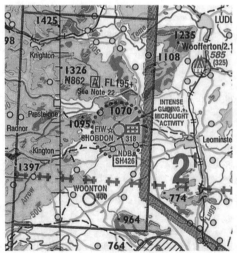 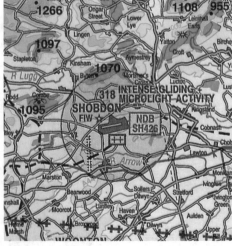

■ *Figure 8-19* **Excerpts from 1:500,000 (left) and 1:250,000 charts**

Scale can be expressed in various ways:

1. **As a representative fraction.** For instance, the WAC and the ONC series are 1: 1,000,000 charts (one to a million), where 1 centimetre on the chart will represent 1,000,000 cm or 10 kilometres on the earth, or where 1 nm on earth is represented by 1 millionth of a nautical mile on the chart. On the ICAO 1:500,000 Aeronautical Charts, an earth distance is represented by one half-millionth of its length; on the UK 1:250,000 Topographical Air Charts, an earth distance is represented by one quarter-millionth of its length.

2. **As a graduated scale line,** which is usually situated at the bottom of the chart. A graduated scale line allows you to measure the distance between two points on the chart and match it against the scale line. Make sure you use the correct scale line (usually nautical miles), since there may be several so that nautical miles, statute miles or kilometres can be measured.

3. **In words** – for instance '1 cm equals 5 nm', which obviously means that 5 nm on the earth's surface is represented by 1 cm on the chart.

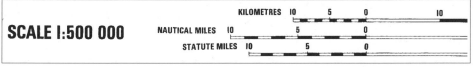

■ *Figure 8-20* **Typical scale lines**

Even if there is no scale line on the chart, you can always compare the distance between two places on the chart with the latitude scale which runs down the side of the chart, remembering that 1′ of latitude = 1 nm, and 1° of latitude = 60 nm.

On conic projections (ICAO 1:500,000), use the latitude scale about mid-way between the two places, because on some charts scale may vary slightly depending on proximity to the standard parallels. In practical terms, however, scale can be considered as constant over all of a 1:500,000 chart.

On the UK transverse Mercator 1:250,000 charts, the scale is exactly correct at the 2°W meridian, and can be considered as constant to about 300 nm either side of this. Since the UK does not have a large east–west spread, the slight variation in scale is not significant.

To all intents and purposes, therefore, scale may be considered constant at all points on both aeronautical chart series, quarter- and half-million.

Converting Chart Length to Earth Distance

While the following calculations are not normally done by pilots, they provide an insight into the making of charts, and you may be examined on them.

EXAMPLE 1 What earth distance is represented by a chart length of 5.2 inches on a 1:250,000 chart?

$$1 \text{ inch on the chart} = 250,000 \text{ inches on the earth}$$

$$= \frac{250,000}{12} \text{ feet (1 ft} = 12 \text{ inches)}$$

$$= \frac{250,000}{12 \times 6,076} \text{ nm (1 nm} = 6,076 \text{ ft)}$$

$$= 3.43 \text{ nm}$$

$$5.2 \text{ inches on the chart} = 5.2 \times 3.43$$

$$= 17.8 \text{ nm on the earth}$$

ANSWER 17.8 nm

EXAMPLE 2 On a 1:500,000 chart, 9 inches represents approximately 62 nm. How many kilometres does 9 inches represent on a 1:250,000 chart?

9 inches = 62 nm on a 1:500,000 chart
therefore, on a 1:250,000 chart (i.e. double the scale):

9 inches = 62 ÷ 2 = 31 nm = 57.5 km (by computer).

ANSWER 57.5 km (your answer should be accurate to ±1 km)

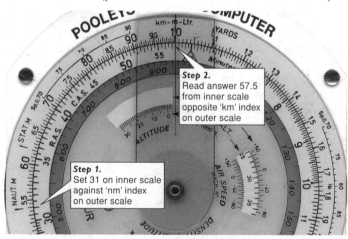

Step 2.
Read answer 57.5 from inner scale opposite 'km' index on outer scale

Step 1.
Set 31 on inner scale against 'nm' index on outer scale

■ *Figure 8-21* **Example 2: 31 nm = 57.5 km**

Now complete **Exercises 8 – The Earth.**

Aeronautical Charts

VFR Charts

The two main charts used for visual navigation in the United Kingdom are:

☐ **1:500,000 ICAO Aeronautical Charts** (the most commonly used); and

☐ **The new CAA 1:250,000 Topographical Air Charts** are suitable for visual navigation up to 5,000 ft amsl).

Amendments to current VFR charts are shown on the CAA's web site: www.caa.co.uk/dap under 'Aeronautical Charts'.

Three ICAO 1:500,000 charts cover the whole of the UK and there are two more of the same scale for the Republic of Ireland. Because of the larger scale of the 1:250,000 charts, it takes a greater number to cover the same area (8 for the UK). The 1:250,000 charts can, however, show much greater detail than the 1:500,000 scale.

ICAO stands for International Civil Aviation Organization – a wing of the United Nations that suggests world aviation standards to ensure commonality of presentation between countries.

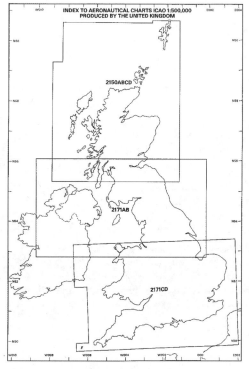

■ *Figure 9-1* **1:500,000 UK Coverage**

CAA 1:250,000 CHARTS. The vertical limit of the series is 5,000 ft altitude. To assist users, airspace with a base of Flight Level 55 (FL55) is shown, *except* where a minimum altitude in excess of 5,000 ft applies. If the QNH is below 1013 mb, controlled airspace not shown on the charts may be below 5,000 ft altitude and you must refer to a 1:500,000 chart to ensure that adequate vertical separation is maintained.

In general, therefore, the 1:250,000 charts are used only for cross-country flying up to 5,000 ft amsl, or when operating at low level in a terminal area. Both series of charts provide:

☐ **topographical information** (mountains, lakes, rivers, coastlines);
☐ **cultural information** (cities, towns, motorways, railway lines);
☐ **aeronautical information** (controlled airspace, Airways, Aerodrome Traffic Zones, Prohibited, Restricted and Danger Areas, airfields, radio beacons). The aeronautical information is printed over the top of the topographical and cultural information, generally in blue and magenta (purple).

Use only the current issue of the chart. Reprints occur periodically (usually every one or two years) and the date of the current chart is specified in NOTAMs (Notices to Airmen). Some items on a chart may change from time to time (for instance, a new radio mast or a new road may be built; airspace may be reorganised) and these changes will be notified to pilots by NOTAM. Your charts should be amended by hand if necessary.

It will help if you now refer to some typical charts; the two that we will use mainly are:

☐ **Aeronautical Chart ICAO 1:500,000** (half million), Sheet 2171AB, Northern England and Northern Ireland (see Note below); and
☐ **Topographical Air Chart** of the United Kingdom 1:250,000 (quarter million) – eight charts cover the UK.

The charts are self-explanatory. Study them thoroughly and become familiar with their legends. As a guide, we will consider the 1:500,000 chart now, with occasional reference to the 1:250,000 series, where applicable.

*Note that the chart excerpts and information in this chapter are for **study purposes only**. For actual flight operations ensure that you have the latest edition of charts, updated by NOTAMs issued since the chart's validity date. Be aware that, once changes are incorporated in the AIP (normally after six months), relevant NOTAMs are cancelled.*

TOPOGRAPHICAL INFORMATION shown is that considered to be of most use to the pilot/navigator. It is obviously impossible to show everything on a chart, so there may be some details on the ground not shown. Features shown on the chart, however, will exist on the ground, e.g. an isolated rock may not be considered significant by the cartographer and therefore will not be shown on the chart. If, however, there is an isolated rock shown on the chart, it will certainly exist on the ground. The same thing may be said about cultural features depicted on UK charts, such as Stonehenge or white horses — if they are shown on the chart, then they exist on the ground and will be suitable as visual landmarks.

DRAINAGE AND WATER FEATURES (hydrographic features). These are generally depicted in blue. Hydrographic features include creeks, streams, rivers, canals, lakes, reservoirs, marshes, shore-lines, tidal flats, etc. Just how they are depicted on the chart is explained by the chart legend, but bear in mind that after heavy rain, for instance, what is shown as a small stream on the chart may in fact have flooded into a raging torrent.

RELIEF. There are various ways of bringing ground contours into relief so that an impression of hills, mountains, valleys, etc., is obtained when you look at the chart. The UK 1:500,000 chart series uses contours — lines joining places of equal elevation above mean sea level — to depict relief. The closer the contour lines are to each other on the chart, the steeper the terrain. The spacing between contour lines is different on the various series of aeronautical charts.

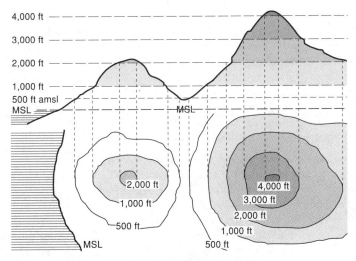

■ *Figure 9-2* **Contour lines represent changes in height amsl**

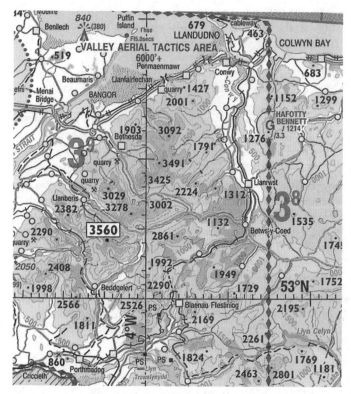

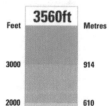

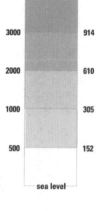

■ *Figure 9-3* **Hypsometric tints to portray relief on a 1:500,000 chart**

Colour or layer tinting is used in conjunction with the contour lines to give even more relief. The colours or tints used for the various ground elevations are shown on a hypsometric tint table at the bottom of the chart. (Hypsometric means establishment of vertical heights or elevations.) The shades of colour generally start with white for low land, then go through light brown and into brown, gradually darkening as the ground becomes higher. Remember that a particular colour may indicate ground elevation up to the level of the next contour above it.

SPOT ELEVATIONS (or spot heights) are shown using a black spot with an adjacent number to indicate the elevation (height amsl – above mean sea level) in feet. These elevations are generally accurate (unless amended by NOTAM). Spot elevations are normally used to show local peaks and other critical elevations that are significantly higher than the surrounding terrain. The highest point on each chart (in this case Mount Snowdon in North Wales) has its elevation printed slightly larger than the rest and is displayed in a white rectangle with a black edge. It also rates a mention on the relief portrayal table.

MAXIMUM ELEVATION FIGURES (MEF) are shown in quadrangles bounded by graticule lines for every half degree of latitude and longitude. The figure is based on the highest known feature in each quadrangle, including terrain and obstacles, and allowing for unknown features. Note that the MEF is *not* a safety height.

HACHURING OR HILL SHADING is used to give a three-dimensional effect on some aeronautical charts. Hachuring consists of short lines running downhill, and is commonly used to portray bluffs, cliffs and escarpments. Hill shading shows darkened areas on the low side of high ground where you would expect to see shadows with the light coming from the northwest (a graphic standard).

■ *Figure 9-4* **Hachuring**

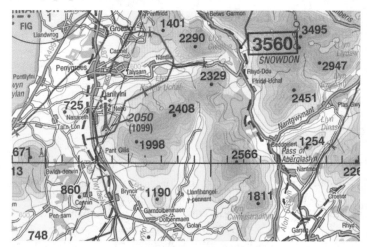

■ *Figure 9-5* **Contours and hill shading in Wales shown on a 1:250,000 chart (sample only)**

On the CAA 1:250,000 charts, hill shading and contours are used, but there is no hachuring. There is no hachuring or hill shading on the UK 1:500,000 series – just contours and layer tints.

Be aware that many continental European charts show contours, elevations and spot heights, not in feet but in metres amsl. When flying in France, for instance, you may need to convert feet to metres, or vice versa. This can be done with a navigation computer, or by using the conversion table that is printed on some charts. The aeronautical charts used in the UK display elevations and heights only in feet.

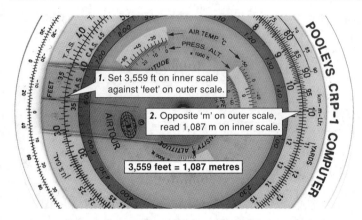

1. Set 3,559 ft on inner scale against 'feet' on outer scale.

2. Opposite 'm' on outer scale, read 1,087 m on inner scale.

3,559 feet = 1,087 metres

■ *Figure 9-6* **Converting feet to metres and vice versa.**

1:500,000 ICAO Aeronautical Charts

Cultural Features on the 1:500,000 Chart
Cultural features are of great help to the pilot/navigator. It is not possible to show every town or every house on the chart, so a choice is made to show what is significant and of value for visual air navigation. A group of 100 houses is of little significance if it lies in the middle of a city the size of Manchester and so will not be specifically depicted on the chart, yet on the moors it may be extremely significant and will be shown.

NOTE Built-up areas are coloured yellow on the full 1:500,000 chart and grey on the equivalent low-level chart.

Roads and railways can be of great assistance to visual navigation. Those that will be most significant will be shown. Distinctive patterns such as curves, roads running parallel to railway lines and then crossing over, junctions, forks, overpasses and tunnels, are especially useful. Even the beds of disused railway lines can be useful, and are shown as broken black lines on charts.

Other useful cultural features, such as the white horses carved into the ground in various parts of England, may also be shown. Study the chart legend and become familiar with the symbols (which differ slightly between the various series of charts).

Figure 9-7 shows some 1:500,000 chart cultural symbols.

Aeronautical Information on the UK 1:500,000 Charts
Most people are familiar with topographical and cultural information, since these are surface features which are shown on a road map and in an atlas. Pilots, however, operate in a three-dimensional environment and therefore require information on the airspace above the surface of the earth as well.

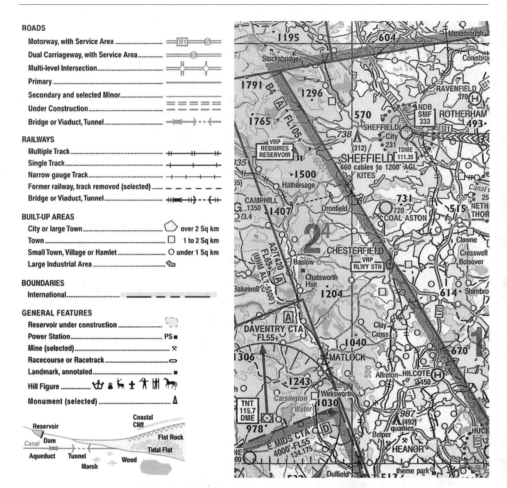

■ Figure 9-7 **Cultural symbols on the UK 1:500,000 series**

Aeronautical information is vital information for pilots, showing not only the position of aerodromes on the ground, but also the division of airspace through which aeroplanes fly, and other useful information. The chart legends explain this information. Memorise the most commonly used symbols, such as aerodromes, airspace, obstructions, etc.

Note that, in the case of the 1:250,000 chart (the low-level chart that shows surface features in great detail), only controlled airspace with a lower limit at or below 5,000 ft amsl or FL55 is shown. If flying above 5,000 ft amsl or FL55, a 1:500,000 chart must be used.

The chart will have all the changes that are effective on the 'Effective Date of Implementation', which is printed on the chart. Out-of-date charts can be dangerous, so always check that you have the latest edition. Check NOTAMs, UK air information publications (such as the Aeronautical Information Circulars – AICs) and the Chart of UK Airspace Restrictions (AIP ENR) for any information affecting the chart after the published date. Note that, once an aeronautical change has been incorporated in the AIP (usually after about six months), the relevant NOTAM or AIC will be cancelled.

NOTE Aerodrome Traffic Zone (ATZs) are only shown on the chart where they lie outside controlled airspace. There is, however, a full list of ATZs on each chart, with the VHF-COM frequency of the responsible Air Traffic Service Unit (ATSU).

AERODROME - Civil .... ⬡

AERODROME - Civil, limited or no facilities .... ○

HELIPORT - Civil .... Ⓗ

AERODROME - Government, available for Civil use. See UK AIP AD 1-1-1 .... ◉

AERODROME - Government .... ◎

HELIPORT - Government .... ⊛

MICROLIGHT FLYING SITES - Intensive Activity also takes place at certain
Licensed and Unlicensed Aerodromes. See UK AIP ENR 1-1 .... Ⓜ

DISUSED or ABANDONED Aerodrome. Shown for navigational
landmark purposes only. See AIC 17/97 (Pink 135) .... ⊗

ELEVATIONS of Active Aeronautical Sites are shown adjacent to the symbol.
Shown in feet above Mean Sea Level 250 250

CUSTOMS AERODROMES are distinguished by a pecked line around   ⌐MANCHESTER⌐
the name of the aerodrome and elevation ....   L 257 ⌐

AERODROME LIGHT BEACON .... ☆FIG ⌐⌐⌐• ☆FIR ⌐⌐⌐•

FOR CURRENT STATUS, AVAILABILITY, RESTRICTIONS AND WARNINGS APPLICABLE
TO AERODROMES SHOWN ON THIS CHART CONSULT AIR INFORMATION PUBLICATIONS
AND AERODROME OPERATORS OR OWNERS. PORTRAYAL DOES NOT IMPLY ANY RIGHT
TO USE AN UNLICENSED AERODROME WITHOUT PERMISSION.

GLIDER LAUNCHING SITES. UK AIP ENR 1-1.
a. Primary activity at locations showing Maximum Altitude of winch launch. AMSL ...... Ⓖ/2.5

b. Additional activity at locations showing Maximum Altitude of
winch launch. AMSL .... ○ G/2.5

c. Additional activity without cables .... ○ G

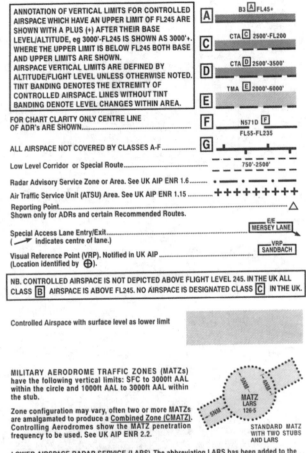

Figure 9-8 *(above & previous page) Sample 1:500,000 legend excerpts*

Figure 9-9, overleaf, illustrates how airspace information is depicted on a chart, showing a busy area of UK airspace – around Manchester and Liverpool. Figure 9-10 shows a section of the airspace around Prestwick and Glasgow.

■ Figure 9-9 *(overleaf) 1:500,000 chart excerpt*

This aeronautical chart contains the following annotation labels:

- **Blackpool Aerodrome:** elevation 34 ft amsl
- **Airway A1 (Class A airspace) above FL65**
- **Manchester Terminal Control Area (TMA), Class A airspace (not available to VFR), above 3,500 ft amsl**
- **Warton Aerodrome Traffic Zone (ATZ)**
- **Warton MATZ: Lower Airspace Radar Information Service freq. 129.525 MHz**
- **Special Access Lane Entry/Exit into Liverpool CTR (blue arrow indicates centre of lane)**
- **Visual Reference Point: Aintree Racecourse**
- **Class A airspace above 3,500 ft amsl**
- **Liverpool Control Zone (CTR), Class D airspace, from surface to 1,500 ft altitude, operating on frequency 119.85 MHz**
- **Manchester Control Area, Class D, (available to VFR), 1,500 ft to 3,500 ft amsl**
- **Restricted Area 311: from surface to 2,200 ft altitude**
- **Low-level Route: max. altitude 1,250 ft on Manchester QNH**
- **Final instrument approach track to Hawarden runway**
- **Wrexham Aerodrome (disused or abandoned)**

Figure 9-10 **1:500,000 chart excerpt**

Further information is given in 'Legend Notes', which should be read carefully. Examples appear in Figure 9–11.

LEGEND NOTES

1. **PROHIBITED AND RESTRICTED AREAS - NORTHERN IRELAND.** Pilots are urgently warned against inadvertent entry into Prohibited or Restricted areas in Northern Ireland. Such entry could entail a danger that the flight might be judged to have a hostile or criminal intent and the aircraft could be liable to counter measures. See UK AIP ENR 5.1.

2. **RESTRICTED AREAS R315, R318, R319, R320, R321, R432 and R504** apply only to Helicopters. See UK AIP ENR 5.1.

3. **FYLINGDALES HIGH INTENSITY RADIO TRANSMISSION AREA.** Up to 8000ft ALT aircraft should not remain for more than one minute within 1·5NM radius of position 542147N 0004012W. See UK AIP ENR 5.3.

■ _Figure 9-11_ **Legend notes from a 1:500,000 chart (sample only)**

HAZARDS TO AVIATION information is also depicted. These hazards include certain aerial activities such as parachuting or hang-gliding, as well as permanent obstructions such as radio masts or cables.

Obstructions that reach 300 ft or more above ground level (agl) are considered to be hazards to aeroplanes and are shown on charts. The numerals in brackets beside the symbol for the obstruction indicate the height of its top agl, and the numerals in italics without brackets indicate the elevation of the top of the obstruction amsl. Obstructions 299 ft agl and lower may not be shown.

Note that, since the first contour is at 500 ft amsl and obstructions less than 300 ft agl may not be shown, it is possible to have an obstruction that is just less than 800 ft amsl not indicated at all on the chart.

HANG/PARA GLIDING - Winch Launch Sites showing Maximum Altitude of
winch launch. AMSL. See UK AIP ENR 1-1.../2.5

WINCH LAUNCHED ACTIVITIES. Maximum Altitude of cables is represented in thousands and hundreds of feet <u>above mean sea level</u> calculated using a minimum cable height of 2000ft AGL plus site elevation. At some sites the cable may extend above 2000ft AGL. Due to the ground-based cable, aircraft should avoid over-flying these sites below the indicated altitude.

> Symbols depicting Non Winch Launch Hang/Para Gliding sites have been removed as they were not an accurate representation of the activity on any given day. Airspace users should be aware that single or groups of soaring or motorised Hang/Para Gliders can be found flying anywhere in the open FIR up to 15,000ft.

FREE-FALL PARACHUTING DROP ZONE. UK AIP ENR 1-1.
Parachutists may be expected within the airspace contained in a circle radius 1.5NM of the DZ <u>up to FL150.</u> Night parachuting may take place at any of the sites shown on this chart.

AIR NAVIGATION OBSTACLES

Exceptionally High Obstacle (Lighted)   *1978*
1000ft or more AGL..(1031)

                                                                         825
Single Obstacle (Unlighted) ....(350)   *1614*
Multiple Obstacle (Lighted) ....(505)
Cable joining Obstacles ....cables

Numerals in italics indicate elevation of top of obstacle above Mean Sea Level. Numerals in brackets indicate height of top of obstacle above local Ground Level. Obstacles annotated 'flarestack' burn off high pressure gas. The flame, which may not be visible in bright sunlight, can extend up to 600ft above the installation.

> KNOWN LAND SITED OBSTACLES ABOVE 300ft AGL ARE SHOWN ON THIS CHART.
> A SMALL NUMBER OF OBSTACLES BELOW 300ft AGL ARE SHOWN FOR LANDMARK
> PURPOSES. PERMANENT OFF-SHORE OBSTACLES ARE SHOWN REGARDLESS OF
> HEIGHT CATEGORY. See UK AIP ENR 1-1.
> WARNING : INFORMATION IS TAKEN FROM BEST AVAILABLE SOURCES BUT IS NOT
> GUARANTEED COMPLETE.

Marine Light..........................● Fl(3)30-0secs   Lightship ....⚓ FlWR12-0secs
(Normally shown if visibility range is not less than 15NM).

■ Figure 9-12 **Hazard and other information on the**
1:500,000 series (sample only)

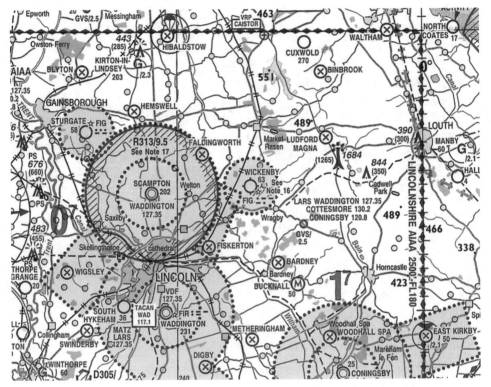

■ *Figure 9-13* ***1:500,000 Lincolnshire excerpt (sample only)***

In the chart extract in Figure 9–13, a number of hazards to aviation are shown, including:

☐ an exceptionally high obstruction (lighted), with a top 1,684 ft amsl, itself being 1,265 ft high (i.e. height agl);

☐ a single unit obstruction just beside it with a top 844 ft amsl and 350 ft agl;

☐ a further obstruction (unlit) to the NE at Louth, with a top 390 ft amsl and 300 ft agl;

☐ a glider launching site with cables at Kirton-in-Lindsey, as well as parachuting just to the north-east at Hilbaldstow.

Other items on the chart excerpt that could be hazardous to aviation, but which are listed elsewhere on the legend, are:

☐ the Wickenby ATZ vertical limit increases from 1,500 ft aal on weekdays to 2,000 ft all at weekends;

☐ numerous disused or abandoned aerodromes, e.g. Bardney.

NOTE Much of the area portrayed lies within the Lincolnshire AIAA (Area of Intense Aerial Activity), which extends from 2,500 ft ALT (amsl) up to Flight Level 180. A Lower Airspace Radar Service (LARS) is available from Waddington, Cottesmore and Coningsby ATS units, on the frequencies shown. These are contact frequencies for flight within the Lincolnshire AIAA. Note also the combined MATZ (CMATZ) of Scampton and Waddington, using Waddington frequency 127.35 MHz.

Airspace Restrictions and other Hazard Information

These are also listed on the legend. If you refer back to Figure 9-9, some Airspace Restrictions were shown (R312 and P311).

A DANGER AREA (D) is airspace of defined dimensions within which activities dangerous to the flight of aircraft may exist at specified times, such as the flying of captive balloons, or weapons ranges, possibly with military aircraft towing targets on long cables. Pilots should avoid Danger Areas and, when flying in their vicinity, keep a sharp lookout for military aircraft.

Charts show only those Danger Areas that extend above 500 ft agl. Many rifle ranges have upper limits less than 500 ft agl, so pilots must ensure that they fly clear of such activities.

A PROHIBITED AREA (P) is an airspace of defined dimensions in which the flight of aircraft is prohibited.

A RESTRICTED AREA (R) is an airspace of defined dimensions within which the flight of aircraft is restricted in accordance with certain specified conditions (see AIP ENR or NOTAMs).

AREAS ACTIVATED BY NOTAM are shown with a broken boundary line.

AIRSPACE RESTRICTIONS Prohibited 'P', Restricted 'R' and Danger Areas 'D' are shown with identification number/ effective altitude (in thousands of feet AMSL). Areas activated by Notam are shown with a broken boundary line.

For those Scheduled Danger Areas whose Upper Limit changes at specified times during its period of activity, only the higher of the Upper Limits is shown. Areas which may be active up to levels below the indicated Upper Limit are depicted by ↑ . Areas whose identification numbers are prefixed with an asterisk (¤) contain airspace subject to byelaws which prohibit entry during the period of activity. See UK AIP ENR 1.1.

BRIEFING INFORMATION Pre-flight information on notifiable activities can be obtained H24 from AIS Heathrow via Tel: 020 8745 3451. Pre-flight information is also available for D508 (indicated on the chart by the prefix ¶) Newcastle ATC 0191 2860966 Ext 3251.

MILITARY LOW FLYING SYSTEM. Military low flying occurs in most parts of the UK at any height up to 2000ft above the surface. However, the greatest concentration is between 250 and 600ft and pilots should avoid flying in that height band whenever possible. Detailed information can be found on Chart of UK AIAA, ATA and Military Low Flying System, (UK AIP ENR 6-5-2-1).

AIAA AND ATA AREAS .... ◆◆◆◆◆◆◆◆◆◆◆ Areas are shown with name, vertical limits and where applicable contact frequency. Pilots of aircraft who transit these areas are strongly advised to make use of the Radar Service.

HIGH INTENSITY RADIO TRANSMISSION AREA (HIRTA). Areas with a radius of 0·5NM or more are shown with name/effective altitude (in thousands of feet AMSL). ....

BIRD SANCTUARIES are shown with name/effective altitude (in thousands of feet AMSL). ....

GAS VENTING OPERATIONS pilots are advised to avoid flying over Gas Venting Sites (GVSs) below specified altitudes. A warning circle is shown on the chart to identify a GVS and the hazard altitude is shown in thousands of feet AMSL. See UK ENR 1.1. ....GVS/3-1

SMALL ARMS RANGES in the UK with a vertical hazard height of 500ft AGL do not attract UK Danger Area status. However, firing at some ranges may constitute a hazard to aircraft below 500ft AGL. Details of the Ranges are listed in the UK AIP at ENR 5.3. Pictorial depiction can be found on the CHART OF UK AIRSPACE RESTRICTIONS. ENR 6-5-1-1.

DANGER AREA CROSSING SERVICE (DACS) is available for certain Danger Areas. The relevant areas (identified on the chart by the prefix †) and Unit Contact Frequencies to be used are shown below. For availability of the services see UK AIP ENR 5.1.

※D201 & D201B	{ ABERPORTH CONTROL 133·5MHz/ INFO. 122·15MHz
	{ LONDON MILITARY 135·15MHz
D402A, D402B & D403	{ WEST FREUGH APP 130·05MHz
	{ SCOTTISH MIL VIA SCOTTISH INFO 119·875MHz
D402C & D403A	WEST FREUGH APP 130·05MHz
D405 &D405A	WEST FREUGH APP 130·05MHz or KIRKCUDBRIGHT RANGE 122·1MHz
D406C	ESKMEALS RANGE 122·75MHz
D411	WEST FREUGH APP 130·05MHz or DAAIS outside hours.
D508	NEWCASTLE APP 124·37MHz
D510	SPADEADAM 122·1MHz

DANGER AREA ACTIVITY INFORMATION SERVICE (DAAIS) is available for certain Danger Areas shown on this chart (identified by the prefix §). The Nominated Air Traffic Service Units (NATSUs) to be used are shown below. See UK AIP ENR 1.1.
Pilots are advised to assume that a Danger Area is <u>active</u> if no reply is received from the appropriate NATSU.

D207	LONDON INFORMATION 124·6MHz
D304	MANCHESTER APP 119·4MHz
D307	DONNA NOOK RANGE CONTROL 122·75MHz
D308	WAINFLEET RANGE CONTROL 122·75MHz
D314	MANCHESTER APP 119·4MHz
※D406 &D406B	LONDON INFORMATION 125·475MHz
※D407 & ※D407A	PENNINE RADAR 128·675MHz
※D408, ※D409	LEEMING APP 127·75MHz or LONDON INFO 125·475MHz
D411	Outside times for DACS, SCOTTISH INFO 119·875MHz
D412	LONDON INFORMATION 125·475MHz
D441	LINTON APP 129·15MHz
D509	WEST FREUGH APP 130·05MHz or SCOTTISH INFO 119·875MHz
D510	NEWCASTLE APP 124·37MHz or CARLISLE TOWER 123·6MHz
※D512 & ※D512A	SCOTTISH INFORMATION 119·875MHz
D513, D513A & D513B	SCOTTISH INFORMATION 119·875MHz
D607, D608 & D609	SCOTTISH INFORMATION 119·875MHz

PORTREE ASR
ALTIMETER SETTING REGION BOUNDARY (ASR) ┅┅   ┿┿ ┿┿ ┿┿ ┿┿
BELFAST ASR
NOTE: The airspace within (and below) all Control Zones, Terminal Control Areas and Control Areas (with the exception of the Worthing and Daventry CTAs) during their notified hours of operation, does not form part of the forecast QNH Altimeter Setting Region System . Pilots flying below the Transition Altitude, should use a QNH of an aerodrome situated within the lateral boundaries of that airspace. Alternatively, when flying within an aerodrome circuit, aerodrome QFE may be used. See UK AIP ENR 1.7.

■ Figure 9-14 **Airspace and hazard information (sample only)**

MILITARY LOW FLYING SYSTEM This occurs in most parts of the UK at any height up 2,000 ft above the surface. However, the greatest concentration is between 250 ft and 600 ft above the surface and civil pilots are advised to avoid this height band whenever possible. Geographic details are given in the UK AIP (ENR 6-5-2-1) on a combined chart called *UK Areas of Intense Air Activity (AIAA), Aerial Tactics Areas (ATA) and Military Low Flying System*.

A BIRD SANCTUARY is airspace of defined dimensions within which large colonies of birds are known to breed. Pilots are requested to avoid these areas, especially during any stated breeding season, and are warned of the high risk of bird strikes. Figure 9-15 shows an example of a bird sanctuary that exists at the mouth of the Severn River from the surface up to 4,000 ft amsl between September and April.

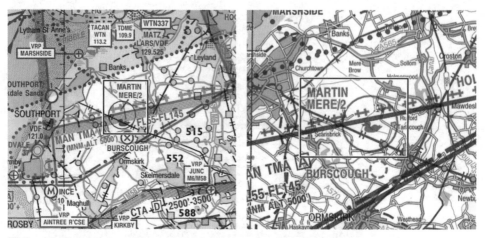

■ *Figure 9-15* **Depiction of the same bird sanctuary on the half- and quarter-million aeronautical charts**

RADIO FACILITIES are also depicted on aeronautical charts, but these will not be significant until you commence training for instrument navigation. Note that the VOR compass roses on the chart are aligned with magnetic north and not true north.

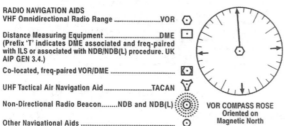

■ *Figure 9-16* **Radio facilities marked on the 1:500,000 series (sample only)**

Position Information

The latitude-longitude graticule is clearly marked on charts.

The east–west parallels of latitude indicating degrees north or south of the equator (north in the UK and Europe) are labelled at either side of the 1:500,000 chart in 1° intervals (i.e. 60 nm intervals). Each degree is divided into 60 minutes, with marks each 5′ and 10′, and a full line across the chart at 30′. In the Northern Hemisphere, latitude is measured up from the bottom of the chart.

The north–south meridians of longitude (which gradually converge as they near the North Pole as a result of the 1:500,000 chart being a conical projection) are labelled at the top and bottom of the chart in degrees east or west of the prime meridian (in the UK, longitudes are both east and west). Each degree is divided into 60 minutes, with marks each 5′ and 10′, and a full line up the chart at 30′. Longitude is measured east or west from the Greenwich meridian. (Do not confuse the meridian with an isogonal.)

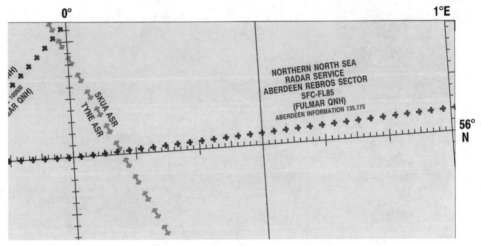

■ *Figure 9-17* ***Graticule of the 1:500,000 series (not to scale)***

HIGH INTENSITY RADIO TRANSMISSION AREA (HIRTA). Airspace of defined dimensions within which there is radio energy of an intensity which may cause interference or damage to radio equipment in the aeroplane. They are best avoided.

AREA OF INTENSE AERIAL ACTIVITY (AIAA). Airspace of defined dimensions, not otherwise protected by Regulated Airspace (Controlled or Special Rules), within which the intensity of civil and/or military flying is exceptionally high, or within which unusual manoeuvres are frequently carried out. Examples are the Vale of York AIAA and the Lincolnshire AIAA.

Airspace Restriction Information is available on the legend of the 1:500,000 chart, and further information can be found in the Aeronautical Information Publication AIP ENR 5, *Chart of UK Areas of Intense Air Activity (AIAA), Aerial Tactics Areas (ATA) and Military Low Flying System* (ENR 6-5-2-1) and on the *Chart of UK Airspace Restrictions and Hazardous Areas* (ENR 6-5-1-1), which is included in the AIP. If necessary, the AIP should be referred to on the ground at the flight planning stage.

To obtain information in flight concerning the activity status of a particular Danger Area, the pilot should call on the appropriate Nominated Air Traffic Service Unit (NATSU) frequency, as listed on the chart legend. (If there is no reply, then assume that the Danger Area is active.)

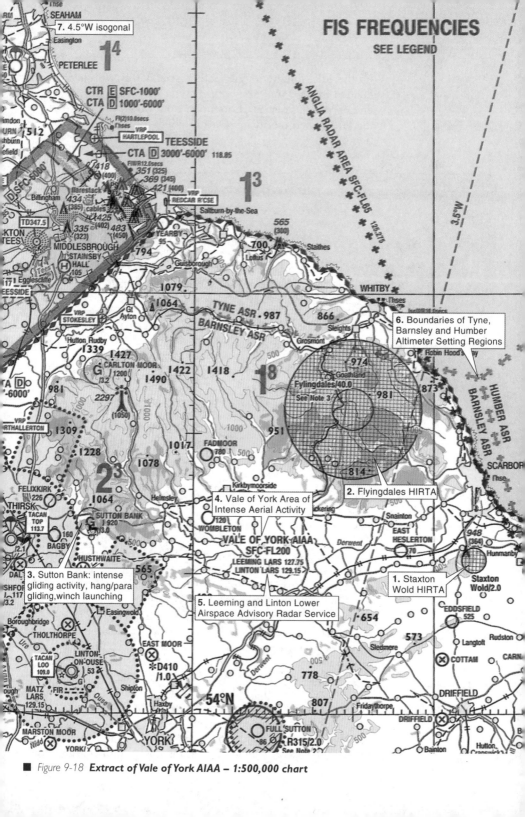

■ Figure 9-18 *Extract of Vale of York AIAA – 1:500,000 chart*

Figure 9-18 shows:

☐ a High Intensity Radio Transmission Area (HIRTA) at Staxton Wold extending up to 2,000 ft amsl (1);

☐ a High Intensity Radio Transmission Area (HIRTA) at Fylingdales, extending up to 40,000 ft (2), which has special conditions specified in Legend Note 3;

☐ intense gliding activity at Sutton Bank, along with hang/para gliding and winch launch activity (3). Note that winch cables may be carried up to altitudes of 3,000 ft amsl.

☐ generally intense aerial activity throughout the area, since it lies in the Vale of York AIAA (4).

Other points of interest (though not hazards) in Figure 9-18:

☐ Lower Airspace Advisory Radar Service frequencies of 127.75 MHz for Leeming and 129.15 MHz for Linton (these are contact frequencies within the Vale of York AIAA) (5);

☐ the boundaries of the Humber, Barnsley and Tyne Altimeter Setting Regions (ASRs) (6);

☐ the 4.5°W isogonal (7).

Magnetic Information on the 1:500,000 Chart

ISOGONALS or isogonic lines (lines joining places of equal magnetic variation, are indicated on the 1:500,000 chart by dashed blue lines. The UK experiences *variation west – magnetic best,* while in Eastern Europe there is *variation east – magnetic least.* For calculation purposes, use the whole degree variation either side of the half-degree isogonal, as appropriate.

THE AGONIC LINE (where true north and magnetic north are the same direction, and variation is zero) lies in between the areas experiencing west variation and those areas experiencing east variation. The agonic line passes through Italy.

Because the magnetic poles are gradually moving, the amount of variation at a particular place will also gradually change over a period of years. Every year the isogonic information on the charts is updated, and the year of the information shown on the chart.

CAA 1:250,000 Topographical Air Charts

The 1:250,000 Topographical Air Charts, published by the CAA, show much more detail, because of their larger scale. This may be useful, especially in busy terminal areas, when you may be operating below 5,000 ft amsl. They show topographical and cultural information, along with low-level aeronautical information (up to 5,000 ft amsl); including:

☐ **all items up to 5,000 ft** amsl shown on the 1:500,000 series;

□ **controlled airspace** with a lower limit at or below 5,000 ft amsl or FL55;

□ **approximate runway layout** at aerodromes, and the main, final instrument approach course at aerodromes outside controlled airspace.

REFERENCE TO AIR INFORMATION

AERODROMES - Field limits with hard runway pattern Civil
GOVERNMENT Aerodromes annotated with a (J) adjacent to the symbol (J) or name indicate availability for Civil use
CUSTOMS AERODROMES are distinguished by a pecked line around the name of the aerodrome [MANCHESTER]
AERODROME LIGHT BEACON ☆ FlG ☆ FlR

HELIPORT Ⓗ Ⓗ

MINOR AERODROME with runway pattern unknown or not portrayable

MICROLIGHT FLYING SITES - Intense Activity also takes place at certain Licensed and Unlicensed Aerodromes. See UK AIP ENR 1.1. Ⓜ

DISUSED or ABANDONED Aerodrome - shown for navigational landmark purposes only. See AIC 17/97 (Pink 135)

GLIDER LAUNCHING SITES - See UK AIP ENR 1.1.
Primary activity at locations Ⓖ cables Ⓖ cables
Additional activity at locations cables cables

HANG/PARA GLIDING - Winch Launch Sites - See UK AIP ENR 1.1.
Primary activity at locations cables cables
Additional activity at locations cables cables
"cables" adjacent to symbols indicate winch launch activity. See Note 3.

FOOT LAUNCH HANG/PARA SITE - most commonly used

ELEVATIONS of Active Aeronautical Sites are shown adjacent to the symbol.
Shown in feet above Mean Sea Level (AMSL). 250 250

FREE-FALL PARACHUTING DROP ZONE - See UK AIP ENR 1.1.
Parachutists may be expected within the airspace contained in a circle radius 1.5NM of the DZ up to FL150.
Night parachuting may take place at any of the sites shown on this chart

FOR CURRENT STATUS, AVAILABILITY, RESTRICTIONS AND WARNINGS APPLICABLE TO AERODROMES SHOWN ON THIS CHART CONSULT AIR INFORMATION PUBLICATIONS AND AERODROME OPERATORS OR OWNERS. PORTRAYAL DOES NOT IMPLY ANY RIGHT TO USE AN UNLICENSED AERODROME WITHOUT PERMISSION.

AIRSPACE RESTRICTIONS Prohibited 'P', Restricted 'R' and Danger Areas 'D' are shown with identification number/effective altitude (in thousands of feet AMSL). Areas activated by NOTAM are shown with a broken boundary line.

For those Scheduled Danger Areas whose Upper Limit changes at specified times during its period of activity, only the higher of the Upper Limits is shown. Areas which may be active up to levels below the indicated Upper Limit are depicted by ↑. Areas whose identification numbers are prefixed with an asterisk (✳) contain airspace subject to byelaws which prohibit entry during the period of activity. See UK AIP ENR 1.1.

DANGER AREA CROSSING SERVICE (DACS) is available for certain Danger Areas. The relevant areas (identified on the chart by the prefix ✳) and Unit Contact Frequencies to be used are shown below. For availability of the services see UK AIP ENR 5.1.

✳D201, D201A & D201B { ABERPORTH CONTROL 133·5MHz / ABERPORTH INFORMATION 122·15MHz or / LONDON MILITARY 135-15MHz
D202 LLANBEDR RADAR 122·5MHz
D406C ESKMEALS RANGE 122.75MHz

DANGER AREA ACTIVITY INFORMATION SERVICE (DAAIS) is available for certain Danger Areas shown on the chart (identified by the prefix §). The Nominated Air Traffic Service Units (NATSUs) to be used are shown below. See UK AIP ENR 1.1. Pilots are advised to assume that a Danger Area is active if no reply is received from the appropriate NATSU.

D304 & D314 MANCHESTER APP 119·4MHz
✳D406 & D406B LONDON INFORMATION 125.475MHz

PRE-FLIGHT INFORMATION is available for certain Danger Areas. Information on notifiable activities can be obtained by telephone H24 from AIS Heathrow, Tel: 0181 745 3451. Pilots are advised to obtain an airborne update of the activity status and obtain a crossing clearance using DACS unit contact frequencies.

RADIO NAVIGATION AIDS
VHF Omnidirectional Radio Range VOR ⊙
Distance Measuring Equipment DME □
(Prefix 'T' indicates DME associated and freq paired with ILS or associated with NDB/NDB(L) procedure. UK AIP COM 0-5.)
Co-located, freq paired VOR/DME ◘
UHF Tactical Air Navigation Aid TACAN ⅄
Non-Directional Radio Beacon NDB and NDB(L)
Other Navigational Aids ⊙

VOR COMPASS ROSE
Oriented on
Magnetic North

ANNOTATION OF VERTICAL LIMITS FOR CONTROLLED AIRSPACE WHICH HAVE AN UPPER LIMIT OF FL245 ARE SHOWN WITH A PLUS (+) AFTER THEIR BASE LEVEL/ALTITUDE, eg 3000'-FL245 IS SHOWN AS 3000'+. WHERE THE UPPER LIMIT IS BELOW FL245 BOTH BASE AND UPPER LIMITS ARE SHOWN. AIRSPACE VERTICAL LIMITS ARE DEFINED BY ALTITUDE/FLIGHT LEVEL UNLESS OTHERWISE NOTED.
FOR CHART CLARITY ONLY CENTRE LINE OF ADR's ARE SHOWN
ALL AIRSPACE NOT COVERED BY CLASSES A-F.

[A] B3 Ⓐ FL45+
[D] CTA Ⓓ 2500'-3500'
[E] TMA Ⓔ 2000'-6000'
[F] N571D Ⓕ
FL55-FL235
[G]

NB. CONTROLLED AIRSPACE IS NOT DEPICTED ABOVE FLIGHT LEVEL 245 IN THE UK. ALL CLASS Ⓑ AIRSPACE IS ABOVE FL245. NO AIRSPACE IS DESIGNATED CLASS Ⓒ IN THE UK. AIRSPACE RESTRICTIONS MAY BE SHOWN ABOVE FL245.

Low Level Corridor or Special Route 750'-2500'
Radar Advisory Service Zone or Area. See UK AIP ENR 1.6.
Reporting Point
Shown only for ADRs and certain Recommended Routes. △
Special Access Lane Entry/Exit E/E
(indicates centre of lane.) MERSEY LANE
Visual Reference Point (VRP). Notified in UK AIP VRP
(Location identified by ⊕). FLEETWOOD

MILITARY AERODROME TRAFFIC ZONES (MATZs) have the following vertical limits: SFC to 3000ft AAL within the circle and 1000ft AAL to 3000ft AAL within the stub. Zone configuration may vary, often two or more MATZs are amalgamated to produce a Combined Zone (CMATZ). Controlling frequencies show the MATZ penetration frequency to be used. See UK AIP ENR 2.2.

MATZ
LARS
126·5

STANDARD MATZ WITH TWO STUBS AND LARS

LOWER AIRSPACE RADAR SERVICE (LARS). The abbreviation LARS has been added to the MATZ frequency to identify those participating MATZ ATS Units. Other participating LARS Units are identified by a LARS frequency box. The Service, Radar Advisory (RAS) or Radar Information (RIS), is available to all aircraft in unregulated airspace up to and including FL95 within approximately 30NM of each participating ATS Unit. See UK AIP ENR 1.6.

AREAS OF INTENSE AIR ACTIVITY (AIAA)
Areas are shown with name, vertical limits and where applicable contact frequency. Pilots of aircraft who transit these areas are strongly advised to make use of the Radar Service.

PORTREE ASR
ALTIMETER SETTING REGION BOUNDARY (ASR) ⟷ ⟷ ⟷ ⟷
NOTE: The airspace within (and below) all Control Zones, BELFAST ASR
Terminal Control Areas and Control Areas (with the exception of the Worthing and Daventry CTAs) during their notified hours of operation, does not form part of the forecast QNH Altimeter Setting Region Number. Pilots flying below the Transition Altitude, should use a QNH of an aerodrome situated within the lateral boundaries of that airspace. Alternatively, when flying within an aerodrome circuit, aerodrome QFE may be used. See UK AIP ENR 1.7.

HIGH INTENSITY RADIO TRANSMISSION AREA (HIRTA). Areas with a radius of 0·5NM or more are shown with name/effective altitude (in thousands of feet AMSL).

BIRD SANCTUARIES are shown with name/effective altitude (in thousands of feet AMSL).

SMALL ARMS FIRING RANGES. May be a hazard to aircraft flying below 500'AGL. Full details are given in UK AIP ENR 5.3. Location of ranges is shown on UK AIP Chart ENR 6-5-1-1.

GAS VENTING OPERATIONS pilots are advised to avoid flying over Gas Venting Sites (GVSs) below specified altitudes. A warning circle is shown on the chart to identify a GVS and the hazard altitude is shown in thousands of feet AMSL. See UK AIP ENR 1.2.1. GVS/3·1

UK AERODROME TRAFFIC ZONES (ATZs)
SERVICES/RT FREQUENCIES (MHz). See UK AIP.

AERODROME TRAFFIC ZONE (ATZ) is regulated airspace from the surface to 2000ft AAL within a circle centred on the notified mid-point of the longest runway, radius 2·0NM (RW≤ 1850m) or 2·5NM (RW≥1850m), where Mandatory Rules apply.
Most Government Aerodrome ATZs are H24.

ABERPORTH (EGUC) AFIS 122·15
BARKSTON HEATH (EGYE) INITIAL CALL CRANWELL ATC 119·375
♦ BIRMINGHAM (EGBB) ATC 118·05
✳ BLACKPOOL (EGNH) INITIAL CALL WARTON ATC 129·525
BLACKPOOL ATC 119·95
CAERNARFON (EGCK) INITIAL CALL VALLEY ATC 134·35, A/G 122·25
CHURCH FENTON (EGXG) ATC 126·5

■ Figure 9-19 **Sample excerpts of 1:250,000 chart (opposite) and legend**

Other Charts

There are other charts that are not used for position plotting or navigation, but to supply specific information. For example:

- ☐ Chart of United Kingdom Airspace Restrictions and Hazardous Areas (AIP ENR 6-5-1-1 and AIP ENR 5).
- ☐ Chart of United Kingdom Areas of Intense Air Activity (AIAA) and Aerial Tactics Areas (ATAs) (AIP ENR 6-5-2-1 and AIP ENR 5).

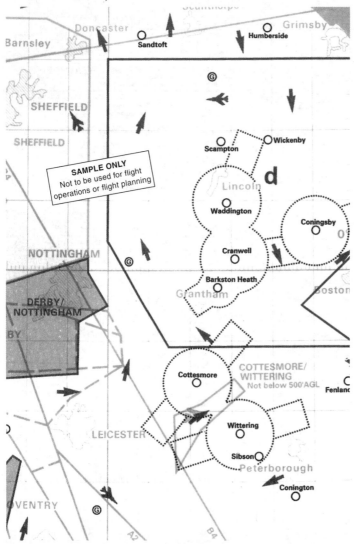

■ Figure 9-20 **Extract from the UK AIAAs and ATAs chart (sample only)**

Useful information regarding civil aerodromes in the United Kingdom 186 can be obtained from *Pooley's Flight Guide.*

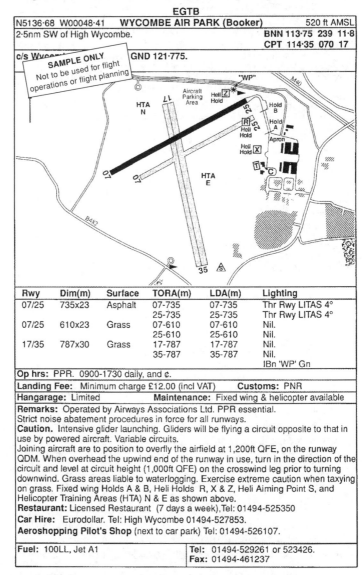

Rwy	Dim(m)	Surface	TORA(m)	LDA(m)	Lighting
07/25	735x23	Asphalt	07-735	07-735	Thr Rwy LITAS 4°
			25-735	25-735	Thr Rwy LITAS 4°
07/25	610x23	Grass	07-610	07-610	Nil.
			25-610	25-610	Nil.
17/35	787x30	Grass	17-787	17-787	Nil.
			35-787	35-787	Nil.
					IBn 'WP' Gn

Op hrs: PPR. 0900-1730 daily, and ¢.

Landing Fee: Minimum charge £12.00 (incl VAT)   **Customs:** PNR

Hangarage: Limited   **Maintenance:** Fixed wing & helicopter available

Remarks: Operated by Airways Associations Ltd. PPR essential.
Strict noise abatement procedures in force for all runways.
Caution. Intensive glider launching. Gliders will be flying a circuit opposite to that in use by powered aircraft. Variable circuits.
Joining aircraft are to position to overfly the airfield at 1,200ft QFE, on the runway QDM. When overhead the upwind end of the runway in use, turn in the direction of the circuit and level at circuit height (1,000ft QFE) on the crosswind leg prior to turning downwind. Grass areas liable to waterlogging. Exercise extreme caution when taxying on grass. Fixed wing Holds A & B, Heli Holds R, X & Z, Heli Aiming Point S, and Helicopter Training Areas (HTA) N & E as shown above.
Restaurant: Licensed Restaurant (7 days a week),Tel: 01494-525350
Car Hire: Eurodollar. Tel: High Wycombe 01494-527853.
Aeroshopping Pilot's Shop (next to car park) Tel: 01494-526107.

Fuel: 100LL, Jet A1   **Tel:** 01494-529261 or 523426.
                                  Fax: 01494-461237

■ *Figure 9-21* **Wycombe Air Park (Booker) aerodrome, as shown in Pooley's Flight Guide**

UNITED KINGDOM
PRIVATE AIRFIELDS

It~~~~ ~~SAMPLE ONLY~~ the airfields and landing fields in this section are mostly
u~ ~~Not to be used for flight~~ **STRICTLY BY PRIOR PERMISSION ONLY** or by
ar~ ~~operations or flight planning~~ ~~ings are~~ made entirely at pilot's own risk. No extracts or part
the~~~~~~may be~~ re-published without the Publisher's and Editor's consent in writing.

1   ABOYNE   N5704·50 W00250·00   460 ft.AMSL
1 nm W of Aboyne. (N of River Dee)   **Op hrs:** PPR
Two parallel tarmac strips 09/27, 540x7 m and 520 x 5·5 m
Remarks: Operated by Deeside Gliding Club, Waterside, Dinnet. Only aircraft
involved in gliding activities permitted. Field grazed by cattle at times. Windsock N of
runway. Gliding site – aerotow only.
Landing fee: £5.00 Gliding Club Business. £10.00 Non Gliding Club Business.
Accommodation: Hotels in Aboyne and Dinnet, both 2 miles.
Fuel: Nil.   **Tel:** Dinnet 013398-85339 or 885236

2   ALLENSMORE   N5200 W00250   300 ft. AMSL
4 nm SW of Hereford.   **Op hrs:** Strictly PPR.
Grass field N/S 550m.
Remarks: Operated by Willox Bridge, Allensmore, Hereford. Contact Mr. Powell.
Prior permission advisable. Care must be taken due to animals grazing. Large letter
'A' on white background on hangar roof at N end of strip.   **Taxi:** 01432-351238
Fuel: Nil   **Tel:** Wormbridge 0198121-203

3   AVIEMORE (Kincraig)   N5706 W00353   850 ft. AMSL
1·5 nm SE of Loch Insh.
Rough grass strip 02/20 approx. 670m.
Remarks: Operated by Miss Jane Williamson, Blackmill, Kincraig, Kingussie,
Invernesshire and Cairngorm Gliding Club. Light aircraft welcome at pilot's own risk,
PPR. Beware steeply rising ground to 4000ft. to East of airfield. Glider flying.
Fuel: Nil.   **Tel:** Kincraig 246

■ Figure 9-22 *Further sample of information included in Pooley's Flight*
Guide

1:1,000,000 Navigation Charts

As you can imagine, charts of this scale (one to one million) cover
a lot of territory compared to quarter- and half-million charts.
This scale is often used when large distances are involved, to provide mainly topographical information (mountains, lakes, rivers,
deserts, coastlines) and cultural information (cities, towns, free-
ways, country roads, railway lines). Aeronautical information is
not shown in detail; aerodromes may be shown, but the division
of airspace, other than FIR boundaries and some restricted airspace, is not.

There are two major series of 1:1,000,000 aeronautical charts:
☐ **Operational Navigation Chart** (ONC) series; and
☐ **ICAO World Aeronautical Chart** (WAC) series.

   Both series use much the same symbols and are based on the
same projection as the half-million charts – the Lambert conformal conic projection – consequently angular relationships and
shapes are preserved and there is a reasonably constant scale over
each chart. Straight lines closely represent the great circle track
between two points on ONCs and WACs.

Items such as isogonals, restricted airspace, obstructions, irrigation channels, railway lines and roads change from time to time, and so they are reprinted regularly – about every two years for busy areas and every five or six years for more remote parts of the world. As with all aeronautical charts, ensure you have the latest edition and study the legend carefully prior to flight.

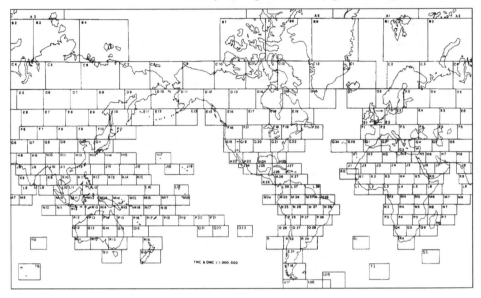

■ *Figure 9-23* **ONC world coverage**

TOPOGRAPHIC BASE
RELIABILITY DIAGRAM

A. Compiled from accurate topographic maps and surveys.

B. Compiled from other available topographic information. Liable to vertical error.

Figure 9-24 **A WAC**

reliability diagram

The series most readily available in the UK is the ONC series. It originates from military sources but is available to civil pilots for most areas of the world. However, ONCs are rarely used in the UK due to the small scale.

The ICAO World Aeronautical Chart (WAC) series originates from civil aeronautical sources. It is widely used in those parts of the world where the 1:1,000,000 scale is better suited to en route navigation, e.g. the Far East, South-East Asia and Australia, due to the large distances involved. Each country producing charts in this series does so according to the ICAO standards.

NOTAM amendments are sometimes issued for WACs, and these are made by hand on the appropriate chart (and called manuscript amendments).

As some areas of the world have not yet been mapped accurately, there is a small 'reliability diagram' at the bottom left-hand corner of each WAC that will alert you to the possibility of unreliable information on the chart.

Measuring Latitude and Longitude

As a pilot/navigator, you sometimes need to determine the latitude and longitude of a place.

To Determine the Latitude of a Place:

1. Lay a straight-edge east–west through the place, parallel to the parallels of latitude.

2. From the latitude scales running north–south down the page you can read off the exact latitude. (It should be the same latitude on the scale either side of the place – this ensures that the straight-edge is placed correctly on the chart.)

NOTE In the Northern Hemisphere the latitude increases towards the north and top of the chart, and the scale lines break up each degree of latitude into 60 minutes, with large marks each 10 minutes. (Make sure that you count from the bottom and up the page, in the direction of increasing latitude.)

To Determine the Longitude of a Place:

1. Lay a straight-edge north–south through the place, parallel to the closest meridians of longitude.

2. From the longitude scales running east–west across the page you can read off the exact longitude. (It should read the same on the scales above and below the place – this checks that the straight-edge is placed correctly on the chart.)

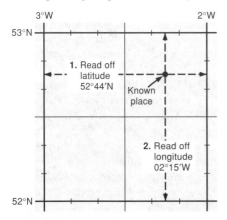

■ Figure 9-25 **Finding the latitude-longitude of a place**

Plotting a Position

The reverse problem of plotting a given latitude and longitude on the chart is just as easy:

1. Find the approximate position of the place on the chart.

2. Mark the latitude given on the two nearest latitude scales either side of the position.

3. Mark the longitude given on the two nearest longitude scales north and south of the position.

4. Join the latitude marks and then join the longitude marks. Their point of intersection is the desired position.

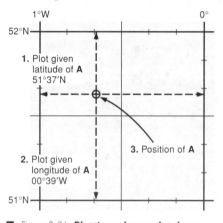

■ Figure 9-26 **Plotting a known lat–long**

NOTE You are required to be able to specify or mark a position to an accuracy of 1 minute of arc.

Great Circles and Rhumb Lines on Charts

The shortest distance between two points on the spherical earth is along a **great circle** (GC). Radio waves also follow great circle paths. Therefore it is convenient for an instrument pilot using radio navigation aids to use aeronautical charts designed so that a straight line closely resembles a great circle track.

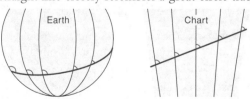

■ Figure 9-27 **Great circles may cross meridians of longitude at varying angles**

Because the ICAO 1:500,000 Aeronautical Chart Series is based on the Lambert conformal conic projection (in which the meridians of longitude converge towards the nearer pole), a straight line drawn on these charts closely resembles a great circle track and will cross the meridians of longitude at varying angles. Thus a pilot wanting to fly a great circle track would have to navigate along a continually changing track direction. This is not a tidy procedure if using a magnetic compass for heading reference.

It is more convenient for a pilot, when using a magnetic compass or direction indicator, to fly a constant track direction. This can be achieved by following a **rhumb line** track, rather than a great circle track. A rhumb line crosses all meridians of longitude at the same angle and will appear on the surface of the Earth as a curved line concave to the nearer pole.

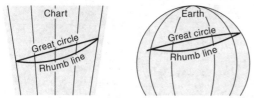

■ *Figure 9-28* **A rhumb line track compared with a great circle track**

A rhumb line track is easier to track along, because you can fly a constant magnetic heading. The disadvantage is that a rhumb line is not the shortest distance between two points on the earth, but over short distances, such as place to place in the UK, the difference is insignificant. A pilot navigating visually using the magnetic compass for heading reference will normally follow the rhumb line track, and an instrument pilot using radio navigation aids will normally follow their great circle track.

NOTE Over short distances (i.e. of less than 200 nm) the rhumb line track and great circle track are almost identical – the rhumb line will be slightly on the equator side of the great circle. The direction of the rhumb line track and the great circle track are identical at the mid-point en route.

Distance Measurement on Charts

Distance may be measured by various methods and you should be able to achieve an accuracy to within 1 nm by using one of the following methods:

1. THE GRADUATED SCALE LINE. This is at the bottom of most charts. Using dividers, or some other means, transfer the distance between the two positions on the chart down onto the scale line.

	KILOMETRES	10	5	0	10
SCALE 1:500 000	NAUTICAL MILES	10		5	0
	STATUTE MILES	10		5	0

■ Figure 9-29 **A graduated scale line is included on aeronautical charts**

2. THE LATITUDE SCALE. This is a graticule found on the side of each chart. At all points on earth for all practical purposes, 1 minute of latitude = 1 nm.

Using dividers or some other means, transfer the distance between the two positions on the chart across onto the latitude scale. (Because the scale over the whole chart may vary slightly from latitude to latitude, use that part of the latitude scale which is about the same as the mid-latitude of the track that you are considering.)

The number of minute divisions then gives you the distance in nautical miles.

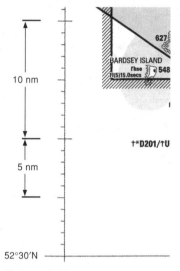

■ Figure 9-30 **Latitude scales**

3. SCALE RULE. Navigation scales rules (and plotters) are designed to measure distances on the 1:500,000 and 1:250,000 (and even 1:1,000,000) charts. Make sure that you are reading the distance off the chart against the correct scale line for that particular chart.

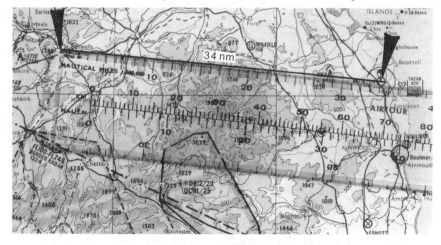

■ Figure 9-31 **Measuring the distance with a scale rule**

Bearing Measurement on Charts

If you are to track between two points, then on the chart you will draw the straight line joining them. This will be an approximate great circle. Its direction will be the same as that of the rhumb line at the mid-meridian of longitude, so it is common practice to measure direction at the mid-meridian. This is usually taken as the meridian that the track crosses closest to the half-way mark.

The true direction can be measured against true north at the mid-meridian of longitude by using a protractor.

Measuring Direction with a Protractor

The best way to measure direction with a protractor is to align its north–south axis with true north along the mid-meridian and then to read off the direction on the outer scale. (You can also measure the direction by aligning the axis of the protractor with the track and measuring the direction against the inner scale.)

Once again it is vital that you have an approximate value in mind prior to using the protractor so that you avoid any gross errors, such as being out by 90° or 180°.

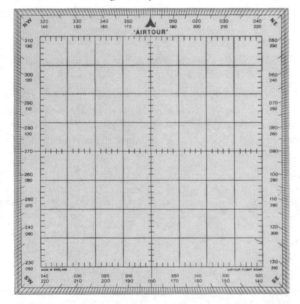

■ Figure 9-32 **The square protractor is the type commonly used in aviation**

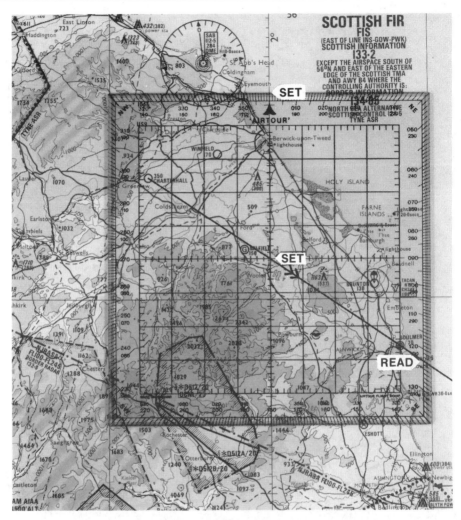

■ *Figure 9-33* **Measuring direction with a protractor**

Measuring Direction with a Plotter

A plotter is a simple device that combines the functions of a scale rule and a protractor. An advantage is that only one instrument is required to measure track and distance, instead of two. This is significant for doing such measurements in the cockpit.

Prior to any accurate measurements of direction, you should always have an idea of the approximate direction (to within 20° or 30°) in mind. This avoids gross errors.

MEASURING DIRECTION WITH A PLOTTER

1. Place the centre of the plotter over the approximate mid-point of the track (where it crosses the mid-meridian).

2. Align the edge of the plotter with the track line.

3. Align the North-South graticule on the rotatable protractor with the True North/True South latitude-longitude grid of the chart, ensuring that the arrowed lines on the protractor point North!

4. Read-off the TRUE Track against the Course Arrow which points in the direction of travel. The other arrow indicates the reciprocal of the desired track.

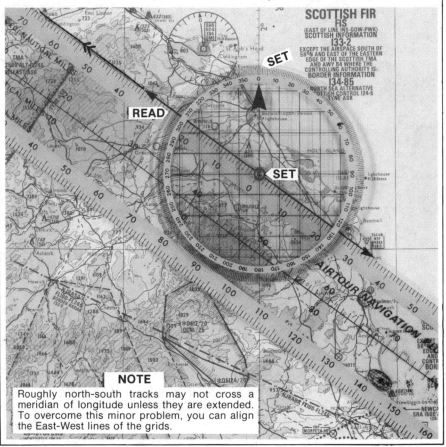

NOTE

Roughly north-south tracks may not cross a meridian of longitude unless they are extended. To overcome this minor problem, you can align the East-West lines of the grids.

■ *Figure 9-34 Measuring track direction with a plotter (note the scales for measuring distance)*

Now complete Exercises 9 – Aeronautical Charts.

Section **Two**

Flight Planning

Introduction to Flight Planning

The aim of flight planning is to assist in a safe and efficient flight; good planning will simplify the flight and reduce your workload in the cockpit. The more thought and preparation given on the ground prior to flight, the more likely that the flight will be completed with ease, safety, confidence and pleasure.

Most PPL pilots act as a sole pilot/navigator. Navigation activity is limited by the confined space of the cockpit and the fact that your attention must be divided between flying the aeroplane, navigating, and handling radio communications. Passengers may also occasionally require attention. Therefore, it is important to keep the navigation activity in the cockpit to a safe minimum.

The better the pre-flight preparation, the less the in-flight workload.

Measuring such things as tracks and distances in flight sometimes requires the pilot to be 'head-down' in the cockpit – though this should be avoided as much as possible. The pilot/navigator needs to be constantly looking out of the cockpit, monitoring the flightpath of the aircraft and watching for other traffic. The better the flight planning, the easier this is to do.

Flight planning is pilot-initiated. You play the active role. To do this, and to take your proper responsibility, you must have a sound understanding of the principles involved in good flight planning, and also be aware of your legal responsibilities as pilot-in-command. These responsibilities include:

- [ ] **that you** are suitably licensed for the flight;
- [ ] **an assessment** that the aeroplane is airworthy, and will remain so for the duration of the flight;
- [ ] **an assessment** that the flight will be safe according to the latest meteorological and operational information, including suitability of the aerodromes;
- [ ] **that sufficient fuel and oil** is carried for the flight, plus an adequate reserve to allow for navigation errors and unplanned diversions;
- [ ] **that the aeroplane** is correctly loaded (at or below maximum weights for take-off and landing, and centre of gravity within limits).

The mental processes required to flight plan, and the methods used to ensure a successful flight, are simple and based on common sense.

Personal Navigation Equipment

The two most important instruments in visual navigation are the magnetic compass and the clock, so always carry a serviceable timepiece. You should also carry a flight case or satchel that fits comfortably within reach in the cockpit and contains your navigation equipment. A typical flight case should contain:

- ☐ **relevant charts** covering at least 50 nm either side of your planned track;
- ☐ **a navigation computer,** scale rule and protractor (or plotter);
- ☐ **pens and pencils;**
- ☐ **relevant CAA documents** and flight information publications (e.g. *Pooley's Flight Guide*);
- ☐ **spare flight log forms;**
- ☐ **clipboard** or kneeboard;
- ☐ **a torch;** and
- ☐ **sunglasses.**

If a flight is planned some days in advance, much of the preparation can be done well before the flight – however sometimes a flight occurs without advance notice. For a short-notice navigation exercise, where there is no time for preparation the night before, a typical routine is:

- ☐ **check** the availability of an aeroplane;
- ☐ **check** the contents of your flight case;
- ☐ **obtain** the appropriate weather forecasts and analyse them;
- ☐ **obtain** the appropriate NOTAMs (Notices to Airmen) and study them;
- ☐ **carry out** the route selection and chart preparation;
- ☐ **complete** a flight log;
- ☐ **consider** Search and Rescue (SAR) aspects (see AIP GEN 3.6);
- ☐ **file a flight plan,** if required.

Weather forecasts NOTAMs may be available at your flying organisation; if not, obtain them from a briefing office or by telephone.

Visual Flight

A basic PPL pilot (with no IMC or Instrument Rating) must comply with the weather minima stated in the licence privileges at all times.

The Visual Flight Rules (VFR) were discussed in detail in Vol. 2 of *The Air Pilot's Manual,* but some additional information is included here as it may affect your flight planning. It concerns a typical private flight outside regulated airspace (i.e. outside all controlled airspace and Aerodrome Traffic Zones) and at an IAS not exceeding 140 knots.

An aircraft may be flown outside controlled airspace under VFR and within the privileges of the Private Pilot Licence at or below 3,000 ft amsl at 140 kt or less indicated airspeed provided it:
- **remains clear of cloud** and in sight of the surface; and
- **has 3 km flight visibility.**

In addition, a minimum cloud ceiling above all obstacles of 1,000 ft is recommended.

More information on VFR flight procedures can be found in UK AIP ENR. While this is a large document and covers many aspects of flight, some sections make interesting reading for a PPL pilot. Your flying instructor will give you guidance.

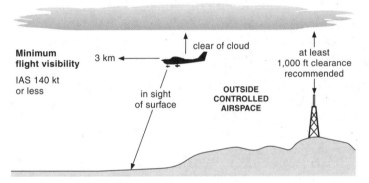

■ Figure 10-1 **Requirements for a typical private flight**

The above criteria are minimum requirements, and a pilot exhibiting good airmanship will increase these according to experience, abilities and limitations. A flight visibility of 3 km, for instance, allows very little room for error, and inexperienced pilots would be well advised to increase their personal minima. Flight visibility of 5 km is a reasonable minimum.

For en route terrain clearance, at least 1,000 ft above obstacles within 5 or 10 nm of track is desirable, though this may not be possible in some congested areas. For example, overlying controlled airspace, such as a Terminal Control Area (TMA), may temporarily restrict the height at which you can fly.

When considering if the forecast (or actual) cloud ceiling at the departure, destination and alternate aerodrome(s) will allow flight in the circuit, the minimum cloud ceiling recommended is the higher of either:
- **600 ft above the highest obstacle** within 4 nm of the aerodrome; or
- **800 ft above aerodrome level** (for aerodromes outside controlled airspace).

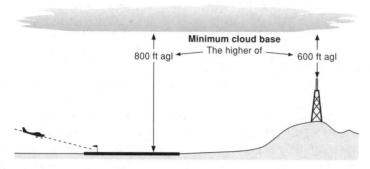

Minimum cloud base
The higher of
800 ft agl ←————————→ 600 ft agl

■ Figure 10-2 **In the circuit of an aerodrome**

VFR Flight Should Occur Only By Day

A check that your flight can be carried out with sufficient daylight remaining is a vital consideration prior to flight.

A VFR flight may not depart before the end of official night, which is **sunrise minus 30 minutes,** and should be well and truly on the ground by the time official night commences – i.e. **sunset plus 30 minutes.** However, basic-PPL holders should plan on arriving at the destination aerodrome well before this latest possible time.

If you are flying locally, at least a 10 minute buffer should be kept and, on longer flights, consider increasing this margin to 20 or 30 minutes. Cloud coverage, mountain shadows and other factors can cause deterioration of the light. Remember that, with a setting sun, it will be much darker at ground level than at altitude. Also, the closing time of your destination aerodrome should be taken into consideration. Many private airfields in the UK close at sunset.

Operational considerations, therefore, commence right from the beginning of planning a flight. For example, if flight time to the destination is one hour, and the latest time of day operations at the destination is 1900 UTC, you should plan on arriving there no later than 1850 UTC. This means a latest departure time of 1750 UTC.

If there is some doubt about weather conditions at your planned destination, allow time to proceed to an alternate aerodrome and make a landing, with a buffer period, before SS+30 (last light). Plan your latest time of departure based on conditions at the destination and alternate aerodromes.

If there is an additional 30-minute flight time from the above destination to an alternate aerodrome, where SS+30 is say 1858 UTC, and you plan to arrive at the alternate no later than 1848, this means that you must plan to depart overhead the destination no later than 1818, and therefore set course from the original aerodrome no later than 1718 UTC. To use a longer and more sensible buffer than 10 minutes, it would be necessary to depart even earlier than this. A 30-minute buffer is good airmanship.

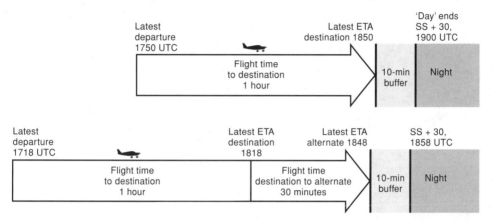

■ *Figure 10-3* **Ascertain the latest time of departure and use a sensible margin as a buffer. The bare minimum is 10 minutes; 30 minutes is better airmanship.**

Summary

Prior to a cross-country flight consider:

1. How much daylight remains?

2. Is the weather satisfactory en route, and at the destination and alternate aerodromes?

3. Are there any operational problems (e.g. runway works in progress at the destination)?

Now complete **Exercises 10 − Introduction to Flight Planning.**

Pre-Flight Briefing

Prior to each cross-country flight, you must carefully consider the weather situation and any operational matters that may affect the proposed flight. A typical pre-flight briefing checklist should include consideration of:

☐ **weather information;**

☐ **current NOTAMs;**

☐ **any changes or additions** to operational procedures (UK AIP);

☐ **serviceability of aerodromes** (including alternates), and prior permission if required (PPR);

☐ **communications frequencies** (on charts, in UK AIP AD, and *Pooley's Flight Guide*);

☐ **airspace restrictions** (see charts, including the normal route chart that you will use, plus the Chart of UK Airspace Restrictions and Hazardous Areas, included in UK AIP ENR);

☐ **hazards to aviation,** existing or likely;

☐ **latest time you can land** – sunset plus 30 minutes, or maybe the destination and/or alternate(s) close earlier, e.g. at sunset; (SR/SS times are available from briefing offices, UK AIP GEN 2-7-1 and there is a table in *Pooley's Flight Guide*).

The Weather

Aerodrome forecasts, reports and forecast charts are now freely available from the Met Office Aviation web site: www.metoffice.gov.uk/aviation

Weather forecasts are a main source of information, but don't be afraid to look at the sky and make your own assessment. If the weather forecast charts or AIRMET teletype text forecasts, plus terminal forecasts, are not available at your departure airfield, then you can take advantage of the AIRMET recorded telephone service, supplemented as necessary by a call to the appropriate weather centre for terminal forecasts and actuals. Note down the details on the published proforma (AIP MET and *Pooley's Flight Guide*). Telephone numbers to use are shown on the AIRMET Areas map.

When analysing the destination aerodrome forecast, particular attention should be given to:

☐ **cloud base;**

☐ **visibility;**

☐ **fog, thunderstorms,** and any other hazards to aviation;

☐ **wind,** especially runway crosswind components.

Remember that the cloud base is given above mean sea level (amsl) in en route forecasts, and above ground level (agl) in aerodrome forecasts.

NOTE Bear in mind that British weather tends to be quite local-ised due to geographical influences – hills, mountains and coastal effects. So it is good practice to study the weather reports from many places to get a thorough picture.

At this stage we suggest you re-read the *Weather Forecasts and Reports* chapter in Vol. 2 of this series. It gives examples of chart and teletype forecasts and reports, and explains how to read them. Aerodrome and Area Forecasts are valuable information.

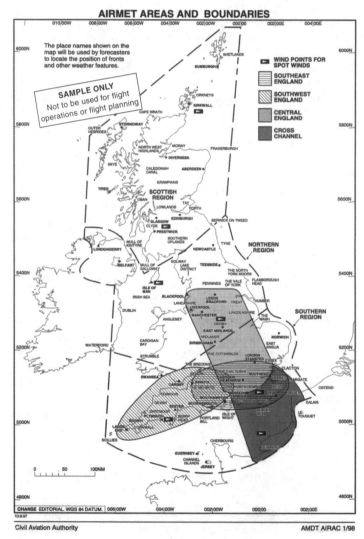

■ *Figure 11-1 **AIRMET areas and boundaries (sample only)***

CIVIL AVIATION AUTHORITY

AIRMET COPY FORM
(for forecasts from 31 March 1995 onwards)

Forecast Number ______ **Valid** ____ / ____ **To** ____ / ____

All temperatures are in degrees Celsius. All heights are AMSL, and all times UTC(Z).

MET SITUATION

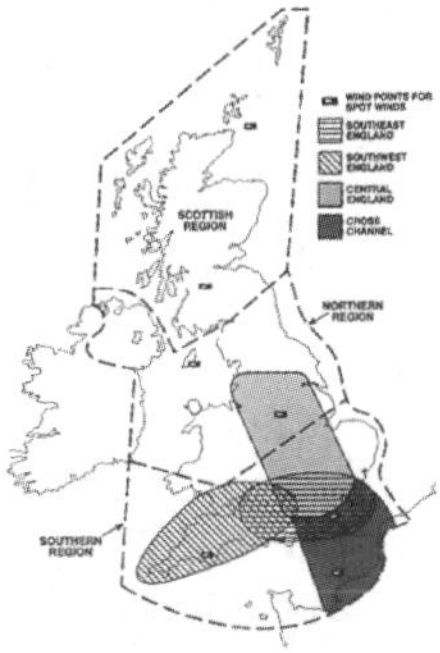

WEATHER CONDITIONS

ALTITUDE	WINDS/TEMPERATURES
1000 Ft	
3000 Ft	
6000 Ft	
10000 Ft	
18000 Ft	
24000 Ft	

FORECAST AREA		
1. SOUTHERN REGION	40	
2. NORTHERN REGION	41	
3. SCOTTISH REGION	42	
4. UK SIG WEATHER	43	
5. UK UPPER WINDS	44	
6. UK UPDATE/OUTLOOK	45	
7. SOUTHWEST ENGLAND	46	
8. SOUTHEAST ENGLAND	47	
9. CROSS CHANNEL	48	
10. CENTRAL ENGLAND	49	

OUTLOOK UNTIL ____ / ____

TELEPHONE NUMBERS

All forecasts between 0530 and 2300 on 0891 77 13 plus two digit code for selected forecasts.

TAFs/METARs
ALDERGROVE 018 494 23275
BIRMINGHAM 0121 717 0580
CARDIFF 01222 390 492
LEEDS 01132 457 687
BRACKNELL 01344 856 267
MANCHESTER 0161 429 0927
GLASGOW 0141 221 6116

All forecasts between 2300 and 0530
PLUS
Consultation for amplification of all forecasts.
BRACKNELL 01344 856 267
MANCHESTER 0161 429 0927
GLASGOW 0141 221 6116

Copies of this form, and of CAA document No 397 AIRMET FORECASTS; USERS NOTES-2nd ISSUE, may be obtained free of charge by writing to: The Technical Secretary, AOPA, 50a Cambridge Street, London SW1V 4QQ, provided a suitable A4 size stamped addressed envelope is enclosed with the request.

■ Figure 11-2 ***Use an AIRMET copy form to take down your AIRMET regional forecast***

Aeronautical Information

Operational matters of long standing are published in the UK Aeronautical Information Publication (AIP) General section (GEN). Recent changes are issued as AIP Supplements such as AIRACs and Class Two NOTAMs (Notices to Airmen).

Pre-Flight Route and Aerodrome Information Bulletins, together with Temporary Navigational Warning Information Bulletins (TNWs) should be readily available at your flying school or aero club. Bulletins are also available on the Internet at http://www.ais.org.uk. Note also that a freephone service for updated information on Royal Flights (RF) and temporary restricted airspace concerning the Red Arrows and similar aerobatic display teams is available daily on 0500 354802.

NOTAMs, Supplements and Bulletins contain vital information on the serviceability of aerodromes, the activation of Danger Areas, the occurrence of Royal Flights, changes in radio frequencies, etc., and should be read carefully.

■ *Figure 11-3* **NOTAMs, Supplements and Bulletins should be checked pre-flight (sample only)**

UK Flight Procedures

While you will be familiar with standard procedures, it may be advisable to revise them and check for any recent changes by reference to the UK AIP.

---

6   **Visual Circuit Reporting Procedures**

6.1   In order that the maximum use may be made of aerodromes for the purpose of landing and taking-off, it is essential that pilots accurately report their positions in the circuit.

6.2   **Standard Overhead Join.** An aircraft which has been instructed to complete a standard overhead join will:

    (a)   Overfly the aerodrome at 2000 ft aal;

    (b)   descend on the 'dead side' to circuit height;

    (c)   join the circuit by crossing the upwind end of the runway at circuit height;

    (d)   position downwind.

SAMPLE ONLY
Not to be used for flight
operations or flight planning

6.3   Position reports are to be made as follows:

    (a)   **Downwind** - Aircraft are to report 'Downwind' when abeam the upwind end of the runway.

    (b)   **Base Leg** - Aircraft are to report 'Base Leg', if requested by ATC, immediately on completion of the turn on to base leg.

    (c)   **Final** - Aircraft are to report 'Final' after the completion of the turn on to final approach and when at a range of not more than 4 nm from the approach end of the runway.

    (d)   **Long Final** - Aircraft flying a final approach of a greater length than 4 nm are to report 'Long Final' when beyond that range, and 'Final' when a range of 4 nm is reached. Aircraft flying a straight-in approach are to report 'Long Final' at 8 nm from the approach end of the runway, and 'Final' when a range of 4 nm is reached.

Note: At grass aerodromes, the area to be used for landing should be regarded as the runway for the purposes of position reporting.

7   **Procedures for Arriving VFR Flights**

7.1   An aircraft approaching an aerodrome under VFR where an Approach Control Service is available should make initial RTF contact when 15 nm or five minutes flying time from the Aerodrome Traffic Zone boundary, whichever is the greater. If the aircraft is not equipped with the Approach frequency, communication on the Aerodrome Control frequency will be acceptable. As well as landing information, ATC will pass information on pertinent known traffic to assist pilots of VFR flights to maintain separation from both IFR and other VFR flights.

7.2   If radar sequencing of IFR flights is in progress, ATC will provide VFR flights with information to enable them to fit into the landing sequence.

7.3   Approach Control will instruct pilots when to change frequency to Aerodrome Control.

■ *Figure 11-4* **Sample excerpts on flight procedures from the AIP**

Aerodromes

The prime source for information on aerodromes is UK AIP AD (Aerodromes), as amended by NOTAM. In the case illustrated in Figure 11-5, Shobdon (designator EGBS) has an asphalt Runway 09/27 with a take-off run available (TORA) of 842 metres and a landing distance available (LDA) of 842 metres.

Further information on local flying regulations, warnings, obstacles, visual ground aids and aerodrome hours of availability is given in AIP AD. The AD contents page will direct you to the various items.

The AIP is too unwieldy to carry in a flight case, but *Pooley's Flight Guide* is a compact source of aerodrome information. It is produced with the assistance of the CAA, is updated regularly, and contains similar information to that described above.

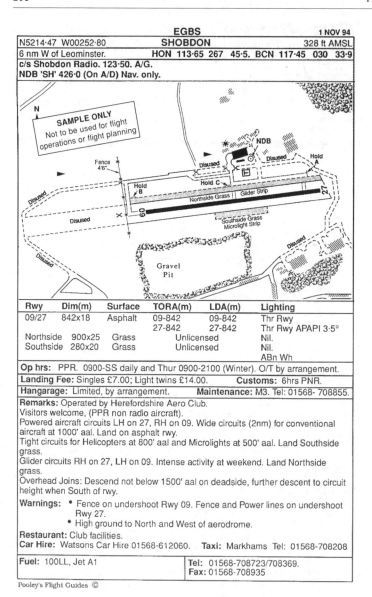

EGBS					1 NOV 94
N5214·47 W00252·80		**SHOBDON**			328 ft AMSL
6 nm W of Leominster.		HON 113·65 267 45·5. BCN 117·45 030 33·9			
c/s Shobdon Radio. 123·50. A/G.					
NDB 'SH' 426·0 (On A/D) Nav. only.					

Rwy	Dim(m)	Surface	TORA(m)	LDA(m)	Lighting
09/27	842x18	Asphalt	09-842	09-842	Thr Rwy
			27-842	27-842	Thr Rwy APAPI 3·5°
Northside	900x25	Grass	Unlicensed		Nil.
Southside	280x20	Grass	Unlicensed		Nil.
					ABn Wh

Op hrs: PPR. 0900-SS daily and Thur 0900-2100 (Winter). O/T by arrangement.

Landing Fee: Singles £7.00; Light twins £14.00.   **Customs:** 6hrs PNR.

Hangarage: Limited, by arrangement.   **Maintenance:** M3. Tel: 01568- 708855.

Remarks: Operated by Herefordshire Aero Club.
Visitors welcome, (PPR non radio aircraft).
Powered aircraft circuits LH on 27, RH on 09. Wide circuits (2nm) for conventional aircraft at 1000' aal. Land on asphalt rwy.
Tight circuits for Helicopters at 800' aal and Microlights at 500' aal. Land Southside grass.
Glider circuits RH on 27, LH on 09. Intense activity at weekend. Land Northside grass.
Overhead Joins: Descend not below 1500' aal on deadside, further descent to circuit height when South of rwy.

Warnings: • Fence on undershoot Rwy 09. Fence and Power lines on undershoot Rwy 27.
     • High ground to North and West of aerodrome.

Restaurant: Club facilities.
Car Hire: Watsons Car Hire 01568-612060.   **Taxi:** Markhams Tel: 01568-708208

Fuel: 100LL, Jet A1	Tel: 01568-708723/708369.
	Fax: 01568-708935

Pooley's Flight Guides ©

■ *Figure 11-5* **Aerodrome information from Pooley's Flight Guide**

UK AIP

2.1	City/Aerodrome	EGLG	PANSHANGER

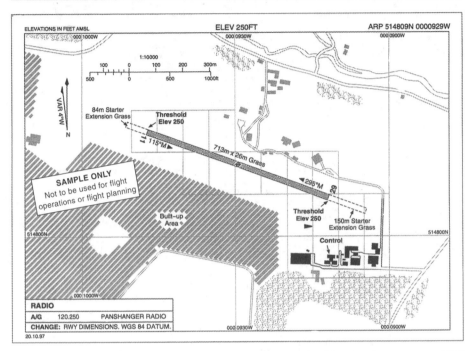

	EGLG AD 2.2 – AERODROME GEOGRAPHICAL AND ADMINISTRATIVE DATA	
2	Direction and distance from city:	2.5 nm W of Hertford.
5	AD Administration: Address:	Professional Flight Management Ltd. Panshanger Airfield, Cole Green, Hertford, Herts, SG14 2NH.
	Telephone: Fax:	01707-391791. 01707-392792.

	EGLG AD 2.3 – OPERATIONAL HOURS	
1	AD:	Winter: 0900-SS or by arrangement. Summer: 0900-SS or by arrangement.
2	Customs and Immigration:	—
7	ATS:	Winter: 0900-SS. Summer: 0900-1600 and by arrangement.
8	Fuelling:	As AD hours.
12	Remarks:	This aerodrome is strictly PPR.

	EGLG AD 2.4 – HANDLING SERVICES AND FACILITIES	
2	Fuel/oil types:	Fuel: AVGAS 100LL.

■ Figure 11-6 **Aerodrome information from AIP AD (sample only)**

AD 2-EGLG-1-2 (1 Jan 98) **PANSHANGER** UK AIP

EGLG AD 2.10 – AERODROME OBSTACLES

	In Approach/Take-off areas			In circling area and at aerodrome		
	1			2		
Runway/Area affected	Obstacle type Elevation Markings/lighting		Co-ordinates	Obstacle type Elevation Markings/lighting		Co-ordinates
a	b		c	a		b
		ft amsl			ft amsl	
11/Approach 29/Take-off	Tree	275	(† 936 ‡ 60R)	Mast (Lgtd)	925	(190°T, 4.2 nm) from ARP
29/Approach 11/Take-off	Trees	360	(†1210 Across RCL)			

3 Remarks: † Distance (m) beyond start of TORA. ‡ Distance (m) Left (L) or Right (R) of extended centre-line.

EGLG AD 2.13 – DECLARED DISTANCES

Runway Designator	TORA (m)	TODA (m)	ASDA (m)	LDA (m)	Remarks
1	2	3	4	5	6
11	797	797	797	713	84 m Starter extension available on Runway 11.
29	863	863	863	713	150 m Starter extension available on Runway 29.

EGLG AD 2.17 – ATS AIRSPACE

SAMPLE ONLY Not to be used for flight operations or flight planning

Designation and lateral limits	Vertical limits	Airspace Classification
1	2	3
Panshanger Aerodrome Traffic Zone (ATZ) Circle radius 2 nm centred on longest notified runway (11/29) 514809N 0000929W.	2000 ft aal SFC	G

4	ATS unit callsign: Language:	Panshanger Radio. English.
6	Remarks:	ATZ hours: 0900-SS (Winter). 0800-1600 (Summer).

EGLG AD 2.19 – RADIO NAVIGATION AND LANDING AIDS

Not applicable.

EGLG AD 2.23 – ADDITIONAL INFORMATION

Aerodrome Regulations. Not applicable.

Warnings. Not applicable.

Flight Procedures

(a) Circuit directions: Runway 29 - RH; Runway 11 - LH. Circuit height: 800 ft aal.

(b) Runway 29 Noise Abatement Routeing: After take-off, turn right to overfly the golf club house and on passing, turn to runway QDM until passing prominent white building (School). Turn right to fly to a square wood (approximately 0.5 mile), then turn downwind to fly between Tewin and Tewin Wood.

■ Figure 11-7 *Aerodrome information from AIP AD (continued)*

Communications

The main Flight Information Service and Air Traffic Control frequencies are published on the 1:500,000 aeronautical charts. Further information is available in UK AIP AD/ENR.

STATION	SERVICE	CALL SIGN OR IDENT	EM	TRANSMITS		RECEIVES		HOURS OF SERVICE		CO-ORDINATES	LOCATION		OPERATING AUTHORITY AND REMARKS
				kHz	MHz	kHz	MHz	WINTER PERIOD	SUMMER PERIOD		MAG	NM	
1	2	3	4	5	6	7	8	9		11	12	13	14
Caernarfon	A/G	Caernarfon Radio	A3E	–	122.250	12		SAMPLE ONLY *Not to be used for flight operations or flight planning*	nent)	–	–	–	Air Caernarfon Ltd.
	NDB	CAE	NONA2A	320	–	–				N5305.98 W00420.32	–	–	On AD. Range 15 nm. Normally radiates H24.

(table header: RADIO COMMUNICATION AND NAVIGATION FACILITIES)

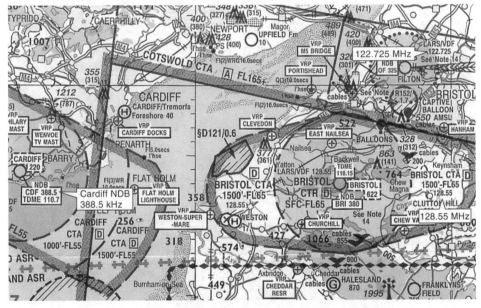

■ Figure 11-8 *Frequencies are found in AIP AD/ENR and on aeronautical charts*

Airspace Restrictions

Aeronautical charts show how the airspace over the UK is divided into controlled airspace of different classes, Danger Areas, etc. Note that the CAA 1:250,000 series of UK charts is only concerned with airspace up to 5,000 ft. The ICAO 1:500,000 series displays airspace up to the base of the UIR–FL245. It may also be necessary to check the other charts in AIP ENR that provide information:

☐ **Chart of UK Airspace Restrictions**; and
☐ **Chart of UK Areas of Intense Aerial Activity and Military Low Flying** system.

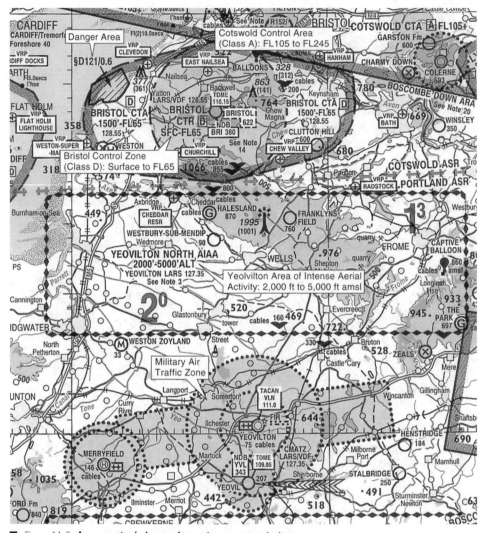

■ *Figure 11-9* **Aeronautical charts show airspace restrictions**

Now complete **Exercises 11 – Pre-Flight Briefing.**

Route Selection and Chart Preparation

Route Selection

When planning a flight, consider the following points when selecting a route.

AIRCRAFT PERFORMANCE is a prime consideration in route selection. There is no point planning a flight from Land's End direct to John o' Groats in an aircraft with a range of only 250 nm; nor of planning to cross the Himalayas when the altitude capability of the aeroplane is only 10,000 ft.

TERRAIN is also a major consideration. A single-engined aircraft flying from the west coast of Wales to Manchester might be safer flying around the coastal route than flying direct, which would take it over rugged, mountainous country. Low cloud and high or rising terrain can rapidly create problems for VFR flights.

WEATHER. A line of thunderstorms or an approaching cold front might cause you to plan via a more favourable route. A low cloud base might also cause problems over high terrain. Have a look at the meteorological forecast before you finally select a route.

AIRSPACE. Always consider the nature of the airspace en route, which can be of various types, such as:
- controlled airspace;
- aerodromes (ATZ, MATZ, non-ATZ, CTR);
- Entry/Exit Access Lanes and Low Level Routes;
- Advisory Routes;
- Prohibited, Restricted and Danger Areas;
- Purple (Royal) Airspace;
- Areas of Intense Aerial Activity, or Aerial Tactics Areas;
- Altimeter Setting Region boundaries.

They are all shown on aeronautical charts and/or the UK AIP. Plan your route to take advantage of them where possible, or to avoid them where advisable.

HAZARDS TO AVIATION. Many things can be hazardous to aviation, and you should consider them. The list includes:
- high terrain;
- obstructions, and their height amsl;
- high intensity radio transmission areas;
- gliding, parachuting, hang gliding, microlight flying, or parascending areas; and
- bird sanctuaries.

It may be advisable to avoid some of these hazards by a considerable distance.

CHECKPOINTS. A route that follows easy-to-identify landmarks or other checkpoints may be preferable to a slightly shorter route on which visual aids to navigation are fewer. Good reporting points are often suggested on aeronautical charts by the manner in which they are depicted. Good visual checkpoints for a VFR flight are:

- ☐ prominent and unique mountains, valleys, rivers;
- ☐ coastlines, especially points, lighthouses, river mouths, bays;
- ☐ bridges, overpasses;
- ☐ railway lines, transmission lines, crossroads;
- ☐ combinations of all of the above, and unique combinations of roads, railway lines, towns, rivers.

ALTERNATE AERODROME(S). Weather conditions, or the doubtful serviceability of your destination aerodrome, or some other reason, may require you to exercise airmanship and carry one or more alternates for your destination. This may force you to fly a different route to the one you would choose if no alternate was included in your pre-flight planning.

NOTE A useful 1:1,000,000 scale *UK Planning Chart* is available, which shows aerodrome locations (among other things). The chart is intended for use in conjunction with *Pooley's Flight Guide,* in which chosen aerodromes can be checked for suitability.

Pooley's Planning Chart is also useful for checking distances when flight planning, and en route, to ascertain coverage of the Lower Airspace Radar Advisory Service (LARS) throughout Britain.

Chart Preparation

What Charts Should I Carry?

You will have been perusing your charts while thinking about route selection, but now that you have decided on the route that you plan to follow, your charts need to be properly prepared to aid your flight planning measurements and calculations, and later your in-flight navigation work. Remember that a minute's work on the ground might save you some anguish later on when in flight.

Good chart preparation is essential.

Carry the appropriate aeronautical charts for your planned flight and any possible diversions (planned or unplanned). They must be current charts. It is advisable to carry charts that give coverage of at least 50 nm either side of the planned track in case of diversions. Also carry information on aerodromes (found in the UK AIP or *Pooley's Flight Guide*).

Ensure that your charts are current.

After selecting the route, mark it in on your charts and make sure that the route is easily visible in flight.

NOTE Many pilots cover their charts with plastic, or even better, purchase them that way. This makes it easier to write on and later to rub out, and prolong the chart life. It also allows you to keep a log on the actual chart without making the chart unusable later on. A 'Chinagraph' pencil is excellent for marking on plastic-coated charts, and can easily be erased. Do not use a red Chinagraph though – red cannot be seen easily in the cockpit at night.

Distance and/or Time Markings Along Track

To allow easy in-flight estimation of flight progress starting at each turning point, or checkpoint, put in 10 nm markers. (Some instructors may suggest that you do this by starting at the destination and working backwards, so that the 'odd man out' is left behind early in each leg, thus making it easy to measure distance-to-run. Either method is simple and satisfactory.)

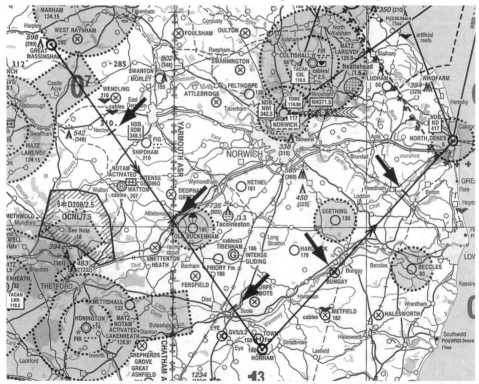

■ Figure 12-1 **10 nm markers on the chart assist estimation of distances**

Some pilots prefer to use time markings, such as your expected position en route every 10 minutes or so, but these change from day to day depending on the wind, the aeroplane and so on, whereas the 10 nm markings for that route will remain the same.

Another approach is to divide each leg up into four; ¼ way, ½ way, ¾ way. This works very well, especially on the short stages common in the UK.

Once again, your flying instructor will give you good advice on which method to use.

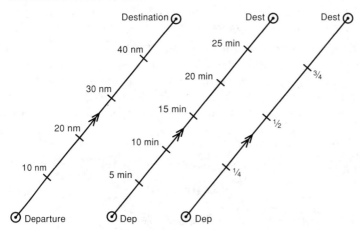

■ *Figure 12-2* **Various distance/time markers**

Track Guides

Navigation in real life never works out precisely as you planned it. Your actual in-flight track made good (TMG) may differ from your desired track (flight-planned track – FPT) marked on the chart. This may be due to reasons outside your control, such as actual in-flight winds differing from those forecast.

To allow for easy estimation of **track error** and **closing angle**, you may like to mark in lines 10 degrees either side of your desired track. Estimation using these track guides (or fan lines) is much easier in flight than having to use a protractor or plotter.

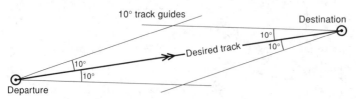

■ *Figure 12-3* **Track guides, or fan lines, assist in estimating track error and closing angle in flight**

NOTE These lines are related to the aircraft's track, and not its heading, consequently be clear that they do *not* show the drift of the aeroplane because drift is related to the aircraft's heading.

Track guides give you an indication of track error and enable you to estimate the closing angle.

Study the Route Prior to Take-Off

It is a good idea to study carefully the route drawn on your chart before you depart, especially if you will be flying through congested airspace. Work slowly along the planned track, noting ground features you should see en route, obstructions, high terrain, Hazardous or Restricted Areas, overlying controlled airspace, and Areas of Intensive Aerial Activity (AIAAs). Also, look for the radio frequencies of the ATS units that you will use, and, if you wish, note them on your flight log form (see Chapter 13).

Folding Your Charts

The final stage in chart preparation is to fold them satisfactorily for cockpit use. When folded, arrange your chart so that, in the cockpit with the chart on your clipboard or knee, you can 'fly up the page'. This means that when you look at the chart, objects that are, for example, ahead and to the right of track should be ahead and to the right of the aircraft when you look out the window. Allow 70 or 80 nm either side of track (1:500,000 scale) to remain visible on the chart. This is a reasonable range for large objects such as mountain ranges, coastlines and so on, that can assist in your navigation.

> **1.** Fold sheet on the long axis, near the mid-parallel, face out, with the bottom part of the chart upward.
> **2.** Fold inwards near the centre meridian.
> **3.** Fold both halves backwards in accordion folds.

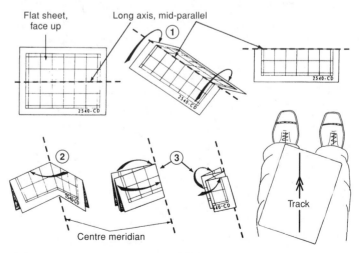

■ *Figure 12-4* **Fold charts so that you 'fly up the page'**

All this may seem like a lot to think about but, in practice, it is quite straightforward. Once you have drawn in the proposed track, each of the above items will be obvious from a close inspection of your chart.

Finally, a further check of the weather forecast and NOTAMs will ensure that the chosen track is suitable from the point of view of cloud on any hills, fog, thunderstorms, and for latest operational information.

Now complete
Exercises 12 – Route Selection & Chart Preparation.

Compiling a Flight Log

Compiling a flight log is a fast and efficient way to plan a cross-country flight. It records the measurements and calculations you made at the flight planning stage and, once airborne, provides you with a plan against which you can compare the actual progress of the flight. A flight log enables you to predict the **time of arrival** at any point en route, and to calculate the **fuel required.**

There are various forms of flight log. Your flying school will provide you with the type it prefers. We have included a number of typical flight logs in this chapter. What follows is a brief explanation of typical entries made on a flight log for a flight from Elstree, to Ipswich, to Cambridge, and return to Elstree. You might like to work through it, using an aeronautical chart for the London area and your own navigation equipment.

NOTE 1 The latitude and longitude of the various aerodromes involved can be found in AIP AD and *Pooley's Flight Guide.*

NOTE 2 Variation decreases by 7–8 minutes annually around the British Isles.

Pilot and Aircraft

At the top of the flight log, insert your name, the aircraft registration and the date.

Pilot H. Lawson				Aircraft G-BATC		Date 1-2-97			ETD 1430 UTC				
From/To	Safety ALT	ALT Temp	RAS	TAS	W/V	TR °T	Drift	HDG °T	Var	HDG °M	GS	Dist	Time	ETA	HDG °C

■ *Figure 13-1* **Put your details on the flight log**

Route Segments

Having marked the planned route on your aeronautical chart:
- ☐ **insert** the turning points, reporting points, and any other en route points for which you want to calculate estimated time intervals (ETIs);
- ☐ **measure** the tracks and distances; and
- ☐ **note** the magnetic variation.

Insert this information on the flight log (see Figure 13-3).

■ *Figure 13-2* **(overleaf) Route of the flight on the 1:500,000 chart (not to scale)**

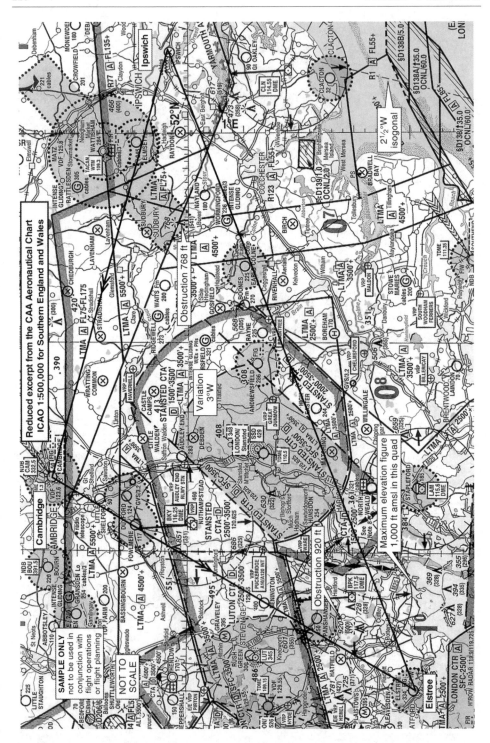

From/To	Safety ALT	ALT	RAS	TAS	W/V	TR °T	Drift	HDG °T	Var	HDG °M	GS	Dist	Time	ETA	HDG °C
		Temp													
Elstree															
						069			3W			60			
Ipswich															
						286			3W			40			
Cambridge															
						208			3W			38			
Elstree															
											Total	**138**			

■ *Figure 13-3* **Tracks, distances, and magnetic variation added**

Measuring the distance is straightforward. First it is a good idea to estimate the distance, and then measure it precisely, using either:

☐ **a scale rule or plotter,** that has the correct scale marked on it; or

☐ **dividers,** which can then be placed against the appropriate scale line at the bottom of the chart, or else down the latitude scale at the side of the chart, to give you the distance.

Engraving a pencil with 10 nm marks (in the correct scale for the chart) helps in distance estimation, particularly in flight.

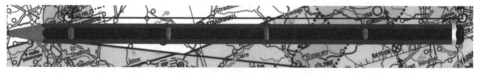

■ *Figure 13-4* **A pencil engraved with 10 nm nicks is very useful**

> Always estimate a direction before you measure it.

Measuring the direction requires strict attention, as an error here can cause serious problems in flight. Always estimate the direction before you measure it. The track from Elstree to Ipswich (now disused) is approximately 070°T. This might seem unnecessary to you, but you would be surprised to know the number of times that reciprocal directions have been inserted on flight logs (250°T instead of 070°T in this case, and who knows where the aeroplane would end up?).

Having estimated the approximate direction, measure it precisely, using either a protractor or plotter. This procedure was explained on page 192.

A straight line on Lambert's conformal conic charts (such as the ICAO 1:500,000 series commonly used in the UK) is an approximate great circle. To obtain the rhumb line direction, measure the straight line track at or near the mid-meridian of the route segment. While this point is not significant on the relatively short legs typically flown in the UK, it is significant on longer legs. (You may fly the Atlantic one day! Magnetic variation will also become very significant then.)

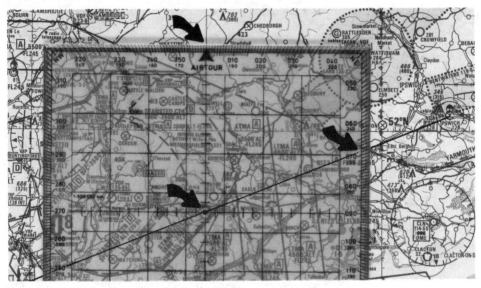

■ *Figure 13-5* **The Elstree to Ipswich leg is 069°T**

When working with the chart, note the magnetic variation indicated by a dashed blue line annotated with 5½°W, 7½°W, or whatever the variation happens to be in that area. (Use the whole number that applies between the isogonals, e.g. 6° between the 5½° and 6½°W isogonals.) Variation is required to convert °T to °M.

Even though most of this chart work can be done well before the flight (at home, for example) in a leisurely manner, you should train yourself to measure tracks and distances fairly quickly so that you can do it efficiently at the aerodrome, or in flight if required.

An unplanned diversion to an alternate aerodrome when airborne, for example, will require an estimate of track and distance, followed by more accurate measurement. Since you will be occupied flying the aeroplane, you must be able to perform such navigation tasks quickly and without error, and in a manner that will not distract you from the main task of controlling the aeroplane's flight path. Incidentally, it is easier to measure track and distance in flight using a plotter rather than a protractor and scale rule.

Determine Safety Altitudes and Select Cruising Levels

It is good airmanship to determine reasonable minimum safe cruising altitudes which will provide an adequate vertical clearance above obstacles on and near the planned route. There are various philosophies about how to estimate this safety height, and you should refer to your flying instructor on this point. Some methods are clearly more conservative than others.

Common procedures for **determining safety altitude** are:

☐ take the highest obstacle within 10 nm of track and add 1,000 ft;

☐ take the highest maximum elevation figure (MEF) en route and add 1,000 ft;

☐ take the highest obstacle within 10 nm track and add 1,500 ft;

☐ take the highest obstacle within 5 nm of track and add 10% of its height plus 1,500 ft;

☐ take the highest obstacle within 10 nm of track and round it up to the next 500 ft.

Calculating a safety altitude requires close inspection of the chart area either side of track (made easier if your transparent rule covers 5 or 10 nm on the chart). For the flight originating from Elstree, the safety altitude is based on a 1,000 ft clearance above obstacles within 10 nm either side of track.

The highest obstacle on the first leg is 6 nm north-east of Elstree, at 920 ft amsl, requiring a minimum safe altitude of 1,920 ft to achieve 1,000 ft clearance.

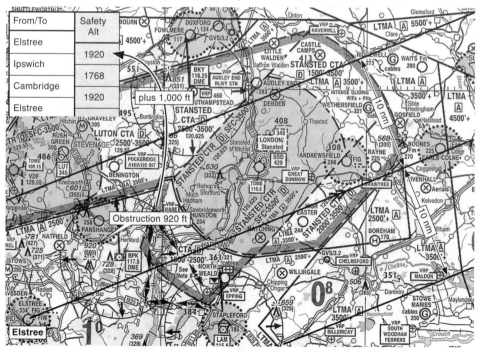

■ *Figure 13-6* **Study the chart and calculate a safety altitude**

NOTE In some congested areas (e.g. Manchester, which has an overlying TMA), flights on some routes may be unable to proceed at or above the safety altitude until clear of the restriction (in this case the overlying TMA) – the minimum safe altitude (MSA) being fairly high due to a high-elevation obstruction near the track.

Naturally, common sense (airmanship) would dictate caution in navigating along the route, especially in conditions of minimum visibility, until able to climb to at least the MSA.

As there is no guarantee that you will be given a clearance to transit controlled airspace (such as Stansted Class D), you should always preplan an alternate route around such zones.

Remember that contours below 500 ft amsl and obstructions below 300 ft agl are not shown on aeronautical charts; in other words, an obstacle that is 799 ft amsl may not be shown, so always keep a sharp lookout, especially in poor visibility.

Having determined the minimum safe cruising altitude for each leg, then select the cruising level which you propose to use. You are constrained:

☐ **on the lower side** by the safety altitude; and
☐ **on the upper side** by perhaps cloud, controlled airspace or a markedly increasing headwind.

Aerodrome Traffic Zones extend up to 2,000 ft above aerodrome level (aal) and Military Aerodrome Traffic Zones extend up to 3,000 ft aal. You may fly through them, of course, but it is good airmanship in some situations to remain clear of an ATZ. There is also no point climbing to a high cruising altitude if your destination is nearby. As a pilot, you must think about vertical navigation as well as horizontal navigation. For this flight, a cruising altitude of 2,400 ft has been selected.

While PPL pilots operating under Visual Flight Rules may cruise at altitude on QNH, they may also choose to fly at flight levels based on 1013 mb when cruising above 3,000 ft amsl, to fit in with Instrument Flight Rules traffic observing the *quadrantal rule* (see page 124).

Insert Met Data on the Flight Log

From the weather forecast, insert the wind and the temperature at your selected cruising level. Remember that forecast winds are given in degrees true. In this case, the wind at 2,400 ft amsl is 270°T/30 kt, and the temperature +10°C (see Figure 13-7).

From/To	Safety ALT	ALT Temp	RAS	TAS	W/V	TR °T	Drift	HDG °T	Var	HDG °M	GS	Dist	Time	ETA	HDG °C
Elstree															
	1920	2400 +10			270/30	069			3W			60			
Ipswich															
	1768	2400 +10			270/30	286			3W			40			
Cambridge															
	1920	2400 +10			270/30	208			3W			35			
Elstree															
										Total	**138**				

■ *Figure 13-7* **Met data added to the flight log**

Calculate the True Airspeed

The pilot flies the aeroplane according to the indicated airspeed, which is shown on the airspeed indicator. To be absolutely precise, the IAS can be corrected to rectified airspeed (RAS), to account for small errors in the particular pitot-static system, and a table to do this is in the Flight Manual. At cruising speeds, this error is usually less than 3 kt, and many pilots consider it unnecessary to refer to an airspeed calibration table like that illustrated below.

For example, at 100 knots indicated airspeed (100 KIAS), the rectified airspeed will be 98 kt (98 KCAS or KRAS) – hardly significant when you consider the minor fluctuations in airspeed occurring with wind gusts, as well as the difficulty in reading the ASI to an accuracy of even ± 1 kt.

AIRSPEED CALIBRATION Normal Static Source											
CONDITIONS: Power required for level flight or maximum rated RPM dive.											
FLAPS UP											
KIAS	40	50	60	70	80	90	100	110	120	130	140
KCAS	46	53	60	69	78	88	98	107	117	127	136

■ *Figure 13-8* **Typical airspeed calibration table**

Using IAS (or the slightly more accurate RAS), the important conversion to true airspeed can be made. This allows for the fact that the aeroplane may be flying in air less dense than at sea level, causing the ASI to indicate a speed less than the actual speed of the aeroplane through the air (TAS). In denser air, the opposite is true, but this is rarely the situation.

The higher the cruising level and the higher the air temperature, the less dense the air, and the greater the TAS for a given IAS. For this flight, cruising at 2,400 ft where the air temperature is +10°C, an IAS (or RAS) of 98 kt provides a TAS of 102 kt. (QNH is 1013). Enter this onto the flight log.

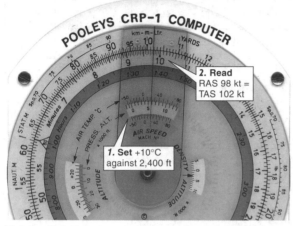

■ *Figure 13-9* **Calculate the TAS on the navigation computer**

From/To	Safety ALT	ALT Temp	RAS	TAS	W/V	TR °T	Drift	HDG °T	Var	HDG °M	GS	Dist	Time	ETA	HDG °C
Elstree															
	1920	2400 +10	98	102	270/30	069			3W			60			
Ipswich															
	1768	2400 +10	98	102	270/30	286			3W			40			
Cambridge															
	1920	2400 +10	98	102	270/30	208			3W			38			
Elstree															
											Total	138			

■ *Figure 13-10* **The flight log at this stage**

Calculate Heading and Groundspeed

Set up the triangle of velocities on the wind side of your navigation computer using your preferred technique (see Chapter 4).

KNOWN:		FIND:
TR	069°T	**HDG and GS**
W/V	270°T/30	
TAS	102 kt	

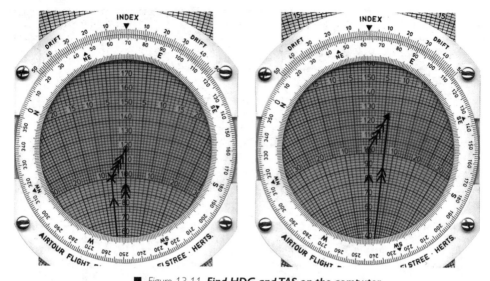

■ *Figure 13-11* **Find HDG and TAS on the computer**

From/To	Safety ALT	ALT Temp	RAS	TAS	W/V	TR °T	Drift	HDG °T	Var	HDG °M	GS	Dist	Time	ETA	HDG °C
Elstree															
	1920	2400 +10	98	102	270/30	069	–6	063	3W		130	60			
Ipswich															
	1768	2400 +10	98	102	270/30	286	–5	281	3W		73	40			
Cambridge															
	1920	2400 +10	98	102	270/30	208	+15	223	3W		84	38			
Elstree															
										Total	138				

■ *Figure 13-12* **Heading and ground speed added to the flight log**

Convert Heading to Degrees Magnetic

With magnetic variation (found on the chart), the HDG in degrees true can be converted to degrees magnetic, which is more useful in the aeroplane since the primary source of direction is the magnetic compass. *Variation west, magnetic best,* therefore, HDG 063°T and variation 3°W, gives HDG 066°M.

When you are in the aeroplane prior to flight, or actually in flight, you can refer to the deviation card and convert degrees magnetic to degrees compass, and enter this on the flight log. As this usually involves less than 3° correction, many pilots choose not to show it on the flight log.

From/To	Safety ALT	ALT Temp	RAS	TAS	W/V	TR °T	Drift	HDG °T	Var	HDG °M	GS	Dist	Time	ETA	HDG °C
Elstree															
	1920	2400 +10	98	102	270/30	069	−6	063	3W	066	130	60			066
Ipswich															
	1768	2400 +10	98	102	270/30	286	−5	281	3W	284	73	40			285
Cambridge															
	1920	2400 +10	98	102	270/30	208	+15	223	3W	226	84	38			228
Elstree															
										Total	**138**				

DEVIATION CARD

	FOR					
N	30	60	E	120	150	
STEER						
001	031	060	089	118	149	

	FOR					
S	210	240	W	300	330	
STEER						
181	213	242	089	301	330	

ON ☒ RADIOS ☐ NO

■ *Figure 13-13* **Headings in °M and °C added to the flight log**

Calculate the Estimated Time Interval for Each Leg

Using the calculator side of your navigation computer, the time taken to cover the distance at the GS calculated above can be determined (see Chapter 5). Prior to using the computer, it is good airmanship to estimate the time mentally so that no gross errors are made.

For instance, at a GS of 130 kt, the 60 nm from Elstree to Ipswich will take just under 30 minutes; by computer, an accurate answer of 28 minutes is obtained. At a GS of 73 kt, the 40 nm from Ipswich to Cambridge will take 33 nm.

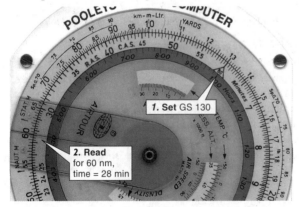

1. Set GS 130

2. Read for 60 nm, time = 28 min

■ *Figure 13-14* **Calculate time for each leg**

All of the individual estimated time intervals (ETIs) can be added up to give a total flight time. Compare this with the total distance and mentally check if the final results are reasonable.

From/To	Safety ALT	ALT Temp	RAS	TAS	W/V	TR °T	Drift	HDG °T	Var	HDG °M	GS	Dist	Time	ETA	HDG °C
Elstree															
	1920	2400 +10	98	102	270/30	069	–6	063	3W	066	130	60	28		066
Ipswich															
	1768	2400 +10	98	102	270/30	286	–5	281	3W	284	73	40	33		285
Cambridge															
	1920	2400 +10	98	102	270/30	208	+15	223	3W	226	84	38	27		228
Elstree															
										Total		138	88		

■ *Figure 13-15* **Estimated time interval for each leg added**

Fuel Planning

The amount of fuel that you carry is extremely important. The **minimum fuel** that should be in the tanks on departure is the amount needed to reach the destination (or an alternate aerodrome) and land, with reserve fuel in intact.

The **maximum fuel** that you can carry is full tanks, but this may limit the number of passengers or weight of baggage for that flight. It is good airmanship to know what minimum amount of fuel is required for each flight, and to ensure that you have at least this amount on board.

A reasonable **fixed reserve** for most light aircraft operations is 60 minutes, or perhaps 45 minutes, calculated at cruise rate, over and above *flight fuel*. This allows for such things as the headwinds en route being stronger than expected, a consumption rate greater than published, minor navigation errors or short diversions. The fixed reserve is usable fuel in the tanks that you should *not* plan on using; think of it as an **emergency reserve.**

While fuel is ordered from the fuel agent and shown on the gauges as a quantity (US gallons, litres, or imperial gallons), it is valuable to know how long this fuel will last in minutes, i.e. the endurance. This of course depends on the consumption rate.

For the flight from Elstree that we are planning, the consumption rate is 7 USG/hour. The flight time has been calculated as 88 minutes, and the required fixed reserve is 45 minutes.

These times can be converted to USG with a simple computer manipulation, and both the time and fuel columns added up to find the minimum fuel required in both minutes and US gallons.

CONSUMPTION RATE	7 USG/hr	
Stage	min	US gal
Route	88	
Reserve	45	
Fuel required		
Margin		
Total carried		

■ *Figure 13-16* **Beginning of the fuel calculations**

CONSUMPTION RATE	7 USG/hr	
Stage	min	US gal
Route	88 →	10.3
Reserve	45 →	5.3
Fuel required		
Margin		
Total carried		

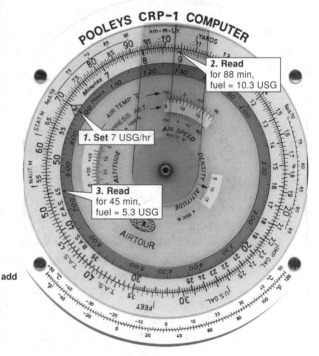

CONSUMPTION RATE	7 USG/hr	
Stage	min	US gal
Route	88	10.3
Reserve	45	5.3	add
Fuel required	133	15.6
Margin		
Total carried		

■ *Figure 13-17* **Calculating fuel required**

Any fuel above the minimum required provides a **margin.** If, for instance 25 USG is loaded, a margin of 9.4 USG over and above the minimum fuel required (15.6 USG) is available. At the consumption rate of 7 USG/hr, this converts to a margin of 80 minutes, providing a total endurance of 213 minutes. This is useful information for the pilot.

1.

CONSUMPTION RATE 7 USG/hr

Stage	min	US gal
Route	88	10.3
Reserve	45	5.3
Fuel required	133	15.6
Margin		
Total carried		25.0 ←

3.

CONSUMPTION RATE 7 USG/hr

Stage	min	US gal
Route	88	10.3
Reserve	45	5.3
Fuel required	133	15.6
Margin	80 ← 9.4	convert
Total carried		25.0

2.

CONSUMPTION RATE 7 USG/hr

Stage	min	US gal
Route	88	10.3
Reserve	45	5.3
Fuel required	133	15.6
Margin		9.4 ⟍ subtract
Total carried		25.0 ⟋

4.

CONSUMPTION RATE 7 USG/hr

Stage	min	US gal
Route	88	10.3
Reserve	45	5.3
Fuel required	133	15.6
Margin	80	9.4	add minutes
Total carried	213	25.0

■ Figure 13-18 **The main fuel calculations completed**

Sometimes you are required to plan for a flight to an alternate aerodrome if, for instance, poor weather does not allow you to land at the planned destination. For the flight from Elstree to Ipswich, with Cambridge as an alternate for Ipswich, the calculations might appear as shown. The alternate fuel is sometimes called diversion fuel.

From/To	Safety ALT	ALT / Temp	RAS	TAS	W/V	TR °T	Drift	HDG °T	Var	HDG °M	GS	Dist	Time	ETA	HDG °C
Elstree															
	1920	2400 / +10	98	102	270/30	069	–6	063	3W	066	130	60	28		
Ipswich															
Ipswich															
	1768	2400 / +10	98	102	270/30	286	–5	281	3W	284	73	40	33		
Cambridge															

■ Figure 13-19 **Cambridge, as alternate for Ipswich**

Stage	min	USG
Destination	28	3.3
Alternate	33	3.9
Flight Fuel	61	7.2
Reserve	45	5.3
Fuel Required	106	12.5

If you load a total of 17 USG, then the final fuel calculations will be:

Stage	min	USG
Destination	28	3.3
Alternate	33	3.9
Flight Fuel	61	7.2
Reserve	45	5.3
Fuel Required	106	12.5
Margin	38	4.5
Total Fuel	144	17.0

Sometimes an allowance for taxi fuel is made (say 1 USG with no time allowance), in which case the fuel table may look like:

Stage	min	USG
Destination	28	3.3
Alternate	33	3.9
Flight Fuel	61	7.2
Reserve	45	5.3
Taxi	–	**1.0**
Fuel Required	106	13.5
Margin	30	3.5
Total Fuel	136	17.0

Some operators like to carry an extra safety margin of 10%, and their fuel calculations may appear thus:

Stage	min	USG
Destination	28	3.3
Alternate	33	3.9
Flight Fuel	61	7.2
Reserve	45	5.3
Total	106	12.5
+10%	**11**	**1.3**
Taxi	–	1.0
Fuel Required	117	14.8
Margin	19	2.2
Total Fuel	136	17.0

This is becoming complicated, but, if you use the one procedure all the time, you soon get used to it.

Weight and Balance, and Performance

Before inserting the final fuel figure, it is good airmanship to consider:

☐ weight and balance; and
☐ take-off and landing performance.

The aeroplane must be loaded so that no weight limitation is exceeded, and so that the centre of gravity lies within approved limits. This is covered in Chapter 33 of Vol. 4 of *The Air Pilot's Manual*. The performance charts should be consulted if necessary to confirm that the aeroplane is able to operate from the planned runways.

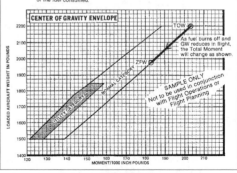

UNITED KINGDOM
SUPPLEMENT

GULFSTREAM AMERICAN
MODEL AA-5A CHEETAH

TAKEOFF DISTANCE (AA-5A United Kingdom)

Sample only
Not to be used
for operational
purposes

ASSOCIATED CONDITIONS:
POWER – MAXIMUM
FLAPS – UP
RUNWAY – HARD SURFACE (LEVEL & DRY)
FUEL MIXTURE – FULL THROTTLE CLIMB, MIXTURE LEANED ABOVE 5000 FT TO SMOOTH ENGINE OPERATION.

NOTES:
1. DECREASE DISTANCE 4% FOR EACH 5 KNOTS HEADWIND. FOR OPERATION WITH TAILWINDS UP TO 10 KNOTS, INCREASE DISTANCE BY 10% FOR EACH 2.5 KNOTS.
2. IF TAKEOFF POWER IS SET WITHOUT BRAKES APPLIED, THEN DISTANCES APPLY FROM POINT WHERE FULL POWER IS ATTAINED.
3. FOR TAKEOFF FROM A DRY, GRASS RUNWAY, INCREASE GROUND RUN AND TOTAL DISTANCE TO CLEAR A 50 FT OBSTACLE BY 12.5% OF THE HARD SURFACE RUNWAY TOTAL TO CLEAR 50 FT OBSTACLE.

WEIGHT KGS	TAKEOFF SPEED KIAS (MPH)		PRESS. ALT FT	0°C (32°F) METRES		10°C (40°F) METRES		20°C (68°F) METRES		30°C (86°F) METRES		40°C (104°F) METRES	
	LIFT OFF	CLEAR 50 FT		GND RUN	50 FT	GND RUN	50 FT	GND RUN	50 FT	GND RUN	50 FT	GND RUN	50 FT
998	56 (64)	63 (73)	SL	230	419	255	464	282	512	311	564	341	618
			2000	273	495	304	549	336	606	370	667	407	732
			4000	326	587	362	651	401	719	442	791	485	868
			6000	391	698	434	774	479	854	529	940	581	1031
			8000	469	832	520	922	575	1018	634	1120	697	1229
907	53 (61)	60 (69)	SL	183	336	203	372	224	411	247	452	272	496
			2000	218	397	241	440	267	486	294	535	323	587
			4000	260	471	288	522	319	576	351	635	386	696
			6000	311	560	345	621	382	685	420	754	462	828
			8000	373	668	414	740	458	817	504	899	554	983
816	50 (58)	57 (66)	SL	142	263	158	292	174	322	192	355	211	389
			2000	169	312	187	345	207	381	229	419	251	460
			4000	202	369	221	409	247	452	273	497	300	546
			6000	241	439	268	486	296	537	326	591	359	649
			8000	290	523	321	580	355	640	392	704	430	773

SAMPLE LOADING PROBLEM	SAMPLE AIRPLANE			YOUR AIRPLANE		
	WEIGHT (LBS.)	ARM (IN.)	MOMENT (LB.-IN. /1000)	WEIGHT (LBS.)	ARM (IN.)	MOMENT (LB.-IN. /1000)
*1. Licensed Empty Weight (Typical)	1262	83.4	105.25			
2. Oil (8 qts.) 1 qt. = 1,875 lbs.	15	32.0	.48		32.0	
3. Fuel (in excess of unuseable) Standard Tanks (37 gal.) Long Range Tanks (51 gal.)	222	90.9 94.81	20.18		90.9 94.81	
4. Pilot and Co-Pilot	340	90.6	30.80		90.6	
5. Rear Seat Passengers	340	126.0	42.84		126.0	
*6. Baggage (in baggage compartment) Max. allowable 120 lbs.	21	151.0	3.17		151.0	
7. Cargo Area Max. allowable 340 lbs.		116.4			116.4	
8. Total Airplane Weight (loaded)	2200	92.17	202.72			
9. Usable Fuel	222	90.9	20.18			
10. Zero Fuel Weight	1978		182.54			

NOTE: If desired, the **Landing Weight and CG position** can be calculated by subtracting from the Take-Off Weight values the weight and moment of the fuel consumed.

CENTER OF GRAVITY ENVELOPE

As fuel burns off and GW reduces in flight, the Total Moment will change as shown.

SAMPLE ONLY
Not to be used in conjunction with Flight Operations or Flight Planning

LOADED AIRCRAFT WEIGHT IN POUNDS

MOMENT/1000 INCH POUNDS

■ *Figure 13-20* **Consult the relevant performance charts and complete a weight and balance calculation**

Some Typical Flight Logs

From/To	Safety ALT	ALT / Temp	RAS	TAS	W/V	TR °T	Drift	HDG °T	Var	HDG °M	GS	Dist	Time	ETA	HDG °C
Elstree															
	1920	2400 / +10	98	102	270/30	069	–6	063	3W	066	130	60	28		066
Ipswich															
	1768	2400 / +10	98	102	270/30	286	–5	281	3W	284	73	40	33		285
Cambridge															
	1920	2400 / +10	98	102	270/30	208	+15	223	3W	226	84	38	27		228
Elstree															
										Total	138	88			

CONSUMPTION RATE	7 USG/hr	
Stage	**min**	**US gal**
Route	88	10.3
Reserve	45	5.3
Fuel required	133	15.6
Margin	80	9.4
Total carried	213	25.0

■ *Figure 13-21* **Completed flight log for the flight from Elstree**

From/To	Safety ALT	ALT / Temp	RAS	TAS	W/V	TR °T	Drift	HDG °T	Var	HDG °M	GS	Dist	Time	ETA	HDG °C
Staverton															
	2770	3000 / +12	90	95	250/20	056	–3	053	5W	058	114	59	31		
Desborough															
	2070	FL35 / +11	90	96	250/20	164	+12	176	4W	180	92	24	16		
Cranfield															
	2570	FL40 / +10	90	96	260/25	231	+7	238	4W	242	73	27	22		
Beckley															
	2570	FL45 / +10	90	97	260/25	299	–9	290	5W	295	76	6	5		
Kidlington															
	2690	FL45 / +10	90	97	260/25	276	–4	272	5W	277	72	31	26		
Staverton															
										Total	147	100			

CONSUMPTION RATE	8.5 USG/hr	
Stage	**min**	**US gal**
Route	100	14.2
Reserve	60	8.5
Fuel required	160	22.7
Margin	122	17.3
Total carried	282	40.0

■ *Figure 13-22* **A flight log for a flight from Staverton**

REGISTRATION			DATE	PILOT		CHOCKS OFF	CHOCKS ON	FLIGHT TIME	
G-BGWY				E. PAPE					
RUNWAY	RH	LH	QFE	QNH	QNH		W/V	VAR	DEV	TAS
24							280 / 25	5	–	90

STAGE	HEADING C	DEPT TIME	LEG TIME	ETA	RTA ATA	SAFE ALT	TRACK T	HDG T	HDG M	GS	DIST
MANCHESTER / CREWE	222		13			1600	201	217	222	82	17
CREWE / WARRINGTON	333		15			"	343	328	333	74	19
WARRINGTON / WIGAN	333		08			"	343	328	333	74	10
WIGAN / BARTON	125		06			"	116	120	125	114	12
BARTON / MANCHESTER	167		05			"	149	162	167	104	8

EMERGENCY 121.5   **CLEARANCES**

CONSPICUITY	4321
EMERGENCY	7700
RADIO FAIL	7600

SAMPLE ONLY
Not to be used in conjunction
with Flight Operations or
Flight Planning

STATION FREQUENCY	CALLSIGN TYPE	POSITION HEADING	ALTITUDE QNH	FROM TO	ESTIMATE	REQUEST
MANCHESTER TOWER 118.70						
MANCHESTER APP. 119.40						
BARTON RADIO 122.70						

CONSUMPTION		5 IGPH
STAGE	TIME	FUEL
FLIGHT	47	4
DIVERSION	30	3
CONTINGENCY	0:45	4
TOTAL		11
+ 10%		1
+ TAXI & TAKE OFF RUN		1
FUEL REQUIRED		13
TOTAL USABLE FUEL		25

■ Figure 13-23 **Flight from Manchester and return**

LEEDS – NEWCASTLE

STAGE	MSA	TR (T)	HDG (T)	VAR	HDG (M)	DIST	GS	TIME	ETA	ATA
WINDS				**RUNWAY**						
2000	*300/20*			QNH			*SAMPLE ONLY* *Not to be used in conjunction* *with Flight Operations or* *Flight Planning*			
5000				QFE						
T.A.S.	*90*			WIND						
TAKE OFF								→		
SET COURSE								→		
HARROGATE	1500	034	021	5°w	026	9	90	6		
SCOTCH CORNER	1500	349	339	5°w	344	28	76	22		
NEWCASTLE ZONE BDY	2000	358	347	5°w	352	30	78	23		
NEWCASTLE	1500	358	347	5°w	352	6	78	5		
ALTERNATE TEESSIDE	*(SEE*	*NEWCASTLE*	*– TEESSIDE*	*SHEET*	*TIME = 20*					
LANDED								→		

```
LEEMING  RADAR   132.4
TEESSIDE  TWR    119.8
          APP    118.85
NEWCASTLE  TWR   119.7
           APP   126.35
```

FUEL REQUIRED
Fuel on Board = *98 ltr*
Consumption   = *24*

	Time	Fuel
Route	*56*	*23*
Alternate	*20*	*8*
Reserve (45 min)	*–*	*18*
TOTAL		*49*

	TWR	APP	RAD	
LEEDS	120.30	123.75	121.05	**DISTRESS 121.50**

■ *Figure 13-24* **Flight log from Leeds, and return**

Planning the Climb

In the previous examples no allowance was made for the increased fuel consumption during the climb. While this is not significant for the low-level flights that have been covered, when you plan a long-range flight at a higher altitude, then, to improve the accuracy of your planning, it will be necessary to calculate fuel, time and distance on the climb and use these in your flight log.

As this is not a requirement as part of your basic PPL training, we have included it in Appendix 2, *Planning the Climb*.

Now complete **Exercises 13 – The Flight Log.**

The Flight Plan Form

The flight plan is an ATC message, compiled by or on behalf of the pilot-in-command to a set CAA format and then transmitted by the appropriate ATC authority to organisations concerned with the flight. It is the basis on which ATC clearance is given for the flight to proceed.

Correct use of the flight plan form is most important. Incorrect completion may result in a delay to processing and subsequently to the flight. Full instructions for the completion of a flight plan form are detailed in an Aeronautical Information Circular (AIC).

Note that a pilot intending to make a flight must contact ATC (or other authority where there is no ATC) at the aerodrome of departure. This is known as **booking out** and is a separate and additional requirement to that of filing a flight plan.

PPL pilots may, if they wish, file a flight plan for any flight. They are advised to file a flight plan if intending to fly more than 10 nm from the coast or over sparsely populated or mountainous areas. Flight plans must be filed for all flights:

☐ **within Class A** airspace (IFR only);
☐ **within controlled airspace** in Instrument Meteorological Conditions (IMC) or at night, excluding Special VFR (SVFR);
☐ **within controlled airspace** in Visual Meteorological Conditions (VMC) if the flight is to be conducted under the Instrument Flight Rules (IFR);
☐ **within Scottish and London** Upper Flight Information Regions (UIRs, i.e. above FL245);
☐ **where the destination** is more than 40 km from departure and the maximum total weight authorised exceeds 5,700 kg;
☐ **to or from the UK** which will cross the UK Flight Information Region (FIR) boundary;
☐ **during which** it is intended to use the Air Traffic Advisory Service.

NOTE The fact that *night flying* is conducted in accordance with IFR procedures does not, of itself, require that a flight plan be filed. Equally, IFR flight in 'open FIR', by day or night, does not of itself require a flight plan.

A flight plan should be filed at least 30 minutes before requesting taxi or start-up clearance (60 minutes in certain cases where the controlling authority is London, Manchester or Scottish Control).

If a pilot who has filed a flight plan lands at an aerodrome other than the destination specified, the Air Traffic Service Unit (ATSU) at the specified destination must be told within 30 minutes of the estimated time of arrival there.

Completing the Flight Plan Form

The pilot should fill in the appropriate white space on the flight plan form using BLOCK LETTERS, or numerals for the time in UTC and the number of persons on board. A typical flight plan could be as follows:

ITEM 7: Insert the aircraft registration, **GMEGS**, five letters with no hyphens.

ITEM 8: Insert V for **Visual Flight Rules**. Insert G for a **general aviation** type of flight.

ITEM 9: Insert, in this case, **PA28** for **type of aircraft** using four characters only, and **L** for **light**-aircraft wake-turbulence category. The first box (two spaces), labelled *number*, is left blank unless there is more than one aircraft in your group.

ITEM 10: Insert V to signify that you have **VHF** communications radio, and C for that category **transponder** for secondary surveillance radar (SSR). The letter S is used to signify **standard** radio equipment, which is considered to be VHF, ADF, VOR and ILS.

ITEM 13: Insert **EGBB** for **Birmingham** (ICAO codes for all aerodromes are listed in the UK AIP and *Pooley's Flight Guide*), and the estimated **off-block** taxiing time of 1210 UTC.

ITEM 15 AND 16: Insert **N0105** to indicate the cruising TAS in **nautical** miles per hour (kt) to the value of 0105 (i.e. TAS is 105 kt), and **A025** to indicate a **cruising altitude** of 2,500 ft amsl, and **DCT** to indicate the **direct** route with no turning points to the destination Northampton (EGBK), which is inserted in item 16, and with the total **estimated elapsed time** of 0026 (00 hours and 26 minutes). The **alternate** aerodrome nominated for Northampton is **Leicester** (EGBG).

ITEM 18: Insert 0 to indicate no other information.

(continued on page 240)

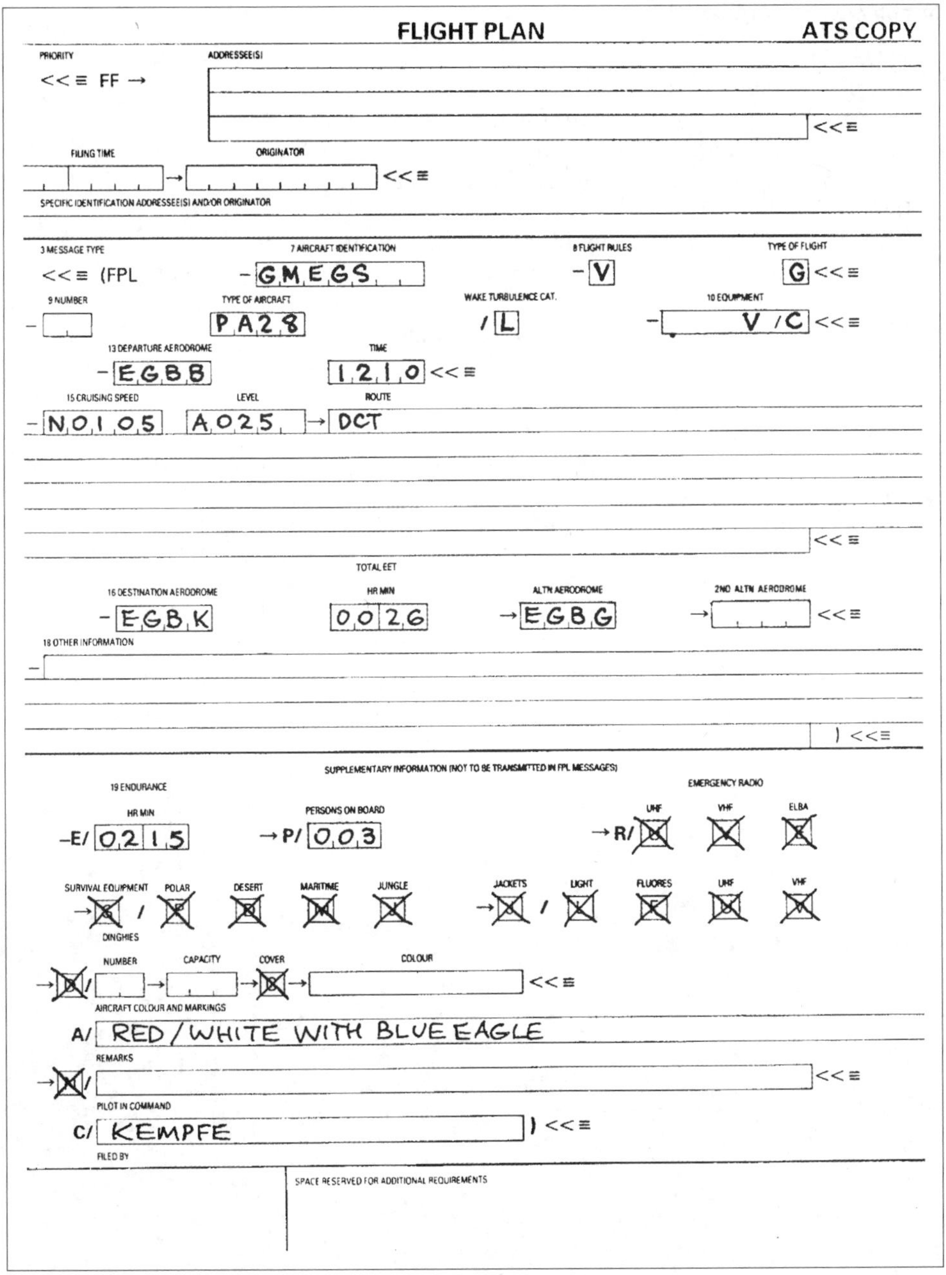

```
                                        FLIGHT PLAN                          ATS COPY
  PRIORITY              ADDRESSEE(S)
  << ≡ FF →

                                                                                    << ≡

     FILING TIME              ORIGINATOR
                          →                                    << ≡
  SPECIFIC IDENTIFICATION ADDRESSEE(S) AND/OR ORIGINATOR


  3 MESSAGE TYPE              7 AIRCRAFT IDENTIFICATION      8 FLIGHT RULES        TYPE OF FLIGHT
  << ≡ (FPL       – G M E G S            – V                 G << ≡
  9 NUMBER              TYPE OF AIRCRAFT        WAKE TURBULENCE CAT.       10 EQUIPMENT
  –              P A 2 8                / L            –          V / C << ≡
          13 DEPARTURE AERODROME         TIME
          – E G B B           1 2 1 0 << ≡
  15 CRUISING SPEED        LEVEL          ROUTE
  – N 0 1 0 5    A 0 2 5    → DCT



                                                                                    << ≡
                          TOTAL EET
  16 DESTINATION AERODROME   HR MIN         ALTN AERODROME        2ND ALTN AERODROME
  – E G B K          0 0 2 6       → E G B G       →            << ≡
  18 OTHER INFORMATION
  –



                                                                                    ) << ≡
              SUPPLEMENTARY INFORMATION (NOT TO BE TRANSMITTED IN FPL MESSAGES)
  19 ENDURANCE                                             EMERGENCY RADIO
     HR MIN            PERSONS ON BOARD            UHF     VHF    ELBA
  – E/ 0 2 1 5    → P/ 0 0 3          → R/ ⊠      ⊠     ⊠
  SURVIVAL EQUIPMENT  POLAR    DESERT  MARITIME  JUNGLE     JACKETS  LIGHT  FLUORES  UHF    VHF
  → ⊠ / ⊠    ⊠     ⊠     ⊠       → ⊠ / ⊠    ⊠     ⊠    ⊠
          DINGHIES
  NUMBER   CAPACITY   COVER         COLOUR
  → ⊠ / [   ] → [   ] → ⊠ → [           ] << ≡
  AIRCRAFT COLOUR AND MARKINGS
  A/ RED / WHITE WITH BLUE EAGLE
  REMARKS
  → ⊠ /                                               << ≡
  PILOT IN COMMAND
  C/ KEMPFE                    ) << ≡
  FILED BY
                     SPACE RESERVED FOR ADDITIONAL REQUIREMENTS
```

Figure 14-1 **Completed flight plan form**

Supplementary Information

ITEM 19:

☐ **Insert endurance** of 0215 (02 hours 15 minutes), and **003** to indicate **three persons on board** (pilot plus two passengers).

☐ **No emergency radio** is carried, so each of these is struck out, as for the survival equipment, none of which is in this particular aeroplane.

☐ **The aircraft's colour and markings** are a distinctive red and white, with a blue eagle on the rear fuselage, so insert these details.

☐ **No further remarks** concerning survival equipment or matters of importance in a search and rescue situation, so strike out the N.

☐ Insert the pilot-in-command's **name.**

For rules to follow in filling in the flight plan correctly refer to the AICs (Aeronautical Information Circulars), AIP and General Aviation Safety Sense leaflet no. 20, *VFR Flight Plans*.

Now complete **Exercises 14 – The Flight Plan.**

Section **Three**

En Route Navigation

En Route Navigation Techniques

Deduced Reckoning

Deduced reckoning is the primary means of visual cross-coun-try navigation. It is commonly known as dead reckoning (DR). It is based on:

☐ **starting** at a known position (called a fix);

☐ **measuring** the track and distance on a chart to the next point chosen along the desired track;

☐ **applying** the best estimate of wind velocity available to deter-mine: the **heading** to steer to achieve the desired track; and the **groundspeed** to find estimated time of arrival over that next point.

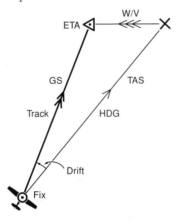

■ *Figure 15-1* **Dead reckoning is the fundamental method of navigating visually. The angle between heading (HDG) and track (TR) is the aircraft's drift.**

Dead reckoning navigation, where the pilot flies the estimated heading for the estimated time interval (both calculated when flight planning), should bring the aeroplane over the next check-point at the appointed time.

Map-reading is used as a backup to dead reckoning. This ena-bles the pilot to pinpoint the aeroplane's position (obtain a fix) over some ground feature en route and evaluate the success of the dead reckoning navigation.

> A **fix** is the geographical position of an aircraft at a specific time, determined by visual reference to the surface of the earth, or by radio navigation equipment.

> A **pinpoint** is the ground position of an aircraft at a specific time
> determined by direct observation of the ground (not by radio navigation
> equipment).

Fixing the aircraft's position is not a continuous process second-by-second throughout the flight, but rather a regular process repeated every 10 or 15 minutes. (This may need to be reduced to 5 minutes or so in areas requiring precise tracking like Entry/Exit Lanes, see Chapter 17.) If you try to identify ground features to obtain a fix at shorter time intervals than this, then you may find yourself just flying from feature to feature without any time being available for the other important navigation tasks, such as planning ahead and monitoring the fuel situation.

For normal en route navigation you should:
- ☐ **fly accurate headings** (by reference to the heading indicator and the ground); and
- ☐ **periodically identify landmarks.**

Unfortunately it is generally the case that the actual track made good (TMG) is not precisely the desired track (or planned track). The difference between the desired track and the actual TMG is known as the **track error** (TE).

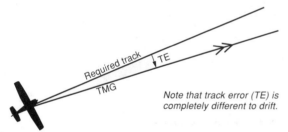

Note that track error (TE) is
completely different to drift.

■ *Figure 15-2* **Track error is the angular difference between required track and track made good**

Wind Effect

Most of the calculations in dead reckoning (DR) navigation are to compensate for wind effect, so if the wind differs in either speed or direction from the expected wind, then a track error will probably result.

Accurate tracking involves compensating for wind effect.

If we assume that there is no wind, then the aeroplane will end up at what we call its **air position** (symbolised by a cross), i.e. its position relative to the air mass.

The wind effect will blow the aeroplane to its **ground position** (symbolised by a small circle), i.e. its position relative to the ground – and this is what we are really interested in.

If we can actually fix or pinpoint the ground position of the aircraft by reference to features on the earth's surface, then we symbolise this on our chart with a small circle.

If this is not possible, we can determine a **DR position** by plotting the calculated track and distance flown since the last fix, and mark this point on our chart as a small triangle.

$+$ $\odot$ $\triangle$
Air position   Ground position   DR position

■ Figure 15-3 **Navigation symbols**

At the flight planning stage, a *forecast* wind was used to calculate a heading for the aeroplane to make good a desired track. This wind will almost certainly not be precisely the same as the actual wind that is experienced in flight. This means that the actual drift in flight (the angle between heading and track made good) will most likely differ from that expected, to a greater or lesser extent.

Also, whether the track made good (TMG) is left or right of the desired track will depend on whether we have allowed too little, or too much, **drift** to counteract the crosswind effect.

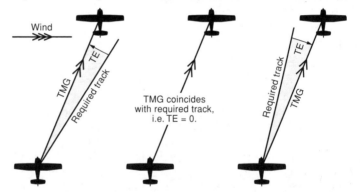

■ Figure 15-4 **Track error results if we allow too little or too much drift**

En route we can counteract a track error by modifying the heading to achieve more accurate DR navigation for the remainder of the flight.

It is also usual to find that the actual in-flight groundspeed (GS) differs from that expected at the flight-planning stage, when all we had at hand was the forecast winds rather than the actual winds that we are experiencing in flight. This means that the original estimated time intervals (ETIs) to cover certain distances will be somewhat in error and will need to be modified once an accurate in-flight check of groundspeed (GS) is obtained. The estimated time of arrival at any point can then be revised.

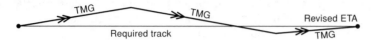

Figure 15-5 _In-flight modification of HDGs and ETIs is usual in dead reckoning navigation_

The most important way to keep in-flight navigation workload to a minimum is to be thorough in your pre-flight preparation (flight planning). For in-flight navigation, concentrate on:

☐ **simple mental calculations;** and
☐ **simple computer operations.**

Flight plan thoroughly.

This will allow you to modify the headings and estimated time intervals (ETIs) calculated at the flight-planning stage without too much 'head-down' work, and the methods that we discuss here will be adequate for most situations.

NOTE Remember that track error and drift are two different things and should never be confused.

Airmanship for the Pilot/Navigator

Airmanship is common sense. Do not become over-engrossed in navigation; as pilot of the aeroplane you are responsible for a safe flightpath.

FLY ACCURATELY. Fly the aeroplane reasonably accurately at all times (heading ±5°; altitude ±100 ft; indicated airspeed ±5 kt). Even though you are looking out of the cockpit most of the time to monitor the altitude and heading of the aircraft, and to check for other traffic, you should periodically check the flight instruments to achieve precise heading, airspeed and altitude.

Setting the correct power and holding the attitude will result in the required performance in general terms but, to fly precisely, you will need to refer to the flight instruments and make suitable minor adjustments to the attitude and the power. This means a quick look at the relevant flight instruments every 10 seconds or so throughout the flight.

Scanning the essential instruments in flight quickly and often is an important skill to develop. A good pilot has a fast scan rate, which is necessary for accurate flying.

LOOKOUT. Keep your paperwork in the cockpit neat and accessible – do not work 'head-down' for more than a few seconds at a time, and keep a good lookout!

Keep a good lookout!

TRIM. Ensure that the aeroplane is in trim, and can fly itself accurately 'hands-off'; not that you will actually fly it hands-off, but correct trimming will considerably lighten your task of maintaining height and heading. Check that the IAS used in your calculations is within 5 kt of that actually being flown, and that the altitude is within 100 ft; if not, do something about it by adjusting power and attitude.

CHECK WEATHER. Continually observe weather conditions, not only ahead of you, but also to either side and behind (just in case you have to beat a hasty retreat). You must assess any deterioration in weather and modify your flight accordingly. Ask Flight Information Service (FIS) or Air Traffic Control (ATC) for an update on the weather en route and at your destination aerodrome if necessary. Their function is to provide a service to pilots.

AVOID HAZARDOUS CONDITIONS. Take appropriate action to avoid hazardous conditions. For instance, it is good airmanship to divert around thunderstorms instead of flying near or under them, and to avoid areas of fog and reduced visibility. Also avoid dense smoke from fires because the visibility will be reduced and the air turbulent.

CHECK POSITION. Obtain a position fix every 10 or 15 minutes if possible and update your headings and ETAs (more frequently in poor visibility and/or congested airspace, e.g. every 5 minutes).

CHECK INSTRUMENTS. Carry out regular en route checks of the:
- **magnetic compass** and heading indicator alignment;
- **engine instruments;**
- **electrical and other systems.**

This en route check can be remembered by the mnemonic FREDA:

FREDA	
F	**Fuel:** on and sufficient; **Fuel tank:** usage monitored; **Mixture:** leaned as required for the cruise; **Fuel pump:** (if fitted), as required.
R	**Radio:** frequency correctly selected, volume and squelch satisfactory; any required calls made.
E	**Engine:** oil temperature and pressure within limits; carburettor heat if required; other systems checked, e.g. the electrical system, suction (if vacuum-driven gyroscopes are fitted);
D	**Direction indicator:** (direction indicator or directional gyro) aligned with the magnetic compass, and your position checked on the map.
A	**Altitude** checked and subscale setting correct (usually Regional QNH).

CHECK TIME. Maintain a time awareness, particularly with respect to fuel and latest time of arrival.

The Flight Sequence

Departure from an Aerodrome

For a trainee pilot, the simplest method of departure is to set heading from directly over the top of the field at cruise speed and at the cruising altitude. Since most VFR cross-country flights in the UK occur at 3,000 ft amsl or below, the appropriate altimeter setting for cruising is the Regional QNH.

The actual method of departing an aerodrome will depend on the circuit direction, and the nature of the aerodrome and surrounding terrain. Information on the particular aerodrome may be found in the UK AIP or in *Pooley's Flight Guide.*

Many aerodromes have no restrictions placed on them, but this is not always the case. For instance, a number of aerodromes lie within the control zones and under the control areas surrounding major airports, and have access lanes for VFR flights which must be adhered to. Obviously if you are navigating to or from one of these aerodromes, you must plan your departure or arrival via one of the points where the access lane leaves or joins the control area. These are indicated on aeronautical charts with an E/E symbol, with the name of the aerodrome. Other aerodromes may have local restrictions due to heavy traffic, high terrain or nearby built-up areas calling for special departure or arrival procedures.

If you depart via an Entry/Exit Access Lane, or by any means other than departing from over the top, then a simple calculation of actual time of departure (ATD) needs to be made. Your en route estimated times of arrival (ETAs) will be based on this (at least initially, until groundspeed checks allow you to update them).

We will consider two possible methods of departing on a track of, for example, 150°M from an aerodrome where the runway in use is Runway 06 and the circuits are left-handed. Assume aerodrome elevation to be 1,200 ft amsl.

Since your compass will be experiencing acceleration and turning errors while setting course, ensure that the gyroscopic heading indicator is aligned with the magnetic compass prior to commencing your take-off roll, and ensure that both the compass and the HI agree at least approximately with the runway direction.

Method 1. Turning in the Direction of the Circuit

After take-off, climb out to 500 ft aal (500 ft on QFE, or 1,700 ft on QNH) and turn left in the direction of the circuit. Continue left turns in the circuit direction and set course overhead the field at a height of at least 1,000 ft aal and climbing clear of the circuit (i.e. 2,200 ft on QNH in this case).

Log the actual time of departure (ATD) in the appropriate place on the flight log. The ATD will be your time of setting course overhead the aerodrome.

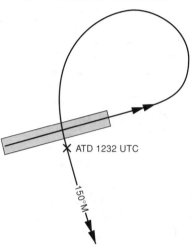

■ *Figure 15-6* **Method 1. Setting course overhead**

Method 2. Climbing Straight Ahead

In this case you will not set course overhead the field, so once you have joined track you will need to estimate your actual time of departure (ATD) as if you had set course from directly overhead. A groundspeed of 120 kt is equivalent to 2 nm per minute, so if you set course at say 4 nm from the aerodrome at time 1234 UTC and your estimated GS is about 120 kt, the ATD would be 2 minutes prior to this at 1232 UTC.

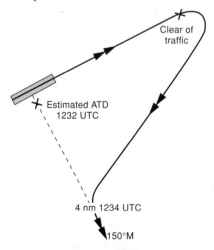

■ *Figure 15-7* **Method 2. Setting course en route and calculating ATD**

If there is a laid down departure route via a specific point, then you can log your time of departure from that point. The main purpose is to have a starting point in time for your en route time calculations (although remember that fuel is being burned from the moment the engine starts).

This second method can be used whenever you intercept track rather than setting course from over the top.

Immediately after setting heading and becoming established on track, you would:

☐ **log the actual time of departure** (ATD) and insert the estimate overhead the first checkpoint, based on the ATD and the flight-planned estimated time interval);

☐ **make a departure report** by radio if required (frequencies are shown on the aeronautical charts).

NOTE The terms estimate and estimated time of arrival (ETA) are used loosely to mean the same thing, i.e. the time of arrival overhead, although in a strict sense ETA applies only to the aerodrome of intended landing.

Rough Check of Departure Track

On departure you should have in mind some ground feature en route that is within 10 or 15 nm of the aerodrome, against which you can check that you indeed are departing in approximately the right direction.

EXAMPLE 1 After take-off from an aerodrome and taking up the calculated heading to achieve your desired track of say 150°T, you should pass slightly left of a large lake at about 8 nm from the aerodrome. To confirm that it is the correct lake, your charts show a large hill and radio mast on its north-west side, so use these to confirm identification of it.

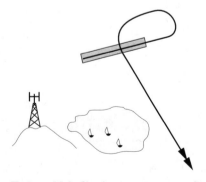

■ Figure 15-8 **Check approximate tracking direction soon after departure**

You should ensure within the first few minutes that you are making good the correct track. If you are in any doubt, check the heading indicator against the magnetic compass. For accuracy, apply the deviation correction found on the card in the cockpit to amend °M to °C.

Set Heading on Departure Visually

If you do not overfly the aerodrome to set heading, then prior to take-off note some features directly on track from the aerodrome and within 5 or 10 nm of it, and then make sure you track over them. You can do this sometimes just prior to take-off by looking in the direction that you intend tracking; otherwise have some feature or checkpoint selected from the chart as in Figure 15-8.

Once clear of the circuit area, aerodrome QFE is of little value, so QNH should be set so that the altimeter reads height above mean sea level and gives you guidance on terrain clearance.

Cruise

On reaching the cruise level you should ensure that Regional QNH is set. If you are cruising above the usual UK transition altitude of 3,000 ft, it may be good airmanship to cruise at a flight level (based on 1013 mb rather than QNH), the same as all the IFR traffic will be doing.

Establish cruise speed and cruise power and trim the aeroplane. Scan all the vital instruments and systems for correct operation. Verify that the gyroscopic HI is aligned with the magnetic compass. It may be a good time to do a full FREHA en route check.

It is good airmanship to check straight away that you are achieving the desired true airspeed (TAS) on the cruise. This may be completed quickly by:

☐ **computer** (by setting pressure altitude against temperature, and reading off TAS on the outer scale against IAS on the inner); or

☐ **approximation** (at 5,000 ft TAS is about 8% greater than IAS, and at 10,000 ft TAS is about 17% greater than IAS);

☐ **setting** the adjustable temp/TAS scale, if fitted on your ASI, so that, as well as reading IAS on one scale, the other scale indicates TAS. This is a feature found on some airspeed indicators in general aviation aeroplanes. It is a scale similar to that on your navigation computer where, by setting pressure altitude against true outside temperature, TAS can be read off against IAS, at least in the cruising range. (See Chapter 2.)

If the achieved TAS is significantly different to that expected then you should check:

☐ **correct power set;**

☐ **correct aircraft configuration** – flaps up, landing gear up (if appropriate), position of cowl flaps.

From two position fixes separated by about 20 to 30 nm, you should be able to establish an accurate groundspeed and determine if your heading is achieving the desired track or not. (Naturally, if you are about to fly over featureless terrain or water, where position fixing will be difficult, there is nothing to stop you using fixes obtained on the climb. Good airmanship is common sense.)

As soon as possible on the cruise obtain a groundspeed check.

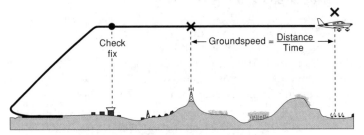

■ *Figure 15-9* **Check groundspeed and track early in the cruise**

If the actual GS is significantly different to that expected at the flight-planning stage, then you will have to revise your ETAs. If the track made good (TMG) differs significantly from the desired track, then you will have to make a HDG change. Make use of the best available information to estimate a suitable heading.

To obtain good fixes you need to select suitable check features and make use of your map-reading skills.

Map-Reading In Flight

The success of map-reading depends on:
- ☐ **Knowledge** of direction, distance and groundspeed.
- ☐ **Selection** and identification of landmarks and check features.

Select good checkpoint features

Landmarks and checkpoints that can be easily identified, which will be within your range of visibility when you pass by them, are best. Just how conspicuous a particular feature may be from the air depends on the:
- ☐ **flight visibility;**
- ☐ **dimensions** of the feature;
- ☐ **relationship** of your selected feature to other features;
- ☐ **angle** of observation;
- ☐ **plan outline** of the feature if you are flying high;
- ☐ **elevation** and side appearance of the feature if you are flying low.

Preferably the feature should be unique in that vicinity so that it cannot be confused with another nearby similar feature. A feature that is long in one dimension and quite sharply defined in another is often useful, because:
- ☐ **if a long feature** (such as a railway line, canal or road) runs parallel to track, it can assist in maintaining an accurate track; and

■ **if a long feature** crosses the track it can be used as a position line to aid in determining an updated groundspeed (GS).

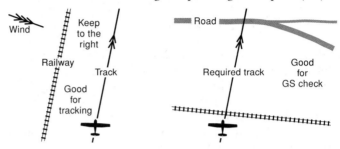

■ *Figure 15-10* **Long, narrow features are particularly useful**

NOTE Remember, when tracking along line features, stay to the right (i.e. keep the line feature on your left where you can best see it out of the captain's seat). Aircraft flying along the same line feature, but in the opposite direction, should be doing the same, thereby minimising collision risk.

The relationship between your selected feature and other nearby ground features is important for a positive confirmation of your position. For example, there may be two small towns near each other, but you have chosen as a feature the one that has a single-track railway line to the west of the town and with a road that crosses a river on the north side of the town, whereas the other town has none of these features. This should make positive identification fairly easy.

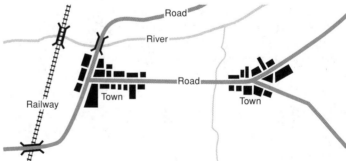

■ *Figure 15-11* **Confirm identification of your selected feature by its relationship with other features**

'Position Lines' Can Be Useful

A position fix is obtained when you can positively identify the position of the aeroplane relative to the ground. A position line is not as specific as a fix because you can only identify the position of the aeroplane as being somewhere along that line, and not actually fixed at a particular point.

> A **position line** is an extended straight line joining two points, somewhere along which the aeroplane was located at a particular time.

You may see a position line referred to as a PL, LoP or a *line of position*. Position lines can be obtained:

- ☐ **from long narrow features** such as railway lines, roads, motorways, coastlines;
- ☐ **from two features** that line up as the aeroplane passes them (known as 'transit bearings');
- ☐ **from magnetic bearings** to (and from) a feature (this need not only be visual, it can also be a radio position line, i.e. a magnetic bearing from an NDB or VOR).

■ *Figure 15-12* **Each of these aeroplanes is on the same position line**

It is usual to show a position line on your map as a straight line with an arrow at either end, and with the time written in UTC at one end.

Ground features   1314 UTC

■ *Figure 15-13* **Marking a position line**

Of course, if you can obtain two position lines that cut at a reasonable angle, then you can obtain a good position fix. For the aeroplane to be on both position lines at the one time, it must be at the point of intersection.

Road

Railway

■ *Figure 15-14* **Two position lines with a good cut can give you a fix**

Select Good Features 10 or 15 Minutes Apart

Do not choose a multitude of landmarks and checkpoints. Just one good checkpoint every 10 or 15 minutes is sufficient. At a groundspeed (GS) of 120 kt, this puts them 20 to 30 nm apart.

Look for a definite feature at a definite time. Choose a unique feature to avoid ambiguity.

Knowing direction, distance and groundspeed, you can think ahead, and anticipate the appearance of a landmark. This anticipation allows time for:

☐ **flying the aeroplane** (HDG, height, airspeed, engine, systems, checking HI against compass); and

☐ **navigation tasks** such as performing simple calculations (estimating new headings, revising ETAs, checking fuel) and then keeping an eye out for the next checkpoint; and then

☐ **looking ahead** at the appropriate time for the checkpoint which should be coming into view.

EXAMPLE 2 From the chart, you choose a small hill with a radio mast as a suitable checkpoint about 4 nm right of the desired track and about 20 nm ahead. The GS is 120 kt, so the 20 nm over the ground should be covered in 10 minutes.

If the present time is 1529 UTC, the estimated time interval (ETI) of 10 minutes gives an estimate at, or abeam, the checkpoint at 1539 UTC. You will, of course, be keeping an eye out for it for some minutes prior to this.

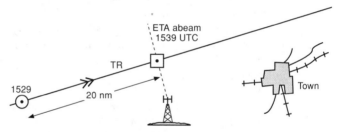

■ *Figure 15-15* **Look for a definite feature at a definite time**

If, instead of passing 4 nm abeam of the feature as expected, the aeroplane passes directly overhead, you recognise from the fix that you are off-track. Confirm that the feature is indeed the selected feature and not another nearby similar one. This can be done by checking the surrounding area for additional ground detail, say a small nearby town with a railway junction, and relating it to the whole picture.

Map-reading is used to assist dead reckoning navigation, not as a replacement for it.

Once certain that you have fixed the position of the aeroplane at a particular time, you can calculate very simply a new heading to achieve the desired track. Two easy ways to do this are by using track guides (or fan lines) already marked on the map by you at the flight-planning stage, or by using the '1-in-60 rule' (to be discussed shortly).

Chart Orientation in the Cockpit

In flight, you must relate land features and their relative bearing from the aircraft to their representations on the chart. To do this it is best to fold the chart so that your desired track is 'up the map'.

If, according to the chart, a landmark is 30° off the track to the right from the present position of the aeroplane, then you should be able to spot it by looking out the aircraft window approximately 30° to the right of track. (Note that it may not be 30° to the right of the heading of the aeroplane because the heading may differ from the track, depending on wind velocity.)

■ *Figure 15-16* **Orientate the chart in the cockpit**

With the chart oriented correctly in the cockpit, the features shown to the right of the track drawn on the map will appear on the right of the aircraft's track as you fly along (hopefully). The only disadvantage is that it may be difficult to read what is printed on the chart, unless you happen to be flying north.

In normal medium-level en route navigation, read from the map to the ground. This means, from the chart select a suitable feature some 10 minutes or so ahead of your present position, calculate an ETA at, or abeam, it and then at the appropriate time (some two or three minutes before the ETA) start looking for the actual feature on the ground. Your chosen landmark need not be in view at the time you choose it, but you should anticipate it coming into view at the appropriate time.

Read from map to ground.

Log Keeping

The purpose of keeping an in-flight log is to record sufficient data:
- ☐ to enable you to **determine your position** at any time by DR;
- ☐ to have readily at hand the **information required** for radio position reporting.

Logged data is invaluable if you are uncertain of the aircraft's position.

Keeping an in-flight log, however simple, helps the methodical navigation sequence:
- ☐ **calculation of HDG** to achieve a desired TR;
- ☐ **calculation of GS and ETI** to determine ETA at the next checkpoint;
- ☐ **anticipation and recognition** of checkpoints;
- ☐ **recalculation of HDG, GS and ETIs** if necessary (and the cycle repeats).

An in-flight log need only be very basic. On a normal cross-country flight you should log:

- ☐ **take-off time** on the flight log;
- ☐ **actual time of departure** (ATD) on the flight log;
- ☐ **fixes** (position and time) on the chart;
- ☐ **track made good** (TMG) on the chart;
- ☐ **changes of HDG** (and airspeed), and time of making them;
- ☐ **calculated GS;**
- ☐ **ETIs and revised ETAs** at the checkpoints;
- ☐ **altitudes.**

This sounds like a lot, but it isn't. Indicating TMG and fixes on the chart simplifies things for you, as these cover the two fundamentals of your progress towards your destination.

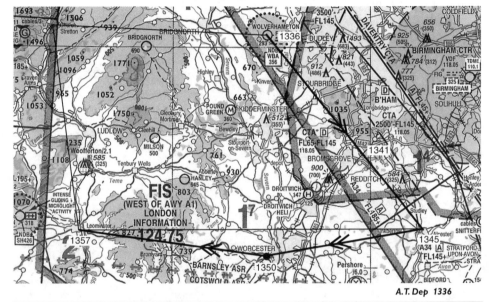

A.T. Dep **1336**

From/To	Safety	ALT	RAS	TAS	W/V	TR	Drift	HDG	Var	HDG	GS	Dist	Time	ETA	HDG
	ALT	Temp				°T		°T		°M					°C
Halfpenny Green	2035	2500	105	106	L&V	141	–	141	4W	145	96	23	13	1349	
Alcester		–5													
Alcester	1904	FL45	104	108	L&V	271	–	271	4W	275	97	32	18		
Leominster		–10													
Leominster	2697	FL45	104	108	L&V	352	–	352	4W	356	97	19	10		
Church Stretton		–10													
Church Stretton	2697	2800	105	106	L&V	099	–	093	4W	099	96	20	11		
Wolver-hampton		–5													
											Total	**94**	**52**		

■ Figure 15-17 **Keeping a log**

Using Position Lines for Groundspeed Checks

You should continually update your groundspeed (GS) as the opportunities arise. Time is of vital importance in navigation and your time of arrival anywhere will depend on the GS that you achieve.

Position lines that are approximately at right angles to your track can assist in updating your GS. Noting the amount of time it takes to cover the distance between the two position lines allows you to calculate the GS.

EXAMPLE 3

1351 UTC: Crossing a railway line perpendicular (at right angles) to track.

1359 UTC: Transit bearing of a radio mast and a bend in a river perpendicular to track 18 nm further on.

18 nm in 8 minutes = GS 135 kt.

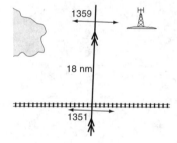

■ *Figure 15-18* **Groundspeed check using position lines perpendicular to track**

These position lines need not only be visual. You could also make use of radio position lines from an abeam NDB or VOR radio navigation station.

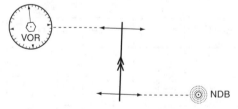

■ *Figure 15-19* **Groundspeed check using radio position lines from abeam radio navigation beacons (NDBs and VORs)**

NOTE As the use of radio beacons for navigation and position fixing is now part of the 'basic–PPL' syllabus, we have included some examples to show that basic navigation techniques are the same no matter where the information comes from. Experienced pilots always use a mix of information sources so as not to get caught out if one source suddenly ceases to be available during the flight. Radio navigation is covered in the final chapter of this book and in Vol. 5 of *The Air Pilot's Manual* series.

You can also carry out simple GS checks using *distance measuring equipment* (DME) radio navaid stations directly on track, either ahead or behind.

EXAMPLE 4

1325 UTC: DTY DME 67 nm and tracking directly towards Daventry DME.

1331 UTC: DTY DME 60 and tracking directly towards Daventry DME.

7 nm in 6 minutes = GS 70

■ *Figure 15-20* **GS check using DME**

Using Position Lines for Estimating Drift

If you have a position line roughly parallel to track you can use it to estimate the drift angle. Tracking directly overhead a long straight railway line makes a visual estimate of your drift angle quite easy, as does tracking along a radio position line to (or from) an NDB or VOR radio navaid station.

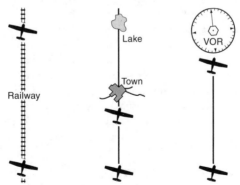

■ *Figure 15-21* **Determining drift angle from position lines parallel to track**

Now complete **Exercises 15 – En Route Nav Techniques-1.**

Off-Track Heading Corrections

It is usual to find that the actual track made good (TMG) over the ground differs from the desired track that you plotted on the chart at the flight-planning stage. If this is the case, then you will have to make some precise corrections to the HDG so that you can return to track at some point further on.

Since the in-flight workload for the pilot/navigator can be quite high, we will concentrate on quick methods of mentally calculating track corrections.

1. The angle between the track made good (TMG) and the required track is called **track error** (TE).

2. The angle at which you want to close on your required track is known as the **closing angle** (CA). The size of the CA will depend on how much further down the track you wish to rejoin it – obviously the sooner you want to rejoin the desired track the greater the CA will have to be.

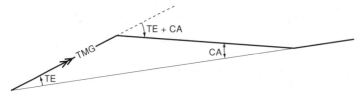

■ *Figure 15-22* **Track error and closing angle**

Figure 15–22 shows that to rejoin the desired track at the chosen position, a track change equal to TE + CA is required. (This makes use of a theorem of geometry you may remember from school which says 'the external angle of a triangle equals the sum of the two interior opposite angles'.)

It is at the point that we make an approximation that simplifies our in-flight calculations. We assume that a track change of, say, 15° can be achieved by a heading change of the same 15°. This is not perfectly accurate because the effect of the wind may cause a different drift angle after making a significant heading change, but within limits it is accurate enough for visual navigation.

> *For angles up to about 15°, assume that a track change can be achieved by an equal heading change.*

The main advantage in doing this is that it allows us to make track corrections without having to calculate the actual wind velocity.

Methods of Estimating Correction Angle

Track Guides

With track guides (or fan lines) already drawn on the chart at the flight planning stage and emanating from certain checkpoints along the route, the estimation of track error (TE) and closing angle (CA) to regain track at that next checkpoint is made easy.

After obtaining a fix, you can estimate TE and CA, which, when added together, will give you the required track change (and the required heading change) to close track at the next checkpoint.

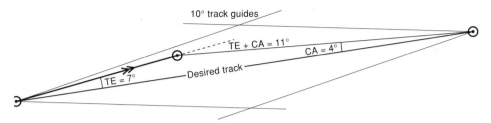

■ Figure 15-23 **Track correction using 'track guides' (or 'fan lines')**

An advantage is that you do not have to measure distance off-track, although this is in fact quite simple to do. A disadvantage is that you must have passed over the point from which the track guides emanate behind and you will rejoin track at the point ahead to which the track guides close. Sometimes this is not the situation and other methods need to be employed.

If 5° and 10° track guides (just 10° adequate if short stage) are drawn either side of your desired track on your map, then estimation of track error in flight becomes easy.

The 1-in-60 Rule

The 1-in-60 rule can be used to estimate correction angle. This is the most useful method of regaining track for VFR pilots. Time spent understanding this method now will make your en route navigation tasks much easier in future. The 1-in-60 rule is based on the fact that:

> *1 nm subtends an angle of 1° at a distance of 60 nm.*

This statement can be extended to say that:

> *5 nm subtends an angle of 5° at 60 nm.*
> *10 nm subtends an angle of 10° at 60 nm.*
> *15 nm subtends an angle of 15° at 60 nm.*

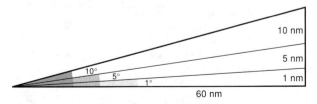

■ Figure 15-24 **The 1-in-60 rule**

We cannot always wait until we have flown 60 nm to find our distance off-track, but that is of no concern because it is *ratios* that we are interested in.

EXAMPLE 5 4 nm off-track in 30 nm distance run is the same as:

8 nm off -track in 60 nm, i.e. a track error of 8°.

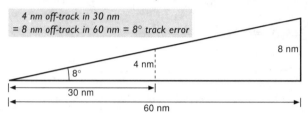

4 nm off-track in 30 nm
= 8 nm off-track in 60 nm = 8° track error

8 nm

4 nm

8°

30 nm

60 nm

■ *Figure 15-25* **Example 5**

To find TE by computer

distance off-track
4

30
distance run

TE angle

60

i.e. a simple ratio

$$\frac{4}{30} = \frac{TE\ angle}{60}$$

■ *Figure 15-26* **The ratios set up on the calculator side**

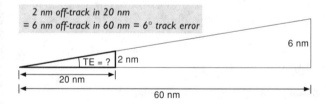

2 nm off-track in 20 nm
= 6 nm off-track in 60 nm = 6° track error

6 nm

TE = ? | 2 nm

20 nm

60 nm

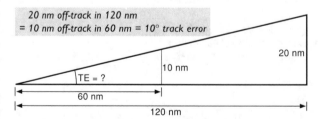

20 nm off-track in 120 nm
= 10 nm off-track in 60 nm = 10° track error

20 nm

10 nm

TE = ?

60 nm

120 nm

■ *Figure 15-27* **Determining track error using the 1-in-60 rule – solve mentally or by flight computer**

Now complete **Exercises 15 – En Route Nav Techniques-2.**

Knowing the Track Error, We Can Parallel Desired Track

If we change our TR by the amount of the calculated track error, we will *parallel track*. (We can do this approximately by changing our HDG by this number of degrees – accurate enough for angles up to 15°.)

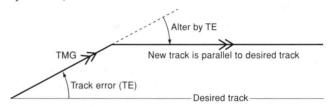

■ *Figure 15-28* **Paralleling track by altering HDG by the angle of TE**

The same 1-in-60 rule can be applied to the closing angle (CA) once we have chosen the point at which we wish to rejoin track.

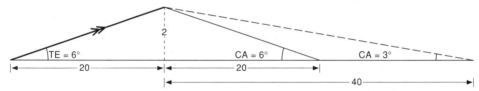

■ *Figure 15-29* **Calculating closing angle by the 1-in-60 rule**

Now, knowing both track error (TE) and closing angle (CA) allows you to make a **heading change** (TE + CA) that should change your track by the same amount.

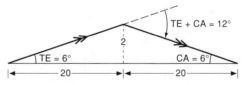

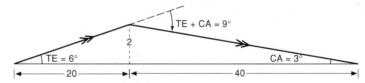

■ *Figure 15-30* **Changing HDG (and TR) by 'TE + CA' to rejoin desired track**

Notice that to regain track at a distance ahead *equal* to the distance already travelled you can simply change heading by *double* the track error (because in this case the closing angle will equal the track error). If you had determined your track error at the halfway point, then this method would bring you back on-track at the next checkpoint.

This is also a convenient method of regaining track if you have to make a diversion, say around a thunderstorm en route. Turn a suitable angle off-track for so many minutes, and then turn back double that angle for the same number of minutes, and you should find yourself roughly back on track (depending on wind effect).

This is an extremely important means of DR navigation for you to understand so we will do a few sample problems.

EXAMPLE 6 After flying 25 nm on a HDG of 085°M, you find yourself 4 nm left of track. What should be your new heading to regain track 25 nm further on?

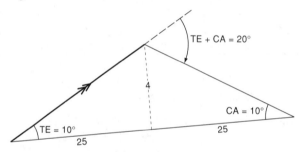

■ *Figure 15-31* **Example 6**

4 nm left of track in 25 nm = TE 10° left.
To close 4 nm in a further 25 nm = CA 10°.
Thus we need to change heading 20° to the right, i.e. to 105°M.

EXAMPLE 7 After 40 nm on HDG 320°M we find ourselves right of track by 4 nm. What heading should we steer to regain track in a further 20 nm?

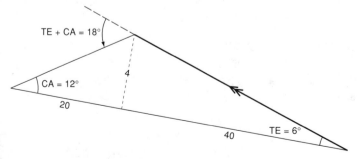

■ *Figure 15-32* **Example 7**

4 nm in 40 = 6 in 60 = 6° TE to the right.
4 nm in 20 = 12 in 60 = 12° CA.
Therefore change heading 18° to the left, i.e. to 302°M.

Now complete **Exercises 15 – En Route Nav Techniques-3.**

EXAMPLE 8 We obtain a fix 6 nm right of track, and 30 nm further on find ourselves 10 nm right of track after flying a steady heading of 065°M. Determine the heading to steer to regain track 40 nm further on.

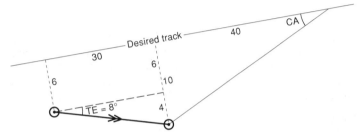

■ *Figure 15-33* **1-in-60 rule, Example 8**

We only have sufficient information to determine the TMG between the two fixes. To find the track error we will have to relate it, not to the desired track itself, but to a line parallel to the desired track.

TE = 4 nm in 30 = 8 in 60 = 8°
CA = 10 nm in 40 nm =15 in 60 = 15°.

Therefore to regain track 40 nm further on we need to change heading by 23° to the left, i.e. to 042°M.

EXAMPLE 9 We obtain a fix 3 nm left of flight planned track (FPT) and take up heading 080°M to rejoin FPT after 50 nm. 20 nm further on, we obtain a second fix 2 nm right of FPT and immediately change heading to rejoin FPT at the 50 nm point (which is now obviously only 30 nm further on). Calculate the new heading.

Since we have no information regarding the tracking of the aeroplane prior to the first fix, we can only be sure of the track made good (TMG) between the two fixes. The track, and therefore the heading, will have to change by an amount equal to TE + CA.

NOTE By definition, track error (TE) is the difference between desired track and TMG, i.e. the angle between FPT and the TMG between the two fixes.

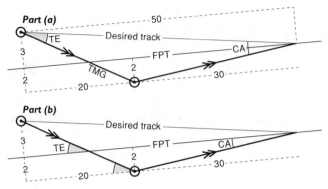

■ *Figure 15-34* **Example 9**

The CA shown in part (a) of Figure 15-34 is the usual closing angle – in this case between desired track from the first fix and desired track from the second fix. The CA shown in part (b) is a different angle – between original FPT and desired track from the second fix.

The sum of TE + CA from part (a) is the same as the sum of TE + CA from part (b). The latter method, part (b), is used in this example because of its simplicity.

Working:

TE = 5 nm in 20 = 15°. CA = 2 nm in 30 = 4°.

Therefore to rejoin track at the desired point we need to alter heading by 19° to the left (to port), i.e. to 061°M.

Now complete **Exercises 15 – En Route Nav Techniques-4.**

The Ratio Method for Estimating Track Corrections

The following rules of thumb, based on the 1-in-60 rule, can help in rapidly estimating closing angles.

☐ **To regain track in the same distance** (or time) since you were last on-track, change heading by double the track error (because the CA will be equal to the TE).

☐ **To regain track in double the distance** that it took you to get off-track, then the CA will be equal to only one-half the TE.

☐ **To regain track in only half the distance** that it took you to get off-track, then the CA will be double the TE.

Figure 15-35 illustrates the **ratio method** of using the 1-in-60 rule.

To regain track after running an equal distance:
1. Alter HDG by TE + CA, i.e. 2 × 8° = 16°
2. Fly for the same time.
3. Alter HDG by the 8°.

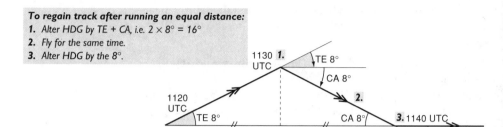

To regain track at a point further along the intended route:
1. Alter HDG by the TE to approximately parallel the flight-planned TR..
2. Alter HDG further by the CA (closing angle) to close on the TR at the chosen point.
3. When TR is regained, alter HDG back by the CA.

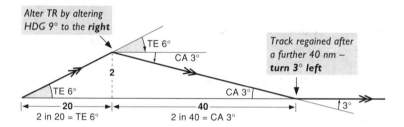

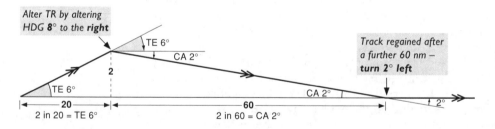

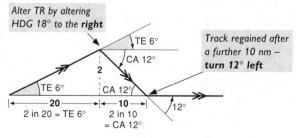

■ Figure 15-35 **Track corrections using the 1-in-60 rule – a summary**

Once the desired track is regained, if we do not alter the heading we used to regain track, we will fly straight through the desired track.

Maintaining a Desired Track (Having Regained It)

From Figure 15-35 it is clear that to remain on track you will have to alter your latest TMG (i.e. the TMG flown as you returned to the desired track) by an amount equal to the chosen closing angle (CA).

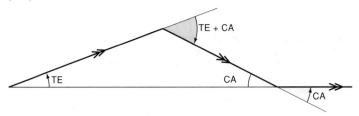

■ *Figure 15-36* **When back on-track, change heading by the chosen closing angle**

Now complete **Exercises 15 – En Route Nav Techniques-5.**

The Inverse-Ratio Method

In the UK, it is seldom possible to fly direct visual routes over long distances because of the presence of controlled airspace, Restricted Areas and Danger Areas. Normally we have to fly a series of shorter tracks with a number of turning points to avoid such areas. It is sound planning to select turning points that can be easily identified, say over a prominent landmark.

With short legs, the 1–in–60 rule can be simplified even further by concentrating on the closing angle (CA) to the next turning point and using what is known as the 'inverse-ratio' method.

Using the Inverse Ratio Method at the Half-Way Point

Previously we saw that, to close track in a distance equal to that already travelled since we were last on track, TE = CA. We would then alter heading by this amount which (since TE = CA) is equal to 2 × CA. This is the situation if we fix the position of the aeroplane at the half-way point along a straight track leg.

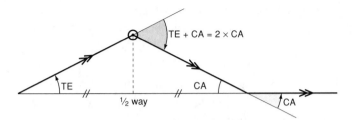

■ *Figure 15-37* **If 'distance-to-go' equals 'distance-gone', then alter heading by '2 × ca'**

Using the Inverse-Ratio Method at Other Points En Route

At any common fraction of the track gone then, to regain track, alter heading by 'CA × the inverse of the fraction of the distance gone'.

☐ At the ½-way point, alter heading by 'CA × 2', as we have just seen.
☐ At the ⅓-way point, alter heading by 'CA × 3'.
☐ At the ¼-way point, alter heading by 'CA × 4'.
☐ At the ⅕-way point, alter heading by 'CA × 5'.

EXAMPLE 10 A track leg is 45 nm. After travelling 15 nm, you are 2 nm left of track. Aim to regain track at the next turning point.

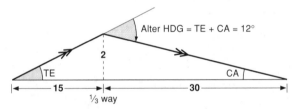

■ *Figure 15-38* **Example 10**

Previous method:

TE is 2 nm in 15 nm = 8 nm in 60 nm = 8° TE.
CA is 2 nm in 30 nm = 4 nm in 60 nm = 4° CA.
Alter heading by TE + CA = 12°.

Inverse-ratio method:

⅓ of track gone.
Alter heading by CA × 3 = 4° × 3 = 12°.

'Eye-Balling' and the Inverse-Ratio Method

Proper preparation of charts makes in-flight track corrections easy.

1. Mark 5° and 10° track guides either side of the desired track from the end of that track;

2. Divide the track into quarters and mark these points.

It is now easy to 'eye-ball' both closing angle and fraction of track gone for any fix that we obtain.

EXAMPLE 11

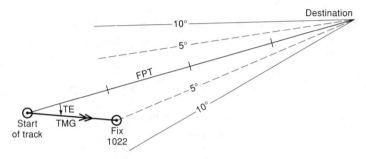

■ *Figure 15-39* **Example 11**

By 'eye-ball', CA = 5° and fraction gone is ¼.
Alter heading by 5° × 4 = 20° to the left.

NOTE The same 'inverse-ratio' method can be used to revise the estimated time interval (ETI). Time gone from start to fix is 7 minutes, therefore total time for leg = 7 × 4 = 28 minutes.

A limitation of the inverse-ratio method is that it only allows for one alteration of heading per stage, and it only regains track at the next turning point. For short legs this is not a significant disadvantage and the method is more than adequate. Its simplicity greatly reduces the workload in the cockpit for just a little extra effort at the flight-planning stage.

Now repeat **En Route Nav Techniques-5**
using the inverse-ratio method.

A Slightly Harder Application of the Inverse-Ratio Method

Some pilots have trouble accurately estimating the fraction of the distance gone. 'Eye-balling' will not be perfect but, as long as your estimate is reasonable, a track correction sufficiently accurate in practical terms can be made.

EXAMPLE 12 Calculating an 'alter heading' and a revised ETA.

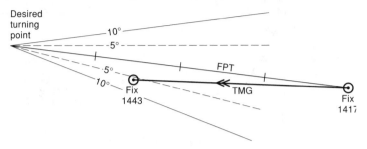

■ *Figure 15-40* **Example 12**

By 'eye-ball': fraction gone ⅔ and CA = 6°

After heading by 6° × 3⁄2 = 9° to the right
(3⁄2 is the inverse ratio of ⅔)

Time gone = 26 min.

Revised total time = 26 × 3⁄2 = 39 min.

Revised ETA = 1417 + 39 = 1456 UTC (GMT).

ANSWER Alter heading by 9° right. Revised ETA 1456 UTC
(and no computer manipulations were necessary).

Diversions

En Route Diversions

Occasionally you will have to divert around such things as thunderstorms, heavy rain showers, and towns. If there are suitable landmarks you can use these to assist you to divert around the 'obstacle' and then to return to track.

If there are no suitable landmarks, then it is a good idea to follow a simple procedure such as:

1. Divert 60° to the desired side of track for a suitable time (and note the HDG and time flown).

2. Parallel track for a suitable time (and note the time flown).

3. Return at 60° for the same time to return to track.

4. Take up a suitable HDG to maintain track.

NOTE A 60° diversion is very convenient because an *equilateral* (equal-sided) triangle's three angles are each 60°.

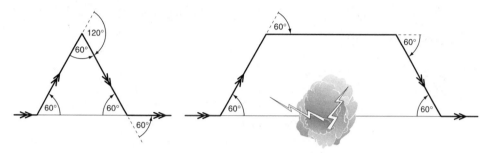

■ Figure 15-41 **The angles of an equilateral triangle are each 60°**

With a 60° diversion followed immediately by a 60° return to track, the actual distance flown on the diversion is double the on-track distance. In nil-wind conditions this will take double the time.

If the initial 60° diversion HDG is flown for 2 minutes, and the 'return to track leg' is flown for 2 minutes, i.e. a total of 4 minutes, this will then exceed the direct on-track time interval by 2 minutes. The ETA at the next checkpoint will therefore be 2 minutes later than previously estimated. If we had flown 5 minutes diversion legs, then it would add 5 minutes to our ETA.

The length of the leg flown parallel to track will not affect the ETA.

NOTE We have assumed nil-wind conditions in this discussion. If a significant wind is blowing, then you have to make appropriate allowances for it.

Diversions to Alternate Aerodromes
Occasionally it may be necessary to divert from your planned destination. Reasons for diverting include deteriorating weather at the destination, the possibility of running out of daylight if you continue to your planned destination, or a suspected mechanical problem that suggests an early landing would be prudent.

If the diversion only entails a small change in HDG (say up to 15°), then using the 1-in-60 rule is adequate.

NOTE An unplanned diversion is part of the PPL Skill Test.

EXAMPLE 13 You are tracking 320°T to your destination aerodrome which is 135 nm further on when you receive a met report to say that a large thunderstorm is approaching it. Your HDG is 315°M and your GS 133 kt.

You decide to divert and land at a small aerodrome which, from your present position, is located 10 nm to the right of track and 42 nm distant. Calculate an approximate HDG to steer and an approximate ETI.

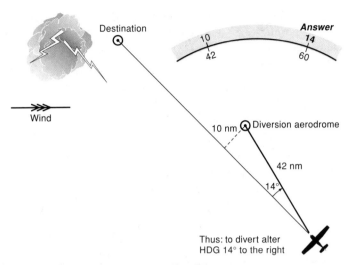

■ *Figure 15-42* **Example of a diversion slightly off the desired track using the 1-in-60 Rule**

10 nm in 42 nm = 14° to the right of your present track.

Because the change in direction is only 14°, a track change of 14° will be achieved reasonably accurately by a HDG change of 14°. (This is because the wind effect will not differ greatly between the two tracks.) Similarly, we can assume the GS to be unaltered due to the similar wind effect on the two reasonably similar tracks.

ANSWER Steer a HDG of (315 + 14) = 329°T to achieve a TR of (320 + 14) = 334°M. 42 nm at a GS of 133 kt = ETI 19 minutes.

If a diversion requires a *significant* change of heading (and this is usually the case), then the wind effect on the new track may differ significantly from that on the original track. The drift experienced may be quite different on the two different headings. In this case it will be necessary to use your computer to calculate the HDG and GS on the new TR using the latest and most accurate W/V that you have.

EXAMPLE 14 En route from Alpha to Bravo. Approaching Charlie, you decide to divert to Delta.

The best technique to use is to maintain HDG and original TR to the next checkpoint (say Charlie) and carry out calculations to enable you to divert from that known position. (5 minutes should be adequate to get yourself organised for an accurate diversion.)

Measure track and distance from your diversion point to the diversion aerodrome, and, using the known TAS and the most accurate wind velocity (W/V) to hand, calculate (on the wind side of your flight computer) the heading (HDG) to steer, and the expected groundspeed (GS), from which you can find an estimated time interval (ETI) and estimated time of arrival (ETA) overhead the aerodrome.

Check your answers with quick mental approximations.

Calculations:
Charlie to Delta, TR 352°T, 27 nm VAR 5°W.
TAS 105, W/V 240°T/30.

By computer:
Drift angle 15° right, Steer HDG 337°T, 342°M.
GS 112 kt, ETI (for 27 nm) 15 min.

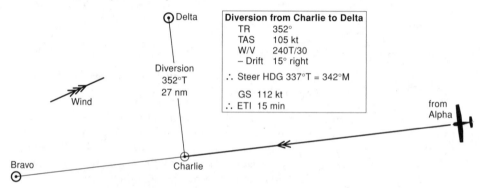

■ Figure 15-43 *A diversion involving a significant change of heading*

Some Practical Hints on Diversions

Diversions sometimes become necessary at the most inopportune moments, possibly when you have other problems on your hands. It therefore pays to have a few tricks up your sleeve to allow you to make quick and practical diversions without having to use your computer and go 'head-down' in the cockpit.

If you can estimate direction and distance by 'eye-balling', then your diversion will be made considerably easier. Direction is most important and, once you have taken up an approximate diversion heading and settled into the diversion track, you can calculate an accurate heading, distance to go, groundspeed, and ETI in a more relaxed atmosphere.

'Eye-balling' Track

Estimation of track is surprisingly easy and, with a bit of practice, you can achieve a ±5° accuracy. In fact, you should always estimate track before measuring it with a protractor or plotter – this will avoid making 180° or 90° errors as has happened from time to time. Estimating before measuring will also develop faith in your ability to estimate to a practical degree of accuracy.

'Halving known angles' is the simplest means of estimating angles. Halving the angle between a quadrantal point and a cardinal point will give you an angle of 22.5°, say 22°, and halving this again will give you 11°. An accuracy of ±5° will be achieved with practice.

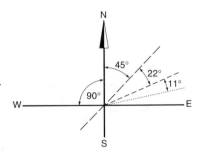

■ *Figure 15-44* **Halving angles as a means of estimating track**

Estimating Distance – Rule of Thumb!

The average adult 'top thumb joint' will cover about 10 nm on a 1:500,000 chart (and 5 nm on a 1:250,000). Check yours! This makes it easy to estimate short distances and times.

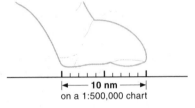

■ *Figure 15-45* **The top thumb-joint covers approx. 10 nm 1:500,000**

A '10-mile thumb' at a groundspeed of 120 kt = 5 min, 100 kt = 6 min, 85 kt = 7½ min, 70 kt = 8½ min, 60 kt = 10 min. For example, an unplanned diversion of 30 nm at groundspeed 100 kt = (3 × 6) 18 minutes.

A full hand span might measure 60 nm on a 1:500,000 chart. Check yours!

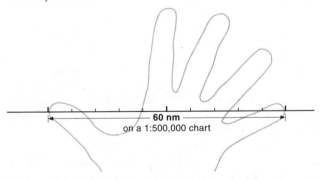

■ *Figure 15-46* **A full hand span is approximately 60 nm on a 1:500,000 chart**

If you have a 60 nm span and a 10 nm top thumb-joint, then you have an in-built 1:60 measuring device, ideally designed to measure 10°.

10 nm in 60 nm = 10°, by the 1-in-60 rule.

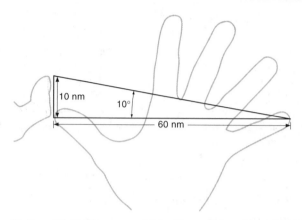

■ *Figure 15-47* **The personal 1-in-60 measuring device for 10°**

As part of your Navigation Flight Test section you will be asked to carry out a diversion. Should you decide to use radio navigation fixes then these will also be examined. Radio navaids need to be thoroughly understood before being used for navigation. (See Chapter 18 of this book and Vol. 5 of *The Air Pilot's Manual*)

Visibility

Cross-country flights by the holder of a basic-PPL (no IMC rating or instrument rating) should only be carried out in good weather conditions which permit continual observations of the ground, according to the specific requirements laid down by the CAA for your licence level. This means that you should generally be able to spot each check feature at an appropriate time prior to actually reaching or passing abeam it.

Poor Visibility

Good visibility decreases the workload on the pilot/navigator, but poor visibility obviously makes things more difficult. As you know from aviation law, it is permissible for a basic-PPL holder to fly, under certain circumstances, in visibility as low as 3 km, which is really quite poor visibility.

As well as making the actual handling of the aeroplane more difficult (no natural horizon to help you hold attitude), poor visibility also means that checkpoints may not come into view until you are almost on top of them and, if the checkpoints are some distance off-track, you may not see them at all.

Poor visibility may be caused by smoke, haze, mist, rain or smog. Sooner or later you will be faced with the problems that reduced visibility brings. Consideration should be given to turning back, or to diverting, if you feel that Visual Meteorological

Conditions (VMC) cannot be maintained, or if the visibility (even if in excess of VFR minimum requirements) is still not adequate for your particular flight and your particular experience.

Consideration should also be given to slowing down and perhaps even extending some flap and adopting the 'precautionary' configuration. A slower speed gives you more time to see things, as well as reducing the radius of turn if manoeuvring is required.

If you are expecting poor visibility en route, it is advisable to select more en route checkpoints that are closer to your desired track. This reduces the time between fixes and removes anxiety if you miss one of the check features, but spot the next one shortly after. If several checkpoints fail to appear, you could have reason to feel 'uncertain of position'.

Uncertain of Position or Lost

Procedure When Uncertain of Position

If you have flown for some time without obtaining a fix (say 20 or 30 minutes), you may feel uncertain of your precise position. You will be able to calculate a DR position (using expected TR and GS), but you may feel anxious that you cannot back this up with a positive fix over or abeam some ground feature. This situation is a normal one and is no reason for immediate anxiety. It is far from being 'lost'.

It is impossible to give a set of rules that covers all possible situations, but the following are general rules that may assist you.

If a Checkpoint Does Not Appear at the Expected Time:

1. Log HDG (compass and heading indicator readings) and time.

2. If the heading indicator is incorrectly set, then you have the information needed to make a fair estimate of your actual position, then reset the HI and calculate a HDG and ETI to regain the desired track. Or:

If the HI is aligned correctly with the compass, then the non-appearance of a landmark, while it will perhaps cause you some concern, need not indicate that you are grossly off-track. You may not have seen the landmark for a perfectly legitimate reason, such as bright sunlight obscuring your vision, poor visibility, or a change in the ground features not reflected on the chart (e.g. removal of a transmission mast, or the emptying of a reservoir). Or if you are navigating above even a small amount of cloud, the inconvenient positioning of some of this cloud may have obscured your check feature.

3. If you consider the situation warrants it, make an **urgency call** (Pan-Pan) on 121.5 MHz. This should enable ATC to fix your position by 'auto-triangulation'.

4. If you obtain a fix, or if the next checkpoint comes up on time, the flight can continue and normal navigation procedures apply once again.

5. If still unable to fix your position, follow the procedure below.

Procedure When Lost

Becoming lost is usually the result of human error. Being lost is totally different to being temporarily uncertain of your position, where you can determine a reasonably accurate DR position.

Once again, it is impossible to lay down a set of hard and fast rules on what to do if you do become lost, but there are some general guidelines you can follow. Remember that careful pre-flight planning and in-flight attention to the normal, simple en route navigation tasks will ensure that the situation of being lost will never arise.

If you are lost, you must formulate a plan of action because it is futile to fly around aimlessly in the hope of finding a pinpoint.

If you are lost, formulate a positive plan of action.

If you change your thinking from one of being *uncertain of position* to one of being *lost,* then make use of the Radar Advisory Service, if available (see point (3) above). If still lost:

1. It is important initially to maintain HDG (if terrain, visibility and what you know of the proximity of controlled airspace permit) and carry out a sequence of positive actions.

2. If a vital checkpoint is not in view at ETA, then continue to fly for 10% of the time since your last positive fix.

3. On deciding what your last positive fix was, check the headings flown since that last fix, ensuring that:
   - the magnetic compass is not being affected by outside influences such as a headset, portable radio, mobile telephone, or other magnetic material place near it;
   - the gyroscopic heading indicator (HI) is aligned with the magnetic compass correctly;
   - magnetic variation and drift have been correctly applied to obtain your HDGs flown;
   - an estimate of track direction on the chart against that shown on the flight plan is correct;

4. Read from ground to chart, i.e. look for significant ground features or combinations of features and try to determine their position on the chart.

Read from ground to chart when lost.

5. Establish a 'most probable area' in which you think you are. There are several ways this can be done. Consult your flying instructor for his or her preferred method.

Finding the Most Probable Area

Estimate the distance flown since the last fix and apply this distance, plus or minus 10%, to an arc 30° either side of what you estimate the probable track made good (TMG) to be.

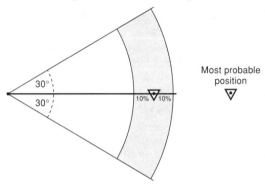

■ *Figure 15-48* **Estimating the most probable area that you are in**

Finding the Most Probable Position

Estimate your 'most probable position' and draw a circle around it of radius equal to 10% the distance flown since the last fix.

■ *Figure 15-49* **Estimating most probable position**

Once the most probable area has been plotted, you should:
☐ **Establish a safety altitude** at which to fly in order to ensure adequate clearance of all obstacles in what you consider the general area to be. Be especially careful in conditions of poor visibility or low cloud.
☐ **Check large features** within this area of the chart with what can be seen on the ground. Try and relate features seen on the ground with those shown on the chart, i.e. read from ground to chart. Confirm the identification of any feature by closely observing secondary details around the feature, e.g. a small irregular lake is confirmed by the position of a small town on a bend in the railway line as it turns from west to south. Double check any fix.

When you do positively establish a fix, re-check your heading indicator (HI) and recommence normal navigation. Calculate the HDG, GS and ETI for the next check feature and set course for it.

At all times continue to fly the aircraft safely, maintaining an awareness of time, especially with respect to the beginning of official night (SS+30) and fuel state.

If you are still unable to fix your position, you should consider taking one of the following actions:

- ☐ **Increase the 'most probable area'** by 10, 15 or even 20% of the distance flown from the last fix.
- ☐ **Climb to a higher altitude** to increase your range of vision.
- ☐ **Turn towards** a known prominent line feature, such as a coastline, large river, railway line or road, and then follow along it to the next town where you should be able to obtain a fix. (Don't forget that it may also lead you into a control zone.)
- ☐ **Steer a reciprocal heading** and attempt to return to your last fix.
- ☐ **Seek navigational assistance** from an Air Traffic Services Unit.

Tell someone if you are hopelessly lost – share the problem!

Airmanship

Note the following important points of airmanship:

RANGE. If you want to cover as much ground as possible with the fuel available, you should fly the aeroplane for best range.

LOG. Keep a navigation log going.

TIME. Remain positively aware of time. Keep your eye on the fuel and on the time remaining until the end of daylight. If darkness is approaching, remember that it will be darker at ground level than at altitude, and that it becomes dark very quickly in the tropics.

LANDING. If you decide to carry out a precautionary search and landing (i.e. a forced landing with the use of power), allow sufficient time and fuel to do this on the assumption that two or three inspections might have to be made before finding a suitable landing area.

Why Did You Become Lost?

If at any stage you became lost, you should systematically try to determine the reason (either in flight or post-flight) so that you can learn from the experience. Common reasons for becoming lost include:

- ☐ **incorrectly calculated HDGs GSs and ETIs** (hence the need for you always to make mental estimates of approximate answers to these items);
- ☐ **incorrectly synchronised heading indicator** (direction indicator) i.e. gyroscopic HI not aligned correctly with the magnetic compass (this should be done every 10 or 15 minutes);

☐ **a faulty compass reading** (due to transistor radios, cameras and other metal objects placed near the compass);

☐ **incorrectly applied variation** (variation west, magnetic best; variation east, magnetic least);

☐ **incorrectly applied drift** (compared to TR, the HDG should be pointing into wind, i.e. flying north with a westerly wind blowing would mean that the HDG should be to the left of track and into-wind);

☐ **a wind velocity** significantly different to that forecast, and not allowed for in flight;

☐ **a deterioration in weather,** reduced visibility, increased cockpit workload;

☐ **an incorrect fix,** i.e. mis-identification of a check feature;

☐ **a poorly planned diversion** from the original desired track;

☐ **not paying attention** to carrying out normal navigation tasks throughout the flight.

With regular checks of heading indicator alignment with the magnetic compass, reasonably accurate flying of heading, and position fixes every 10 or 15 minutes, none of these errors should put you far off-track. It is only when you are careless and let things go a bit too far that you become lost.

Further Points on En Route Navigation

Range and Endurance Flying

The performance of most aeroplanes is fairly flexible, and you would operate your aeroplane in the best manner for your purposes according to your own judgement. Guidance is given in the various manuals associated with the aeroplane.

If your desire is to fly a given route using the minimum amount of fuel (or conversely, fly the maximum distance on a given amount of fuel) then you would fly for range.

Range flying is concerned with distance and fuel.

If you want to stay in the air for the maximum time possible, with the distance covered not a consideration, then you would fly for endurance – for example, holding near an aerodrome waiting for some bad weather to pass, or holding due to traffic before you make your approach.

Endurance flying is concerned with time and fuel.

Performance figures for range or endurance cruising will usually be found in the Pilot's Operating Handbook for your aircraft. See Vol. 4 of *The Air Pilot's Manual,* Chapter 32.

The Air Plot

Pilots mainly use the **track plot,** which is the path over the ground described by track and groundspeed. Occasionally the **air plot** is used, where passage relative to the air mass is plotted, i.e. wind effect is not taken into account. The symbol for an *air position* is a cross **+**.

An air plot may be used for an aircraft that has requested navigation assistance because of being lost. By plotting HDGs and TASs flown since the last fix (i.e. the passage of the aeroplane relative to the air mass), it is possible to determine where the aeroplane would have been if there was nil-wind.

By applying an appropriate wind vector for this time to the final air position, a DR ground position for the aeroplane may be deduced. The wind blows the aeroplane from its air position to its ground position.

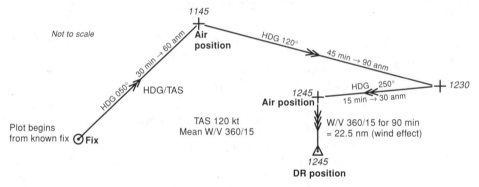

■ *Figure 15-50* **Example of an air plot**

NOTE It is not usual when navigating visually to use an air plot, although it may be of use when flying over featureless terrain or the sea, where obtaining fixes or tracking information is difficult. The principle, however, is fairly simple.

Mental Dead Reckoning

If you develop the skills of mental dead reckoning, then it becomes less likely that you will ever make a gross navigation error. Each time you are flying, not only on cross-countries but also out in the local training area, practise estimating tracks, distances and heights.

Wind Components Applied to TAS and Desired Track

When flight planning and also en route, it is a good idea to keep a mental check on all your heading and GS calculations. Some formulae based on trigonometry can be memorised, but this is too involved at PPL level.

What you can do quite easily, however, is remember the following:

☐ **a headwind component** reduces groundspeed to less than true airspeed;

☐ **a tailwind component** increases groundspeed to more than true airspeed;

☐ **to achieve the desired track,** the aeroplane must be headed somewhat into wind.

EXAMPLE 15 Your desired track is west and the wind is from 220°. Having a headwind component, your GS should be less than TAS.

Your heading must be into-wind compared to desired track and so will be to the left of west, i.e. a bearing less than 270°. With this in mind, you check that your flight plan and en route calculations reflect this, i.e. GS less than TAS, and HDG less than the desired TR in this case.

Estimating Distances

Also good to keep in mind is that a 'sight-down' angle of 45° from the horizon gives a horizontal distance equal to your height agl – either ahead or to the side.

EXAMPLE 16

☐ **If you are 7,000 ft** above terrain which is 1,000 ft amsl, height agl is 6,000 ft (approx. 1 nm), so a sight-down of 45° gives a horizontal distance of 1 nm.

☐ **At 12,000 ft agl,** a sight-down angle of 45° gives 2 nm.

☐ **At 3,000 ft agl,** a sight-down angle of 45° gives 0.5 nm.

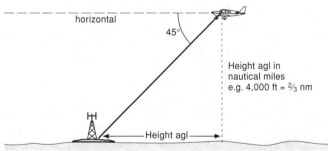

■ *Figure 15-51* **Estimating distances using slight down angle 45° below the horizon**

Low-Level Navigation

Low-level navigation means navigation at about 500 ft agl. It is conducted in the same way as normal pilot navigation at higher altitudes, with a few special considerations.

At a low level you will have a limited field of vision. You will also have to keep a constant lookout due to your close proximity to terrain. This means that at the pre-flight stage you should study your charts carefully and choose suitable check features, reasonably close to track and perhaps greater in number than for a similar flight at a higher altitude.

The elevation of nearby features above the general level of the surrounding terrain is more important for a low-level flight, because they will be seen side-on rather than from above as in normal en route navigation at a higher level.

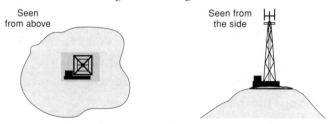

■ *Figure 15-52* **The side elevation of check features is important in low-level navigation**

Spot heights such as radio masts, factory chimneys and church steeples are very useful at low level, but may be almost invisible when flying at high altitudes. Railway lines at the bottom of cuttings may be very visible from altitude, but not visible from low level unless you are directly over them.

The presence of unusually high and difficult-to-see obstructions and built-up areas must be anticipated and avoided.

The limited field of vision means that you need to anticipate the sighting of check features and recognise them quickly (hence the need for a very careful study of your charts before commencing the low-level navigation exercise).

If a ground feature fails to appear at its ETA, there will not be time to search for it. Assume that it has been passed and concentrate on looking for the next check feature which should not be too far ahead. The number of check features required for low-level navigation should in general be greater than for normal higher-level navigation. Only if you fail to spot several consecutive check features should you become 'uncertain of your position'. Mental DR in such a situation is invaluable in determining the probable position.

Log keeping on a low-level exercise will necessarily have to be restricted because of the greater concentration required on things outside the cockpit. Due to aircraft handling considerations, and the need to keep a good lookout, it may at times be impossible to make any but the briefest log entries or marks on your charts.

NOTE Be aware of the Low Level Civil Aircraft Notification Procedure (CANP), a service aimed at improving the information available on low-level civil aircraft to be disseminated to military operators to assist them in planned avoidance. It pertains mainly to such low-level localised operations as crop-spraying and banner-towing; however, check if your flying instructor considers it affects your planned flight. CANP is described in AIP ENR 1-10-13.

Descents From Higher Levels

Most visual (as distinct from instrument) flights in the UK are made at 3,000 ft and below, which makes an accurate descent calculation rather academic. Since it is so straightforward, however, we will consider a few simple cases for those times when you do cruise high.

EXAMPLE 17 If your rate of descent is 500 feet per minute (ft/min or fpm), how long will it take to descend from 8,000 ft amsl to 2,500 ft amsl?

Time to descend (8,000 – 2,500)
= 5,500 ft at 500 ft/min
= 11 mins

■ *Figure 15-53* **Example 17**

EXAMPLE 18 In the above case, if your estimated groundspeed (GS) on descent is 162 kt, how far from the aerodrome should you commence descent to arrive overhead at 2,500 ft amsl?

This would be a typical situation on arrival at an aerodrome of elevation 500 ft amsl, where you wanted to overfly at 2,000 ft above aerodrome level (i.e. 2,500 ft amsl, prior to joining the circuit for an approach and landing).

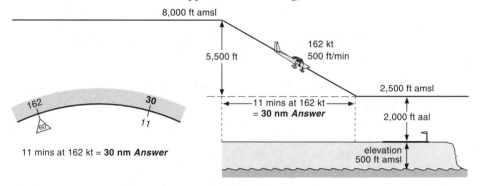

■ *Figure 15-54* **A simple descent calculation**

EXAMPLE 19 Your estimated time interval (ETI) to a nearby diversion aerodrome (elevation 142 ft amsl) is 8 minutes and you want to begin descent immediately from 5,000 ft amsl to overfly at 2,000 ft above aerodrome level (aal). What average rate of descent should you maintain?

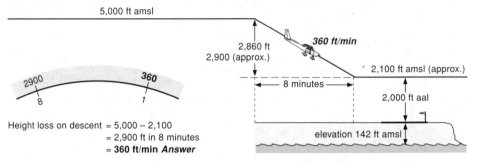

Height loss on descent = 5,000 − 2,100
               = 2,900 ft in 8 minutes
               = **360 ft/min Answer**

■ *Figure 15-55* **Another simple descent calculation**

EXAMPLE 20 You are at FL75, 18 nm from an aerodrome (elevation 21 ft amsl, QNH 980 mb) and you want to commence descent immediately to arrive overhead the aerodrome at 2,000 ft aal. If your true airspeed on descent is 127 kt with a tailwind component of 25 kt, what rate of descent do you require?

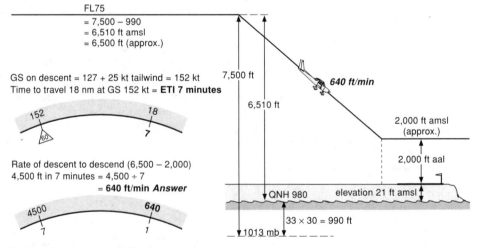

GS on descent = 127 + 25 kt tailwind = 152 kt
Time to travel 18 nm at GS 152 kt = **ETI 7 minutes**

Rate of descent to descend (6,500 − 2,000)
4,500 ft in 7 minutes = 4,500 ÷ 7
                    = **640 ft/min Answer**

■ *Figure 15-56* **Example 20**

EXAMPLE 21 You are to descend at 500 ft/min from 8,500 ft with a GS of 157 kt, to overfly an aerodrome, elevation 730 ft, at 2,000 ft aal. At what distance from the field should you commence your descent?

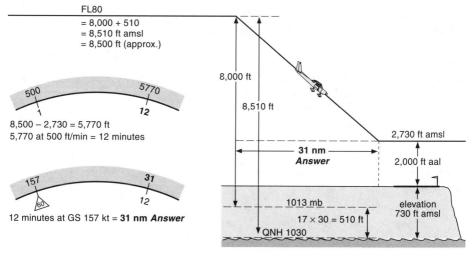

FL80
= 8,000 + 510
= 8,510 ft amsl
= 8,500 ft (approx.)

8,500 – 2,730 = 5,770 ft
5,770 at 500 ft/min = 12 minutes

12 minutes at GS 157 kt = **31 nm** *Answer*

8,000 ft

8,510 ft

2,730 ft amsl

◀— **31 nm** —▶
Answer

2,000 ft aal

1013 mb

17 × 30 = 510 ft

QNH 1030

elevation
730 ft amsl

■ *Figure 15-57* **Example 21**

Now complete **Exercises 15 – En Route Nav Techniques-6.**

Navigation In Remote Areas

One day, you may fly into one of the world's remote and fea-tureless areas, such as North Africa, the Middle East, India or even the Australian outback. The transition from cross-country flying in the more heavily populated areas of the UK to flying in the featureless areas should not be taken lightly. Navigation in remote areas is not necessarily more difficult, but the lack of land-marks requires more disciplined flight planning and flying.

A number of accidents have occurred when inexperienced pilots encountered navigation difficulties in remote areas of the world. A common theme has been:

☐ lack of experience; coupled with
☐ inadequate flight preparation; and
☐ poor in-flight navigation technique.

EXPERIENCE. Where does one gain experience? Pilots are faced with 'lack of experience' many times in their flying careers. How do we gain experience, except by reading and studying and then finally 'doing'? First solo and first cross-country flight as a single pilot/navigator are stages in extending ourselves to new limits, and in the process gaining experience.

Often we learn some lessons that have been learned many times before by other pilots. Listen to them! But make your own oper-ational judgements. *Biggles* stories may contain lessons for you. Read reports of trips where things did not go as planned (and learn from other pilots' experiences rather than your own).

The term 'lack of experience' is used here in reference to nav-igation experience. We assume that, as a responsible pilot, you would only venture forth into a remote area in an aeroplane in which you had recent flying experience and whose systems (fuel system, electrical system, etc.) you were fully conversant with.

FLIGHT PREPARATION. There is no excuse for inadequate flight preparation, even for the most inexperienced pilot. You must do your homework properly for a particular route, so that you can make reasonably correct in-flight decisions when the unexpected occurs. Of course, with proper pre-flight preparation, the unex-pected seems to occur less often.

IN-FLIGHT NAVIGATION TECHNIQUE. Flying in remote and fea-tureless areas requires some good DR flying. Following dirt tracks that meander through the desert and then peter out is a poor nav-igation technique for remote areas.

This is not to say that following the only railway line up to Alice Springs or the one-and-only sealed road across to Perth in Australia shouldn't be done – this is an area for your own operational judgement – but we are referring here particularly to areas where such features are not available.

What can you, a pilot-in-command, do to avoid the pitfalls that can occur in remote area flying?

Flight Plan Carefully

'Day-Before' Pre-Flight Planning

☐ Allow plenty of time to flight plan carefully without any pressure of time being placed on you.

☐ Ensure that your charts are current and adequate for your intended route, plus or minus any reasonable planned or unplanned diversions.

☐ Examine your charts carefully for landmarks and distinguishing features along your proposed route, and to either side of track.

☐ Ensure that you are up to speed on your computer usage, especially in calculating headings, groundspeeds and times.

☐ Ensure that you carry the required radio and survival equipment and that it is in good condition and you know how to operate it.

☐ Make use of the local knowledge of other pilots and briefing officers who know the area you intend flying over. Determine suitable fix points and obtain as much information as possible on suitable landing areas along the route. Ensure that the information is reliable and up to date, because it is not unknown for landing grounds in remote areas to be abandoned and possibly unusable.

☐ If practicable, plan your route over suitable landing areas.

Obtain a Thorough Met Briefing

☐ Ensure that you are briefed thoroughly on the route and for your destination and alternate aerodromes.

☐ Do not be embarrassed if you do not understand all aspects of the Area Forecasts or Aerodrome Forecasts, or some of the abbreviations. Ask for clarification!

☐ Be wary of areas where visibility may be reduced in dust or haze.

☐ Do not plan on flying above a low layer of cloud for long periods where your visual navigation could be impeded.

☐ In hot, desert areas, try and determine an appropriate altitude above which you will be out of the convective turbulence layer and its associated 'bumpy ride' for the time at which your flight will occur.

Obtain a Thorough Operational Briefing

☐ ATSU personnel are aviation professionals. They are trained to a high standard and it is their job (and usually their pleasure) to assist you in any way possible. It is up to you to request their assistance.

☐ Pay particular attention to landing area and aerodrome serviceability along your proposed route, especially following rain.

☐ Determine availability of the correct fuel at appropriate landing points.

☐ Determine if any military activity is planned in the area. Military jet low-level navigation exercises do occur at high speed in remote areas — some of these aircraft are camouflaged fighters that are hard to see, and some of them large bombers. It is nice to know if they are around.

☐ Verify the time of last light for your destination.

Submit a Flight Plan

☐ Check tracks and distances mentally following your computer calculations to ensure there are not gross errors, e.g. tracks wrong by 90° or 180°. Apply magnetic variation correctly (variation east — magnetic least).

☐ Check that drift has been allowed for in the correct direction and that ETIs are approximately correct.

☐ Plan on flying as high as is practicable because:

– a better picture of the country can be obtained;

– on hot days, the flight should be smoother;

– VHF radio coverage is better.

☐ Allow adequate fuel, plus reserves — not only for the planned flight, but for any possible alternative action, including what procedures you will follow in case selected fix-points are not located as expected.

☐ Allow sufficient time for the planned flight plus any possible alternative action, especially if flying in the latter part of the day when last light is a consideration. Only a foolishly over-confident visual pilot would allow a mere 10-minute buffer prior to last light for arrival over the destination.

☐ Early departure times in the desert areas generally produce better flights. Cooler air gives better take-off performance and a smoother ride. Visibility may be better and the pressure of impending last light removed. The benefit of the early start can be lost if you dawdle along, though, wasting time with inefficient flight planning, refuelling, etc.

☐ Allow for proper food and rest at appropriate intervals. It is not only the aeroplane that needs fuel.

In-Flight Navigation Technique

☐ Fly estimated headings accurately. Do not allow the aircraft to wander off-track simply through inattention. Have in your mind an awareness of approximate direction – and check that drift is applied in the correct direction for your desired track and the wind experienced. Check for drift soon after departure and adjust your heading as necessary.

☐ Map-read carefully as the flight progresses, but do not let this distract you from flying an accurate heading. Be aware that, following heavy rains in remote areas, large uncharted rivers and lakes may appear and disappear within a few days. Even if you cannot pinpoint yourself visually at all times due to the lack of landmarks, at least know your dead reckoning (DR) position at all times based on estimated TR and GS since your last fix.

☐ Maintain an in-flight log, recording all HDGs flown and the time of any significant changes. It takes a few seconds to complete and may prove invaluable.

☐ Maintain a general sense of direction and ensure that the heading indicator is re-aligned with the magnetic compass at regular intervals (every 10 or 15 minutes).

☐ Do not deviate from your flight plan without any real justification. A flight plan should be adhered to unless a positive fix indicates that you are off-track, or unless you change your intentions in flight and prepare a new flight plan. With a positive fix, you have data that enable you to make a reasoned correction to your heading.

☐ Anticipate your fix points some minutes ahead of your estimate for them and commence a good lookout, not just ahead but also to each side of track. Do not just wait for planned fix points to show up – anticipate them. Continually study the surrounding countryside, but not to the extent that it disturbs your accurate heading keeping.

☐ Positively establish your position in relation to a selected fix point before continuing to the next fix point.

▢ If you are unable to locate your selected fix point and you are uncertain of your position, commence your planned alternative action, being aware of fuel and time in particular. This alternative action could be to return to the last positive fix or to divert to some prominent landmark, even if some distance away. In these circumstances you may have to abandon your original plan for proceeding to your original destination, in favour of a destination that is easier to locate and in a more accessible area. Maintain an accurate log in this procedure.

▢ If you depart from your original flight plan, notify your new intentions to the appropriate ATSU, but do this after you have planned on your new course of action and flying the aeroplane is well in hand.

If Things Do Not Work Out As Planned ...

▢ Do not become flustered. With reasonable planning, you should have allowed fuel and time to sort out this sort of problem. Establish the fuel state and time remaining to last light.

▢ Do not assume that you are in a particular place simply because that is where you want to be. Keep an open mind and study the surrounding countryside carefully. Log all significant changes of heading, and the times they are made.

▢ Follow the procedures suggested in the previous chapter on what to do if you are uncertain of your precise position or if you become lost.

▢ Advise the ATSU of the headings and times flown since your last positive fix; the SAR (search and rescue) organisation can plot your flight using the latest wind data and assist in establishing your position.

▢ If, despite your precautions, things go unexpectedly wrong and you are caught with insufficient fuel or daylight to reach your destination or a suitable alternate, be intelligent in the use of your resources.

▢ Carry out a precautionary search and landing while you still have adequate fuel and daylight available. Stay with the aircraft and activate the emergency locator transmitter.

The Emergency Locator Transmitter (ELT)

In remote areas visual searches can be difficult. The emergency locator transmitter (ELT), if properly used, can allow the search area to be reduced quickly so that the visual search can be concentrated in a small area.

ELT is a generic (family) term covering devices known as crash locator beacons, emergency locator beacons, etc. They all operate on both 121.5 and 243 megahertz.

A few common sense points on the use of the ELT are:

☐ Know how to use the ELT. Revise the operating instructions for your particular transmitter prior to flight.

☐ Ensure that the battery is fully charged.

☐ Ensure that the ELT is capable of operating properly (tests are restricted, so seek the advice of the authorities before activating a test, as it may result in the commencement of unnecessary SAR action, such as scrambling of aircraft, etc.).

☐ If you are forced down, however, do not be reluctant to activate the ELT at an appropriate time.

Now complete **Exercises 16 – Navigation In Remote Areas.**

Entry/Exit Lanes and Low-Level Routes

Special Entry/Exit Access Lanes and Low-Level Routes are provided for light aircraft to allow exit from and entry to some aerodromes that lie within Control Zones (CTRs) or under controlled airspace. They are established to allow easier access for training aircraft, for example.

There may be other routes legitimately usable which do not infringe Restricted Areas or controlled airspace, but the established Access Lanes provide a readily identifiable channel through complex sections of airspace.

Entry/Exit Lanes and Low-Level Routes are designed to simplify navigation and operational procedures for non-IMC-rated pilots flying near or into busy Control Zones.

Basic Rules

You should refer to the relevant aerodrome listing in AIP AD and/or *Pooley's Flight Guide* for instructions.

- **Follow the published instructions.**
- **Adhere to the published tracks** and entry/exit points (labelled 'E/E').
- **Conform with the general flight rules** regarding terrain clearance, flight over populous areas, danger areas, etc.
- **Operate no higher than the altitude specified** as the upper limit in the section being flown.
- **Keep to the right** (traffic separation may not be provided by ATC).

Navigating an Access Lane or Low-Level Route is based on the normal visual navigation procedure of flying accurate headings and backing up with frequent visual fixes.

Flight Plan Accurately

Entry/Exit Access Lanes and Low-Level Routes are very confined areas. Control Zones (CTRs) that you must avoid entering are adjacent. The traffic in the area may be concentrated in the lane or route. For these (and other) reasons extra attention must be paid to keeping a good lookout outside the cockpit compared to normal cross-country flying, and to map-reading with more than the usual number of fixes.

The easiest way to achieve this is to flight plan accurately and thoroughly.

☐ Study the weather forecasts and actual reports thoroughly. Note any significant weather, visibility, cloud ceiling and wind. Relate the weather conditions to the terrain or built-up areas that you will have to fly over, ensuring that adequate terrain clearance and clearance from cloud is available. Be aware that strong winds may give rise to turbulence in the low levels where you will be flying.

☐ Request an operational briefing from your instructor, checking to see if any special considerations need to be made for your flight.

☐ Select the best route. Sometimes there are several Access Lanes to choose from, and sometimes you may choose to avoid one and fly a completely different route. Prevailing conditions may make a more circuitous route, offering easier navigation, flatter terrain, better visibility, higher cloud base, more separation from controlled airspace, etc., more suitable than the published Access Lanes, although generally they are perfectly suitable.

☐ Study the chart carefully for suitable landmarks and specified points in or near the Lane. Read all relevant operational comments in the AIP AD or *Pooley's Flight Guide*.

☐ Identify a landmark on the approach to the lane over which you can accurately position the aeroplane to commence the transit of the lane; this point is best chosen to be, say, 5 nm prior to the commencement of the lane to allow you room to manoeuvre without penetrating controlled airspace.

☐ Check all computer work for accuracy, and do mental checks of all HDGs, GSs and ETIs.

☐ Have an alternative plan of action ready in case poor weather or some other reason makes a transit of the lane undesirable.

☐ Aim to reduce the in-flight workload to a minimum.

Navigate Accurately

☐ You need to keep on track in an Access Lane, because of the proximity of Control Zones in most cases, where both large and small aircraft may be operating.

☐ Accurately position your aeroplane (over a landmark if possible) prior to entering the lane. This is your starting point for accurate track-keeping through the lane.

☐ Aim to have all other tasks (such as after-take-off checks, a departure or position report, copying the landing information off the ATIS, aligning the heading indicator with the magnetic compass) completed prior to entering the lane.

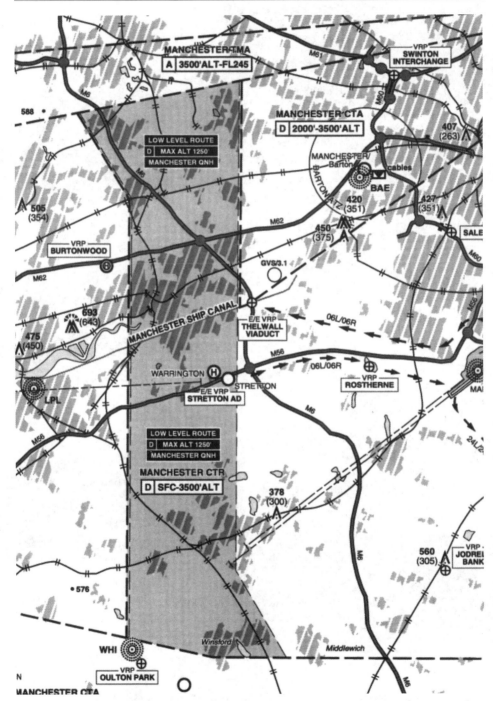

■ Figure 17-1 **Manchester Low-Level Route, as shown in the UK AIP**

Coming up to VRP Junc. M6/M58 (at left)

Passing the canal at Warrington

Haydock Racetrack and M6 junction

VRP Stretton (airfield at right)

Approaching Warrington

Lake north of Northwich

Entering the Low-Level Route by Winsford

Navigating the Manchester Low-Level Route (views when tracking northbound)

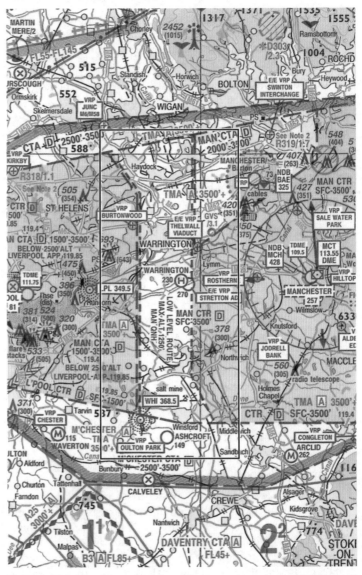

■ Figure 17-2 **Manchester Low Level Route as shown on 1:500,000 chart**

☐ Check the weather ahead to see if it is clear enough for a safe transit of the lane. If not, adopt your alternative course of action, which might be to return to the aerodrome of departure, or to try another track.

☐ Ensure that your heading indicator is aligned with the magnetic compass in straight and level unaccelerated flight.

☐ From your commencement point, steer your calculated or estimated HDG and continue with steady map-reading. Adjust your HDG to maintain the desired track and to avoid straying into controlled airspace.

☐ Be suspicious of any HDG that differs more than 10° from what you calculated was necessary at the flight-planning stage. Many pilots have tracked visually along wrong railway lines, when a quick HDG check would have alerted them to an incorrect track.

☐ Look ahead for navigation features. If you miss one, look ahead for the next one, flying your best estimate of HDG. This is essential if visibility deteriorates.

☐ You should aim to stay on-track and within the confines of the lane by identifying the various features and either tracking over them or tracking abeam them on the correct side. Check that your HDG approximates the HDG that you calculated.

☐ Concentrate on navigation, but keep a sharp lookout for other aircraft and for landmarks.

☐ Don't forget an occasional en route check of other items such as engine settings, fuel state, etc. (the FREHA check).

☐ Listen on the radio for other traffic, and broadcast your own intentions if you consider it necessary.

☐ If you feel uncertain of your position, do not be reluctant to request assistance. You will often be in radar environments, and if you are experiencing navigation difficulties because unexpected poor visibility is making visual fixes difficult to obtain, call for help! A request for a radar vector (HDG) to steer to remain in the lane or route may prevent an inadvertent penetration of a Control Zone.

These remarks have been directed at a pilot who is not familiar with a particular Entry/Exit Lane. An experienced pilot in good weather may feel quite happy tracking visually through a familiar lane with little planning, but if visibility decreases unexpectedly or some other unforeseen situation arises, these procedures give him something to fall back on. Local experience can count for a lot, but not always.

We all know very calm and proficient pilots who always seem to be on top of the task at hand, no matter what situation arises. These pilots are usually the ones who have done their homework and have done as much preparation on the ground as possible to minimise their in-flight workload. Having cards up your sleeve and alternative plans of action ready allow you to look calm.

Entry/Exit Lanes and Low-Level Routes require extra vigilance, and it is good to plan on a minimum in-flight workload so that your extra capacity is available to cope with any unforeseen distractions, which do occasionally occur.

Now complete
Exercises 17 – Entry/Exit Lanes and Low-Level Routes.

Section **Four**

En Route Navigation
with Radio Navaids

NOTES

1 The material in this section is intended only for PPL candidates. IMC and Instrument Rating candidates should refer to Vol. 5 of *The Air Pilot's Manual* for full details on instrument flying techniques, let-downs and the instrument landing system etc.

2 For the PPL Skill Test, you are not required to be fully conversant with all the radio navigation facilities described in this section – the requirements will vary depending on the geographic location of your flying school. Your flying instructor will advise you on which sections to study.

Introduction to Radio Navigation Aids

Having achieved a high standard in visual attitude flying, it is now time to apply this ability to cross-country navigation with reference to radio navigation instruments.

It is, in fact, possible to fly cross-country using attitude flying only, without referring to any radio navigation instrument in the cockpit, simply by following instructions passed to you by a radar controller.

Instructions such as "Turn onto heading three four zero, and descend now to eight hundred feet," can be followed, even to the point of a cloudbreak for a straight-in landing on a particular runway.

Radar is the first of the radio navigation aids, or *radio navaids,* that we consider in this section, since it does not involve a great deal of understanding before you can benefit from it. As well as explaining how radar can be of use to you, we also discuss the basic theory of its operation, along with the transponder in the aircraft.

It is possible that your instructor may follow an order of study different to that presented here. If so, simply bypass the other chapters and proceed to the one desired. Each chapter is self-contained, and reading earlier chapters is not necessary to understand the content of a later one.

VHF direction finding (VDF), which, like radar, does not require additional instrumentation in the cockpit, may also be used for cross-country flying. By requesting ATC to provide you with a magnetic bearing to the station, known as a QDM, which can be determined at some aerodromes by detecting the direction from which your VHF radio communications are received, a track to or from the station can be flown. The procedure used is a little more complicated than simply steering radar headings, so we have left it until the end of this section.

Radio navigation aids covered that do require cockpit instruments include:

- the **non-directional beacon (NDB)** and **automatic direction finder (ADF)** combination. The ADF has various cockpit presentations, such as the relative bearing indicator (RBI) and radio magnetic indicator (RMI).
- the **VHF omni range (VOR)**;
- **distance-measuring equipment (DME)**.

We also introduce an RNAV (area navigation) system – pseudo-VOR/DMEs.

It may sound a little complicated at this stage, but careful consideration of each of these radio navigation aids one at a time will make it easy for you. There is a certain amount of jargon, but it will not take long before you are familiar with all the terms.

The main function of this section of the manual is for you to understand how the aids work, and how to use them, especially for tracking to or from a ground station.

Radar

Most air traffic control in busy airspace occurs in a *radar environment*. This means that the air traffic controller has a radar map of the area showing the position of the various aircraft within it, bringing enormous advantages, such as:

☐ A significant reduction in the amount of air–ground communication. For instance, there is no need for pilots to transmit regular position reports.

☐ The ability to handle an increased number of aeroplanes in the same airspace, with reduced, but still safe, separation distances.

☐ The ability to 'fix' an aircraft's geographic position.

☐ The ability to *radar vector* an aeroplane along various tracks by passing headings to steer to the pilot.

☐ The ability to feed aeroplanes onto final approach to land, either to the commencement of an instrument approach such as an ILS (instrument landing system) or until the pilot becomes 'visual', without the need for excessive manoeuvring, and with more than one aeroplane on the approach at any one time.

This use of radar is known as **surveillance radar.** Surveillance radar, although extensively used in air traffic control, is not confined to controlled airspace. Wide areas of the UK have radar coverage, and you may, even if operating in uncontrolled airspace, take advantage of services such as the Lower Airspace Radar Advisory Service (LARS).

Most aeroplanes are now fitted with a secondary surveillance radar **transponder,** which transmits a unique signal in response to a radar signal from the ground, thereby allowing the radar controller to identify a particular aeroplane on a radar screen. You are probably familiar with the operation of the transponder – if not, it is considered in detail towards the end of this chapter. The name *transponder* is derived from *transmitter/responder.*

■ *Figure 19-1* ***A typical SSR transponder***

At certain aerodromes, the surveillance radar controller can provide tracking guidance and height information down final approach in what is called a surveillance radar approach (SRA). This is a common approach for an IMC-rated pilot.

Radar Vectoring

Radar vectoring is when a radar controller passes a heading to steer to a pilot with an instruction such as:

> Charlie Delta
> Steer heading two five zero

Bear in mind that the radar controller is trying to get you to achieve a particular track over the ground and, because he does not know precisely what the wind at your level is and the amount of drift that it is causing, he will occasionally request a modification to your heading while radar vectoring your aeroplane.

No radio navigation instruments are required in the aeroplane for it to be radar vectored, but radio communication is necessary. The pilot concentrates on attitude flying (maintaining the desired heading, altitude and airspeed), while the radar controller concentrates on the aeroplane achieving the desired track over the ground. This is not to say that you should not be very aware of where your track is taking you, especially if high terrain is in the vicinity, and you should always maintain a picture of where the aeroplane is with respect to the aerodrome. This is essential in case of radio communication failure.

The termination of radar vectoring is indicated by the phrase:

> Resume own navigation

How Radar Works

The remainder of this chapter discusses the theory of radio waves and of radar. It is not essential knowledge but it will help your understanding of radio, radar and radio navigation aids.

Radio uses the ability to transmit electromagnetic energy, in the form of radio waves, from one place to another. Radio has played a pivotal part in the development of aviation, and radar is an important type of radio system.

Waves of electromagnetic energy emanating from a radio transmitter can carry information, such as speech, music and Morse code, out into the surrounding environment. Radio receivers tuned to the *same* frequency can detect and use these signals, often at long distances from the transmitter.

Common uses for radio in aviation are:
- ☐ air–ground voice communication; and
- ☐ radio navigation (the ADF/NDB combination, VOR and ILS).

■ *Figure 19-2* **Radio is the transmission of electromagnetic energy and the reception of it at a distant location**

The Reflection of Radio Waves

Electromagnetic radiation can be reflected from certain surfaces. Light waves, for instance, will be reflected by the metallic coating on a mirror. Similarly, radio waves of certain frequencies will be reflected from metallic and other surfaces, with some of the radio energy returning to the point from which it was transmitted as a return echo. Other surfaces and objects, such as wood, may not cause reflection of the radio waves, which will simply pass through like X-rays pass through a body.

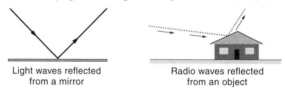

Light waves reflected
from a mirror

Radio waves reflected
from an object

■ *Figure 19-3* **Radio waves, like light waves, can be reflected**

Radar

Detection of the reflected radio waves at the point from where they were originally transmitted is known as radar.

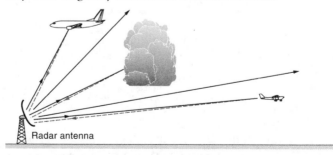

Radar antenna

■ *Figure 19-4* **Radar is the transmission of electromagnetic radio energy and the detection of some of the reflected energy back at the point of transmission**

The principle of radar has been known since the mid–1930s, and was used with devastating effect during World War II (1939–45) to detect objects such as aeroplanes and measure their range. Indeed, the name *radar* was devised from *radio detection and ranging*.

The combined transmitter-receiver used in radar is usually a parabolic dish that is very efficient both in transmitting radio energy in a particular direction and then receiving the reflected radio energy from the same direction. The best results are obtained with ultra-high frequency radio energy. The whole sky can be scanned systematically if desired, simply by slowly rotating the radar dish.

■ *Figure 19-5* **A typical radar antenna**

The Relationship of Time and Distance

All electromagnetic energy travels at the speed of light, 300,000 kilometres per second (162,000 nautical miles per second), the equivalent of almost eight journeys around the world in one second. Some common forms of electromagnetic energy are light, radio waves, X-rays, ultra-violet radiation and infra-red radiation.

By measuring the elapsed **time** between the transmission of a bundle or *pulse* of radio energy and the reception back at the source of its reflected echo, it is a simple mathematical calculation (knowing velocity) to determine the **distance** or *range* of the object causing the echo.

Radar converts an *elapsed time* to a *distance*.

$$\frac{distance}{time} = speed$$

Multiplying both sides of this equation by *time* gives an expression for *distance* in terms of the known speed of light and the measured elapsed time.

$$distance = speed \times time$$

During the elapsed time between transmission of the pulse and reception of its reflection (measured electronically at the radar site), the distance between the radar site and the object will of course have been travelled twice – once out and once back – so the elapsed time needs to be halved, and this is also done electronically.

The speed of light, being so great, means that the times involved are extremely short. This allows a stream of pulses to be transmitted, with only short time intervals between the pulses when no transmission occurs, to allow for reception of any echo. As a matter of interest, the time taken for a radar pulse to travel to and from a reflector 20 nm away (a total of 40 nm) is 0.000250 seconds, or 250 millionths of a second.

$$40 \text{ nm } (2 \times 20) \text{ at } \textit{speed of light } 162{,}000 \text{ nm/sec } = \frac{40}{162{,}000} \text{ sec}$$
$$= 0.000250 \text{ sec}$$

At what Range can Radar Detect Targets?

Radar uses ultra-high frequency (UHF) transmissions, which are basically *line of sight,* and so propagation will be interrupted by buildings, high terrain and the curvature of the earth. These will cause **radar shadows,** and objects in these shadow areas may not be detected.

Bearing in mind the curvature of the earth, the higher an aeroplane is flying, the greater the distance at which it can be detected by radar. An approximate maximum distance in nautical miles is given by the relationship:

$$Radar \ range \ = \ \sqrt{1.5 \times height \ agl \ in \ feet \ (nm)}$$

NOTE $\sqrt{1.5 \ height}$ is the same as $1.22 \sqrt{height}$, which some people prefer. It is a similar expression, since the square root of 1.5 is 1.22.

EXAMPLE 22 At 5,000 ft agl over flat terrain with no obstruction, an aeroplane will be detected up to approximately 87 nm away.

$$
\begin{aligned}
Radar \ range \ &= \ \sqrt{1.5 \ \text{ht in feet}} \\
&= \ \sqrt{1.5 \times 5{,}000 \ \text{ft}} \\
&= \ \sqrt{7{,}500 \ \text{ft}} \\
&= \ 87 \ \text{nm}
\end{aligned}
\qquad
\begin{aligned}
or \quad &= \ 1.22 \ \sqrt{\text{ht in feet}} \\
&= \ 1.22 \ \sqrt{5{,}000 \ \text{ft}} \\
&= \ 1.22 \times 71 \ \text{nm} \\
&= \ 87 \ \text{nm}
\end{aligned}
$$

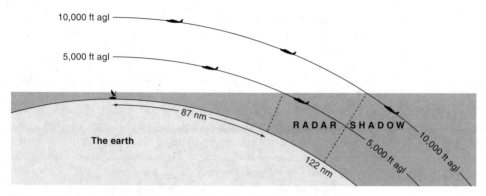

■ Figure 19-6 **Radar detection range for aircraft at 5,000 and 10,000 ft**

EXAMPLE 23 At 10,000 ft agl over flat terrain with no obstructions, an aeroplane will be detected up to approximately 120 nm.

$$\text{Radar range} = \sqrt{1.5 \text{ ht in ft}} \qquad \overset{or}{} \quad = 1.22 \sqrt{\text{ht in ft}}$$

$$= \sqrt{1.5 \times 10,000 \text{ ft}} \qquad\qquad = 1.22 \sqrt{10,000 \text{ ft}}$$

$$= \sqrt{15,000 \text{ ft}} \qquad\qquad\qquad = 1.22 \times 100 \text{ nm}$$

$$= 122 \text{ nm} \qquad\qquad\qquad\qquad = 122 \text{ nm}$$

NOTE These are expected ranges under ideal conditions; in reality, the range of a radar may be significantly less than this, and it may experience *blind spots* and *radar shadows*.

Radar range may be increased if the radar antenna is sited at a high elevation, both to raise it above nearby obstacles that would cause shadows, and to allow it to 'see' further around the curvature of the earth. Hence radar dishes are to be seen on the tops of hills and buildings. The range at which an aeroplane can now be detected by a radar sited well above a uniform surface is given approximately by:

$$\text{Radar range} = \sqrt{1.5 \text{ height of radar dish}} + \sqrt{1.5 \text{ height of aircraft}}$$

    or

$$\text{Radar range} = 1.22 \sqrt{\text{height of radar dish}} + 1.22 \sqrt{\text{height of aircraft}}$$

EXAMPLE 24 At 5,000 ft agl over flat terrain with no obstructions, an aeroplane will be detected up to approximately 99 nm if the radar dish is elevated 100 ft above a uniform surface.

$$Radar\ range = \sqrt{1.5 \times 100} + \sqrt{1.5 \times 5,000}\ ft$$
$$= (\sqrt{150} + \sqrt{7,500})$$
$$= (12 + 87)\ nm$$
$$= 99\ nm$$

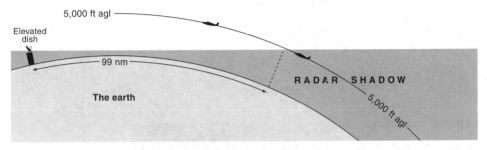

■ Figure 19-7 **Radar range is increased if the radar dish is elevated**

Radar that makes use of reflected radio energy is known as **primary radar,** and it is used for a number of purposes in aviation, including:

- **surveillance radar** to provide an overview of a whole area, and used in surveillance radar approaches (SRA) for azimuth and height guidance on final approach to land; and
- **precision approach radar** (PAR) for extremely accurate azimuth and slope guidance on final approach to land.

Direction by Radar

If the direction from which the reflected signal comes can be determined, as well as its range, then the **position** of the object can be pinpointed. This is achieved by slowly rotating the radar dish, a typical rate being two revolutions per minute, during which time it will have fired out many millions of pulses in its radar beam and received almost instantaneously any reflected returns. The angle of the radar antenna compared to north at the time the return echo is received indicates the horizontal direction (or *azimuth*) of the object. These *returns* are displayed as *blips* on a screen.

Primary Surveillance Radar

Surveillance radar is designed to give a radar controller an over-view of his area of responsibility. It does not transmit pulses in all directions simultaneously, but rather as a beam, which is slowly rotated. For an aeroplane to be detected, the beam must be directed roughly towards it. If the radar controller has his radar tilted up, then it may miss lower aircraft at a distance; conversely, nearby high aeroplanes may not be detected if the tilt is down.

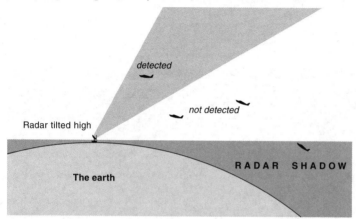

■ Figure 19-8 **To be detected, aircraft must be within the radar transmitter's beam**

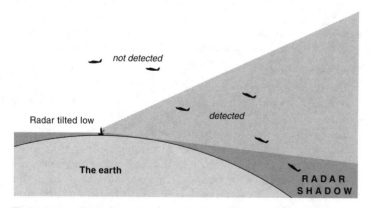

■ Figure 19-9 **Radar tilted low cannot detect targets directly above**

The Radar Screen

Most radar screens are simply cathode ray tubes (CRT) that resemble circular television screens. Using the same principle as television, a beam of electrons is directed onto the fluorescent coating of the CRT to provide a radar picture.

Radar controllers generally have circular displays showing the position of the radar antenna in the centre, with range marks to aid in estimating distance. The radar screen is also known as a **plan position indicator (PPI)**.

The actual radar dish may be located away from the position of the radar controller, possibly on a nearby hill or tower. As the radar antenna rotates slowly, the small electron beam in the controller's CRT also rotates, leaving a faint line or trace on the screen in a direction aligned with the direction of the antenna at that moment. Any radar return signal appears as a *blip* or *paint* at the appropriate spot on the screen.

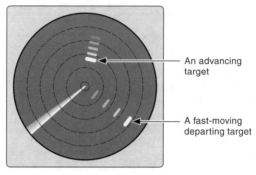

An advancing target

A fast-moving departing target

■ *Figure 19-10* **A radar screen**

An indication of north on the screen allows the controller to estimate the direction of the target, and the range marks assist in estimating its distance. The *paint* of the target remains visible for some seconds after the small trace line has moved on, and will still be visible (but fading) as its next *paint* occurs in the following revolution. This fading trail of blips allows the controller to determine the motion of the target in terms of direction and speed.

In areas of high traffic density, the radar responsibility may be divided between various controllers, each with their own screen and radio communications frequency, and will go under such names as:
- **Approach Control**; and
- **Zone Control.**

Other markings besides the range circles may be superimposed on the screen as a video map to indicate the location of nearby controlled airspace, aerodromes, radio navigation aids such as VORs and NDBs, Restricted Areas, etc.

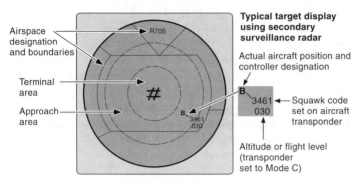

■ Figure 19-11 *A typical ATC radar screen*

Some Disadvantages of Primary Radar

While a big advantage of primary radar is that no special equipment is required in an aeroplane, it does have some operational disadvantages, including:

☐ **clutter** from precipitation and high ground;

☐ **uneven returns** from different aircraft; and

☐ **blind spots.**

The radio energy in the reflected signal received at the radar dish may be quite small, depending on the strength of the original transmission, how good a reflector the target is, its distance from the radar antenna, and so on. A radar that is sensitive enough to pick up weak returns from targets may also pick up returns from terrain and precipitation, leading to *ground clutter* and *weather clutter* on the screen. During periods of heavy rain, primary radar may be significantly degraded.

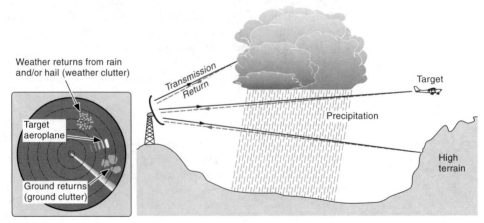

■ Figure 19-12 *Primary surveillance radar is subject to clutter*

Some radars incorporate an electronic sifting device known as a **moving target indicator** (MTI) that only allows signals from moving targets to be shown on the screen, in an attempt to eliminate clutter from stationary objects.

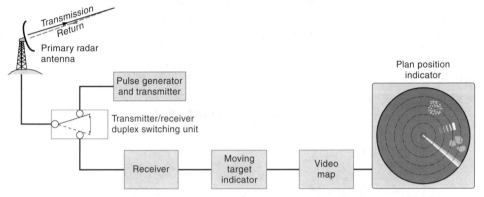

■ *Figure 19-13* **Diagrammatic layout of a primary radar system**

With primary radar only, it is often difficult for the radar controller to distinguish between various signals, and he may have to request one aeroplane to carry out a manoeuvre such as a turn to distinguish its radar blip from that of another aeroplane. A typical request could be:

> *Golf Sierra Delta*
> *For identification*
> *Turn left thirty degrees*
> *Heading zero six zero*

Once the controller observes this turn on the screen:

> *Golf Delta Sierra*
> *Identified one two miles northwest of Exeter*

Secondary Surveillance Radar (SSR)

Secondary surveillance radar removes most of the limitations of primary radar simply by adding energy to the return pulse from the aeroplane, using a device carried on board the aeroplane known as a **transponder.**

Primary radar detects radar energy passively reflected from a target and displays it as a blip, or fading series of blips, on a screen; this is a similar process to a searchlight operator at night seeing an aeroplane in the beam of the searchlight.

Secondary radar is much more than this, and the target is far from passive. It is as if each time the searchlight strikes the target, the target is triggered to light itself up very brightly in response, and not just passively reflect some of the energy transmitted from the ground site. Secondary radar is really two radar sets talking to each other.

Because only a small amount of energy transmitted from the ground is required to act as a trigger for the airborne SSR transponder, the secondary radar ground transmitter and antenna system can be quite small (unlike the large primary radar dish and powerful transmitter in a system which depend on reflected echoes proportional to the original power of transmission). A long and narrow secondary surveillance radar antenna can often be seen above the large primary radar dish.

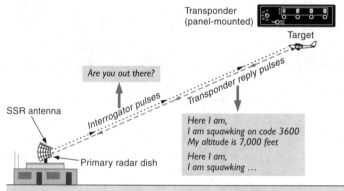

■ Figure 19-14 **SSR is two radars talking to each other**

The SSR ground equipment consists of:

☐ **an interrogator** that provides a coded signal asking a transponder to respond;

☐ a highly directional rotating radar **antenna** that transmits the coded interrogation signal, then receives any responding signals, and passes them back to the interrogator; and

☐ **a decoder,** which accepts the signals from the interrogator, decodes them and displays them on the radar screen.

The SSR aircraft equipment consists of a transponder carried in the individual aeroplane.

The originating signal transmitted from the ground station triggers an automatic response from the aeroplane's transponder. It transmits a strong answering coded signal which is then received at the ground station. This response signal is much, much stronger than the simple reflected signal used in primary radar. Even a very weak signal received in the aircraft will trigger a strong response from the transponder.

The secondary responding pulse from the aeroplane's transponder can carry coding that distinguishes the aeroplane from all others on the radar screen. Depending on the code selected in the transponder by the pilot, it can also carry additional information, such as:

- the identity of the aeroplane;
- its altitude; and
- any abnormal situation such as radio failure, distress, emergency, etc.

A significant advantage is that SSR is not degraded to the same extent as primary radar by weather or ground clutter, it presents targets of the same size and intensity to the controller, it allows the controller to select specific displays, and the system has minimal blind spots.

Unfortunately, not all aircraft are fitted with transponders, yet they may be flying in the same airspace. For this reason, both primary and secondary surveillance radar information will be presented to a radar controller on the one screen.

SSR Symbols on the Radar Screen

We recommend that you visit a radar control centre to see the system in action from the air traffic controller's point of view. Understanding his task and how it interacts with yours as pilot-in-command will lead to greater professionalism.

Sometimes ATC need to distinguish a particular aeroplane from others in its vicinity. This situation may arise with a number of aircraft holding in the one area, or with a light aircraft that is having navigational difficulties and has requested assistance. ATC will then assign a code (such as 1700 or 4000) to this particular aircraft.

Technological advances are being made and already many aeroplanes and some SSRs are equipped for altitude reporting and the like. For instance, some aircraft squawk specific codes, e.g. code 3916 applies to only one particular aeroplane, and on certain advanced SSR screens this will show up as that aeroplane, with a read-out of its altitude and groundspeed. Under less sophisticated radar coverage, the older SSR screens will show this only as belonging to the 3000 family, i.e. as a large circle.

All of these symbols are continually shown on the screen as a result of the coding selected on the aircraft transponder, except for the large *squawk* triangle which appears on the radar screen for 15 to 20 seconds only when a pilot presses the IDENT button.

"Squawk ident" is often requested by ATC when they want positive identification of an aeroplane on their screen. For this reason you should only press the IDENT button on your transponder when specifically requested to do so by ATC.

Using the Transponder in the Cockpit

Usually the transponder is warmed up in the STANDBY position during the taxi, the code to be used (a four-figure number) selected, and then switched ON just prior to take-off.

Even though transponders produced by various manufacturers vary slightly in design, they are operated in basically the same manner. As a responsible pilot, you will become familiar with your particular transponder.

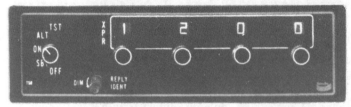

■ *Figure 19-15* **Transponders from various manufacturers**

The Function Selector Knob

The function selector knob enables you to select the transponder to one of its various operation modes, e.g. OFF, ON, STANDBY, ALT. Typical transponder modes include:

OFF: switches the transponder off.

STANDBY: warmed up, and ready for immediate use. This is the normal position until you are ready for take-off, when you would select ALT or ON (if transponder is to be used in flight).

ON: transmits the selected code in Mode A (aircraft identification mode) at the normal power level.

ALT: (altitude) may be used if the altitude-reporting capability (known as mode C) is installed in your aircraft. This is a special **encoding altimeter** which feeds your altitude to the transponder for transmission on to the ATC radar screen.

(If an encoding altimeter is not installed, the transponder still transmits in Mode A, i.e. aircraft identification without altitude reporting.)

TST: tests that the transponder is operating correctly and if so, illuminates the reply monitor light. It causes the transponder to generate a self-interrogating signal to check its operation.

Code Selection

Knobs are provided for you to select the appropriate squawk code for your transponder, and the selected code is prominently displayed in digital form.

An important procedure to follow when selecting and altering codes is to avoid passing through vital codes (such as 7700 for emergencies, 7600 for radio failure) when the transponder is switched ON. This can be avoided by selecting STANDBY while the code is being changed. Your flying instructor will explain further.

The Reply-Monitor Light

The reply light will flash to indicate that the transponder is replying to an interrogation pulse from a ground station.

The reply-monitor light will glow steadily when you:

☐ press the TEST button or move the function switch to the TEST position (depending on the design of your particular transponder) to indicate correct functioning; or

☐ transmit an IDENT pulse.

The IDENT Switch or Button

When the IDENT button is pressed by the pilot on request from the radar controller to SQUAWK IDENT, a special pulse is transmitted with your transponder's reply to the interrogating ground station. This causes a special symbol to appear for a few seconds on the radar screen around the return from your aircraft's transponder, thus allowing positive identification by the radar controller.

NOTE Your particular transponder may have minor variations to that described above, but will certainly be fundamentally the same. It may for instance have a separate mode selector to select Mode A (position reporting) or Mode C (position and altitude reporting). These variations are easily understood.

Squawk

The term *squawk* that you will often hear is confined to transponder usage, and the instruction following squawk is usually quite clear, for instance: "Squawk ident"; "Squawk code 4000"; "Squawk Mayday" (7700), etc.

Typical Transponder Radio Calls

ATC: "(CALLSIGN), SQUAWK IDENT". Pilot response is to press the transponder IDENT button, allowing the radar controller to identify you positively on his screen.

ATC: "(CALLSIGN), SQUAWK CODE 7340". Pilot response is a read-back of the assigned code: "(callsign), code 7340", and to select the transponder to that code.

ATC: "(CALLSIGN), SQUAWK STANDBY". Pilot response is to move the function switch to STANDBY from ON or ALT position, for a temporary suspension of transponder operation (maintaining present code).

ATC: "(CALLSIGN), SQUAWK NORMAL". Pilot response is to reacti-vate the transponder from STANDBY to ON or ALT, as appropriate, retaining the existing code.

Further information on SSR operating procedures appears in UK AIP ENR 1-6-2-1.

Now complete **Exercises 19 – Radar.**

DME

Slant Distance

Distance-measuring equipment (DME) can provide you with extremely useful information: the distance of your aircraft from a DME ground station. DME uses radar principles to measure this distance, which is the *slant distance* rather than the horizontal distance (or range). For most practical purposes, the DME distance can be considered as range, except when the aeroplane is within a few miles of the DME ground station.

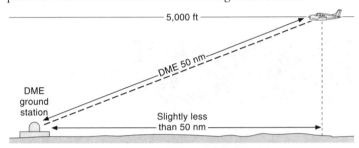

■ *Figure 20-1* **DME measures slant distance**

Passing directly over the DME ground station, the DME indicator in the cockpit will either show the height of the aeroplane in nautical miles (1 nm = 6,000 ft approximately), or the DME indication will drop out.

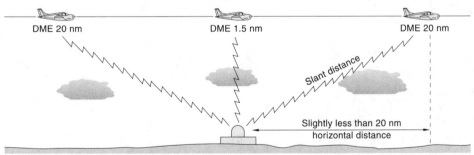

■ *Figure 20-2* **Passing overhead a DME ground station**

DME Cockpit Displays

DME distance is usually displayed in the cockpit as a digital readout. The pilot generally selects the DME using the VHF-NAV radio (since most DMEs are paired with a VOR frequency or a localizer frequency). Once the DME is *locked on,* and a DME reading and *ident* obtained, the DME indications can be used for distance information irrespective of whether the VOR (or local-izer) is used for tracking or orientation purposes.

Some airborne DME equipment is capable of computing the rate of change of DME distance (the *rate of closure* of the aeroplane with the DME ground station), and displaying this rate of closure on the DME cockpit instrument. If it is assumed that slant distance equals horizontal distance, and that the aeroplane is tracking either directly towards or directly away from the DME ground station, then the rate of closure read-out will represent **groundspeed (GS),** a very useful piece of information. Some DME indicators can also display **time to the station (TTS)** in minutes at the current rate of closure, by comparing the ground-speed with DME distance.

> *DME measures rate of closure to the ground station and displays your groundspeed and time to the station.*

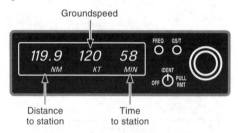

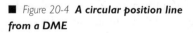

■ *Figure 20-3* **A digital DME panel**

If the DME equipment in the aeroplane does not give a groundspeed read-out, then simply note the DME distance at two particular times, and carry out a simple calculation of GS = distance/time either mentally or on your navigation computer.

EXAMPLE 1 You note DME distance and time as you track towards a DME ground station. Calculate groundspeed.

DME 35	Time 0215 UTC	
DME 25	Time 0220 UTC	
10 nm	5 min	= **GS 120 kt**

Circular Position Lines

The DME provides a circular position line. If the DME reads 35 nm, for instance, then you know that the aeroplane is somewhere on the circumference of a 35 nm circle centred on the DME ground station.

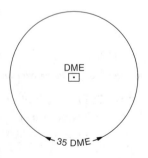

■ *Figure 20-4* **A circular position line from a DME**

Information from another radio aid may assist in positively fixing the position of the aeroplane, provided the two position lines give a good 'cut' (angle of intercept).

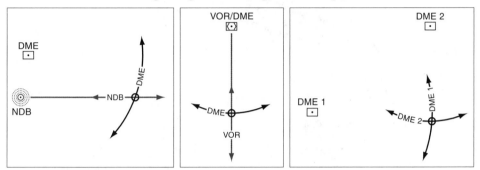

■ *Figure 20-5* **Using two radio navaids to fix position**

How DME Works

DME uses the principle of secondary radar. Radar is covered thoroughly in Chapter 19, where both primary and secondary radar are discussed. **Primary radar** detects one of its own transmissions that is reflected from some object; **secondary radar** detects a *responding transmission* from a **transponder** activated by an *interrogation* signal.

Distance measuring equipment operates by the airborne transmitter (the *interrogator*) sending out a stream of radio pulses in all directions on the receiving frequency of the DME ground station transponder.

At the target DME ground beacon, these pulses are passed through an electronic *gate*. If the pulses and the gate match up, the DME ground beacon (or transponder) is triggered, and responds by transmitting a strong answering signal. The airborne DME equipment detects this answering signal and measures the time between the transmission of the interrogating pulse from the aircraft and the reception of the ranging reply pulse from the DME ground station. It converts this time to a *distance in nautical miles* and the DME indicator, when it displays this distance with the red OFF flag out of view, is said to have latched on or locked on.

NOTE Do not confuse the DME transponder at the DME ground station (and associated with the airborne DME equipment) with the SSR transponder carried in the aircraft (operated by the pilot and associated with the ground-based secondary surveillance radar).

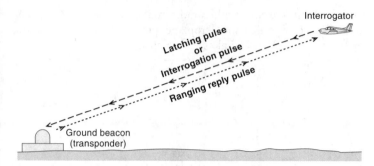

■ *Figure 20-6* **Operation of the DME**

Each DME ground transponder can cope with about 100 different aeroplanes at any one time before becoming saturated, and the system is designed so that there is no possibility of interrogation pulses from one aeroplane causing an incorrect range indication in another aeroplane. Also, because the frequencies are carefully chosen so that stations with like frequencies are situated far apart geographically, there is no likelihood of interference from the wrong DME ground station. DME signals are line-of-sight transmissions (like VHF radio communications, radar and VOR). The approximate usable range in nautical miles is the square root of (1.5 × height in ft).

> *You must positively identify a DME ground station before using it for navigation.*

DME Frequencies

DME operates in the UHF (ultra-high frequency) band from 962 MHz to 1,213 MHz which, with 1 MHz spacing, gives 252 possible frequencies. Each DME channel consists of two frequencies (an interrogation frequency from the aeroplane and a paired response frequency from the ground station).

There are 126 channels currently in use, numbered from 1 to 126, and with X or Y classification after them. You may see references such as DME CH 92Y or DME CH 111X in the AIP, but there is no need for you to know these details, since these numbers are not used by the pilot to select the DME – the DME is automatically selected on many types of VHF-NAV units when you select the VHF-NAV to an appropriate VOR or ILS frequency.

VOR/DME Pairing

Each VOR frequency has a specific DME channel paired with it. For instance, VOR frequency 112.00 MHz has DME channel 57X paired with it, so that the VOR's associated DME will automatically be interrogated when you select the VOR frequency 112.00 on the VHF-NAV. The purpose of this pairing is to reduce your workload in the cockpit, with only one selection instead of two required, and to reduce the risk selecting the right VOR but the wrong DME station. It is normal for only **co-located** VORs and DMEs to be frequency paired. Co-located VORs and DMEs are situated within 800 metres of each other, and each will have the same Morse code ident.

A paired VOR and DME give a very good position fix:
☐ the radial from the VOR; and
☐ the distance from the DME.

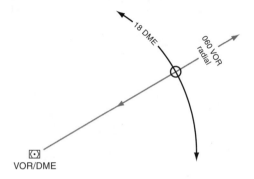

VOR/DME

■ *Figure 20-7* **Fixing position with VOR and DME**

DME Station Information
Further information on individual DME ground stations appears in the ENR 4-1-1 section of the UK AIP.

ENR 4.1 — RADIO NAVIGATION AIDS — EN-ROUTE						
Manchester VOR/DME (4.8°W - 1996)	MCT	113.55 MHz (Ch 82Y)	H24	AD Purpose: 532125.29N 0021544.24W ENR Purpose: 532125N 0021544W	282 ft amsl	APCH Aid to Manchester. DOC 90 nm/50000 ft.

■ *Figure 20-8* **Information from AIP ENR 4-1-1 for the Midhurst DME station**

Now complete **Exercises 20 – DME.**

The NDB and the ADF

General Description

The non-directional beacon (NDB) is the simplest form of radio navigation aid used by aircraft. It is a ground-based transmitter that transmits radio energy in all directions, hence its name – the **non-directional beacon.**

The **automatic direction finder** (ADF), fitted in an aeroplane has a needle that indicates the direction from which the signals of the selected NDB ground station are being received. This is extremely useful information for pilots flying in instrument conditions and/or at night. In days past, the combined ADF/NDB system was referred to as the **radio compass.**

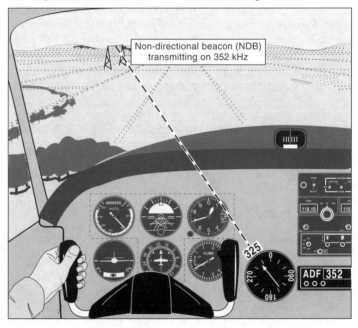

Non-directional beacon (NDB) transmitting on 352 kHz

■ *Figure 21-1* **A correctly tuned ADF indicates the direction of the selected NDB from the aircraft**

Flying to an NDB in an aeroplane is similar to following a compass needle to the North Pole – fly the aeroplane towards where the needle points and eventually you will arrive overhead.

■ *Figure 21-2* **Flying to a station is straightforward**

Flying away from the North Pole, however, with the magnetic compass needle pointing behind, could take the aeroplane in any one of 360 directions. Similarly, flying away from the NDB using only the ADF needle will not lead the aeroplane to a particular point (unlike flying *to* an NDB). The aeroplane could end up anywhere! Further information is required.

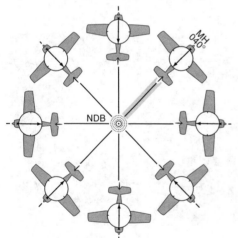

■ *Figure 21-3* **Flying away from a station requires more information than just the needle on the tail**

The ADF and the Heading Indicator

The extra information required by the pilot, in addition to that supplied by the ADF needle, comes from the magnetic compass, or more commonly, from the heading indicator. Accurate navigation can be carried out using the aircraft **ADF needle** which points at an NDB ground station, and a **heading indicator** which indicates the aeroplane's magnetic heading (MH).

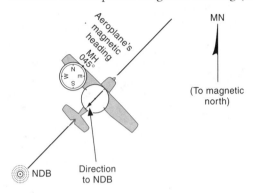

■ *Figure 21-4* **The ADF/NDB combination needs support from a magnetic compass (or from a heading indicator)**

NOTE Since a heading indicator will most probably drift slowly out of alignment, it is essential that you periodically realign it with the magnetic compass in straight flight at a steady speed, say every 10 or 15 minutes.

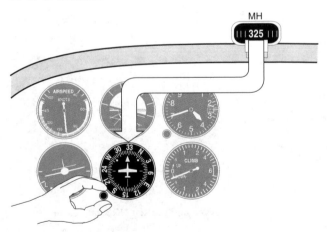

■ *Figure 21-5* **Periodically realign the DI with the magnetic compass in steady flight**

The NDB/ADF Combination

Before using an ADF's indications of the bearing to a particular NDB, the aeroplane must be within the promulgated range of the NDB and you must have:

☐ **correctly selected** the NDB frequency;

☐ **identified** its Morse code ident; and

☐ **tested** the ADF needle to ensure that it is indeed 'ADFing'.

If the NDB is 40° to the left of the aeroplane's magnetic heading, say MH 070°M, then the situation can be illustrated as shown in Figure 21-6. The NDB, since it is 40° left of the nose, will have a magnetic bearing (MB) of 030°M from the aeroplane.

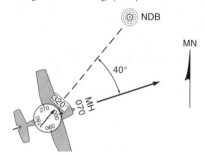

■ *Figure 21-6* **A diagrammatic representation**

The ADF/NDB combination, in conjunction with the heading indicator, can be used:
- **to track** to the NDB on any desired track, pass overhead the NDB, and track outbound on whatever track is desired; or
- **to fix** the aeroplane's position.

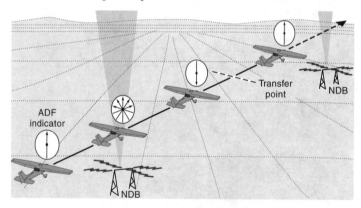

■ *Figure 21-7* **Flying towards, over, and past an NDB, and on to the next one**

The ADF in the aeroplane should, whenever possible, be selected to an NDB relevant to the desired path of the aeroplane. If tracking en route between two NDBs, the point of transfer from one NDB to the next would reasonably be the half-way point, depending of course on their relative ranges.

If the ADF needle points up, the NDB is ahead.

If the ADF needle points down, the NDB is behind.

If the NDB is ahead, the ADF needle will point up the dial; if the NDB is behind, the ADF needle will point down the dial. As the aeroplane passes overhead the NDB, the ADF needle will become very sensitive and will swing from ahead to behind.

The NDB/ADF combination is the simplest form of radio navigation in theory, yet it takes a good instrument pilot to use it accurately. Other more advanced systems, such as the VOR, are more complicated in principle but easier to use.

The NDB

The NDB is a ground-based transmitter.

The non-directional beacon (NDB) is the ground-based part of the combination. It is called *non-directional* because no particular direction is favoured or differentiated in its transmissions; the NDB radiates identical electromagnetic energy in all directions. Each NDB transmits on a given frequency in the low-frequency or medium-frequency LF/MF bands (somewhere between 200 to 1,750 kHz). The transmission aerial is either a single mast or a large 'T-aerial' slung between two masts.

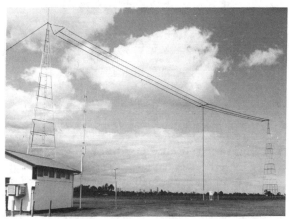

■ *Figure 21-8* **NDB transmission aerials**

Identify an NDB before using it for navigation.

To avoid confusion between various NDBs, and to ensure that the pilot is using the correct beacon, each NDB transmits its own particular identification signal (or **ident**) in the form of a two- or three-letter Morse code signal, which you should monitor periodically in the cockpit.

EXAMPLE 1 The Plymouth NDB has a frequency of 396.5 kHz and is identified by listening to, and identifying the Morse code symbols for PY, which are: *"dit-dah-dah-dit dah-dit-dah-dah"* or:

NDB Range

For long-range en route navigation where no other aids are available, a fairly strong NDB with a range of 100 nm or more is usually required. Some NDBs used for long-distance overwater tracking, for instance in the Pacific area, may have a range of 400 nm. In the UK, however, where routes are relatively short and there are many navigation facilities, most NDBs have only a short range.

Lichfield NDB, for instance, near Birmingham, has a range of only 50 nm. The range of each non-directional beacon (NDB) is listed in AIP ENR 4-1-1, and within this promulgated range the NDB should provide bearings accurate to within ±5°. The promulgated range also provides guidance as to when you should shift your attention to the next aid.

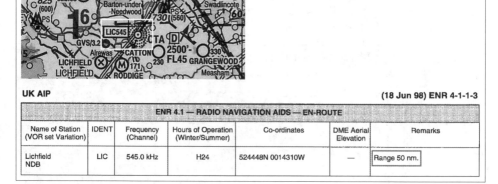

UK AIP   **(18 Jun 98) ENR 4-1-1-3**

ENR 4.1 — RADIO NAVIGATION AIDS — EN-ROUTE						
Name of Station (VOR set Variation)	IDENT	Frequency (Channel)	Hours of Operation (Winter/Summer)	Co-ordinates	DME Aerial Elevation	Remarks
Lichfield NDB	LIC	545.0 kHz	H24	524448N 0014310W	—	Range 50 nm.

■ *Figure 21-9* **Many NDBs have only a short range**

For manoeuvring in the vicinity of aerodromes, only lower-powered NDBs are required. NDBs used for approaches are referred to as locators. Such low-powered beacons are listed in AIP Aerodrome Section (AD 2) and seldom have a range greater than 20 nm.

The range of an NDB depends on:
- **transmission power** (10–2,000 watts);
- **transmission frequency;** and
- **atmospheric conditions** existing at the time – electrical storms, as well as the periods of sunrise and sunset, can distort or reflect the signals from an NDB.

NDB Signal Accuracy

An ideal NDB signal received by an aircraft may be accurate to ±2°; however, various factors may reduce this accuracy considerably. These factors include:

THUNDERSTORM EFFECT causes the ADF needle to be deflected towards a nearby electrical storm (cumulonimbus cloud) and away from the selected NDB.

NIGHT EFFECT when strong skywaves from the NDB returning to earth from the ionosphere cause interference with the surface waves from the NDB, possibly resulting in a fading signal and a wandering ADF needle (most pronounced at dawn and dusk).

INTERFERENCE from other NDBs transmitting on similar frequencies.

MOUNTAIN EFFECT due to reflections of the NDB signals from mountains.

COASTAL EFFECT caused by the NDB signal bending slightly towards the coastline when crossing it at an angle.

NDB Identification

Each NDB or locator is identifiable by a two- or three-letter Morse code identification signal which is transmitted along with its normal signal. This is known as its **ident.**

You must identify an NDB before using it for any navigational purpose within its promulgated range and, if using it for some length of time, periodically re-identify it.

If a test or incorrect ident is heard, the NDB must not be used.

The lack of an ident may indicate that the NDB is out of service, even though it may still be transmitting (say for maintenance or test purposes), and it must not be used for navigation. If an incorrect ident is heard, then those signals must not be used.

	L	L	
	'LUT' 345	'TD' 347.5	'NH' 371.5
Morse code	• — • • • • — — —	— — — • •	— • • • • •

Monitor the ident frequently if an NDB is the only navaid you are using, as a signal failure will not be indicated on the ADF display.

To identify most NDBs, simply select AUDIO on the ADF, listen to the Morse code signal, and confirm that it is the correct one. (Morse code sheets are included on the legend of the ICAO 1:500,000 aeronautical chart series.)

Different NDBs have different ident characteristics which are associated with the type of transmission.

All NDBs in the UK can be identified with the ADF mode selector in the ADF position. In Continental Europe, however, there are some NDBs that require the pilot to select BFO (beat frequency oscillator) to enable identification. The BFO imposes a tone onto the NDB carrier wave to make it audible.

Some NDBs carry voice transmissions, such as the automatic terminal information service (ATIS) at some aerodromes. It is also possible, in a situation where the communications radio (VHF-COM) has failed, for ATC to send voice messages to the pilot on the NDB frequency. They can be received on the ADF if AUDIO is selected.

NOTE Broadcasting stations such as the BBC and commercial stations may also be received by an ADF, since they transmit in the LF/MF bands. But it is not good airmanship to use a broadcasting station as a navigational aid, since they are difficult to identify precisely. Even if an announcer says "This is BBC Radio 2", it is possible that the transmission is coming, not from the main transmitter, but from an alternative or emergency transmitter located elsewhere, or even a relay station many miles away from the main transmitter. To use information from a radio broadcasting station, you must be absolutely certain of its geographical position – something which is difficult to determine. It is not good airmanship to listen to a broadcasting station in flight, as it will distract you from operational tasks and responsibilities.

The ADF

The airborne partner of the NDB is the automatic direction finder, usually referred to as the ADF. It operates on the *radio compass* principle whereby the ADF needle indicates the direction from which the signals are coming.

> The ADF is a receiver in the aircraft.

The automatic direction finder has three main components:

THE ADF RECEIVER, which the pilot tunes to the frequency of the desired NDB and verifies with the ident.

THE AERIAL SYSTEM, consisting of a **loop aerial** (or its modern equivalent), plus a **sense aerial,** which together determine the direction from which the signal is coming.

THE ADF COCKPIT DISPLAY, either a fixed-card or a rotatable compass card with a pointer or needle indicating the direction from which the signals are coming. The cockpit instrument is fitted into the instrument panel, usually to the right of the attitude flight instruments, with the top of the dial representing the nose of the aeroplane, and the bottom of the dial representing its tail. Ideally, the ADF needle will point continuously and automatically towards the NDB ground station.

Combined loop and sense aerial

ADF antenna mounted under fuselage

ADF control panel

ADF card and pointer

■ *Figure 21-10* **The airborne ADF equipment**

ADF Aerials

Improved reception on a portable radio is sometimes possible by rotating it to a particular position, because of the directional properties of its receiving antenna. The automatic direction finder works on the same principle.

The ADF Control Panel

ADF units vary from type to type, so you must become familiar with the set you will be using prior to flight.

■ Figure 21-11 **Typical ADF control panel**

You must be able to select and positively identify the NDB that you want to use, and then verify that the ADF needle is indeed responding to the signals from that NDB. The correct procedure, any time a new NDB is to be used, is to confirm (verbally if so desired):

☐ selected;
☐ identified; and
☐ ADFing (and giving a sensible bearing).

The Mode Selector or Function Switch

The mode selector switches between ADF modes of operation:

OFF. Switches the ADF off.

ADF. The normal position when you want bearing information to be displayed automatically by the needle. Most NDBs can be identified with the mode selector in this position (and the volume knob adjusted suitably).

The ADF mode selector is usually selected to ADF.

ANT or REC. Abbreviations for **antenna** or **receiver**. In this position, only the signal from the sense antenna is used, with no satisfactory directional information being available to the ADF needle. The reason for this function position is that it gives the best audio reception to allow easier identification, and better understanding of any voice messages. Never leave the mode selector in this position if you are navigating using the ADF – the ADF needle will remain stationary with no obvious indication that it is not responding! It is possible, however, to identify most NDBs with the mode selector in the ADF position (which is a safer position), and for the ANT position to be avoided.

BFO or CW. Abbreviations for **beat frequency oscillator** or **carrier wave.** This position is selected when identifying the few NDBs that use A0/A1 or A1 transmissions, which are unmodulated carrier waves whose transmission is interrupted in the pattern of the NDB's Morse code identification. Since no audio message is carried on an unmodulated carrier wave, the BFO (as part of the airborne equipment) imposes a tone onto the carrier wave signal to make it audible to the pilot so that the NDB signal can be identified. Again, do not leave the mode selector switch in this position when navigating using the ADF.

TEST. Switching the mode selector to the TEST position will deflect the ADF needle from its current position. Placing the mode selector back to ADF should cause the needle to swing back and indicate the direction of the NDB. This function should be tested everytime as part of the *selected, identified, ADFing* tuning procedure. Some ADF sets have a separate TEST button which only needs to be pressed to deflect the needle, and then released to check the return of the needle.

NOTE On some ADF equipment, the TEST function is achieved using the ANT/REC position, which drives the needle to the 090 position. Returning the mode selector to ADF should see the needle start 'ADFing' again.

VOL. The **volume** knob will probably be separate from the mode selector. With audio selected to the pilot's headset or to the cockpit speakers, the VOL should be adjusted so that the ident or any voice messages on the NDB may be heard. If signal reception is poor in ADF, then try ANT/REC; if there is no signal reception, try BFO/CW. But remember to return the mode selector to ADF!

Frequency Knobs

NDBs transmit on a frequency in the range 200–1,750 kHz, the most common band being 200–400 kHz. To allow easier and accurate selection of any particular frequency, most modern ADFs have knobs that allow digital selection, in 100, 10 and 1 kHz steps. Some ADFs may have a band selector (200–400; 400–1,600 kHz), with either a tuning knob or digital selection for precise tuning.

ADF Cockpit Displays

The basic purpose of an automatic direction finder in an aeroplane is for its needle to point directly towards the selected NDB ground station.

The ADF cockpit display is a card or dial placed vertically in the instrument panel so that:

■ if the ADF needle points up, the NDB is ahead;

■ if the ADF needle points down, then the NDB is behind;

■ if the ADF needle points to one side, then the NDB is located somewhere to that side of the fore–aft axis of the aeroplane.

To convey this information to the pilot, various presentations are used, three of which we will consider:

1. The fixed-card ADF, or relative bearing indicator (RBI);

2. The rotatable-card ADF (the poor man's RMI); and

3. The radio magnetic indicator (RMI).

The Relative Bearing Indicator (RBI)

A fixed-card display has an ADF needle that can rotate against the background of a fixed azimuth card of 360° with 000° (360°) at the top, 180° at the bottom, and so on. The fixed-card ADF is also known as the relative bearing indicator (RBI), and is common in many general aviation aircraft.

> On the fixed-card ADF, the needle indicates the relative bearing of the NDB from the aeroplane.

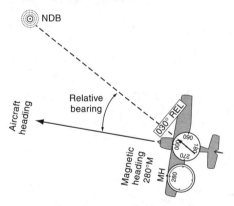

■ Figure 21-12 **A fixed-card ADF is a relative bearing indicator (RBI)**

The **relative bearing** of the NDB from the aircraft is the angle between the aircraft's heading and the direction of the NDB. Usually relative bearings are described clockwise from 000° to 360°, but it is sometimes convenient to describe the bearing of the NDB relative to the nose or tail of the aeroplane.

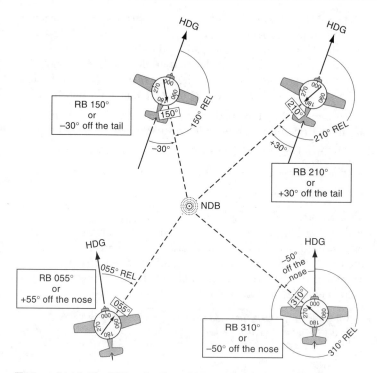

■ *Figure 21-13* **The RBI or fixed-card ADF shows relative bearings**

Each time the aeroplane changes its magnetic heading, it will carry the fixed card with it. Therefore:

> With each change of magnetic heading, the ADF needle will indicate a different relative bearing (RB).

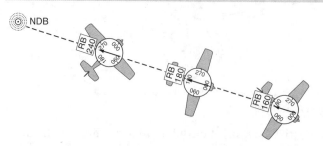

■ *Figure 21-14* **Each time heading is changed, the relative bearing also changes**

Orientation using the RBI

The aeroplane can be orientated with respect to the NDB if you know:

☐ the **magnetic heading** (MH) of the aeroplane (from the compass or heading indicator); plus

☐ the **relative bearing** (RB) of the NDB from the aeroplane.

In practice, magnetic heading is flown using the heading indicator, which should be realigned with the magnetic compass in steady flight every 10 minutes or so. Our illustrations will therefore display the DI instead of the magnetic compass.

In Figure 21-15, the aeroplane is heading 280°M, and the ADF indicates RB 030° to the Bristol locator, i.e. MH 280 and RB 030.

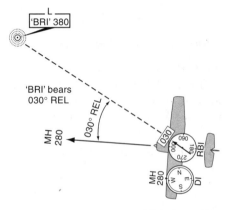

■ *Figure 21-15* **Orientation (Where am I?) using an RBI**

MH 280	+	RB 030	=	310°M to NDB
Aircraft magnetic heading	**+**	**Relative bearing of NDB from aircraft**	**=**	**Magnetic bearing of NDB from aircraft**

Visualising Magnetic Bearing To the NDB (QDM)

The magnetic bearing of the NDB from the aeroplane is also known as QDM, and in this case is QDM 310.

A quick pictorial means of determining QDM using a relative bearing indicator and a heading indicator is to translate the ADF needle onto the DI, by paralleling a pencil or by using your imagination.

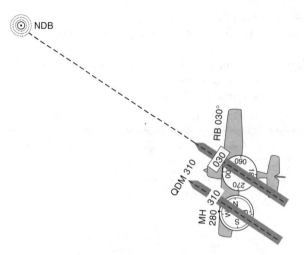

■ *Figure 21-16* **A pictorial (but clumsy) method of finding QDM**

Visualising Magnetic Bearing From the NDB (QDR)

The magnetic bearing of the aircraft from the NDB, i.e. the reciprocal to QDM, is known as the QDR, and in Figure 21-16 is QDR 130. QDR can be visualised as the tail of the pencil (or needle) when it is transferred from the RBI onto the DI.

NOTE An easier method of finding reciprocals than adding or subtracting 180°, is to either:
☐ add 200 and subtract 20; or
☐ subtract 200 and add 20.

EXAMPLE 2

QDM 310	QDM 270	QDM 085
−200	−200	+200
+20	+20	−20
QDR 130	QDR 090	QDR 265

The Rotatable-Card ADF

The rotatable-card ADF is an advance on the fixed-card ADF, because it allows you to rotate the card so that the ADF needle indicates, not relative bearing, but magnetic bearing to the NDB (also known as QDM). Do this by aligning the ADF card with the DI compass card each time the aeroplane's magnetic heading is changed.

To align a rotatable-card ADF:

☐ note magnetic heading on the heading indicator; then
☐ rotate the ADF card, setting magnetic heading under the index.

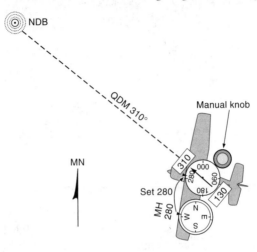

■ *Figure 21-17* **Using a rotatable-card ADF**

When the ADF card is aligned with the DI, the ADF needle will indicate QDM, the magnetic bearing to the NDB. This eliminates any need for mental arithmetic. Note also that the tail of the needle, 180° removed from its head, indicates QDR, the magnetic bearing of the aeroplane from the NDB.

> Any time the aircraft changes magnetic heading, you must manually align the ADF card with the DI (ensuring, of course, that the DI is correctly aligned with the magnetic compass).

If desired, the rotatable card can still be used as a fixed card simply by aligning 000 with the nose of the aeroplane and not changing it.

The next step up from a rotatable card is one that remains aligned automatically, a radio magnetic indicator (RMI).

The Radio Magnetic Indicator (RMI)

The RMI display has the ADF needle superimposed on a card that is continuously and automatically aligned with magnetic north. It is, if you like, an automatic version of the rotatable-card ADF – an automatic combination of the direction indicator and RBI.

The RMI is the best ADF presentation, and the easiest to use, but unfortunately the most expensive and usually only encountered in more sophisticated aircraft.

The RMI **needle** will always indicate QDM, the magnetic bearing **to** the NDB.

The **tail** of the RMI needle will indicate QDR, the magnetic bearing **from** the NDB.

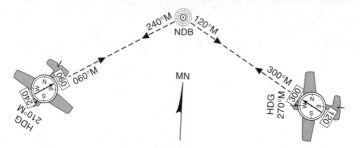

■ Figure 21-18 **The RMI compass card remains aligned with magnetic north**

As an aeroplane turns and its magnetic heading alters, the RMI card (which automatically remains aligned with magnetic north) will appear to turn along with the ADF needle. In reality, of course, it is the compass card and the RMI needle that remain stationary, while the aeroplane turns about them. Before, during and after the turn, the RMI's needle will constantly indicate the current QDM.

Now complete **Exercises 21 – The NDB and the ADF.**

The Relative Bearing Indicator (RBI)

Tracking

Tracking Inbound to an NDB

The ADF/NDB combination is often used to provide guidance for an aeroplane from a distant position to a position overhead the NDB ground position. This is known as **tracking**. Just how you achieve this depends to a certain extent on the wind direction and speed, since an aeroplane initially pointed directly at the NDB will be blown off course by a crosswind.

Tracking Towards an NDB, with No Crosswind Effect

With no crosswind, a direct track inbound can be achieved by heading the aeroplane directly at the NDB. This is achieved with a heading that maintains the ADF needle on the nose of the aeroplane (RB 000).

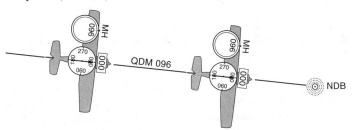

■ *Figure 22-1* **Tracking inbound, with no crosswind**

If there is no crosswind to blow the aeroplane off track, then everything will remain constant as in Figure 22-1 – the magnetic heading 096, the relative bearing of 000, and the QDM 096 will all remain constant. This will be the situation in:

▢ nil-wind conditions;

▢ a direct headwind; or

▢ a direct tailwind.

Tracking Inbound with a Crosswind

WITH NO CORRECTION FOR DRIFT made by the pilot, and the aeroplane headed directly at the NDB so that the ADF needle indicates a relative bearing of 000, any crosswind will cause the aeroplane to be blown off track.

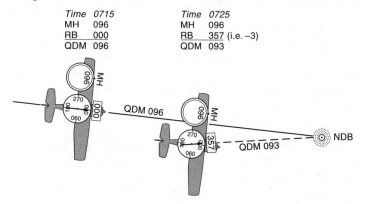

Time	0715	Time	0725
MH	096	MH	096
RB	000	RB	357 (i.e. –3)
QDM	096	QDM	093

■ *Figure 22-2* **Crosswind causes drift**

In Figure 22-2, the wind, with a northerly component, has blown the aeroplane to the right of track. This is indicated by the ADF needle starting to move down the left of the dial. To return to track, the aeroplane must be turned towards the left, i.e. towards the direction in which the head of the needle is moving.

If the pilot turns left to RB 000 to put the NDB on the nose again, then after a short while the aeroplane will again have been blown to the right of track, and the ADF needle will move to the left of the nose. A further turn to the left will be required – and the process will need to be repeated again and again.

In this way, the track made good (TMG) to the NDB will be curved, the aeroplane finally approaching the NDB heading roughly into-wind, and a longer distance will be travelled compared to the direct track from the original position. This rather inefficient means of arriving overhead the NDB is known as **homing** (keeping the NDB on the nose). It is not a very tidy procedure. Professional pilots rarely use it.

WITH CORRECT DRIFT CORRECTION made by the pilot – a far better procedure than homing is to **track direct to the NDB** by heading into wind and laying off a wind correction angle (WCA) to counteract drift. If 5° left is indeed the correct WCA, the aeroplane can achieve a track of 096°M direct to the NDB by the pilot steering MH 091.

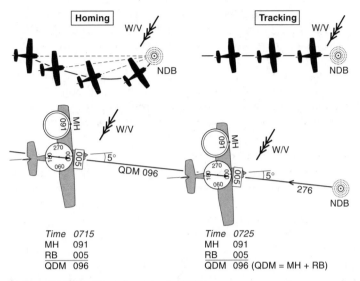

Time 0715
MH   091
RB   005
QDM   096

Time 0725
MH   091
RB   005
QDM   096 (QDM = MH + RB)

■ Figure 22-3 **Tracking direct to the NDB**

Different Winds Require Different Wind Correction Angles

An aeroplane is on track when the relative bearing is equal and opposite to the difference between the actual magnetic heading and the desired track. This is illustrated in Figure 22-4. In each situation, the aeroplane is on the desired track of 010°M, but using a different wind correction angle to counteract the drift under different wind conditions.

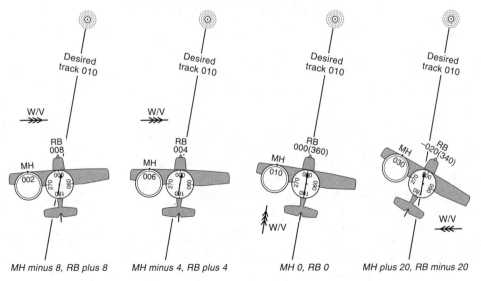

■ Figure 22-4 **Laying off drift to achieve the desired track**

If the precise wind effect is not known, then use a 'best guess' WCA estimated from the available information as an initial WCA. For the same crosswind, slower aeroplanes will need to allow a greater WCA then faster aeroplanes.

It is possible that the wind effect will change as you track towards an NDB, so regular adjustments to the heading may be required. This is often the case as an aeroplane descends using the NDB as the tracking aid, due to variations in wind velocity and true airspeed.

WITH INCORRECT DRIFT CORRECTION made by the pilot, the aeroplane will move off the desired track, i.e. the QDM (magnetic track to the NDB) will change. If a steady heading is being flown, this will become obvious through a gradually changing relative bearing, with the ADF needle moving left or right down the dial.

Suppose, for instance, the pilot steers a heading with a 5° wind correction angle to the left to counteract the effect of a wind from the left. If the wind effect turns out to be less than expected, then the aeroplane will gradually move to the left of the desired track to the NDB, and the QDM will gradually increase. Typical cockpit indications could be:

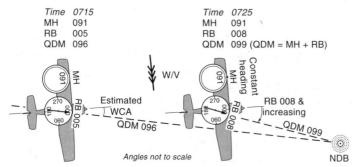

■ *Figure 22-5* **An incorrect wind correction angle causes QDM to change**

The head of the ADF needle falling away to the right indicates that a turn right must be made to track to the NDB. Conversely, the head of the ADF needle falling away to the left indicates that a left turn must be made to track to the NDB. Just how great each correcting turn should be depends on the deviation from track.

NOTE Be careful of terminology. *Drift* is the angle between heading and the actual track made good, which may not be the desired track. The perfect *wind correction angle* will counteract any drift exactly, and the actual TMG will follow the desired track, which is usually the aim of tracking.

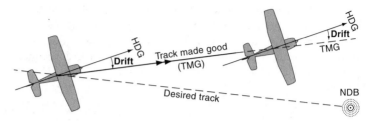

■ *Figure 22-6* **Drift is the angle between heading and TMG**

Maintaining Track

Flying straight and level usually consists of many tiny climbs and descents as the pilot attempts to maintain the desired altitude perfectly. Similarly, it is almost impossible to maintain a perfect track, and so many small turns will usually have to be made by the pilot in an attempt to do so, by correcting any deviations from track.

Re-intercepting a track, having deviated from it, involves the same procedure as the initial intercept of a new track, except that the angles will be smaller provided you are vigilant and do not allow large deviations to occur. Realising that the aeroplane is diverging from the direct track to the NDB, you have several options. You may either:

1. Track direct from the present position (along a new track); or

2. Regain the original track.

1. TO TRACK DIRECT TO THE NDB from the present position (even though it is not the originally desired track) turn slightly right (say 3° in this case), and track direct to the NDB from the present position. In most NDB tracking, this technique is used only when very close to the station (say 1 or 2 nm from the NDB), when there is insufficient distance remaining to regain track.

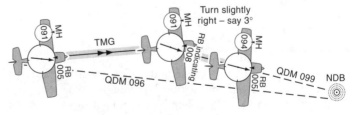

■ *Figure 22-7* **Flying a new track to the NDB**

> *Needle head falling right; turn right.*

2. TO REGAIN THE ORIGINAL TRACK, turn further right initially (say 5° onto MH 096), re-intercept the original track by allowing the wind to blow the aeroplane back onto it and, once the track is regained, turn left and steer a heading with a different wind correction angle (say WCA 3° left instead of 5° left), MH 093 instead of MH 091. This is a very moderate correction, something you would expect to see from an experienced instrument pilot, who would have noticed any deviation from track fairly quickly.

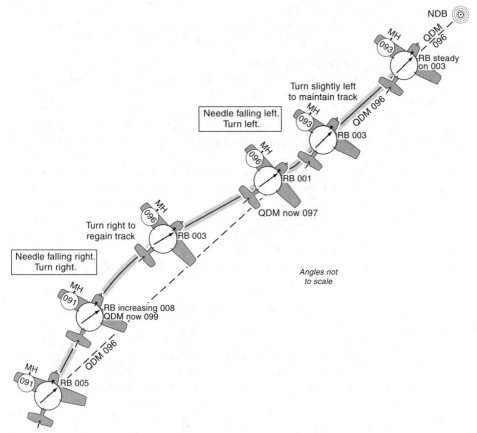

■ *Figure 22-8* **Regain the desired track**

Attempting to maintain the desired track (or remain on the one QDM) is the normal navigational technique when at some distance from the NDB. If, when maintaining a steady magnetic heading, the ADF needle near the top of the dial indicates a constant relative bearing, then the aeroplane is tracking directly to the NDB, and no correction to heading is necessary.

If MH + RB = desired QDM constantly, then ADF tracking is good.

CORRECTING TURNS TO MAINTAIN TRACK. Just how great each correcting turn should be depends on the deviation from track. A simple method is to double the error. If the aeroplane has deviated 10° left indicated by the RBI moving 10° right, then alter heading by 20° to the right. (If you alter heading by only 10° to the right, the result will probably be a further deviation to the left, a further correction to the right, with this being repeated again and again, resulting in a curved *homing* to the NDB).

Having regained track, turn left by only half the correcting turn of 20°, i.e. turn left 10° to intercept and maintain track. This leaves you with a WCA different to the original one (remembering that the original WCA caused you to deviate from track). The new WCA should provide reasonable tracking. If not, make further minor corrections to heading!

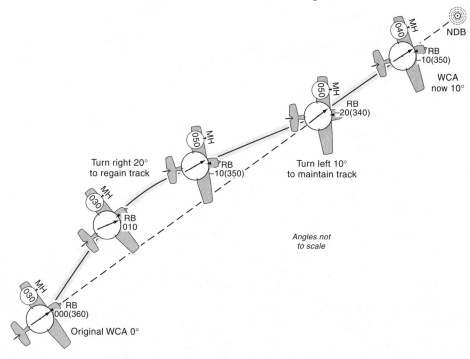

■ Figure 22-9 **Regaining track by 'doubling the error', and maintaining track thereafter**

Bracketing Track

In practice, an absolutely perfect direct track is difficult to achieve. The actual track made good will probably consist of a number of minor corrections such as those just described, a technique known as **bracketing** the track, i.e. making regular corrections, left or right as required, to maintain or regain the desired track.

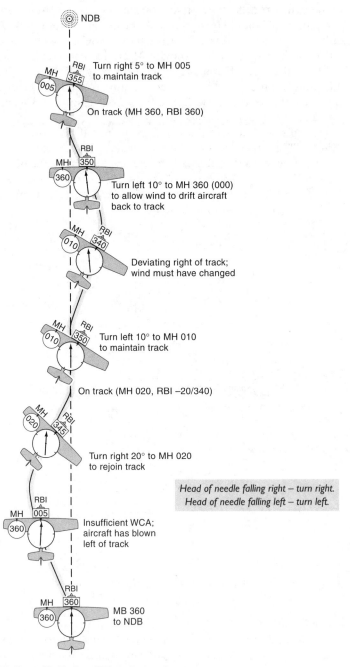

NDB

Turn right 5° to MH 005
to maintain track

On track (MH 360, RBI 360)

Turn left 10° to MH 360 (000)
to allow wind to drift aircraft
back to track

Deviating right of track;
wind must have changed

Turn left 10° to MH 010
to maintain track

On track (MH 020, RBI –20/340)

Turn right 20° to MH 020
to rejoin track

Head of needle falling right – turn right.
Head of needle falling left – turn left.

Insufficient WCA;
aircraft has blown
left of track

MB 360
to NDB

■ *Figure 22-10* **Bracketing the track**

The aim of bracketing is to find the precise WCA needed to maintain track. If, for instance, a WCA of 10° right is found to be too great and the aeroplane diverges to the right of track, and a WCA of only 5° right is too little and the wind blows the aeroplane to the left of track, then try something in between, say WCA 8° right.

Monitor the tracking of the aeroplane on a regular basis, and make corrections earlier rather than later. The result will be a succession of small corrections rather than just one big correction. However, if a big correction is required as may be the case in strong winds, make it. Be positive in your actions!

Wind Effect

If the wind direction and strength is not obvious, then the best technique is to initially **steer track as heading** (make no allowance for drift). The effect of the wind will become obvious as the ADF needle moves to the left or right. Observe the results, and then make heading adjustments to bracket track.

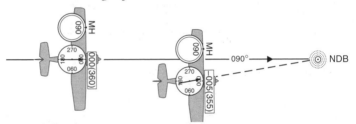

■ Figure 22-11 **If uncertain of wind, initially steer track as heading**

Tracking Overhead an NDB

The ADF needle will become more and more sensitive as the NDB station is approached. Minor displacements left or right of track will cause larger and larger changes in relative bearing and QDM, and the ADF needle becomes 'agitated' as the NDB is approached. For a very precise track to be achieved, you must be prepared to increase your scan rate as the NDB is approached, and to make corrections more frequently.

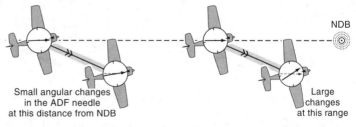

■ Figure 22-12 **Approaching the NDB, the ADF needle becomes more sensitive**

Close to the station and just prior to passing overhead, however, the ADF needle becomes very sensitive. At this point, you can relax a little and steer a steady heading until the aeroplane passes overhead the NDB, indicated by the ADF needle moving towards the bottom of the dial and settling down.

Having passed overhead the NDB, tracking *from* the NDB should be checked and suitable adjustments made to heading. If the track outbound is different to that inbound, then a suitable heading change estimated to make good the new desired track could be made as soon as the ADF needle falls past the 090 or 270 position on its way to the bottom of the dial.

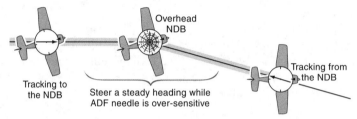

Overhead NDB

Tracking to the NDB

Steer a steady heading while ADF needle is over-sensitive

Tracking from the NDB

■ *Figure 22-13* **Do not overcorrect when close to the station**

The ADF needle becoming extremely active and then falling rapidly to the bottom of the dial indicates that the aeroplane has passed directly overhead the NDB.

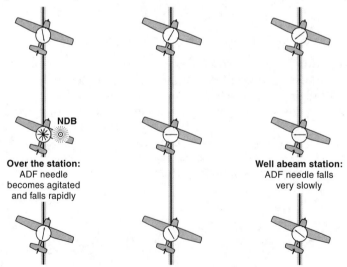

NDB

Over the station:
ADF needle becomes agitated and falls rapidly

Well abeam station:
ADF needle falls very slowly

■ *Figure 22-14* **Good ADF tracking (left); reasonable and poor tracking**

The ADF needle moving gradually to one side and slowly falling to the bottom of the dial indicates that the aeroplane is passing to one side of the beacon – the rate at which the needle falls being an indication of the aeroplane's proximity to the NDB. If it falls very slowly, then perhaps your tracking could have been better. Time overhead (or abeam) the NDB can be taken as the needle falls through the approximate 090 or 270 position.

Tracking Away From an NDB

When tracking away from an NDB, the head of the ADF needle will lie towards the bottom of the dial.

Tracking Away From an NDB with No Crosswind Effect

If you track overhead the NDB and then steer track as heading, the aeroplane will track directly away from the NDB with the head of the ADF needle steady on 180, and the tail of the ADF needle steady at the top of the dial on 000.

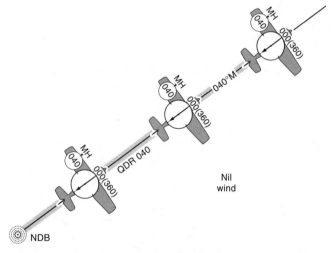

Figure 22-15 **Tracking away from an NDB with no crosswind effect**

The aeroplane shown in Figure 22-15 has a QDR of 040 (magnetic track from the station to the aeroplane), and a QDM of 220 (magnetic track from the aeroplane to the station).

Tracking Away From an NDB with a Crosswind

Suppose that the desired track outbound from an NDB is 040°M, and you estimate that a WCA of 5° to the right is necessary to counteract a wind from the right. To achieve this, you steer MH 045, and hope to see the tail of the ADF needle stay on –005 (i.e. 355). The magnetic track away from the station (QDR) is found from:

QDR = MH ± deflection of the tail of the needle.

In this case, MH 045 − 005 tail = QDR 040, and the chosen WCA and magnetic heading to steer are correct.

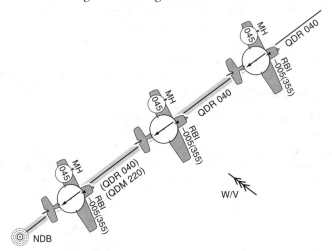

■ *Figure 22-16* **Tracking away from an NDB, with a WCA of 5°**
into wind

If the estimated WCA is incorrect, then the track made good by the aeroplane will differ from that desired. If, in Figure 22-16, the wind is stronger than expected, the aeroplane's actual TMG may be 033°M, and to the left of the desired track of 040°M.

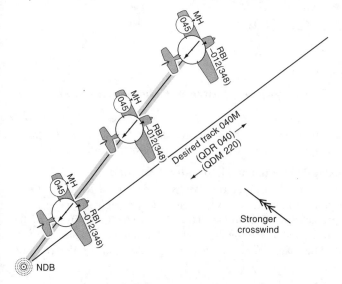

■ *Figure 22-17* **Tracking away from an NDB with an incorrect**
wind correction angle

Whereas inaccurate tracking *to* an NDB is indicated by the ADF needle falling, incorrect tracking away *from* an NDB can occur with the ADF needle indicating a steady reading. Having passed overhead the NDB, an aeroplane can track away from it in any direction. You must always ensure that you are flying away from the NDB along the correct track, and the easiest way to do this is to calculate QDR or QDM using the DI and the RBI.

Regaining Track Away from an NDB in a Crosswind

If an incorrect wind correction angle is flown, the aeroplane will be blown off track. A vigilant pilot will see the incorrect TMG, probably by visualising QDR (from the NDB) or QDM (to the NDB) while a constant magnetic heading is flown.

EXAMPLE 3 In Figure 22-18, the pilot is flying track as heading, i.e. initially making no allowance for drift. If the head of the ADF needle moves right from 180 into the negative quadrant, then the aeroplane must be turned right to regain track.

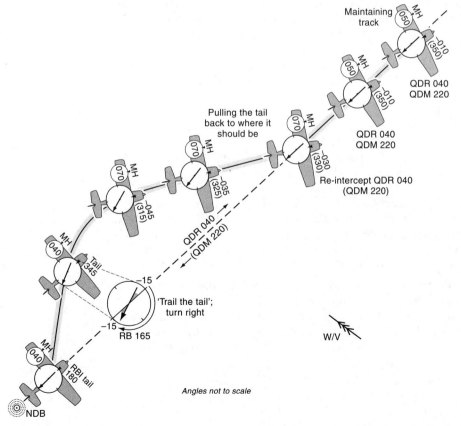

■ Figure 22-18 **Turning right to 'trail the tail' or 'pull the tail around'**

NOTE It is generally easier to work off the top of the dial, since that is where the aeroplane is going, rather than off the bottom of the dial. The right turn necessary to regain track, turning right towards the head of the needle and therefore away from the tail of the needle, can be thought of as *pulling the tail of the ADF needle around* or *trailing the tail*. Some instructors, however, prefer to say that if the head of the needle is moving left, then turn left (and vice versa), even though the head of the needle is at the bottom of the dial. Your instructor will recommend a method.

In Figure 22-18, the aeroplane has been blown to the left of track. The off-track QDR is given by:

MH 040 – 015 tail = QDR 025;
which is left of the desired QDR 040.

To regain track, the pilot has turned right by 30° (double the error) from MH 040 to MH 070, which causes a simultaneous change in the relative bearing of the NDB, the ADF needle tail moving from –015 (345) to –045 (315). (The head of the needle, indicating relative bearing, will move from 165 to 135, but this is not a calculation for the pilot to make, only an observation.)

The relative bearing will naturally change as the aeroplane is turned but, once the aeroplane is flown on its steady intercept heading of MH 070, the tail of the needle will be gradually pulled around.

The pilot will continue with the intercept heading until the aeroplane approaches the desired track, QDR 040. This is indicated to the pilot by MH 070 and the tail of the needle moving up towards –030 (since QDR 040 = MH 070 – 030 tail). For a 30° intercept of 040°M outbound, the pilot is steering + 30 (040 + 30 = MH 070), waiting for the tail of the needle to rise to –030.

Flying track plus 30, waiting for minus 30 on the needle.
As the desired outbound track is approached, the pilot turns left to maintain QDR 040. Estimating a WCA of 10° into wind to be sufficient, the pilot steers MH 050 and checks regularly that the needle tail stays on –010.

EXAMPLE 4 If, on the other hand, the head of the ADF needle moves left from 180 into the positive quadrant, then the aeroplane must be turned left to regain track. Looking at the top of the ADF dial and the tail of the needle, turn left and 'trail the tail'.

In Figure 22-19, the aeroplane has been blown to the right of track. The off-track QDR is given by:

MH 040 + 015 tail = 055;
which is right of the desired QDR 040.

To regain track, the pilot has turned left by 30° from MH 040 to MH 010, which causes a simultaneous change in the relative bearing of the NDB, the tail of the ADF needle moving from 015 to 045.

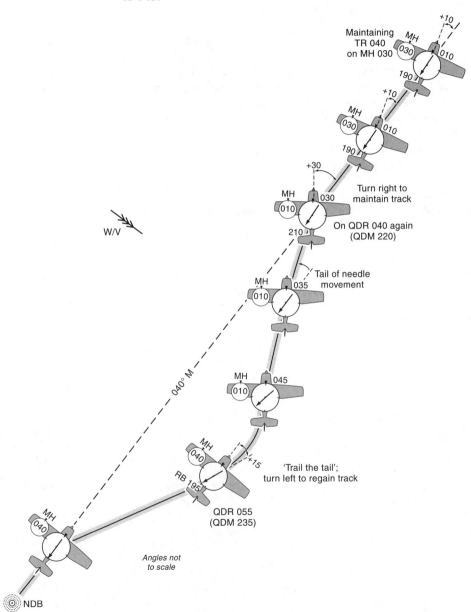

Maintaining TR 040 on MH 030

+10

Turn right to maintain track

On QDR 040 again (QDM 220)

+30

Tail of needle movement

W/V

040° M

'Trail the tail'; turn left to regain track

QDR 055 (QDM 235)

Angles not to scale

NDB

■ Figure 22-19 **Turning left to 'trail the tail' or 'pull the tail around'**

The relative bearing will naturally change as the aeroplane is turned but, once the aeroplane is flown on its steady intercept heading of MH 010, the tail of the needle will be gradually pulled around. For a 30° intercept of 040°M outbound, the pilot is steering −30 (040 − 30 = MH 010), waiting for the tail of the needle to rise to + 030.

Flying track minus 30, waiting for plus 30 on the needle.

The pilot will continue with the intercept heading until the aeroplane approaches the desired track, QDR 040. This is indicated by MH 010 and the tail of the needle moving up towards 030 (since QDR 040 = MH 010 + 030 tail).

As the desired track outbound is approached, the pilot turns right to maintain QDR 040. Estimating a WCA of 10° into wind to be sufficient, the pilot steers MH 030 and checks regularly that the needle tail stays on +010.

Now complete
Exercises 22 – The Relative Bearing Indicator (RBI).

The Radio Magnetic Indicator (RMI)

The RMI significantly reduces pilot workload.

The radio magnetic indicator combines the relative bearing indicator and heading indicator into one instrument, where the ADF card is aligned automatically with magnetic north. This considerably reduces pilot workload by reducing the amount of visualisation and mental arithmetic required. Even the rotatable card (which allows you to align the ADF card manually with magnetic north) lightens the workload, since it also reduces the amount of visualisation and mental arithmetic required.

The discussion that follows applies to both the RMI and the rotatable-card ADF, except that whereas:

- **the RMI** is continuously and automatically aligned with magnetic north;
- **the rotatable card** must be re-aligned with the DI by hand following every heading change (and of course the DI must be re-aligned with the magnetic compass by hand every 10 minutes or so).

■ *Figure 23-1* **Radio magnetic indicators with single and double pointers. The RMI card is automatically aligned with magnetic north.**

■ *Figure 23-2* **The rotatable-card ADF**

Orientation

An RMI gives a graphic picture of where the aeroplane is:

☐ **the head** of the RMI needle displays QDM (magnetic track *to* the NDB); and

☐ **the tail** of the RMI needle displays QDR (magnetic track *from* the NDB).

EXAMPLE 1 Orientate an aeroplane with MH 320 and RMI 050. Determine the QDM, QDR and QTE (true track from the NDB). The magnetic variation is 7°W.

NOTE RMI 050 means QDM 050°M to the NDB (whereas RBI 030 or ADF 030 means a relative bearing of 030 to the NDB, i.e. relative to the nose of the aeroplane and its heading).

QDM is 050, QDR is 230.

Variation west, magnetic best; so true track from the NDB is given by:

QTE = QDR 230 – 7°W variation = QTE 223.

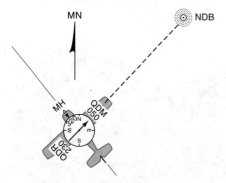

■ *Figure 23-3* **Orientation with an RMI is quite straightforward**

QTE is really only of value for plotting a position line on a visual chart, and so is rarely used in instrument flying.

The Initial Interception of Track

Intercepting an Inbound Track

A common use of the RMI, after you have used it to orientate yourself with respect to the NDB, is to **track to the NDB.** The RMI makes it easy for you to visualise:

☐ where you are;

☐ where you want to go; and

☐ how to get there.

EXAMPLE 2 Your aeroplane has MH 340 and RMI 030. You are requested to intercept a track of 090 to the NDB.

Step 1. Orientating the aeroplane is made easy by the RMI. The QDM (magnetic track to the NDB) in the present position is 030. If you now imagine a model aeroplane attached to the tail of the needle, and on the actual heading (which in this case is MH 340), then you have a very good picture of the situation.

The desired track to the NDB, 090°M-*to*, is ahead of the present position of the aeroplane. If you visualise the desired track on the RMI, with the model aeroplane on the tail of the needle tracking as desired, it becomes quite clear what turns are required to intercept the desired track.

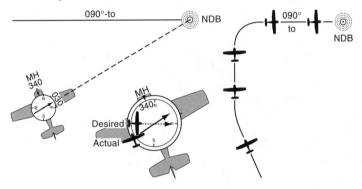

■ *Figure 23-4* **Visualising track on an RMI**

Step 2. To intercept the track 090 to the NDB, the aeroplane should be turned onto a suitable intercept heading, such as one of those illustrated in Figure 23-5.

Step 3. Maintain the chosen intercept heading and periodically observe the RMI needle as it falls towards the desired inbound track of 090°M.

Step 4. As the 090 track is approached, indicated by the RMI needle approaching 090, turn right to take up the desired track to the NDB, allowing for any estimated crosswind effect on tracking. In this case, a WCA of 10° right has been used. With MH 100, and the RMI steady on 090, the aeroplane now tracks 090 to the NDB.

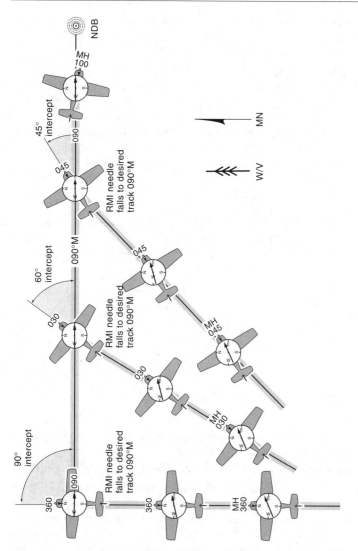

■ *Figure 23-5* **Intercepting track at 90°, 60°, or 45°**

EXAMPLE 3 An aeroplane is given a radar vector by ATC to steer a heading of 010°M, and then to make an intercept 055°M inbound to an NDB.

Visualising the situation confirms that radar vector 010 will intercept the 055-*to* track, and it will in fact be a 45° intercept (055 − 010 = 45). The RMI needle falls towards 055 approaching the desired track inbound, and you should commence a turn shortly before reaching it to avoid overshooting it. This is known as **leading in** (which is really anticipating), and the amount of lead-in can be judged by the *rate* at which the needle is falling, and the distance required for the aeroplane to turn onto a suitable heading to track inbound. Another way to achieve a smooth intercept is to reduce the closing angle as the desired track is approached, say from 45° to 30° to 15° and, finally, to zero as it is intercepted.

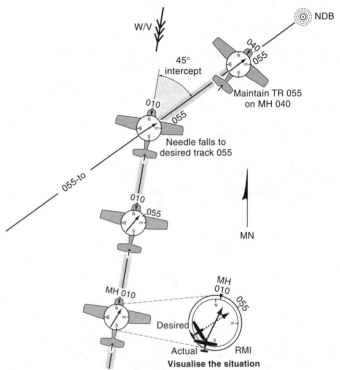

■ *Figure 23-6* **Intercepting 055°M inbound from radar vector 010**

In this case, the pilot has chosen to track inbound with a WCA of 15° left to counteract drift caused by a strong northerly wind. Correct tracking to the NDB will be confirmed by the RMI needle staying on 055.

Intercepting an Outbound Track

EXAMPLE 4 The pilot is given a radar vector of 340 to intercept 280 outbound from an NDB.

Step 1. Orientate the aeroplane.

Step 2. Consider the intercept, 60° in this case (340 − 280 = 60). Visualise the situation. Again, the model aeroplane imagined on the tail of the needle helps.

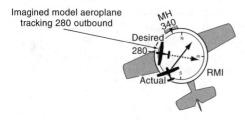

■ *Figure 23-7* **Visualise the situation**

Step 3. Monitor the intercept by steering a steady MH 340 and periodically checking the tail of the RMI needle rising to 280.

Step 4. As the desired track 280 outbound (or QDR 280) is approached and as the tail of the needle approaches 280, the pilot turns left to pick it up, in this case allowing no wind correction angle, since no crosswind effect is expected.

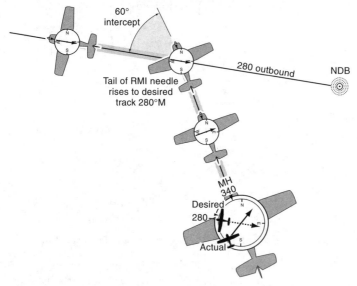

■ *Figure 23-8* **Intercepting 280 outbound off radar vector 340**

Maintaining Track

Tracking Towards an NDB, with No Crosswind Effect

With no crosswind, a direct track inbound can be achieved by heading the aeroplane directly at the NDB. The magnetic heading will, in this case, be the same as the desired track, and the RMI needle will be on the nose indicating the track.

If there is no crosswind to blow the aeroplane off track, then everything will remain constant as in the case shown in Figure 23-9 – the magnetic heading 250 and the RMI 250 will remain constant. This will be the situation in:

- nil-wind conditions;
- a direct headwind; or
- a direct tailwind.

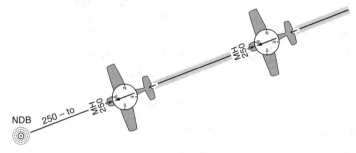

■ Figure 23-9 **Tracking inbound on 250°M using an RMI, with no crosswind**

Tracking Inbound with a Crosswind

WITH NO CORRECTION FOR DRIFT made by the pilot, and the aeroplane headed straight at the NDB with the RMI needle initially on the nose, any crosswind will cause the aeroplane to be blown off track.

Time 0715	Time 0725
MH 250	MH 250
RMI 250 (QDM)	RMI 255 (QDM)

In the case shown in Figure 23-10, the wind, with a northerly component, has blown the aeroplane to the left of track. This is indicated by the head of the RMI needle starting to move down the right of the dial. To return to track, the aeroplane must be turned towards the right, i.e. towards the direction in which the head of the needle is moving.

If the pilot turns left to put the NDB on the nose again (MH = RMI 255), then after a short period the aeroplane will again be blown to the left of track, and the RMI needle will move to the right of the nose. Another turn to the right will be required.

In this way the path to the NDB will be curved, with the aeroplane finally approaching the NDB heading roughly into wind, and a longer distance will be travelled compared to the direct track from the original position. This is known as **homing** (keeping the NDB on the nose). It is not a very tidy procedure. Professional pilots rarely use it!

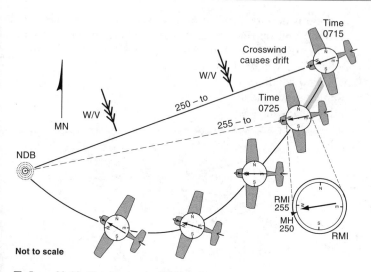

■ Figure 23-10 **Homing to the NDB**

WITH CORRECT DRIFT CORRECTION made by the pilot – a much better procedure than homing – the aeroplane tracks direct to an NDB by heading into wind and laying off a wind correction angle (WCA) to counteract drift. If 15° right is indeed the correct WCA, then the aeroplane will track 250°M direct to the NDB by steering MH 265.

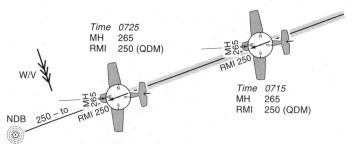

■ Figure 23-11 **Tracking direct to the NDB**

Different Winds Require Different Wind Correction Angles

An aeroplane is on track when the RMI indicates track. This is illustrated in Figure 23-12. In each situation, the aeroplane is on the desired track of 355°M, but using a different wind correction angle to counteract the drift under different wind conditions.

If the precise wind effect is not known, then use a 'best guess' WCA estimated from the available information as an initial WCA. For the same crosswind, slower aeroplanes will need to allow a greater WCA than faster aeroplanes.

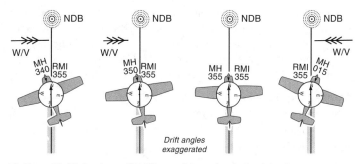

Drift angles exaggerated

■ Figure 23-12 **Laying off drift to achieve the desired track**

It is possible that the wind effect will change as you track towards an NDB, and so regular alterations of heading may be required. This is often the case as an aeroplane descends using the NDB as the tracking aid.

WITH INCORRECT DRIFT CORRECTION made by the pilot the aeroplane will move off the desired track, i.e. the QDM (magnetic track to the NDB) will change. This will become obvious through a gradually changing RMI reading (as the RMI indicates QDM).

Suppose, for instance, you steer a heading with a 5° wind correction angle to the right to counteract the effect of a wind from the right. If the wind effect turns out to be greater than expected, the aeroplane will gradually deviate to the left of the desired track to the NDB, and the RMI reading (QDM) will gradually increase. Typical cockpit indications could be:

> *Modify the wind correction angle to maintain course by altering heading.*

Time 0715	Time 0725
MH 020	MH 020
RMI 015 (QDM)	RMI 018 (QDM)

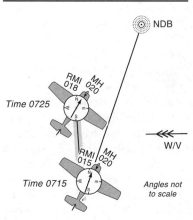

■ Figure 23-13 **An incorrect wind correction angle causes RMI reading (QDM) to change**

The head of the RMI needle falling away to the right indicates that a right turn must be made to track to the NDB. Conversely, the head of the RMI needle falling away to the left indicates that a left turn must be made to track to the NDB. Just how great each correcting turn should be depends on the deviation from track.

Maintaining Track

Re-intercepting a track, once having deviated from it, uses the same procedure as the initial intercept of a new track, except that the angles will be smaller, provided you are vigilant and do not allow large deviations to occur. Realising that the aeroplane is diverging from the direct track to the NDB, you have several options. You may either:

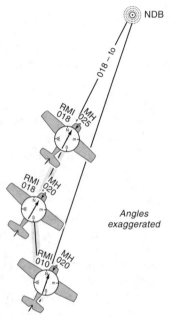

1. Track direct to the NDB from the present position even though it is slightly off the original track; or

2. Regain the original track.

METHOD 1. Turn slightly right (say 5° in this case), and track direct to the NDB from the present position, even though it is not on the originally desired track. In most NDB tracking this technique is used only when very close to the station (say 1 or 2 nm).

■ *Figure 23-14* **Method 1: flying a new track to the NDB**

> Needle falling right; turn right.

METHOD 2. Turn further right initially (say 10° onto MH 030), and re-intercept the original track, indicated by the RMI needle moving down to read 015 again. Once track is regained, turn left (say by half the correcting turn of 10°) onto MH 025. This is a very moderate correction, something you would expect to see from an experienced instrument pilot. (See Figure 23-15.)

> If the MH maintains a constant (correct) RMI indication then the ADF tracking is good.

Attempting to maintain the desired track (or remain on the one QDM) is the normal navigational technique when at some distance from the NDB. If the RMI remains on a steady reading, then the aeroplane is tracking directly to the NDB.

CORRECTING TURNS. Just how great each correcting turn should be depends on the displacement from track and the distance from the station. A simple method is to initially alter heading by double the error. If the aeroplane has deviated 10° left (indicated by the RMI moving 10° right), then alter heading by 20° to the right. (If you alter heading by only 10° to the right, the result will probably be a further deviation to the left, a further correction to the right, resulting in a curved homing to the NDB.)

HAVING REGAINED TRACK, turn left by only half the correcting turn of 20°, i.e. turn left 10° to intercept and maintain track. This leaves you with a WCA different to the original one (that caused you to deviate from track), and one that should provide reasonable tracking. If not, make further corrections to heading!

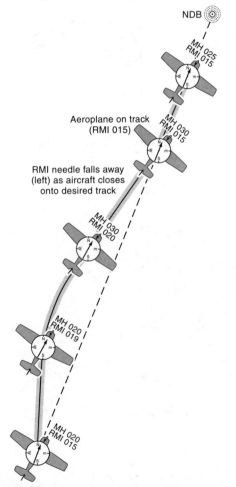

■ *Figure 23-15* **Method 2: regain the desired track**

Bracketing Track

In practice, an absolutely perfect direct track is difficult to achieve. The actual track made good will probably consist of a number of minor corrections such as those just described, a technique known as **bracketing** the track, i.e. making regular corrections, left or right as required, to maintain or regain the desired track.

The aim of bracketing is to find the precise WCA needed to maintain track. If, for instance, a WCA of 10° right is found to be too great and the aeroplane diverges to the right of track, and a WCA of only 5° right is too little and the wind blows the aeroplane to the left of track, then try something in between, say WCA 8° right.

A precise instrument pilot will monitor the tracking of the aeroplane on a regular basis and make corrections earlier rather than later, the result being a number of small corrections rather than just one big correction.

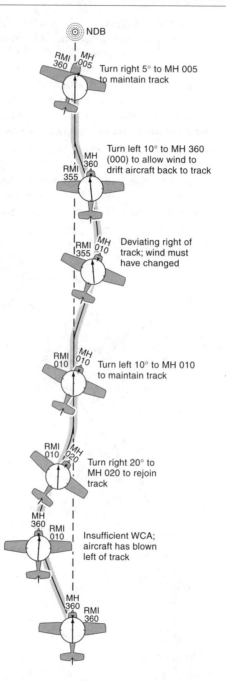

■ Figure 23-16
Bracketing the track

Head of needle falling right – turn right.
Head of needle falling left – turn left.

Wind Effect

If the wind direction and strength is not obvious, then a useful technique is to initially steer the track to the station as heading (i.e. make no allowance for drift), observe the results, and then make heading adjustments to bracket track. This is illustrated in Figure 23-16.

Tracking Overhead an NDB

The RMI needle will become more and more sensitive as the NDB station is approached, minor movements left or right of track causing larger and larger changes in the RMI reading; i.e. the RMI needle becomes 'agitated' as the NDB is approached. For a very precise track to be achieved, you must be prepared to increase your scan rate and respond more frequently.

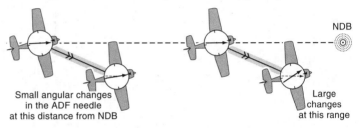

■ *Figure 23-17* **Approaching the NDB, the RMI needle becomes more sensitive**

Close to the station and just prior to passing overhead, however, you can relax a little and steer a steady heading until the RMI needle moves towards the bottom of the dial and settles down, at which time tracking from the NDB should be checked and suitable adjustments made to heading. If the track outbound is different to that inbound, then a suitable heading change estimated to make good the new desired track could be made as soon as the RMI needle falls past the mid-position on its way to the bottom of the dial.

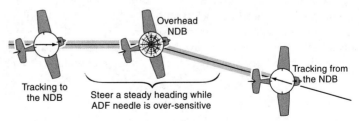

■ *Figure 23-18* **Do not overshoot when close to the station**

The RMI needle becoming extremely active and then falling rapidly to the bottom of the dial indicates that the aeroplane has passed directly overhead the NDB. The RMI needle moving gradually to one side and slowly falling to the bottom of the dial indicates that the aeroplane is passing to one side of the beacon, the rate at which the needle falls being an indication of the aeroplane's proximity to the NDB. If it falls very slowly, then perhaps your tracking could have been better. Time overhead (or abeam) the NDB can be taken as the needle falls through the approximate mid-position.

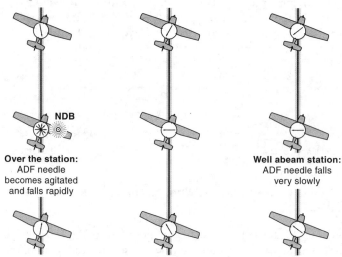

Over the station:
ADF needle
becomes agitated
and falls rapidly

Well abeam station:
ADF needle falls
very slowly

■ Figure 23-19 **Good ADF tracking (left); reasonable and poor tracking**

Tracking Away From an NDB

When tracking away from an NDB, the head of the RMI needle will lie towards the bottom of the dial, and the tail of the RMI needle will be towards the top of the dial.

Tracking Away From an NDB with No Crosswind Effect

If you track overhead the NDB and then steer track as heading, the aeroplane will track directly away from the NDB with the head of the RMI needle steady at the bottom of the dial, and the tail of the RMI needle steady at the top of the dial under the MH lubber line.

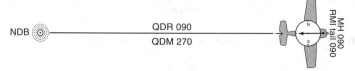

NDB · ──────── QDR 090
                QDM 270

MH 090
RMI tail 090

■ Figure 23-20 **Tracking away from an NDB with no crosswind effect**

The aeroplane in Figure 23-20 has a QDR of 090 (magnetic track from the station to the aeroplane) indicated by the tail of the RMI needle, and a QDM of 270 (magnetic track from the aeroplane to the station) indicated by the head of the RMI needle. Since it is track *outbound* that is being considered here, the position of the *tail* of the needle is of more use.

Tracking Away From an NDB with a Crosswind

Suppose that the desired track outbound from an NDB is 340°M, and you estimate that a WCA of 12° to the right is necessary to counteract a wind from the right. To achieve this, you steer MH 352, and hope to see the tail of the RMI needle stay on 340, the desired outbound track.

In Figure 23–21, the chosen WCA and MH are correct, and the desired track of 340°M outbound is maintained.

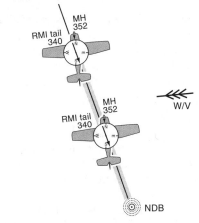

■ *Figure 23-21* **Tracking away from an NDB with a WCA of 12° into wind**

If the estimated WCA is incorrect, then the actual track made good by the aeroplane will differ from that desired. If the wind is stronger than expected, the aeroplane's actual TMG may be 335°M, and to the left of the desired track of 340°M (Figure 23-22).

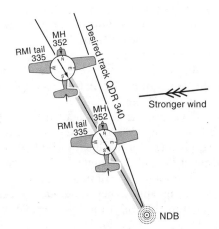

■ *Figure 23-22* **Tracking away from an NDB with an incorrect wind correction angle**

Whereas inaccurate tracking *to* an NDB is indicated by the ADF needle falling, incorrect tracking away *from* an NDB can occur with the RMI needle indicating a steady reading – but the aeroplane may be on the *wrong* QDR. Having passed overhead the NDB, an aeroplane can track away from it in any direction. You must always ensure that you are flying away from the NDB along the correct track, and the easiest way to do this is to *observe the QDR on the tail of the RMI needle.*

Regaining Track Away from an NDB in a Crosswind

If an incorrect wind correction angle is flown, then the aeroplane will of course be blown off track. The vigilant pilot/navigator will observe the incorrect TMG (track made good), probably by noting that the tail of the RMI needle is indicating something other than the desired outbound track.

NOTE It is generally easier to work off the top of the dial, since that is where the aeroplane is going, rather than off the bottom of the dial. The left turn necessary to regain track (turning left towards the head of the needle and therefore away from the tail of the needle) can be thought of as *pulling the tail of the RMI needle around* or *trailing the tail.* Some instructors, however, prefer to use the head of the needle – in this case, the head of the needle (now at the bottom of the dial) moves left, indicating that a correcting turn to the left is required. Your instructor will recommend a method.

EXAMPLE 5 In the situation illustrated in Figure 23-23, the pilot is flying track as heading, i.e. initially making no allowance for drift. If the tail of the RMI needle moves right, then the aeroplane must be turned left to regain track.

In Figure 23-23, the aeroplane has been blown to the right of the desired track QDR 035, onto QDR 043 indicated by the tail of the RMI needle.

To regain track, the pilot has turned left by 16° (double the error) from MH 035 to MH 019. As the aeroplane is flown on its steady intercept heading of MH 019, the tail of the needle will be gradually pulled around.

The pilot will continue with the intercept heading until the aeroplane approaches the desired track, QDR 035. This is indicated by the tail of the RMI needle moving up the dial towards 035.

As the desired track outbound is approached, the pilot turns right to maintain the RMI tail on 025, i.e. QDR 035. Estimating a WCA of 8° into wind to be sufficient, the pilot steers MH 027 and checks regularly that the tail of the RMI needle stays on 035.

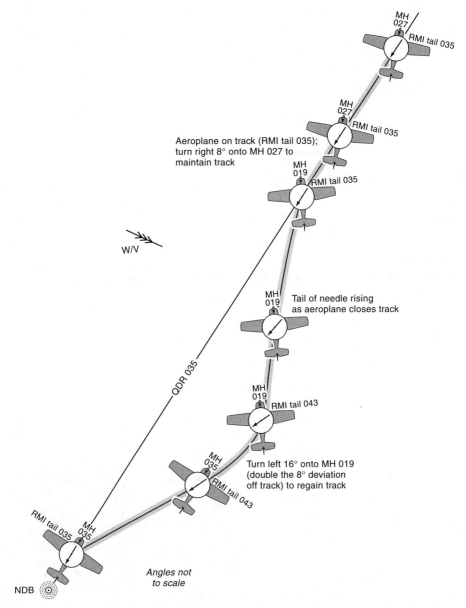

MH
027
RMI tail 035

MH
027
RMI tail 035

Aeroplane on track (RMI tail 035);
turn right 8° onto MH 027 to
maintain track

MH
019
RMI tail 035

W/V

Tail of needle rising
as aeroplane closes track

MH
019

QDR 035

MH
019
RMI tail 043

Turn left 16° onto MH 019
(double the 8° deviation
off track) to regain track

MH
035
RMI tail 043

RMI tail 035   MH
035

Angles not
to scale

NDB

■ *Figure 23-23* **Turning left to 'trail the tail' or 'pull the tail around'**

Similarly, if the tail of the RMI needle is left of where it should be, then the desired track is out to the right, and a right turn should be made to trail the tail (Figure 23–24).

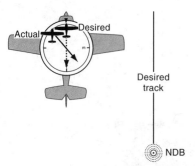

Desired
track

NDB

■ *Figure 23-24* **Turn right to 'trail the tail'**

NOTE If using the head of the needle is the preferred technique, then the need for a left turn is indicated by the head of the needle moving to the left of the datum QDM 215.

Now complete

Exercises 23 – The Radio Magnetic Indicator (RMI).

The VOR

The VOR (pronounced *"vee-oh-are"*) is a very high frequency radio navigation aid that is extensively used in instrument flying. Its full name is the **very high frequency omni-directional radio range,** commonly abbreviated to the VHF omni range, VOR, or omni.

A VOR ground station can be selected on the VHF-NAV radio set.

Each VOR ground station transmits on a specific VHF frequency between 108.00 and 117.95 megahertz (MHz), which is a lower-frequency band than that used for VHF communications. A separate VHF-NAV radio is required for navigation purposes, but is usually combined with the VHF-COM in a NAV-COM set.

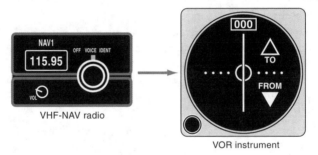

VHF-NAV radio

VOR instrument

■ *Figure 24-1* **Cockpit VOR equipment**

The VOR was developed in the United States during the late 1940s, and was adopted by the International Civil Aviation Organisation (ICAO) as the standard short-range radio navigation aid in 1960. When introduced, it offered an immediate improvement over existing aids such as the ADF/NDB combination, most of which operated in lower frequency bands than the VOR and suffered significant limitations, such as night effect, mountain reflections, interference from electrical storms, etc.

Principal advantages of the VOR include:
- **reduced susceptibility** to electrical and atmospheric interference (including thunderstorms);
- **the elimination of night effect,** since VHF signals are line-of-sight and not reflected by the ionosphere (as are NDB signals in the LF/MF band).

The reliability and accuracy of VOR signals allows the VOR to be used with confidence in any weather conditions, by day or by night, for purposes such as:
- **orientation** and position fixing (Where am I?);

- **tracking** to or from a VOR ground station;
- **holding** (for delaying or manoeuvring action); and
- **instrument approaches** to land.

Many VORs are coupled with a DME (distance-measuring equipment providing a measure of distance from the station in nautical miles), so that selection of the VOR on the VHF-NAV set in the cockpit also selects the DME, thereby providing both tracking and distance information.

> *VORs are often paired with a DME.*

How the VOR Works

The VOR ground station transmits two VHF radio signals:

1. **the reference phase,** which is omni-directional (the same in all directions); and

2. **the variable phase,** which rotates uniformly at a rate of 1,800 revolutions per minute, with its phase varying at a constant rate throughout the 360°.

The aerial of the VOR aircraft receiver picks up the signals, whose **phase difference** (the difference between the wave peaks) is measured, this difference depending on the bearing of the aeroplane from the ground station. In this manner, the VOR can determine the **magnetic bearing** of the aeroplane from the VOR ground station.

■ *Figure 24-2* **Typical VOR aerials**

■ *Figure 24-3* **A VOR ground station (Brookmans Park, near London)**

The two signals transmitted by the VOR ground station are:
- in phase on magnetic north, which is the reference for VOR signals;
- 90° out of phase at magnetic east 090°M;
- 180° out of phase at magnetic south 180°M;
- 270° out of phase at magnetic west 270°M; and
- 360° out of phase (back *in* phase) at magnetic north 360°M, or 000°M.

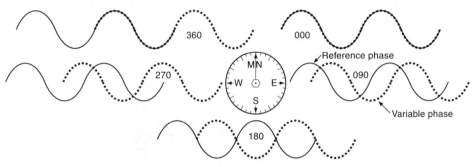

■ *Figure 24-4* **The VOR transmits two VHF signals with a phase difference between them**

Check the Morse code ident before using a VOR.

Every 10 seconds or so a Morse code **ident** signal is transmitted, allowing you to positively identify the VOR. Some VORs may also carry voice transmissions with a relevant automatic terminal information service (ATIS).

The VOR is a very high frequency aid operating in the frequency band 108.0 MHz to 117.95 MHz. It allows high-quality *line-of-sight* reception as there is relatively little interference from atmospheric noise in this band. Reception may be affected by the terrain surrounding the ground station, the height of the VOR beacon, the altitude of the aeroplane and its distance from the station.

VOR Range

The VOR signal is line-of-sight.

The approximate maximum range of a VHF signal is given by the formula (which you do not need to remember):

$$VHF\ range\ in\ nm\ =\ \sqrt{1.5 \times altitude\ in\ feet}$$

EXAMPLE 1 At 7,000 ft amsl, approximate VHF range:

$$= \sqrt{1.5 \times 7,000}$$
$$= \sqrt{10,000}$$
$$= 100\ nm$$

Different VOR stations may operate on the same frequency, but they should be well separated geographically so that there is no interference between their VHF line-of-sight signals. The higher the aeroplane's altitude, however, the greater the possibility of interference. The AIP specifies a designated operational coverage (DOC) for each VOR above which interference is possible. Within the DOC coverage, VOR reception should be reliable. *Detling VOR,* for instance, has a DOC of 60 nm/50,000 ft (see AIP ENR 4-1-1).

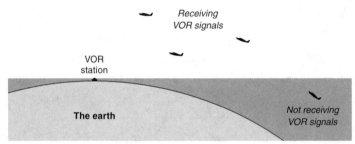

■ *Figure 24-5* **VHF line-of-sight signals**

Tracking with a VOR

The VOR can be used to indicate the **desired track** and the aeroplane's **angular deviation** from that track. For a desired track of 015°M, expect to steer a heading of approximately 015°M, plus or minus a wind correction angle (WCA). By selecting an omni bearing of 015 under the course index of the VOR cockpit display, you can obtain tracking information, as illustrated in Figures 24-6 and 24-7.

The VOR cockpit display is not heading sensitive, which means that the display will not change as a result of the aeroplane changing heading. Figure 24-7 shows the same aeroplane as Figure 24-6, except that a wind correction angle of 10° right is being used by the pilot to counteract a wind from the right, and so the aeroplane's magnetic heading is now MH 025 (rather than MH 015 previously).

Note that:
☐ the VOR indication depends on the **angular deviation** of the aeroplane relative to the selected track;
☐ the VOR indication will *not* change with any heading change of the aeroplane.

It is usual, when tracking en route from one VOR to another, to select the next VOR when the aeroplane is approximately halfway between them, as in Figure 24-8. This allows the use of the stronger signal, although intervening mountains which might shield the signal of a VOR may affect your decision in this regard.

Change VORs at the approximate mid-point between them.

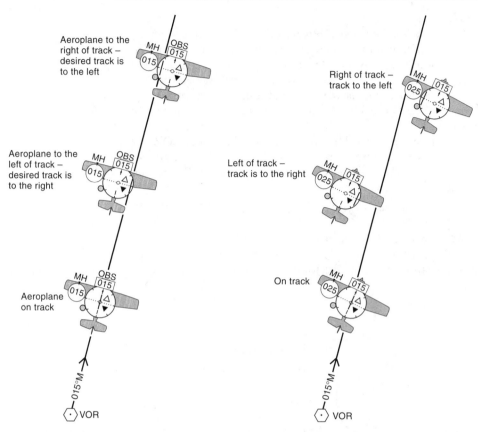

■ Figure 24-6 **The VOR is used to indicate track**

■ Figure 24-7 **The VOR cockpit display is not heading sensitive**

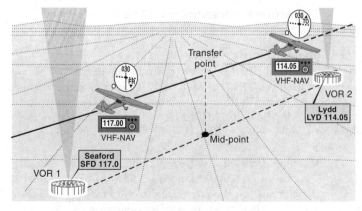

■ Figure 24-8 **Tracking between two VORs**

VOR Radials

As its name *omni* suggests, a VOR ground transmitter radiates signals in all directions. Its most important feature, however, is that the signal in any particular direction differs slightly from all the adjacent signals. These individual directional signals can be thought of as *tracks* or *position lines* radiating out from the VOR ground station, in much the same way as spokes from the hub of a wheel.

By convention, 360 different tracks away from the VOR are used, each separated from the next by 1°, and each with its direction related to magnetic north. Each of these 360 VOR tracks or position lines is called a radial.

> A **radial** is the magnetic bearing outbound FROM a VOR.

NOTE A specific VOR radial is the same as QDR. For instance, the 293 radial is QDR 293, which is a track of 293° magnetic away *from* the VOR ground station.

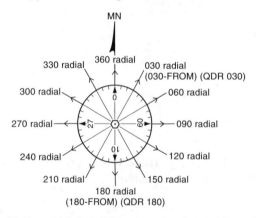

■ *Figure 24-9* **A radial is a magnetic bearing from the VOR ground station (QDR)**

VORs on Aeronautical Charts

Most aeronautical charts show the position, frequency and Morse code identification (ident) of each VOR ground station. Information on a particular VOR may be found in the UK Aeronautical Information Publication (AIP ENR 4-1-1), and any changes to this information will be referred to in NOTAMs (to which you may refer prior to flight).

A VOR ground station may be represented in various ways on a chart – the common representations are shown in Figure 24-10. Since magnetic north is the reference direction for VOR radials, a magnetic north arrowhead usually emanates from the VOR symbol, with a compass rose heavily marked each 30°, and the

> *VOR radials are based on magnetic north.*

radials shown in 10° intervals on the rose. This is generally adequate for in-flight estimation of track to an accuracy of ±2°; however, when flight planning, it is advisable to be more accurate.

At the flight planning stage, use a protractor or plotter for precise measurement of track, although in some cases this may not be necessary because some much-used tracks are published on Radio Navigation Charts (RNCs) in degrees magnetic. If you measure the track in degrees true (°T), then magnetic variation needs to be applied to convert to degrees magnetic (*variation west, magnetic best*).

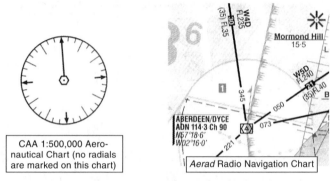

CAA 1:500,000 Aeronautical Chart (no radials are marked on this chart)

Aerad Radio Navigation Chart

■ *Figure 24-10* **A VOR and its radials represented on different charts**

It is usual for instrument-rated pilots to use the Radio Navigation Charts (published by *Aerad* and *Jeppesen*), and IMC-rated pilots to use the CAA 1:500,000 (half-million) ICAO Topographical Charts, already well known from visual navigation.

Further Information on VORs

The UK AIP carries information regarding radio navigation aids in its ENR 4-1-1 section. For example, the AIP extract for *Goodwood*, shown in Figure 24-11, includes:

☐ Frequency, 114.75 MHz (also found on the charts).
☐ Callsign, or identification, 'GWC' (also found on the charts) which, in Morse code, is *"dah-dah-dit dit-dah-dah dah-dit-dah-dit"*.
☐ Hours of service (24 hours a day, summer and winter).
☐ Location in latitude and longitude (if you cannot find it on the chart).
☐ Remarks that:
   – the VOR is an approach aid to Chichester/Goodwood aerodrome (and there will therefore be an instrument approach chart available for it from *Jeppesen, Aerad* and the CAA); and
   – it has a designated operational coverage (DOC) of 80 nm up to 50,000 ft amsl, above which there may be interference from distant VORs using the same frequency.

ENR 4.1 — RADIO NAVIGATION AIDS — EN-ROUTE						
Name of Station (VOR set Variation)	IDENT	Frequency (Channel)	Hours of Operation (Winter/Summer)	Co-ordinates	DME Aerial Elevation	Remarks
1	2	3	4	5	6	7
Goodwood VOR/DME (4.0°W - 1994)	GWC	114.75 MHz (Ch 94Y)	H24	AD Purpose: 505118.78N 0004524.25W ENR Purpose: 505119N 0004524W	113 ft amsl	APCH Aid to Chichester/ Goodwood. DOC 80 nm/50000 ft.

■ *Figure 24-11* **UK AIP ENR extract for Goodwood VOR**

ENR 4.1 — RADIO NAVIGATION AIDS — EN-ROUTE						
Name of Station (VOR set Variation)	IDENT	Frequency (Channel)	Hours of Operation (Winter/Summer)	Co-ordinates	DME Aerial Elevation	Remarks
1	2	3	4	5	6	7
Guernsey VOR/DME (4.4°W - 1996)	GUR	109.40 MHz (Ch 31X)	H24	AD Purpose: 492613.45N 0023613.67W ENR Purpose: 492613N 0023614W	347 ft amsl	APCH Aid to Guernsey. DOC 60 nm/50000 ft (80 nm/ 50000 ft in Sector 022°-067°M).

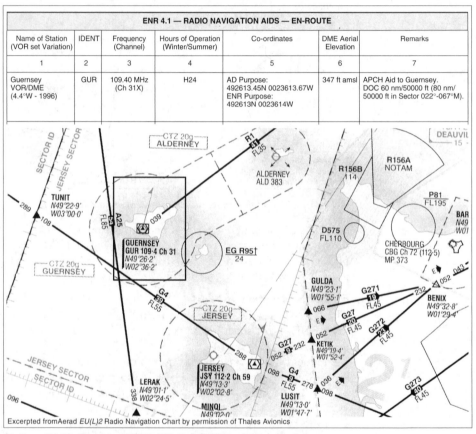

Excerpted fromAerad *EU(L)2* Radio Navigation Chart by permission of Thales Avionics

■ *Figure 24-12* **Guernsey VOR/DME, in AIP ENR and Aerad chart**

Also, the beginning pages of AIP ENR advise not to use any VOR if it cannot be identified by its Morse code ident. It may be that the VOR is radiating signals on test, in which case the ident is suppressed or the Morse letters 'TST' (for test) are transmitted, to indicate that the facility is not to be used for navigation.

VORs that have a DME (distance-measuring equipment) station associated with them may be described as VOR/DMEs.

The DME is automatically tuned when you select the VOR frequency on the VHF-NAV radio. Guernsey has such a facility, see the AIP ENR and chart extract in Figure 24-12.

As the VOR is a VHF radio navigation aid, its line-of-sight signals can be stopped or distorted by high mountains in some locations. AIP ENR should contain a warning, as is the case in Figure 24-13, where Inverness VOR has reduced coverage in the sector between 154°M and 194°M from the VOR ground station.

ENR 4.1 — RADIO NAVIGATION AIDS — EN-ROUTE						
Name of Station (VOR set Variation)	IDENT	Frequency (Channel)	Hours of Operation (Winter/Summer)	Co-ordinates	DME Aerial Elevation	Remarks
1	2	3	4	5	6	7
Inverness VOR/DME (6.7°W - 1997)	INS	109.20 MHz (Ch 29X)	H24	AD Purpose: 573233.45N 0040229.55W ENR Purpose: 573233N 0040230W	58 ft amsl	APCH Aid to Inverness. On Inverness AD. DOC 60 nm/25000 ft. Reduced coverage in Sector RDL 154°-RDL 194°. Flag alarms may occur in this Sector when aircraft are 30 nm or more from the VOR and flying at or below 7000 ft. DME co-located and freq paired with VOR and unmonitored outside Inverness ATC hours of operation. Available for approach and landing purposes only during the hours of APP. Due to terrain effects the DME may unlock in Sector RDL 154° to RDL 194° when aircraft are at

■ *Figure 24-13* **AIP ENR extract for Inverness**

VOR Cockpit Instruments

There are various types of VOR cockpit display, but they are all reasonably similar in terms of operation. The VOR cockpit display is often referred to as the **omni bearing indicator,** or **OBI.** It displays the omni bearing selected by the pilot on the course card using the **omni bearing selector** (OBS), a small knob which is geared to the card.

If the aeroplane is on the selected radial, then the VOR needle, known as the **course deviation indicator** or **CDI,** will be centred. If the aeroplane is not on the selected track, then the CDI will not be centred.

Whether the selected track would take the aeroplane to or from the VOR ground station is indicated by the TO/FROM flags.

The OBI is only to be used for navigation if:
- the red OFF warning flag is hidden from view;
- the correct Morse code ident is heard.

When a VOR is operating normally, the radials are transmitted to an accuracy of at least ±2°.

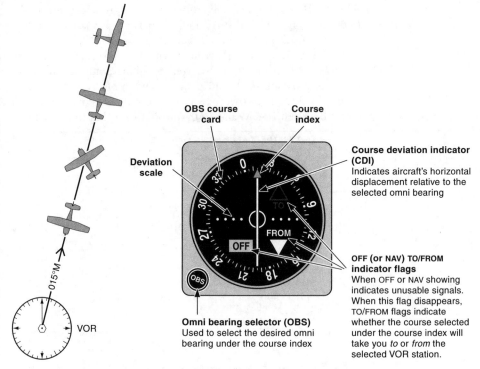

■ Figure 24-14 *The VOR cockpit display (OBI) for aeroplanes on the*
015 radial

NOTE *Course* is an American term with the same meaning as *track*.
Since most aviation radio equipment is manufactured by US
companies, American terminology is used. In the UK, *course*
sometimes refers to heading; however, it will not be used in this
sense in *The Air Pilot's Manual*.

Course Deviation Indicator (CDI)

The course deviation indicator (CDI) in the VOR cockpit instrument indicates off-track deviation in terms of *angular deviation from
the selected track*. At all times, the reference when using the VOR
is the selected track under the course index. (This is a totally
different principle to that of the ADF needle which simply points
at an NDB ground station and indicates its relative bearing.)

The amount of *angular* deviation from the selected track is
referred to in terms of *dots*; there are 5 dots either side of the
central position. The inner dot on both sides is often represented
by a circle passing through them. Each dot is equivalent to 2° track
deviation.

- If the aeroplane is on the selected track, the CDI is centred.
- If the aeroplane is 2° off the selected track, the CDI is displaced 1 dot from the centre (i.e. on the circumference of the inner circle).
- If the aeroplane is 4° off the selected track, the CDI is displaced 2 dots.
- If the aeroplane is 10° or more off the selected track, the CDI is fully deflected at 5 dots.

> A 1-dot deviation of the CDI on the VOR cockpit display represents 2°.
> Full-scale deflection at 5 dots represents 10° or more.

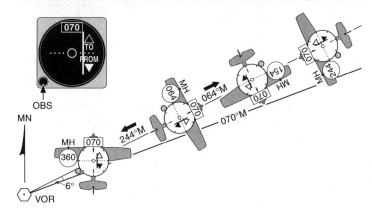

■ Figure 24-15 **Each of these aeroplanes is displaced 6° from the 070 radial**

Since the CDI indicates *angular* deviation, the actual *distance* off track for a given CDI indication will be smaller the closer the aeroplane is to the ground station. In a manner of speaking, the aeroplane is 'funnelled' in towards the VOR ground station.

To or From

The 090 radial, which is QDR 090 (a magnetic bearing away *from* the station) of 090°M, is the same position line as QDM 270 *to* the station. If an aeroplane is on this position line, then the CDI will be centred when *either* 090 *or* 270 is selected with the OBS. Any ambiguity in your mind regarding the position of the aeroplane relative to the VOR ground station is resolved with the TO/ FROM indicators.

The TO or FROM flags or arrows indicate whether the selected omni bearing will take you *to* the VOR ground station, or away *from* it.

In Figure 24-16, the pilot could centre the CDI by selecting either 090 or 270 (reciprocals) with the OBS. A track of 090°M would take the aeroplane *from* the VOR, whereas a track of 270°M would lead it *to* the VOR.

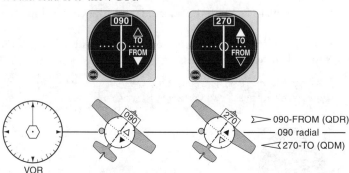

■ *Figure 24-16* **Using the TO/FROM flag**

EXAMPLE 2 Illustrate two indications on the omni bearing indicator that would inform you that the aeroplane is on the 235 radial. The 235 radial is either:

▢ 235°M *from* the VOR; or
▢ 055°M *to* the VOR.

So, with the CDI centred, the VOR cockpit display could indicate either 235-FROM or 055-TO.

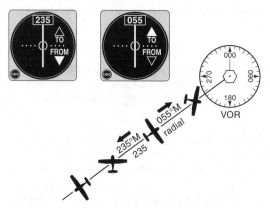

■ *Figure 24-17* **Indications that the aeroplane is on the 235 radial**

> At all times, the reference when using the OBI is the track
> selected under the course index. It determines:
> • CDI deflection; and
> • whether the TO or the FROM flag shows.

Different Presentations of the Omni Bearing

There are various presentations of VOR information. In all cases, full-scale deflection is 10° either side of the selected omni bearing (a total arc of 20°), with five dots either side of centre. In many VOR cockpit displays the two inner dots are joined by the circumference of a circle.

The course deviation indicator (CDI) may also differ between instruments. It may move laterally as a whole, or it may hinge at the top and swing laterally.

Similarly, the means of displaying the selected omni bearing may differ between instruments. It may be shown under a course index, or it may be shown in a window. In some equipment, the TO and the FROM flags may be displayed in the one window, in others they may have separate windows.

The VOR cockpit display usually doubles as the ILS (instrument landing system) display, with vertical dots marked to indicate glideslope (GS) deviation (using a second needle which lies or is hinged horizontally so that it can move up or down). When being used for the VOR (and not the ILS), the glideslope cross bar (or needle) may be biased out of view, and there may be a **red GS warning flag** showing.

Operational Use of the VOR

Preparing the VOR for Use

Always select, tune and identify a VOR before use.

A radio navigation aid is of little value if you do not use it correctly. Prior to using the VOR, you must:

- ensure electrical power is available, and switch the VHF-NAV ON;
- select the desired frequency (e.g. 114.3 MHz for Aberdeen VOR as found on navigation charts or in AIP ENR);
- identify the VOR (*dit-dah dah-dit-dit dah-dit,* which is ADN in Morse code as shown on the navigation charts for AberDeeN);
- check that the OFF flag is not showing (i.e. the signal is usable, otherwise the OFF flag would be visible).

Orientation

Using a Single VOR Position Line

Orientation means 'to determine one's approximate position'. The first step in orientation is to establish a position line (PL) along which the aircraft is known to be at a particular moment.

To obtain a position line using the VOR display:

- rotate the OBS (omni bearing selector) until the CDI (course deviation indicator) is centred; and
- note whether the TO or the FROM flag is showing.

EXAMPLE 3 You rotate the OBS until the CDI is centred – this occurs with 334 under the course index and the TO flag showing. Illustrate the situation.

Could another OBI (omni bearing indicator) reading be obtained with the course deviation indicator centred?

In the aircraft's location, the CDI will be centred with either:
- 334-TO; or
- 154-FROM.

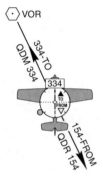

■ *Figure 24-18* **On the 154 radial**

Using Two Position Lines to Fix Position

One position line alone does not allow you to positively fix the position of the aircraft overhead a particular point, it only provides a line somewhere along which the aircraft lies.

It requires two or more position lines to positively fix the position of an aircraft. Also, to be of any real value for position fixing, the two PLs need to intersect at an angle of at least 45°. Any 'cut' less than this decreases the accuracy of the fix.

Radio position lines can be provided by any convenient radio navigation aid, including VORs, NDBs and DMEs.

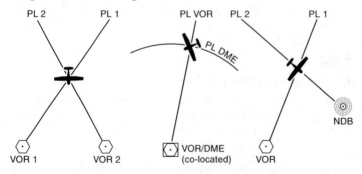

■ *Figure 24-19* **Fixing position requires two position lines with a good 'cut' (angle of at least 45°)**

Two VORs

Some aeroplanes are fitted with two independent VHF-NAV systems, enabling two different VORs to be tuned at the same time, and thus two PLs from two different VOR ground stations can be obtained simultaneously. In an aeroplane fitted with only one VHF-NAV set, you can obtain two PLs using the one VHF-NAV by retuning it from one VOR to another.

EXAMPLE 4 An aeroplane fitted with two VHF-NAVs is tracking 134°M from Prestwick to Manchester via Dean Cross, and obtains the following indications:

■ VOR 1. Dean Cross 115.2 is selected, and the CDI centres with 134-TO.

■ VOR 2. Talla 113.8 is selected, and the CDI centres with 220-FROM.

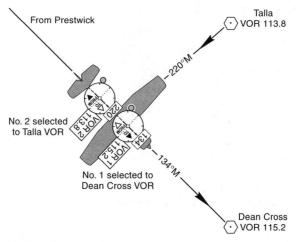

■ *Figure 24-20* **Fixing position using two VORs**

Figure 24-20 shows that the aeroplane is on track (134°M between Prestwick and Dean Cross) and passing the Talla 220 radial. The two position lines cut at a good angle, and the pilot has a fairly positive indication of where the aeroplane is.

VOR and a DME

Probably the most common form of en route position fixing between aids is the VOR/DME fix, based on a ground station where the DME (distance-measuring equipment) is co-located with the VOR ground station. The VOR can provide a straight position line showing the radial that the aeroplane is on, and the DME can provide a circular position line showing the distance that the aeroplane is from the ground station. The intersection of the lines is the position of the aeroplane.

EXAMPLE 5 An aircraft tracking north from Brecon (ident BCN, frequency 117.45 MHz) has the cockpit indications of:

☐ BCN VOR 008-FROM; and
☐ BCN DME 31 nm.

Where is the aircraft?

As can be seen from Figure 24-21, the aircraft is at the RADNO position, an in-flight position determined purely by radio navaids.

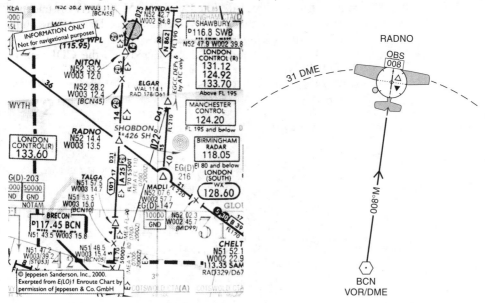

■ Figure 24-21 **Fixing position using a co-located VOR/DME**

Overhead a VOR

As an aircraft approaches overhead a VOR, the CDI will become more and more agitated as the ±10° funnel either side of track becomes narrower.

As the aircraft passes through the **'zone of confusion'** over the VOR ground station, the CDI may flick from side to side, before settling down again as the aircraft moves away from the station. The TO/FROM flag will also change from TO to FROM (or vice versa), and the red OFF flag may flicker in and out of view because of the temporarily unusable signal.

The zone of confusion can extend in an arc of 70° overhead the station, so it may take a minute or so for the aircraft to pass through it before the CDI and the FROM flag settle down, and the OFF flag totally disappears.

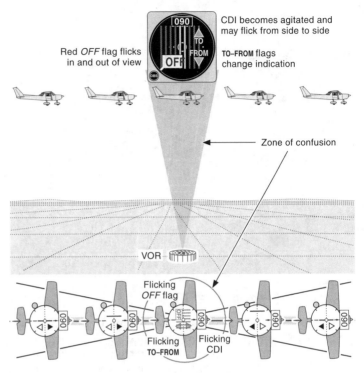

■ Figure 24-22 **Fixing position overhead a VOR**

Passing Abeam a VOR

A common means of checking flight progress is to note the time passing abeam (to one side of) a nearby VOR ground station. The most straightforward procedure is to:

☐ select and identify the VOR; and
☐ under the course index, set the radial perpendicular (at 90°) to your track.

EXAMPLE 6 An aircraft is tracking 350°M, and will pass approximately 20 nm abeam a VOR ground station out to its right. The VOR radial perpendicular to track is the 260 radial, and so 260 should be set with the OBS. The CDI will be fully deflected to one side if the aircraft is well away from the abeam position, and will gradually move from full deflection one side to full deflection on the other side as the aircraft passes through the ±10° arc either side of the selected radial. The aircraft is at the abeam position when the CDI is centralised.

The abeam position can also be identified by setting the QDM *to* the VOR under the course index (rather than the QDR or radial *from* the VOR), in which case the movement of the CDI will be from the opposite side.

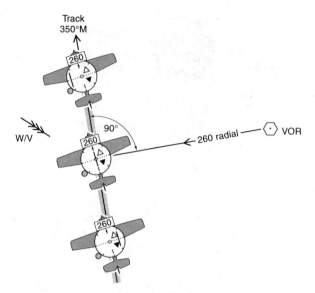

■ *Figure 24-23* **Passing abeam a VOR**

The 1-in-60 rule, frequently used in navigation, states that 1 nm off-track in 60 nm subtends an angle of 1°. In rough terms, this means that, as the aircraft flies at right angles through the 10° from when the CDI first starts to move to when it is centred, it will travel approximately 10 nm abeam the VOR when it is located 60 nm from the VOR ground station (or 5 nm at 30 nm, etc.). At say GS 120 kt (2 nm/min), passing through a 10° arc abeam the VOR will take 5 minutes at 60 nm, or 2.5 minutes at 30 nm.

Crossing a Known Radial from an Off-Track VOR

It is a simple procedure to identify passing a known radial from an off-track VOR and, indeed, some en route reporting points are based on this.

EXAMPLE 7 Upton reporting point en route on the track between Ottringham and Wallasey VORs is specified by the 330 radial from Gamston VOR.

- With two VOR displays in the cockpit, it would be normal procedure to track using VOR 1 on Ottringham (and later Wallasey), and check UPTON using VOR 2 tuned to Gamston.
- With only one VOR set fitted in the aircraft, it would be normal procedure to leave it on the main tracking aid (Ottringham) until almost at UPTON (say two minutes before ETA), and then select Gamston and the 330 radial. Having crossed this radial, the VOR could be selected to a tracking aid (Ottringham or Wallasey).

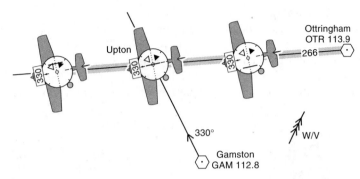

■ *Figure 24-24* **Crossing a known radial**

If a 1:500,000 aeronautical chart is being used (rather than a Radio Navigation Chart), you can construct your own check-points along track using nearby off-track VORs. In Figure 24-25, the pilot has chosen to check position crossing the 105, 075 and 045 radials from an off-track VOR. By measuring the distance between these planned fixes en route and noting the time of reaching them, the pilot can calculate the groundspeed and revise estimates for positions further along track.

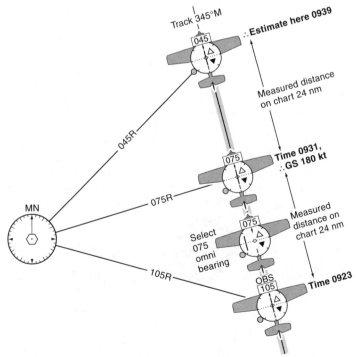

■ *Figure 24-25* **Using an off-track VOR to monitor progress**

The VOR Display

The VOR indicates the position of the aeroplane with respect to the selected VOR track, and the VOR display in the cockpit will be the same irrespective of the aeroplane's heading. Each of the aeroplanes in Figure 24-26 will have the same VOR display, provided the same track is set under the course index with the OBS.

> *The CDI position will **not** change as the aeroplane changes heading.*

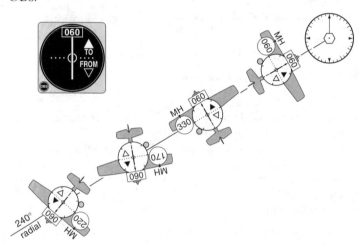

■ Figure 24-26 **The VOR cockpit display is not heading sensitive**

Orientation Without Altering the OBS

It is possible, without altering the omni bearing selector, to determine which quadrant the aeroplane is in with respect to the selected track. In Figure 24-27, the selected omni bearing is 340.

▢ The CDI is deflected left, which indicates that, when looking in direction 340, the aeroplane is out to the right (of the line 340–160); and

▢ The FROM flag indicates that tracking 340 would take the aeroplane *from* the VOR ground station, i.e. the aeroplane is ahead of the line 250–070 when looking in the direction 340.

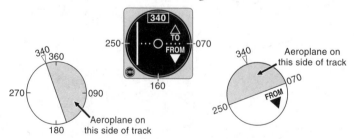

■ Figure 24-27 **Using the CDI and the TO/FROM flag for orientation without moving the omni bearing selector**

This puts the aeroplane in the quadrant away from the CDI, and away from the TO/FROM flag – between 340 and 070 radials (omni bearings from the VOR ground station).

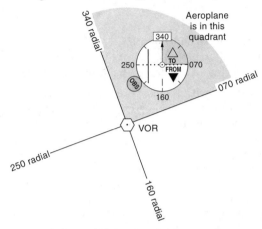

■ *Figure 24-28* **The aeroplane is in the quadrant away from the CDI and TO/FROM flag**

NOTE No information is available from the VOR cockpit display regarding aeroplane heading. Heading information in °M must be obtained from the heading indicator.

EXAMPLE 8 With 085 under the course index, the OBI reads CDI deflected right with the TO flag showing. Position the aeroplane with respect to the VOR.

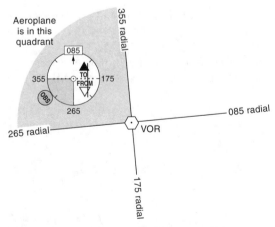

■ *Figure 24-29* **The aeroplane is between the 355 and 265 radials**

This method is a quick way to determine the approximate position of the aeroplane in relation to the VOR ground station.

VOR Tracking

Tracking To a VOR

To track *to* a VOR:

- **select** the VOR frequency;
- **identify** the station (Morse code ident);
- **check** that the red OFF warning flag is not displayed; and
- **select the omni bearing** of the desired track with the OBS.

Orientate the aeroplane with respect to the desired track, and then take up a suitable intercept heading using the heading indicator (aligned with the magnetic compass). If the aeroplane is heading approximately in the direction of the desired track, the centre circle will represent the aeroplane, and the CDI the desired track. To intercept track in this case, turn towards the CDI.

This is using the OBI as a **command instrument**. This commands you to turn towards the CDI to regain track. Be aware, however, that this only applies when the aeroplane's heading is roughly in the same direction as the selected omni bearing.

On intercepting track, steer a suitable heading to maintain it, considering wind direction and strength. If the desired track is maintained, the CDI will remain centred.

EXAMPLE 9 In Figure 24-30, with the desired track 030 set in the OBI, the CDI is out to the right. Since the aeroplane's initial heading agrees approximately with the track of 030, the pilot concludes that the track is out to the right of the aeroplane. The CDI out to the right *commands* a right turn to regain track and centre the CDI.

The pilot has taken up a heading of 050°M to intercept a track of 030 *to* the VOR, which will give a 20° intercept. This is satisfactory if the aeroplane is close to the track.

If the aeroplane is well away from track, then a 60° or 90° intercept might be more appropriate. This would be MH 090 or MH 120.

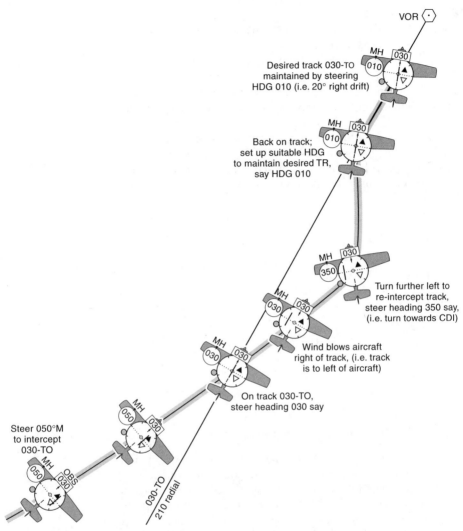

VOR

MH 030
010
Desired track 030-TO
maintained by steering
HDG 010 (i.e. 20° right drift)

MH 030
010
Back on track;
set up suitable HDG
to maintain desired TR,
say HDG 010

MH 030
350
Turn further left to
re-intercept track,
steer heading 350 say,
(i.e. turn towards CDI)

MH 030
030
Wind blows aircraft
right of track, (i.e. track
is to left of aircraft)

MH 030
030
On track 030-TO,
steer heading 030 say

MH 050
030
Steer 050°M
to intercept
030-TO

MH 050
OBS 030
030-TO
210 radial

■ *Figure 24-30* **Using the VOR indicator as a command instrument**

Determining Drift Angle

When tracking inbound on 360 *to* a VOR with 360 set under the course index, MH 360 will allow the aeroplane to maintain track provided there is no crosswind component.

If, however, there is a westerly wind blowing, then the aeroplane will be blown to the right of track unless a wind correction (WCA) is applied and the aeroplane steered on a heading slightly into wind. This is MH 352 in the centre diagram of Figure 24-31.

If, on the other hand, there is an easterly wind blowing, the aeroplane will be blown to the left of track, unless a wind correction angle (WCA) is applied and the aeroplane steered on a heading slightly into wind, such as MH 005 in the right-hand diagram of Figure 24-31.

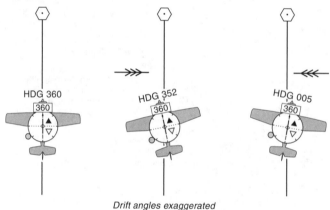

Drift angles exaggerated

■ *Figure 24-31* **Tracking inbound and allowing for drift**

Just how great the WCA need be is determined in flight by trial and error (although any pre-flight calculations using the navigation computer when flight planning may suggest a starting figure for WCA). If the chosen WCA is not correct, and the aeroplane gradually departs from track, causing the CDI to move from its central position, then heading should be altered, the track regained (CDI centred), and then a new magnetic heading flown with an improved estimate of WCA. This process of achieving a suitable WCA is known as **bracketing**.

Of course, in the real world the wind frequently changes in both strength and direction, and so the magnetic heading required to maintain track will also change from time to time. This becomes obvious by gradual movements of the CDI away from its central position, which you will notice in your regular scan of the radio navigation instruments, and correct by changes in magnetic heading. See Figure 24-32.

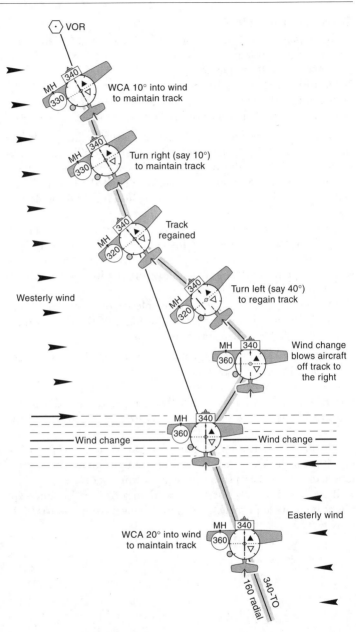

⊘ VOR

WCA 10° into wind
to maintain track

Turn right (say 10°)
to maintain track

Track
regained

Westerly wind

Turn left (say 40°)
to regain track

Wind change
blows aircraft
off track to
the right

Wind change — Wind change

Easterly wind

WCA 20° into wind
to maintain track

160 radial

340-TO

■ *Figure 24-32* **Tracking inbound through a wind change**

Tracking From a VOR

To track *from* a VOR (assuming the VOR has not already been selected and identified):

- **select** the VOR frequency;
- **identify** the station (Morse code ident);
- **check** that the red OFF warning flag is not displayed; and
- **select the omni bearing** of the desired track with the OBS.

Orientate the aeroplane with respect to the desired track, and then take up a suitable intercept heading using the heading indicator (aligned with the magnetic compass). If the aeroplane is heading approximately in the direction of the desired track, the centre circle will represent the aeroplane, and the CDI the desired track.

To intercept track in this case, turn toward the CDI. This is using the OBI as a **command instrument**. This commands you to turn towards the CDI to regain track. Be aware, however, that this only applies when the heading is roughly in the same direction as the selected omni bearing.

On intercepting track, steer a suitable heading to maintain it, considering the wind direction and strength. If the desired track is maintained, the CDI will remain centred.

EXAMPLE 10 In Figure 24-33, with the desired track 140 set in the OBI, the CDI is out to the right.

Since the aeroplane's initial heading agrees approximately with the track of 140, the pilot concludes that the track is out to the right of the aeroplane (or, in this case, straight ahead and to the right).

The pilot has taken up a heading of 220°M to intercept a track of 140 *from* the VOR, which will give an 80° intercept. This is satisfactory if the aeroplane is well away from the track.

If the aeroplane is close to track, then a 60° or 30° intercept might be more applicable, which, in this case, would be MH 200 or MH 170.

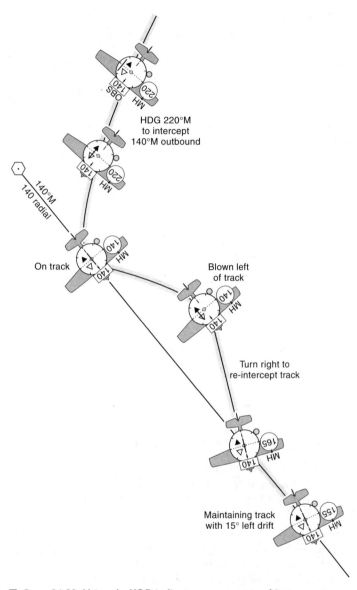

HDG 220°M
to intercept
140°M outbound

140°M
140 radial

On track

Blown left
of track

Turn right to
re-intercept track

Maintaining track
with 15° left drift

■ *Figure 24-33* **Using the VOR indicator as a command instrument**

Use the OBI as a Command Instrument

Use the OBI as a **command instrument** whenever possible. With the desired track set in the OBI, and the aeroplane headed at least roughly in the same direction as the selected track, the omni bearing indicator will act as a command instrument. By flying *towards* the deflected CDI, you can centre it, and thereby regain track. For example:

- ▣ tracking 060 *to* the VOR, set 060 under the course index;
- ▣ tracking 030 *from* the VOR, set 030 under the course index.

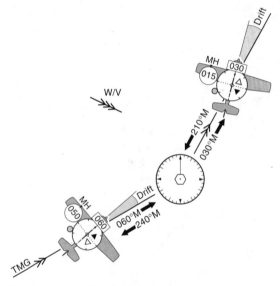

■ *Figure 24-34* **Use the OBI as a command instrument**

A minor complication can arise when the aeroplane is steered on a heading approximating the *reciprocal* of the omni bearing selected on the OBI. It causes the VOR cockpit display to be no longer a command instrument.

EXAMPLE 11 You have been tracking 140 *from* a VOR, with 140 selected in the OBI and by steering MH 140. The aeroplane has drifted left of track, and so the CDI will be deflected to the right of centre. To regain the 140-FROM track, you must turn towards the needle, in this case towards the right, i.e. heading and OBI selection are similar, so it is used as a command instrument.

The VOR indicator is not
heading sensitive.

Now you want to return to the VOR ground station on the reciprocal track, which is 320 *to* the VOR, so turn through approximately 180° onto MH 320 without altering the 140 set under the course index. The omni bearing indicator, because it is not heading sensitive, indicates exactly as it did before the turn, with the CDI as seen by the pilot out to the right of centre.

A non-command VOR
setup is difficult to
interpret and use.

To regain track on this reciprocal heading, turn, not towards the CDI, but away from it. Turning towards the CDI on this reciprocal heading to the selected track would take you further away from the selected track, i.e. it is no longer a command instrument, which is a pity!

This inconvenience can be easily removed, and the OBI returned to being a command instrument, by selecting the new desired track under the course index, 320, which approximates the heading being flown. The immediate effect will be for:

- the TO flag to appear, replacing the FROM flag, and
- the CDI to swing across to the other side.

A command VOR setup is
easy to interpret and use.

The CDI will now be out to the left, and a turn towards it will bring the aeroplane back towards the selected track. The OBI is once again a command instrument, easier to understand, and easier to fly.

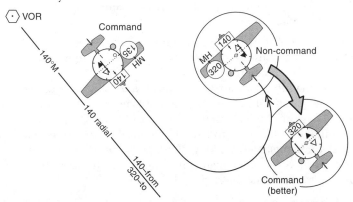

■ *Figure 24-35* **For ease of operation, use the OBI as a command
instrument**

Intercepting a Track using the VOR

Orientation

You need to know:

- Where am I?;
- Where do I want to go?; and
- How do I get there?

The easiest method of orientating the aircraft using the VOR is to rotate the OBS until the CDI centres. This can occur on one of two headings (reciprocals of each other); choose the one with the omni bearing that most resembles the aircraft's magnetic heading. If the aircraft is heading towards the VOR ground station, then the TO flag will show; if it is heading away from the VOR, then the FROM flag will show.

Select the desired track in °M using the omni bearing selector (OBS). Determine which way to turn to intercept the desired track, and then take up a suitable intercept heading.

Intercepting an Outbound Track

The VOR is just as useful tracking away from a VOR ground station as tracking towards it, and it is much easier to use than the NDB/ADF combination. The next example illustrates the normal method of doing this.

EXAMPLE 12 You are tracking inbound on the 170 radial to a VOR (350-TO). ATC instructs you to take up a heading to intercept the 090 radial outbound (090-FROM).

Orientation is not a problem since you already know where you are (the usual situation). The best way to track inbound on the 170 radial (which is the same as QDR 170, making the inbound QDM 350), is to have 350 set in the OBI course index, since the aeroplane is tracking 350 *to* the VOR. This ensures that the indicator is a command instrument (fly towards the CDI needle to regain the selected track).

Visualise the situation:

- tracking northwards towards the VOR;
- the desired track, 090-FROM, lies ahead to the right.

To intercept the 090-FROM track:

- set 090 under the course index;
- take up a suitable intercept heading (MH 030 for a 60° intercept); and
- maintain MH 030 until the CDI moves from full-scale deflection towards the centre. To avoid overshooting the track, anticipate the interception, and 'lead-in' by commencing a turn just prior to intercepting track.

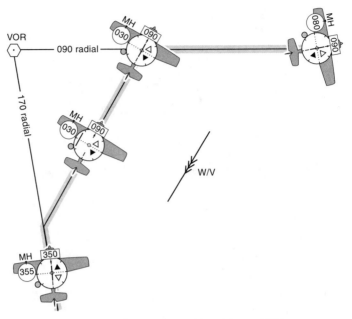

■ *Figure 24-36* **Intercepting a track outbound from a VOR**

Intercepting an Inbound Track

EXAMPLE 13 ATC instructs you to track inbound on the 010 radial to a particular VOR.

Select and identify the VOR; then

▢ Orientate yourself with respect to it (perhaps by centring the CDI suitably).

▢ Set the desired track under the course index – *inbound* on the 010 radial (QDR) is 190-TO (QDM) – and determine the position of this track.

▢ Take up a suitable intercepting heading, and wait for the CDI to centre.

In Figure 24-37:

▢ the CDI centres on 050-FROM (it would also centre on 230-TO);

▢ you have chosen a 90° intercept, steering MH 280 to intercept 190-TO; and

▢ as the CDI starts to move (within 10° of the selected track), lead in to smoothly join track, and allow a wind correction angle of 5°.

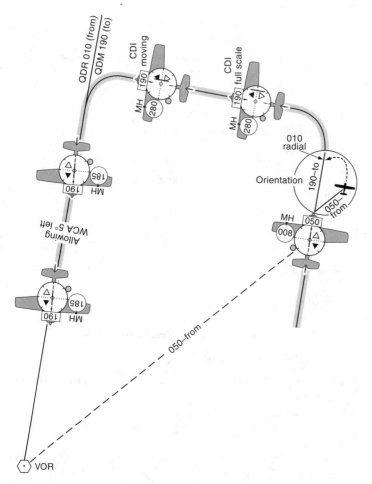

■ Figure 24-37 *Intercepting an inbound track to a VOR*

Now complete **Exercises 24 – The VOR.**

VHF Direction Finding (VDF)

General Principle

Some aerodromes are equipped with radio aerials that can sense the direction of VHF-COM signals (normal voice signals) received from an aeroplane.

This information is presented to the air traffic controller (usually the approach controller) as a radial line on a cathode ray tube similar to a radar screen or, with the most modern VDF equipment, as a very accurate digital readout of bearing.

VDF enables a controller to determine the direction a VHF-COM signal is coming from.

The controller can then give the pilot the bearing of the aircraft relative to the aerodrome. This is known as **very high frequency direction finding,** and is often abbreviated to VDF or VHF D/F.

An advantage of VDF is that no specific aircraft equipment is required other than a VHF-COM – normal VHF communications radio.

A typical VDF air–ground exchange would be a pilot requesting ATC to provide QDM (magnetic bearing to the ground station), followed by the controller advising it. For example:

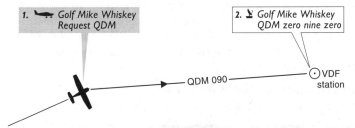

■ *Figure 25-1* **QDM is magnetic bearing to the VDF ground station**

By steering the QDM, the pilot is able to *home to,* or head towards, the ground station.

Ground stations that are equipped to provide VDF are designated by the term **homer,** e.g. *Shoreham Homer,* which operates on the VHF communications frequency of 123.15 MHz.

Whereas no special equipment is required in the aeroplane for VDF other than a VHF-COM radio, it does require a special installation at the ground station. Two typical designs for VDF aerials at aerodromes are the H-type aerial (a double-H dipole aerial in technical terms), or the Doppler-type VDF aerial.

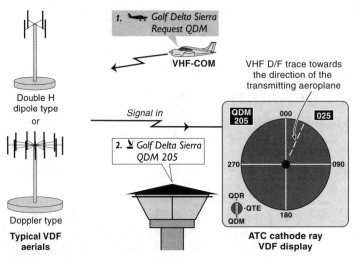

■ *Figure 25-2* **Ground equipment for VHF direction finding**

VDF ground equipment from years ago was known as a **manual homer,** and used an ADF-type null-seeking aerial which the operator had to rotate manually to determine the direction of the aeroplane. It also required long transmissions from the aeroplane while the operator sought the null position.

Modern equipment is fully automatic. The direction of the aeroplane is displayed automatically following only a short VHF-COM transmission from the pilot.

Information Available from VDF

Bearings that a pilot may request from a VDF operator are:

VDF BEARINGS	
QDM	*magnetic bearing **to** the station*
QDR	*magnetic bearing **from** the station (the reciprocal of the QDM)*
QTE	*true bearing **from** the station*

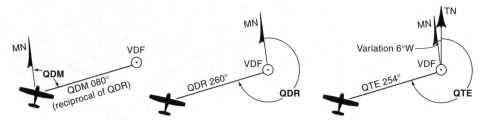

■ *Figure 25-3* **QDM, QDR and QTE**

QDR

QDR, the magnetic bearing from the station, is useful for orientation (Where am I?). QDR is similar information to a VOR radial. QTE, the true bearing from the station, is useful if you want to plot a position line from the VDF ground station to the aeroplane on a map (against true north). However, it is QDM, the magnetic bearing to the station, that is the most commonly used and requested VDF bearing.

QDM

QDM is the most commonly requested bearing. It is the heading to steer direct to the VDF station provided no crosswind exists. In a crosswind, however, a wind correction angle (WCA) into wind must be used to counteract the drift if a reasonably straight track is to be achieved, rather than a curved (and inefficient) homing.

At typical light aircraft speeds, it is reasonable for the pilot to request a QDM each half-minute or so to check tracking, and to modify heading if necessary.

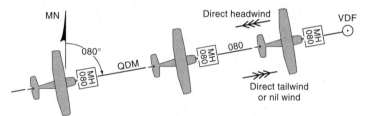

■ *Figure 25-4* **Steering QDM to a VDF ground station in nil-crosswind conditions is satisfactory**

If QDM is steered as heading in crosswind conditions, then the aeroplane will drift downwind, and its QDM will gradually change. The next QDM passed by the ground operator will be different from the first.

In Figure 25-5, an original QDM 080 has become QDM 075, and so the pilot would turn slightly left from a heading of 080°M to a heading of 075°M (the new QDM) to continue homing to the station.

There would be further changes to QDM advised by the operator as the aeroplane continued on, the end result being a curved path with the aeroplane arriving overhead the ground station heading roughly into wind – not a particularly professional arrival!

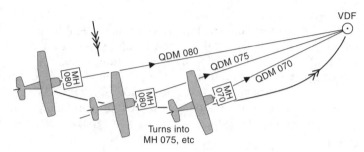

■ *Figure 25-5* **An inefficient homing to a VDF ground station**

A more efficient arrival can be achieved by allowing for wind effect, i.e. tracking using a wind correction angle into wind to counteract drift, rather than homing to the station by flying a continually changing QDM as heading.

VDF Bearing Accuracy

The quality of the bearings obtained by VDF is classified by the VDF ground operator to the pilot as:

Class A	*Accurate to within ±2°*
Class B	*Accurate to within ±5°*
Class C	*Accurate to within ±10°*
Class D	*Less accurate than Class C (CAP 46 lists some Class D VDF stations with accuracy less than ±10°)*

Most modern equipment is generally accurate to ±1°, although accuracy may be decreased by:

▢ **VDF site errors** such as reflection from nearby uneven ground, buildings, aircraft or vehicles; and

▢ **VHF propagation errors** caused by irregular propagation over differing terrain, especially if the aeroplane is at long range from the VDF ground station.

VDF Tracking

Tracking Inbound using QDM

To achieve a desired track to a VDF ground station, the pilot should try to maintain a **datum QDM** which is the same as the **desired track.** For instance, to maintain a track of 080°M to the VDF ground station, the pilot should fly a heading so that QDM 080 is consistently maintained.

While VDF ground operators can advise QDM, they will not advise heading to steer to counter any crosswind effect. The pilot must determine this if a direct track to the VDF station is to be achieved. If the selected WCA is perfectly correct, then the ground operator will advise, on request for QDM, the same QDM as previously.

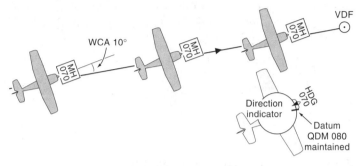

■ Figure 25-6 **Perfect allowance for drift**

The supply of QDMs by ATC may be thought of as a 'talking RMI'. You can, by mentally placing the QDM onto the direction indicator, form the same picture as that given to you by an RMI.

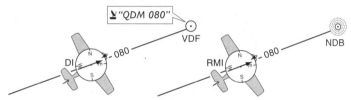

■ Figure 25-7 **The stated QDM is like a talking RMI**

If the stated QDM moves to the right of the datum QDM, then the aeroplane has drifted to the left of the desired track, and should be turned right to re-intercept the desired track (to re-establish the datum QDM). This is exactly the same response as for the head of an RMI needle moving to the right of the datum QDM.

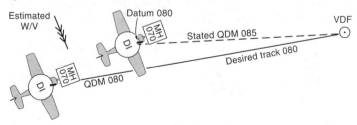

■ Figure 25-8 **Tracking towards a VDF ground station; if QDM moves right of the datum, turn right**

In this case, while flying on a magnetic heading of 070, the actual QDM has moved to the right of the datum QDM 080, indicated by ATC stating QDM 085. To regain the desired track, the pilot should turn right and increase heading (to say MH 090), and then request QDMs until the desired QDM 080 is reached. At this time, a more suitable heading to maintain QDM 080 would be flown, say MH 075.

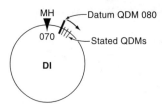

■ Figure 25-9 **If QDM moves right of datum, turn right**

If the stated QDM moves to the left of the datum QDM, then the aeroplane has drifted to the right of the desired track, and should be turned left to re-intercept the desired track (to re-establish the datum QDM). This is exactly the same response as for the head of an RMI needle moving to the left of the datum QDM.

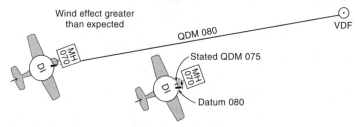

■ Figure 25-10 **Tracking towards a VDF ground station; if QDM moves left of the datum, turn left**

In this case, the stated QDM has moved left of the datum QDM 080 to 075. The pilot should turn left and decrease heading (to say MH 060), and request QDMs until the desired QDM 080 is reached. At this time, a more suitable heading to maintain QDM 080 would be flown, say MH 065.

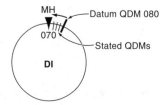

■ Figure 25-11 **QDM moving left of datum, turn left**

IN KNOWN WIND CONDITIONS, use a 'best-guess WCA' as a starting point in estimating a magnetic heading to maintain the datum QDM, making modifications to heading if the actual or stated QDM gradually moves away from the datum QDM.

IN UNKNOWN WIND CONDITIONS, when unable to estimate a suitable wind correction angle to counter drift, a simple procedure is to steer the QDM as heading, and see what develops. Suitable corrections can then be made as changes in the QDM become apparent.

WHEN TRACKING TOWARDS THE VDF STATION:

> • *turn right if actual QDM moves to the right of datum;*
> • *turn left if actual QDM moves to the left of datum.*

The aim is to establish a wind correction angle that allows for drift and results in the desired track being maintained – indicated by the QDM remaining constant. The process of finding a suitable WCA by trial and error is known as **bracketing.** Typically, it will take a number of heading changes to establish the WCA required to maintain track.

Changes to heading will also be required if the wind effect changes, which is often the case. Like most instrument flying, VDF tracking will consist of a continuing series of small (and sometimes not so small) corrections.

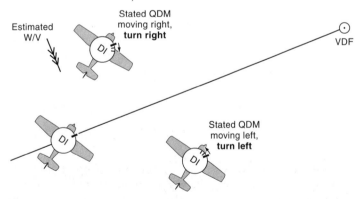

■ *Figure 25-12* ***Tracking towards a VDF ground station***

Tracking Outbound

When tracking away from a VDF ground station, the datum QDM is the reciprocal of the outbound track. For instance, to maintain a track of 060°M away from the VDF ground station, the aeroplane should be flown so that datum QDM 240 is maintained.

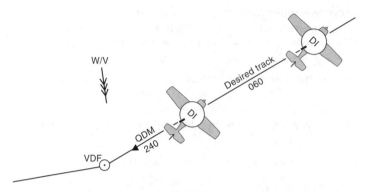

■ *Figure 25-13* **Tracking away from a VDF ground station**

If the stated QDM moves to the right of the datum QDM, the aeroplane has drifted to the left of the desired track, and should be turned right to re-intercept the desired track (to re-establish the datum QDM). This is exactly the same response as for the head of an RMI needle moving to the right of the datum QDM.

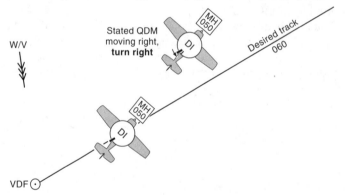

■ *Figure 25-14* **Tracking away from a VDF ground station; if QDM moves right of the datum, turn right**

In this case, the pilot would turn right and increase heading (to say MH 060), which would allow the wind to blow the aeroplane back onto track, and request QDMs until the desired QDM 240 is reached. At this time, a more suitable heading to maintain datum QDM 240 would be flown, say MH 055.

If the stated QDM moves to the left of the datum QDM, the aeroplane has drifted to the right of the desired track, and should be turned left to re-intercept the desired track (to re-establish the datum QDM). This is exactly the same response as for the head of an RMI needle moving to the left of the datum QDM.

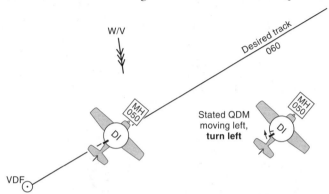

■ *Figure 25-15* **Tracking away from a VDF ground station; if QDM moves left of the datum, turn left**

In this case, since MH 050, allowing for an estimated 10° of drift, has taken the aeroplane to the right of track, the pilot should turn left and decrease heading (to say MH 040), and then request QDMs until the desired QDM 240 is reached. At this time, a more suitable heading to maintain QDM 240 should be flown, say MH 045, allowing a WCA of 15° into wind.

IN KNOWN WIND CONDITIONS, use a 'best-guess' WCA as a starting point in an attempt to maintain the datum QDM, making modifications to heading if the actual QDM changes from the datum.

IN UNKNOWN WIND CONDITIONS, when unable to estimate a suitable wind correction angle to counter drift, a simple procedure is to steer the reciprocal of the QDM as heading, and see what develops. Suitable corrections can then be made as changes in the QDM become apparent.

WHEN TRACKING AWAY FROM THE VDF STATION:

> • *turn right if actual QDM moves to the right of datum;*
> • *turn left if actual QDM moves to the left of datum.*

Note that these are exactly the same rules as for tracking towards the VDF ground station.

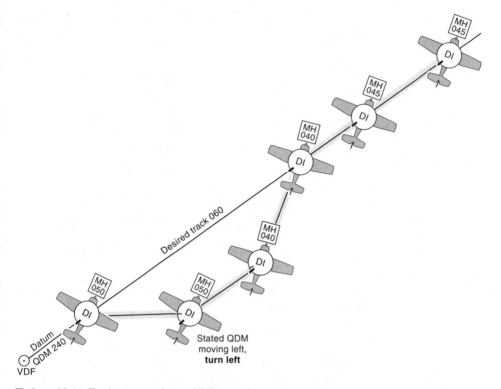

■ *Figure 25-16* ***Tracking away from a VDF ground station***

VDF Tracking Rules

1. Determine datum QDM for the desired track;
   - inbound: datum QDM = desired track;
   - outbound: datum QDM = reciprocal of desired track.

2. Use best-guess WCA to establish an initial heading in an attempt to maintain datum QDM.

3. Both inbound and outbound from the VDF ground station:
   - if stated QDM moves left of datum, turn left;
   - if stated QDM moves right of datum, turn right; (treat the stated QDM on the DI as a command instrument).

Flying Overhead the VDF Ground Station

As the aeroplane passes overhead (or near to overhead) the VDF ground station, the ground operator will be unable to determine the direction from which VHF-COM signals are received, even though the actual voice communications will be received normally. He will report this to the pilot as "No bearing".

If the outbound track differs significantly from the inbound track, then the pilot will need to take up a suitable intercept heading until the datum QDM for the outbound track is established, at which time normal tracking to maintain it should occur.

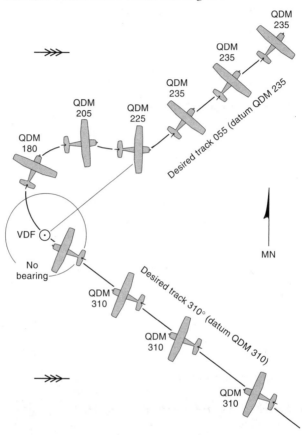

■ *Figure 25-17* **Flying overhead the VDF ground station, and intercepting an outbound track**

Requests for QDM by the pilot should be more frequent the closer the aeroplane is to the ground station so that suitable adjustments to heading can be made.

Other Uses for VDF

Bearings obtained by VDF can be used for a number of common navigational purposes. For instance, you may request a QDM from an abeam VDF station to verify that you are indeed flying abeam it.

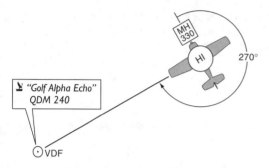

"Golf Alpha Echo"
QDM 240

VDF

■ *Figure 25-18* **QDM abeam a ground station**

A position line given by a VDF bearing can be used together with another position line from say a VOR, NDB or even another VDF station to fix the position of the aeroplane.

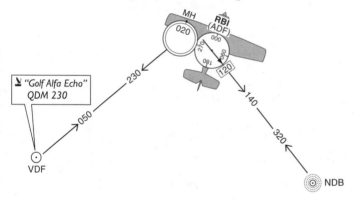

"Golf Alfa Echo"
QDM 230

VDF

NDB

■ *Figure 25-19* **Fixing position with VDF**

Now complete **Exercises 25 – VHF Direction Finding (VDF).**

Introduction to RNAV and GPS

General Description

A waypoint is a geographical position used to define a route.

Area navigation (RNAV) allows you to fly point-to-point on a direct course without having to overfly ground-based radio aids. Instead of flying from VOR/DME-to-VOR/DME along or beneath airways on what might be a circuitous route, you can fly direct from your departure airport to the destination airport, or from waypoint-to-waypoint, using RNAV. A **waypoint** is a geographical position usually specified by latitude and longitude, or by radial and distance from a VOR/DME, and used to define a route.

Some RNAV systems can define a waypoint internally when the pilot inserts the desired waypoint latitude and longitude into the computer. The RNAV system then derives data from navigation systems such as LORAN, inertial navigation systems (INS), VLF/Omega systems, and Doppler radar which enables the airplane to be flown to the desired waypoint. Other RNAV systems define waypoints relative to a VOR/DME, using radial and distance (or latitude and longitude) to create 'phantom' VOR/DMEs, known as pseudo-VOR/DMEs.

Pseudo-VOR/DMEs

Many general aviation aircraft have a course line computer system which, when used in conjunction with the VHF-NAV radio selected to a VOR/DME, can electronically relocate that VOR/DME, so that a pseudo-VOR/DME is created at any desired waypoint. It does this by electronically adding a vector (radial and distance) to the position of the actual VOR/DME.

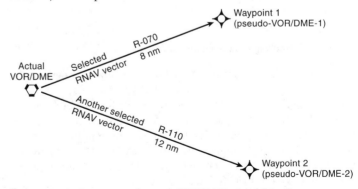

■ *Figure 26-1* **Creating a phantom VOR/DME electronically**

Operational Use

You can locate pseudo-VOR/DMEs wherever you like, provided they are within signal reception range of the parent VOR/DME, and thereby create a series of waypoints along your desired route.

> *You can create your own pseudo-VOR/DME as a waypoint.*

The normal VHF–NAV receiver is selected to the parent VOR/DME, and the computer is programmed to electronically add the vector (radial and distance) to received VOR/DME signals. How this is done depends on the actual equipment in the cockpit – refer to equipment information in your Pilot's Operating Handbook.

The course deviation indicator (CDI) in the cockpit receives its input via the computer, and indicates deviation from course between the waypoints – not an angular deviation as for normal VOR flying, but a lateral deviation in nautical miles, or fractions thereof.

The course between waypoints is maintained by keeping the CDI centered. Because it indicates lateral deviation in nautical miles, known as crosstrack error, rather than angular deviation, there is no 'funneling' effect using the RNAV CDI.

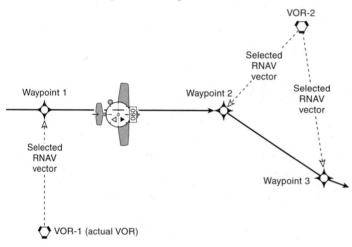

■ *Figure 26-2* **Tracking between waypoints**

Distance to the waypoint is shown on the normal DME indicator.

The waypoints can normally be preset on the RNAV equipment, and then instantaneously recalled as you need them. As the flight progresses, you will proceed through the waypoints in order, keeping within signal range of each parent VOR/DME by flying at a suitable altitude and distance from it. If the usable signal range is exceeded, the CDI OFF flag will show.

Typical RNAV systems can provide you with:
- crosstrack deviation from the selected course in nm with TO/FROM information;
- distance to the waypoint in nm;
- groundspeed in knots;
- time-to-waypoint in minutes.

■ Figure 26-3 **A typical RNAV display**

Global Positioning System (GPS)

General Description

The global positioning system (GPS) is an extremely accurate area navigation aid for all classes of aviation as well as other modes of transport. GPS was developed for the United States Department of Defense, but has now been made available for civil use.

In early 1994 the Federal Aviation Administration approved the use of GPS as an operational in-flight navigational aid. With an FAA-approved GPS system and supporting software, GPS may now be used to fly en route under Instrument Flight Rules, and, in some cases in the USA, for nonprecision instrument approaches. The GPS instrument approach procedures are presently overlayed on other established instrument approach procedures, such as VOR approaches. Dedicated GPS approaches will soon be introduced with a potential accuracy of 10 metres! No doubt the UK and Europe will follow.

GPS should not be used as the primary navigation method.

VFR pilots may also use GPS as an aid to visual navigation, to provide information relating to aircraft speed and track over the ground, wind velocity and distance/time to waypoints or the destination. GPS is very accurate, but as satellites can become unservicable etc., it should not be considered as such for more than 95% of the time. Therefore GPS should not be used as the primary navigation method, only as an aid to other methods.

Basically, GPS is comprised of three elements:
- a space element, consisting of a constellation of 21 active satellites orbiting the earth every 12 hours, in six orbital planes with four in each plane, at an altitude of 11,000 nm (21,300 km);
- a satellite control ground network (control station plus monitor stations), responsible for orbital accuracy and control; and

■ navigation receiver/computers in aircraft capable of receiving and identifying signals from satellites in view at a particular time and place.

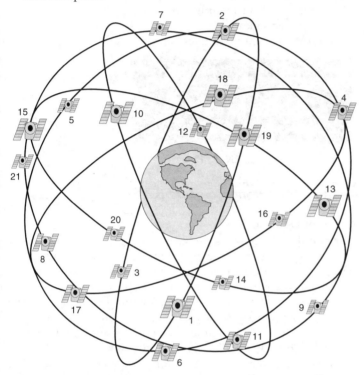

■ *Figure 26-4* **The orbital configuration of the 21 GPS satellites**

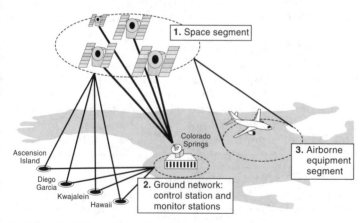

■ *Figure 26-5* **The GPS consists of three basic segments**

Basic Operating Principle

Each satellite transmits its own computer code packet on frequency 1575.42 MHz (for civilian use), 1,000 times per second. The satellite continually broadcasts its position and the exact time UTC. By knowing the exact position of the satellite at the time of transmission, and then by measuring the time taken for the data packet to reach the receiver from the satellite, the distance between the satellite and the receiver can be determined. The satellite constellation configuration usually guarantees that at least four satellites are in view at any given time.

Each transmitted data packet contains a precise timing reference. GPS receivers use accurate clocks and appropriate software to ascertain position by receiving and computing data from at least three satellites for a two-dimensional fix, and four satellites for a three-dimensional fix, such as ground position and altitude.

■ Figure 26-6 **Signals from satellites are received to establish position**

Now complete **Exercises 26 – Introduction to RNAV and GPS.**

The Navigation Skill Test

The Navigation Flight Test is undertaken at the end of your PPL training and when all your theoretical exams have been passed (including Radiotelephony Theory and Practical). It is undertaken either as part of the whole PPL Test, or as a separate section (with the agreement of the Examiner).

The Flight Test route will be new to you. Expect the first leg to be 40–50 nm; The second leg will be 50–60 nm, and will proceed for at least 10 minutes before diverting to an unplanned destination at least 20 nm away. You will be allowed approximately 1 hour to complete all aspects of the planning phase.

Normally there will be no intermediate landings and the route may penetrate regulated airspace or MATZ zones. However, no navigation assistance may be provided by radar controllers since your preflight planning should be sufficiently thorough to enable you to comfortably complete the flight without assistance.

Your navigation plan and in-flight log must be completed so that the flight could be 'reconstructed' at the end of the detail.

In cases where the navigation element is elected to be performed as a separate entity, the pre-flight planning, departure, approach and landing procedures will assessed (or reassessed).

During the flight, it is of prime importance to maintain the planned headings accurately and make sensible off-track heading corrections. Mental calculations or computer calculations of heading changes should be backed-up by common sense. For example, if you are off-track to the left it will be necessary to make a correcting turn to the right to regain track. During your early navigational dual training, your flying instructor will advise you on how to reach (and surpass) the required standard.

The aim of the Navigation Flight Test is to check your ability to:
- apply simple visual navigation techniques;
- continue to navigate safely when forced by weather or other constraints to vary the planned flight profile;
- carry-out an in-flight diversion; and
- liaise with ATC.

The following excerpt on the Navigation Flight Test element is reprinted from the CAA Standards Document 19 (version 1): *Notes for the Guidance of Applicants taking the Skill Test for the Private Pilot Licence (Aeroplanes).*

5.4.   THE FLIGHT

5.4.1   Throughout the flight the applicant will be assessed on the general flight management including use of check lists, prevention of engine icing and airmanship.   The Examiner will remind the applicant that the flight is assumed to be the first flight of the day and that he should point out any items that he is checking. The applicant will be expected to proceed with the checks at a practical pace and refer to the authorised check list.   Expanded check lists are not permitted.   Where visual checks are made each check should be detailed to the Examiner.

5.4.2   **Pre - Departure Procedure**
The applicant will be expected to carry out a safe and practical inspection of the aeroplane prior to flight, and must be aware of the servicing operations that he is entitled to carry out on the aeroplane.   Pre-start and after-start checks should include all the items detailed in the check list.   The ability to tune radio aids can be observed during ground checks of the equipment and these checks should embrace all the equipment which the applicant proposes to use during the flight.   The applicant should assume that the Examiner is a passenger and may not be fully acquainted with the aeroplane and therefore he should explain the position and method of the use of emergency exits; safety belts; safety harnesses; oxygen equipment; life jackets; and all other devices required by the CAP 383 Air Navigation Order and intended for use by passengers in the case of emergency.   The applicant should instruct the Examiner in the emergency action which he should take in the unlikely event of   a real emergency on the ground.

NOTE: The applicant must be prepared to deal with actual or simulated Abnormal or Emergency Operations at any stage.   The Examiner may simulate, for example, an engine fire during start up or brake failure during taxying.

5.4.3   **Take-off and Departure.**
When ready for departure the applicant should assess the cross wind component and confirm this to the Examiner.   The departure should comply with any instructions given by ATC.   The following points should also be observed:-

(a)   Correct use of cross-wind take-off techniques where appropriate.

(b)   Correct use of take-off safety, rotation and initial climb speeds;

(c)   Correct power settings for the climb;

(d)   and completion of the after take-off checks.

5.4.4 En Route Procedures

During this section of the flight the aeroplane is assumed to be on a private passenger carrying operation under Visual Flight Rules (VFR). When the aeroplane has achieved cruising altitude and is on heading for the first turning point, the applicant should confirm to the Examiner the heading, altitude, and ETA, thereafter advising any changes and the relevant information on which these changes are made. For instance, "2 minutes late at my halfway point - the revised ETA is now..."etc. The applicant is expected to use a definitive method of navigation. The following points should also be observed:-

(a)   Appropriate altimeter settings;

(b)   Observance of minimum height rules or safety altitudes (MSA) and minimum levels;

(c)   Compliance with regulations and liaison with ATC. A safe practical approach to ATC liaison is required; the applicant would not, for example, be expected to enter a MATZ without contacting the controlling authority simply because no legal requirement exists to do so;

(d)   Accuracy of flying, altitude, speed, heading control;

(e)   Cruise checks as appropriate, carburettor icing; mixture control; fuel management (range and endurance) etc;

(f)   Map reading and assessment and correction of errors;

(g)   Log Keeping. (The Examiner may ask to see the applicant's flight and RT logs after the flight) (see para 2.4.1);

(h)   Achievement of ETA's;

(i)   Engine handling.

(j)   Observation and anticipation of deteriorating weather conditions.

5.4.5   The applicant is expected to navigate by visual positioning in a practical way, not to feature crawl. Numerous heading changes that are the result of poor heading control, or poor flying generally, may constitute a fail in this section. Radio navigation aids may not be used during this first part of the navigation route.

5.4.6   **Diversion.** During the en route procedure, at an appropriate time either before or on reaching the planned destination, or second turning point, the applicant will be instructed to carry out a diversion. A specific airfield or prominent position for the diversion will be pin-pointed by the Examiner on the applicant's chart. The applicant will be given reasonable time to assess his position and calculate the necessary navigation data before altering heading towards the diversion point. Applicants may use their own grids, graticules or plotters for navigation purposes in the air provided control of the aeroplane is satisfactorily maintained while doing so. When the aeroplane is established on heading for the diversion point, the applicant will be expected to advise the Examiner of the heading, altitude, and ETA, thereafter advising any changes. At some stage during the diversion, the Examiner may require the applicant to establish position by using a radio navigation aid. Followed by a short period of radio aid track as specified by the Examiner.

Should the Examiner not require the applicant to fix and track using radio aids during the navigation, a demonstration of radio aid tracking will be required at another point during the test. The applicant will be required to comply with the appropriate ATC clearances and other regulations throughout the diversion phase.

5.4.7 **Simulated IMC.** The Examiner will simulate inadvertent entry into cloud, by means of screens, visors or goggles and the applicant will be required to execute a turn on instruments through 180° to return the aircraft to VMC on a suitable heading. Applicants are expected to show consideration of the safety factors necessary for flight in IMC.

You may find the checklist opposite helpful when preparing for the PPL Skill Test.

PPL SKILL TEST CHECKLIST

Operations A/C	Cleaned
	Refuelled
	Serviceable
	Two headsets
Candidate/Ops	Certificate of Airworthiness
	Certificate of Registration
	Certificate of Release to Service (airframe, engine(s), compass)
	Certificate of Maintenance Review
	Certificate of Radio Installation
	Certificate of Aircraft Insurance
	Noise Certificate
	Weight and Centre of Gravity Schedule
	Aircraft Flight Manual
	Technical Log (check hours agree)
	Deferred Defect Sheet
	Two checklists
	PPL training records available
Candidate	Current Medical Certificate
	All written exams passed and in date
	Radiotelephony written and practical tests passed
	All solo and dual training completed
	Pilot's Logbook
	Screens, foguls or hood available
	Current 1:500,000 chart
	Weight & balance + fuel plan considered
	Aircraft Check 'A;
	Clean cloth, fuel strainer
	Windscreen clean
	Deviation card present

Planning the Climb

At the time of printing, in the CAA Examination on Air Navigation (and Meteorology) you will not normally be required to consider the climb, but will treat the whole flight as a cruise. On an actual flight, however, especially when you plan to cruise at a high altitude with a significant climb involved, you should allow time (and fuel) for the climb in your flight log calculations.

Note that no allowance need be made for descent of a light aircraft – it is usual to plan as if the cruise continues to overhead the destination. The slight gain of the descent is offset by the fuel used in manoeuvring and approach.

Climb TAS Is Usually Less than Cruise TAS

It is usual to set climb power and climb at a particular climb indicated airspeed (CLIAS). From Chapter 2, you will recall that for the same indicated airspeed (IAS), the true airspeed (TAS) increases with increase in density altitude, and that the profile of the climb gradually flattens out – especially as you near the performance ceiling of the aeroplane. On a climb at an approximately constant IAS:

▢ **true airspeed** gradually increases with altitude for the same indicated airspeed; and

▢ **rate of climb** (RoC) gradually decreases.

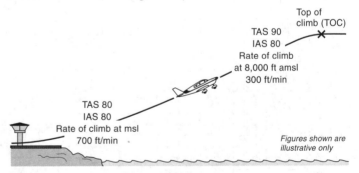

■ *Figure 1* **At a constant climb IAS, TAS progressively increases and the climb gradually flattens out**

A typical climb IAS for a light aircraft is 80 kt.

DENSITY ALTITUDE	IAS/TAS	RATE OF CLIMB
Under ISA MSL conditions	*80 kt IAS = 80 kt TAS*	*RoC 700 ft/min*
At 5,000 ft density altitude	*80 kt IAS = 86 kt TAS*	*RoC 470 ft/min*
At 10,000 ft density altitude	*80 kt IAS = 94 kt TAS*	*RoC 240 ft/min*

Because the rate of climb will decrease as you climb into the higher altitudes, it is usual to consider:

- **the average climb TAS** to be ⅔ of the way to cruise altitude;
- **the average wind effect** on the climb to be that of the wind at ⅔ of the way to your cruising altitude. (To determine this wind, either extract it for the ⅔ height approximately from the Area Forecast, or simply take ⅔ of the wind strength at cruise level, which will usually be accurate enough.)

Once you have achieved your cruise altitude the normal procedure, having accelerated to the expected cruise indicated airspeed, is to set cruise power and let the speed settle. A typical cruising TAS for a smaller aircraft might be 110 KTAS (and at cruise altitude, the IAS shown on the airspeed indicator would be less than this TAS).

Presentation of Performance Data

Performance data may be presented in either graphical or tabular form. Either presentation is easy to use. We show the graphical presentation for the Piper Warrior and the tabular presentation of the Cessna 172.

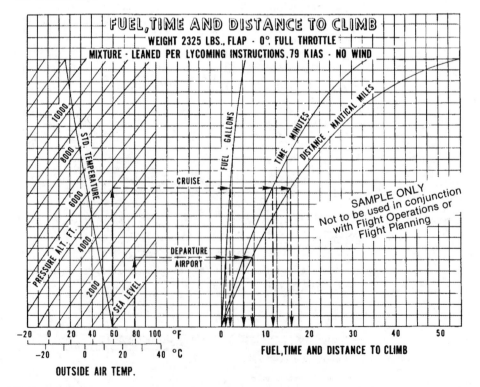

■ *Figure 2* ***Fuel, time and distance to climb – Piper Warrior II***

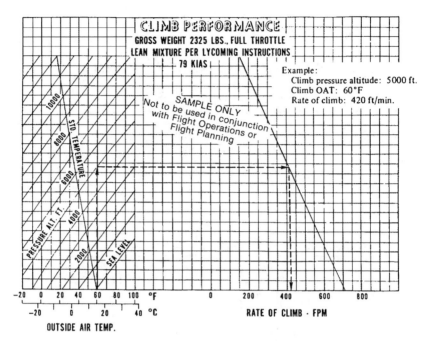

■ *Figure 3* **Climb performance graph – Piper Warrior II**

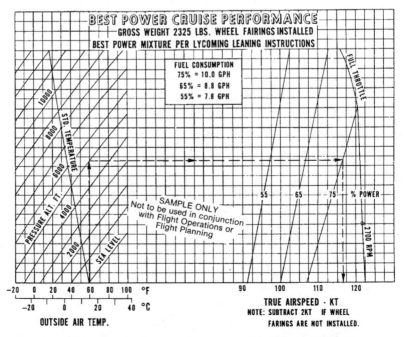

■ *Figure 4* **Best power cruise performance – Piper Warrior II**

CESSNA
MODEL 172P   PERFORMANCE

TIME, FUEL, AND DISTANCE TO CLIMB

MAXIMUM RATE OF CLIMB

CONDITIONS:
Flaps Up
Full Throttle
Standard Temperature

SAMPLE ONLY
Not to be used in conjunction
with Flight Operations or
Flight Planning

NOTES:
1.   Add 1.1 gallons of fuel for engine start, taxi and takeoff allowance.
2.   Mixture leaned above 3000 feet for maximum RPM.
3.   Increase time, fuel and distance by 10% for each 10°C above standard temperature.
4.   Distances shown are based on zero wind.

WEIGHT LBS	PRESSURE ALTITUDE FT	TEMP °C	CLIMB SPEED KIAS	RATE OF CLIMB FPM	FROM SEA LEVEL		
					TIME MIN	FUEL USED GALLONS	DISTANCE NM
2400	S.L.	15	76	700	0	0.0	0
	1000	13	76	655	1	0.3	2
	2000	11	75	610	3	0.6	4
	3000	9	75	560	5	1.0	6
	4000	7	74	515	7	1.4	9
	5000	5	74	470	9	1.7	11
	6000	3	73	425	11	2.2	14
	7000	1	72	375	14	2.6	18
	8000	-1	72	330	17	3.1	22
	9000	-3	71	285	20	3.6	26
	10,000	-5	71	240	24	4.2	32
	11,000	-7	70	190	29	4.9	38
	12,000	-9	70	145	35	5.8	47

■ Figure 5 **Tabular climb data format – Cessna 172**

PERFORMANCE

CRUISE PERFORMANCE

CONDITIONS:
2400 Pounds
Recommended Lean Mixture

SAMPLE ONLY
Not to be used in conjunction
with Flight Operations or
Flight Planning

PRESSURE ALTITUDE FT	RPM	20°C BELOW STANDARD TEMP			STANDARD TEMPERATURE			20°C ABOVE STANDARD TEMP		
		% BHP	KTAS	GPH	% BHP	KTAS	GPH	% BHP	KTAS	GPH
2000	2500	- - -	- - -	- - -	76	114	8.5	72	114	8.1
	2400	72	110	8.1	69	109	7.7	65	108	7.3
	2300	65	104	7.3	62	103	6.9	59	102	6.6
	2200	58	99	6.6	55	97	6.3	53	96	6.1
	2100	52	92	6.0	50	91	5.8	48	89	5.7
4000	2550	- - -	- - -	- - -	76	117	8.5	72	116	8.1
	2500	77	115	8.6	73	114	8.1	69	113	7.7
	2400	69	109	7.8	65	108	7.3	62	107	7.0
	2300	62	104	7.0	59	102	6.6	57	101	6.4
	2200	56	98	6.3	54	96	6.1	51	94	5.9
	2100	51	91	5.8	48	89	5.7	47	88	5.5
6000	2600	- - -	- - -	- - -	77	119	8.6	72	118	8.1
	2500	73	114	8.2	69	113	7.8	66	112	7.4
	2400	66	108	7.4	63	107	7.0	60	106	6.7
	2300	60	103	6.7	57	101	6.4	55	99	6.2
	2200	54	96	6.1	52	95	5.9	50	92	5.8
	2100	49	90	5.7	47	88	5.5	46	86	5.5
8000	2650	- - -	- - -	- - -	77	121	8.6	73	120	8.1
	2600	77	119	8.7	73	118	8.2	69	117	7.8
	2500	70	113	7.8	66	112	7.4	63	111	7.1
	2400	63	108	7.1	60	106	6.7	58	104	6.5
	2300	57	101	6.4	55	100	6.2	53	97	6.0
	2200	52	95	6.0	50	93	5.8	49	91	5.7
10,000	2600	74	118	8.3	70	117	7.8	66	115	7.4
	2500	67	112	7.5	64	111	7.1	61	109	6.8
	2400	61	106	6.8	58	105	6.5	56	102	6.3
	2300	55	100	6.3	53	98	6.0	51	96	5.9
	2200	50	93	5.8	49	91	5.7	47	89	5.6
12,000	2550	67	114	7.5	64	112	7.1	61	111	6.9
	2500	64	111	7.2	61	109	6.8	59	107	6.6
	2400	59	105	6.6	56	103	6.3	54	100	6.1
	2300	53	98	6.1	51	96	5.9	50	94	5.8

■ *Figure 6* **Cruise performance data – Cessna 172**

Planning a Typical Climb

Consider a climb from a sea-level aerodrome to a cruising altitude of 7,500 ft by a Piper Warrior under ISA conditions. (Assume the conditions such as weight, etc., are as specified on the climb performance graph above.)

From the area forecast, the winds are light and variable at all altitudes. Our first checkpoint is, say, 45 nm from our departure aerodrome.

Climb from MSL to 7,500 ft (from graph)

☐ 2.5 USG, 15 minutes, 21 nm, and since there is nil significant wind, this will mean 21 gnm (nm over the ground).

☐ There is no need to determine the average TAS on the climb, but if you do it is quite easy: 21 anm in 15 min = TAS 84 kt.

■ Figure 7 **Computer set-up**

Cruise (65% power) from Top of Climb (TOC) to First Checkpoint (at, say, 45 nm)

☐ Cruise TAS = 108 kt, nil wind, therefore groundspeed 108 kt.

☐ Distance from TOC to first checkpoint = 45 − 21 = 24 nm. 24 nm at GS 108 = ETI 13 min at 8.8 GPH = 1.9, say 2 US gallons.

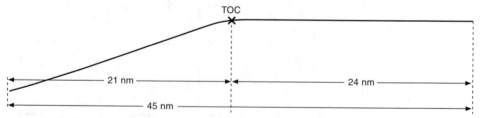

■ Figure 8 **Profile of the first leg**

☐ Time from departure
  to first checkpoint = 15 min climb + 13 min cruise
                      = 28 min

☐ Fuel burn from departure
  to first checkpoint = 2.5 USG + 2 USG
                      = 4.5, say 5 USG

What If We Had Not Considered the Climb?

If we had treated the whole of this first leg as a cruise, then:
- ETI is: 45 nm at GS 108 kt = 25 minutes ETI;
- Fuel burn is: 25 min at 8.8 GPH = 3.7 USG.

At the first checkpoint in this case, there is a 3 minute difference in ETI due to the consideration of the 7,500 ft climb. Fuel burn as a result of climbing will exceed that of a pure cruise by (4.5 − 3.7) = 0.8, say 1 USG.

What Do We Do About This?

Your flying instructor will give you advice on how to allow for the climb in your particular aeroplane. It may be that:
- for short climbs, no consideration of climb is required; and
- for longer climbs – a time and fuel allowance is made; or
  - a mean TAS is used for the leg; or
  - a full climb calculation is done.

Typical Climb and Cruise Calculation – Piper Warrior

Departure aerodrome:
- Elevation 1,334 ft, QNH 1005, OAT +30°C
  (so pressure altitude = 1,574 ft).

Cruise altitude:
- 7,500 ft, regional QNH 1009 (so pressure altitude is 7,620 ft), OAT + 10°C (use 65% power).

Winds from the Area Forecast:
- 5,000 ft: 10 kt headwind.
- 7,000 ft: 20 kt headwind.
- 10,000 ft: 25 kt headwind.

Climb

- From MSL to 7,620 ft PA (OAT + 10°C) =
  3 USG / 18 min / 27 anm
- From MSL to 1,574 ft PA (OAT + 30°C) =
  1 USG / 6 min / 8 anm;
- So, from 1,574 ft PA to 7,620 ft PA =
  2 USG / 12 min / 19 anm

Note that both pressure altitude and temperature come into this calculation, i.e. we are really considering density altitude. (The performance of an aeroplane, from both the engine point of view and the flying ability or airframe point of view, depends on air density.)

To obtain our actual climb figure from 1,500 ft to 7,500 ft amsl we need to subtract one from the other (since the climb from mean sea level to 1,500 ft does not actually occur – our take-off is at PA 1,500 ft).

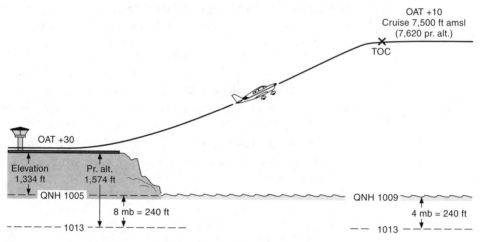

OAT +10
Cruise 7,500 ft amsl
(7,620 pr. alt.)
TOC

OAT +30

Elevation
1,334 ft

Pr. alt.
1,574 ft

QNH 1005

8 mb = 240 ft

1013

QNH 1009

4 mb = 240 ft

1013

■ Figure 9 **Climb profile**

In this case we do not have nil-wind conditions. We will take the average wind for the climb to be that ⅔ of the way up to cruising altitude.

The climb from 1,500 to 7,500 = 6,000 ft, ⅔ of which = 4,000 ft, so our average wind will be at 1,500 + 4,000 = 5,500 ft. All of this is very approximate, so we will use the forecast 5,000 ft wind of −10 kt (i.e. a headwind component of 10 kt).

☐ In 1 hour (60 minutes), the wind effect would be 10 nm.

☐ Since our climb lasts 12 minutes, the wind effect will be:
¹²⁄₆₀ of 10 = ⅕ of 10 = 2 nm.

☐ Since it is a headwind, the 19 air nautical miles on our climb will be reduced to 19 − 2 = 17 ground nautical miles.

To continue our flight plan to the first checkpoint, say 70 nm from the departure aerodrome, the remaining cruise distance is 70 − 17 = 53 nm, and we proceed with the cruise calculations.

Now complete **Exercises – Climb Planning.**

The Air Pilot's **Manual**

Volume 3

Exercises and Answers

Air Navigation

Exercises 1

The Pilot/Navigator

1 Since time is of vital importance to a pilot/navigator, you must ensure that you have an accurate and serviceable w.... or c..... .

2 The basis of a confident cross-country flight and navigation exercise is s.... prep........ .

3 The length of the shortest line joining two points around the surface of the earth is called the .... between them.

4 For most navigation purposes, distance is stated in n........ m..... .

5 One nautical mile travelled over the ground or water is sometimes referred to as a ....

6 One nautical mile travelled through an air mass is called an ... .

7 What is the abbreviation for nautical mile?

8 The abbreviation for a ground nautical mile is .... .

9 The abbreviation for an air nautical mile is .... .

10 The usual navigation unit for airspeed is the ...., which is 1 .... per hour.

11 The accepted unit of length for shorter distances such as runway length is the m..... .

12 The accepted unit for altitude and elevation of aerodromes is the .... .

13 A circle on the earth's surface, whose centre is the centre of the earth, is called a ....

14 A circle may be divided into .... degrees and each one of these degrees may be further subdivided into .... minutes.

15 Great circles on the earth's surface, that pass through the North and South Geographic Poles, are known as meridians of ....

16 Position on the surface of the earth is specified by reference to a graticule in terms of la...... and lo........ .

17 Parallels of latitude (do/do not) run parallel to the equator and to each other.

18 1 minute of arc of a great circle on the earth's surface has a length of .... nm.

19 While the usual navigation unit for distance between places on earth is the nautical mile, shorter distances are referred to by different units. For instance, distance from cloud in the Visual Flight Rules is specified in f..., and runway length is referred to in m...... .

20 1 nautical mile = ... metres.

21 As a simple method of expressing direction, we divide a full circle into 360 degrees and number them from 000 through 090, 180, 270 to 360 in a .....wise direction.

22 If 000 (and 360 of course) are aligned with north, then 090 is .... .

23 If 360 is aligned with north, then 180 is ....

24 If 000 is aligned with north, then 270 is .... .

25 The speed of the aeroplane relative to the air mass is called its t... a..s...., which is abbreviated to .... .

26 To completely specify the motion of an aeroplane relative to an air mass we need to specify two things: its h...... and its t... a..s..... .

27 The heading /true airspeed vector is symbolised by a s.....-headed arrow.

28 The movement of an air mass relative to the ground is called w.... .

29 The wind direction, by convention, is the direction that the wind blows ..... .

30 A northerly wind blows (from/towards) the north.

31 A westerly wind blows (from/towards) the west.

32 The passage of an aeroplane over the ground is called its t.... .

33 The speed of an aeroplane relative to the ground is called its g.....s.... .

34 The direction in which an aeroplane points is called its ....

35 The direction of travel over the ground is called an aeroplane's ..... .

36 The aeroplane is blown from its heading to its track by the .... effect.

37 The angle between the direction an aeroplane is pointing (its heading) and the direction in which it is travelling over the ground (its track) is called the ..... angle.

38 Label the shaded angle shown in Figure 1.

39 Is this drift left (port) or right (starboard)?

40 Sometimes the actual drift experienced in flight differs from that expected and the aeroplane makes good a track (TMG) different to the desired track. The difference between desired track and TMG is called the ....

41 Label the shaded angle in Figure 2.

42 Is this track error left or right?

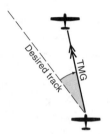

■ Figure 2

43 In Figure 3, label the vectors A and B and the angle D with their appropriate navigation terms.

44 Which statement best fits the situation in Figure 3?

    (a)   TAS exceeds GS.

    (b)   GS exceeds TAS.

    (c)   Drift is left (port).

    (d)   The wind is easterly.

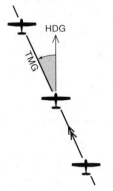

■ Figure 1

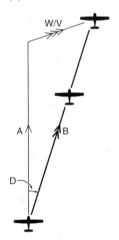

■ Figure 3

Exercises 2

Speed

Speed-1

1 The rate of progress of an aeroplane through an air mass is called its t... a..s..... .

2 The speed of an aeroplane relative to the ground is called its g.....s.... .

3 The reason that there may be a difference between TAS and GS is due to the effect of ..... .

4 The cockpit instrument used to measure airspeed is called an .... indicator and its abbreviation is .... .

5 The speed that a pilot reads on the airspeed indicator is called the .... airspeed and its abbreviation is .... .

6 Performance of the aeroplane depends on its (indicated/true) airspeed.

7 Navigation and flight planning depend on (indicated/true) airspeed.

8 The airspeed indicator is usually graduated in ....

9 If a pilot corrects the indicated airspeed read on the airspeed indicator for errors such as the instrument error and position error peculiar to that particular ASI, the result is r........ airspeed, which is also known as the c......... airspeed.

10 Errors in modern airspeed indicators are generally not significant and we can usually assume that the i........ and r........ (or c.........) airspeeds are the same value.

11 The speed that a pilot reads on the ASI is called the:

    (a) IAS.

    (b) RAS or CAS.

    (c) TAS.

    (d) GS.

Speed-2

1 Air density will normally (increase/decrease) with altitude.

2 Air density is affected by both t.......... and p........ .

3 Airspeed indicators are calibrated to read correctly only under I............ Standard Atmosphere m... s.. l.... conditions.

4 At high altitudes the true airspeed will be (greater than/less than) the airspeed indicated on the ASI in the cockpit.

NOTE For the following questions, assume that the instrument and position error for the airspeed indicator is zero, and therefore rectified airspeed is equal to the indicated airspeed. IAS may be taken to mean RAS (or CAS).

5 At 5,000 ft density altitude, your TAS will exceed the indicated airspeed by about .... %.

6 An IAS of 100 kt at density altitude 5,000 ft will give you a TAS .... kt.

7 A RAS of 200 kt at density altitude 5,000 ft will give you a TAS .... kt.

8 A RAS of 120 kt at density altitude 5,000 ft will give you TAS .... kt.

9 At 10,000 ft density altitude, your TAS will exceed the IAS by about ....%.

10 At density altitude 10,000 ft, RAS = 100 kt, your TAS will be .... kt.

11 At density altitude 10,000 ft, RAS = 200 kt, your TAS will be .... kt.

12 At density altitude 10,000 ft, RAS = 120 kt, your TAS will be .... kt.

Speed-3

1 Complete Table 1 below:

Pressure altitude	Temp.	RAS	TAS
3,000 ft	+2°C	134 kt	
3,000 ft	+6°C	134 kt	
3,000 ft	−10°C	134 kt	
5,000 ft	−10°C	134 kt	
5,000 ft	+10°C	134 kt	

■ *Table 1* **Speed-3, Question 1**

NOTE If you are given a question where altitude is stated, but not QNH, then you may assume altitude to mean pressure altitude. The difference in answers for TAS, neglecting the effect of QNHs other than 1013 mb, is generally not operationally significant. Also, if temperature is given as an ISA deviation, convert it to a straight temperature before applying it to your navigation computer.

2 If you are cruising at pressure altitude 6,500 ft with an indicated airspeed of 162 kt, and outside air temperature of −5°C, your true airspeed is:

   (a)   162 kt.

   (b)   176 kt.

   (c)   180 kt.

   (d)   194 kt.

3 You are flying at FL50 (pressure altitude 5,000 ft). Outside air temperature (OAT) is ISA+5. IAS(RAS) is 98 kt. Determine the TAS.

4 You are a passenger in the cockpit of a Cessna 421 that is flying at FL140, ISA+10. The speed indicated on the aircraft's airspeed indicator is 154 kt. What is its TAS?

5 At altitude 8,500 ft amsl on QNH 999 mb and temperature ISA−5, what rectified airspeed is required to achieve a true airspeed of 150 kt?

6 At altitude 8,500 on QNH 1030 mb, OAT is −8°C, what RAS is required to achieve TAS 150 kt?

Exercises 3

Direction

1 The standard for measuring direction is to start at north and proceed in a clockwise direction for .... degrees until you are back at north again.

2 The direction 090 degrees clockwise from north is called .... .

3 The direction 180 degrees clockwise from north is called .... .

4 The direction 270 degrees clockwise from north is called .... .

5 The earth rotates on its axis and the two points where this axis meets the earth's surface are called the geographic N.... Pole and the geographic S.... Pole. They are also referred to as t... n.... and t... s.... .

6 Any 'straight' line drawn on the earth's surface between the two geographic poles (e.g. longitude meridians) will run in a true .....−..... direction.

7 Near the earth's true geographic poles are areas from where the earth's magnetic field emanates. These two points are called the n.... m....... p... and the s.... m....... p... .

8 A bar magnet, like that in a simple magnetic compass, will align itself approximately with m....... n.... and m....... s.... .

9 The angular difference from true to magnetic north is called v........ .

10 If magnetic north lies to the east of true north, then variation is .... .

11 If magnetic north lies to the west of true north, then magnetic variation is said to be .... .

12 Lines drawn on a chart joining places of identical magnetic variation are called i........ .

13 Variation east, magnetic .....; variation west, magnetic ..... .

14 Complete Table 2 below:

HDG(T)	Variation	HDG(M)
090°T	7°W	
273°T	7°W	
359°T	7°W	
005°T	7°W	
156°T	5°W	
	5°W	270°M
	5°E	082°M
	4°W	003°M

■ *Table 2* **Direction, Question 14**

15 Due to local magnetic fields in the aircraft, the magnetic compass may not point directly towards magnetic north but rather towards c...... north.

16 The degree to which the magnetic compass is deviated from magnetic north by these local magnetic fields is called ....

17 The angular difference between a magnetic heading and a compass heading is called c...... d........ .

18 Given the following deviation card, fill in the blank spaces in Table 3 below:

19 To achieve a true heading of 330°T in an area where the magnetic variation is 7°W, what compass heading must be steered if the deviation is 2°W?

20 If the aircraft is headed 097°C and experiences 8° starboard (right) drift, calculate its true track, given deviation 1°W on that heading, and variation 5°W.

21 If the aircraft is headed 358°C and experiences 4° starboard drift, calculate its true track, given deviation 2°E on that heading, and variation 7°W.

22 If the aircraft is headed 358°C and experiences 5° port (left) drift, calculate its true track, given deviation 2°E on that heading, and variation 6°W.

23 Storing your transistor radio and a spare set of headphones near the magnetic compass (is/is not) a good practice.

24 If you are taking off on Runway 34, your compass (provided you are not turning or accelerating) should read about:

(a) 034.

(b) 340.

(c) 000.

(d) 160.

For	Steer	HDG (T)	Varn.	HDG (M)	HDG (C)
N(360)	003	012°T	8°W	020°M	
E(090)	087	270°T	8°W	278°M	
S(180)	181	189°T	8°W		
W(270)	272	285°T	7°W		
		100°T		106°M	
			7°W		280°C

Table 3 **Direction, Question 18**

25 Acceleration errors in the direct reading magnetic compass are greatest on a
   heading of:
   (a) north.
   (b) south.
   (c) east.
   (d) west.
   (e) north and south.
   (f) east and west.

26 Turning errors in the direct reading
   magnetic compass are greatest on a
   heading of:
   (a) north.
   (b) south.
   (c) east.
   (d) west.
   (e) north and south.
   (f) east and west.

27 When accelerating on a heading of due
   east in the UK, the magnetic compass
   will indicate:
   (a) a turn to the left (towards north).
   (b) a turn to the right (towards south).
   (c) correctly.

28 When accelerating on a heading of due
   west in the UK, the magnetic compass
   will indicate:
   (a) a turn to the left (towards south).
   (b) a turn to the right (towards north).
   (c) correctly.

29 When accelerating on a heading of due
   north in the UK, the magnetic compass
   will indicate:
   (a) a turn to the left.
   (b) a turn to the right.
   (c) correctly.

30 When accelerating on a heading of due
   south in the UK, the magnetic compass
   will indicate:
   (a) a turn to the left.
   (b) a turn to the right.
   (c) correctly.

31 After having accelerated on a heading
   of 090°C and settled down to a new
   steady cruising speed, the magnetic
   compass will have:
   (a) read correctly throughout the
        acceleration.
   (b) initially indicated a false heading
        change towards north, before grad-
        ually returning to a correct reading
        of 090°C.
   (c) initially indicated a false heading
        change towards south, before grad-
        ually returning to a correct reading
        of 090°C.
   (d) initially indicated a false heading
        change towards north, and will
        continue to indicate incorrectly
        even after the speed settles down.

32 When turning through north in the
   UK, the pilot should:
   (a) undershoot the desired heading.
   (b) overshoot the desired heading.
   (c) stop the turn immediately when
        the compass indicates the desired
        heading.

33 When turning through north in the
   UK, the magnetic compass will:
   (a) indicate correctly throughout.
   (b) under-indicate the amount of turn,
        requiring the pilot to stop the turn
        before the desired heading is indi-
        cated.
   (c) over-indicate the amount of turn,
        requiring the pilot to stop the turn
        after the desired heading has been
        indicated.

34 When turning through south in the UK, the pilot should:

(a) undershoot the desired heading.

(b) overshoot the desired heading.

(c) stop the turn immediately when the compass indicates the desired heading.

35 When turning through east in the UK, the magnetic compass will:

(a) indicate correctly.

(b) over-indicate the amount of turn, requiring the pilot to stop the turn before the desired heading is indicated.

(c) under-indicate the amount of turn, requiring the pilot to stop the turn after the desired heading has been indicated.

36 When turning onto an easterly heading in the UK, the pilot should:

(a) undershoot the desired heading.

(b) overshoot the desired heading.

(c) stop the turn when the compass indicates east.

37 When turning through west in the UK, the magnetic compass will:

(a) indicate correctly.

(b) over-indicate the amount of turn, requiring the pilot to stop the turn before the desired heading is indicated.

(c) under-indicate the amount of turn, requiring the pilot to stop the turn after the desired heading has been indicated.

38 When turning onto a westerly heading in the UK, the pilot should:

(a) undershoot the desired heading.

(b) overshoot the desired heading.

(c) stop the turn when the compass indicates west.

39 When turning through north in the UK, the direct reading magnetic compass will:

(a) indicate correctly throughout the turn.

(b) show an exaggerated turn when turning either left or right.

(c) show an exaggerated turn when turning left, but under-indicate a right turn.

(d) show an exaggerated turn when turning right, but under-indicate a left turn.

(e) under-indicate turns both left and right.

40 When turning through south in the UK, the direct reading magnetic compass will:

(a) indicate correctly throughout the turn.

(b) show an exaggerated turn when turning either left or right.

(c) show an exaggerated turn when turning left, but under-indicate a right turn.

(d) show an exaggerated turn when turning right, but under-indicate a left turn.

(e) under-indicate turns both left and right.

41 When turning through east in the UK, the direct reading magnetic compass will:

(a) indicate correctly.

(b) show an exaggerated turn when turning either left or right.

(c) show an exaggerated turn when turning left, but under-indicate a right turn.

(d) show an exaggerated turn when turning right, but under-indicate a left turn.

(e) under-indicate turns both left and right.

42 When turning through west in the UK, the magnetic compass will:

(a) indicate correctly.

(b) show an exaggerated turn when turning either left or right.

(c) show an exaggerated turn when turning left, but under-indicate a right turn.

(d) show an exaggerated turn when turning right, but under-indicate a left turn.

(e) under-indicate turns both left and right.

43 Turning from north-east to north-west by the shortest way, a magnetic compass will:

(a) indicate correctly.

(b) over-indicate the number of degrees turned.

(c) under-indicate the number of degrees turned.

44 The gyroscopic heading indicator should be aligned with the magnetic compass (once per flight/every 10 or 15 minutes).

45 You (should/should not) align the HI with the compass when the aeroplane is turning.

46 Once aligned with the compass, the HI is (easier/harder) than the magnetic compass to use for turning onto a new heading, because the HI is not subject to turning and acceleration errors like the magnetic compass.

47 The direction of an object related to the nose of the aeroplane is called the r....... b...... of the object from the aeroplane.

48 If a radio mast bears 60° to the right of the nose of the aircraft, then its relative bearing is .... REL.

49 If a small township bears 80° to the left of the nose of the aircraft, then its relative bearing is .... REL.

50 If a hill bears 50° to the right of the aircraft's nose, then its relative bearing is .... REL and, if the aircraft's HDG is 035M, then the magnetic bearing of the hill from the aircraft is .... M.

51 In what direction would someone on the hill look to see the aeroplane?

Exercises 4

Wind Side of the Navigation Computer

Wind Side-1

1 Label the sides marked A and B in Figure 4.

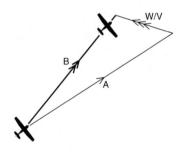

■ Figure 4

2 The wind blows an aeroplane from its .... to its ....

3 At the flight planning stage, we measure the direction on our chart of the d...... t..... .

4 Using the forecast wind velocity given in knots and degrees true, and knowing the true airspeed that we can expect from our aeroplane at the selected altitude, we can calculate h...... and g.....s..... .

5 Calculate the true heading and groundspeed for:
TAS 98 kt;
W/V 280°T/35; and
track 340°T.

6 Calculate the true heading and groundspeed for:
TAS 98 kt;
W/V 280°T/35; and
track 251°T.

7 Calculate the true heading and groundspeed for:
TAS 98 kt;
W/V 280°T/35; and
track 100°T.

8 Calculate the true heading and groundspeed for:
TAS 98 kt;
W/V 280°T/35; and
track 072°T.

9 If you wish to maintain a groundspeed of 120 kt on track, calculate the true heading and TAS required if W/V is 280°T/35 and track 072°T.

10 If you wish to maintain a groundspeed of 80 kt on track, calculate the true heading and TAS required if W/V is 090°T/20 and track 180°T.

11 Complete Table 4 below, doing your computer manipulations using degrees true, to find true heading and ground-speed, then convert the true heading to a magnetic heading.
(This is the procedure you will use when completing a flight log form prior to flight).

TAS	track(T)	W/V(T)	HDG(T)	Variation	HDG(M)	GS
120	085°T	055°T/36		7°W		
120	055°T	055°T/36		7°W		
140	120°T	350°T/30		6°W		
140	300°T	350°T/30		6°W		

■ Table 4 **Wind Side-1, Question 11**

12 If you wish to maintain a groundspeed of 120 kt on track, calculate the true heading and TAS required if W/V is 280°T/35 and track 072°T.

13 If you wish to maintain a groundspeed of 80 kt on track, calculate the true heading and TAS required if W/V is 090°T/20 and track 180°T. What rectified airspeed (CAS, or IAS if the airspeed indicator is perfect) would this require at pressure altitude 5,000 ft and temperature +12°C?

14 To achieve a track of 300°T, calculate the magnetic heading and groundspeed if you plan to cruise at FL100 (pressure altitude 10,000 ft), where the forecast wind velocity and temperature is 280°T/25 and +6°C, at an indicated airspeed of 100 kt. Variation is 6°W.

15 Some flying instructors prefer to convert to degrees magnetic as early as possible, and then do all of the working that follows in °M, i.e. the track, heading and wind direction set up on the computer are **all** in magnetic (rather than **all** in true). If this is the case, then you would perform the calculations in the following manner. Note that you end up with the same answers for HDG(M) and GS as in the previous question. Complete the table:

TAS	track(T)	Variation	TR(M)	W/V(T)	W/V(M)	HDG(M)	GS
120	085°T	7°W		055°T/36			
120	055°T	7°W		055°T/36			
140	120°T	6°W		350°T/30			
140	300°T	6°W		350°T/30			

■ *Table 5* **Wind Side-1, Question 15**

Wind Side-2

1 You are flying at TAS 125 kt on HDG 280°T. From two position fixes you calculate your TMG and GS to be 286°T and 144 kt. Calculate the wind velocity.

2 Calculate the W/V if heading is 290°T, TAS 110 kt, GS 95 kt and drift 5° port (left).

3 Calculate the W/V if heading is 356°T, TAS 100 kt, GS 93 kt and track made good 010°T?

4 Calculate the W/V if heading is 070°T, TAS 96 kt, GS 108 kt and drift 7° starboard (right).

Wind Side-3

1 Complete the following table where you are given HDG/TAS and W/V, and have to find TR/GS.

TAS	W/V(T)	HDG(T)	TR(T)	GS
120	055°T/36	076°T		
140	350°T/30	110°T		
140	350°T/30	310°T		
120	055°T/36	104°T		
120	055°T/36	014°T		
120	055°T/36	055°T		

■ *Table 6* **Wind Side-3, Question 1**

2 You are flying over featureless terrain at TAS 157 kt on a HDG 346°M. The forecast wind is 315°T/30. What is your dead reckoning true TR and GS? Variation is 7°W.

Wind Side-4

1 The tower passes you a surface wind of 050°M/30. What are the headwind and crosswind components on Runway 34?

2 If your aircraft has a crosswind limitation of 15 kt, could you take off on RWY 34 under these circumstances?

3 Would RWY 03 or RWY 21 be suitable under the circumstances of Question 2?

Exercises 5

Calculator Side of the Navigation Computer

Calculator-1

1 At a GS of 147 kt, how far will you travel in 11 minutes?

2 At a GS of 183 kt, how far will you travel in 17 minutes?

3 At a GS of 120 kt, how far will you travel in 10 minutes?

Calculator-2

1 If you cover 23 nm over the ground in 9 minutes, what is your GS?

2 If you cover 17 nm over the ground in 11 minutes, what is your GS?

3 If you cover 18 nm over the ground in 6 minutes, what is your GS?

4 If you cover 9 nm over the ground in 3 minutes, what is your GS?

5 If you travel 20 nm over the ground in 8 minutes, what is your GS and what is the estimated time interval (ETI) to fly a further 30 nm in the same direction, assuming no change in GS?

6 If you cover 22 gnm in 10 minutes, what is your GS and how long will it take you to reach the next checkpoint which is still 73 nm further on in the same direction?

7 If you cover 25 nm in 12 minutes, how long will it take you to cover 31 nm in the same direction?

8 At a GS of 137 kt, how long will it take you to travel 27 nm?

9 At a GS of 153 kt, how long will it take you to travel 33 nm?

10 The distance from Alpha to Bravo is 107 nm. 10 minutes after leaving Alpha the aeroplane has travelled 16 nm towards Bravo. How much longer until it reaches Bravo if the same GS is maintained?

11 The distance from Bournemouth to Cardiff is 68 nm. If an aeroplane departs Bournemouth at time 1230 UTC, and passes over the disused aerodrome at Henstridge, 23 nm en route, at time 1242 UTC, what is the estimated time of arrival (ETA) overhead Cardiff if the same ground-speed is maintained?

12 The distance from Edinburgh to Prestwick is 50 nm. If an aeroplane departs Edinburgh at time 0807 UTC and passes over the railway line at Motherwell, 22 nm from Edinburgh, at time 0816 UTC, what is the estimated time of arrival (ETA) overhead Prestwick if the same TAS is maintained and the W/V does not change?

Calculator-3

1 If you burn fuel at the rate of 32 litres/hour, how much will you burn in 25 minutes?

2 If you burn fuel at the rate of 28 litres/hour, what fuel will you burn in 8 minutes?

3 If you burn 15 litres of fuel in 34 minutes, what is your rate of fuel consumption?

4 If you burn 5 US gallons of fuel in 40 minutes, what is your rate of fuel consumption?

5 If you burn 12 litres of fuel in 24 minutes, what is your rate of fuel consumption, and how long would it take to burn 17 litres?

6 If full tanks is 48 USG of usable fuel and the average consumption rate is 8 USG/hr, calculate the safe endurance for flight if you wish to retain 1 hour's fuel as reserve

7 If full tanks is 26 USG of usable fuel and the average consumption rate is 5.5 USG/hr, calculate the safe endurance for flight if you wish to retain 1 hour's fuel as reserve.

8 If full tanks is 36 USG of usable fuel and the average consumption rate is 7.5 USG/hr, calculate the safe endurance for flight if you wish to retain 45 minutes' fuel as reserve.

9 What total fuel is required if GS is 120 kt, distance 300 nm, average fuel consumption 7.3 USG/hr and you wish to carry 1 hour's fuel as reserve? If you refuelled to a whole number of gallons, how much fuel would you carry?

10 What total fuel is required if GS is 98 kt, distance 130 nm, average fuel consumption 6.5 USG/hr and you wish to carry 1 hour's fuel as reserve? If you refuelled to a whole number of gallons, how much fuel would you carry?

11 If there is 27 USG on board and the average fuel consumption is 6.8 USG/hr, how far can you fly at a GS of 93 kt and still have 1 hour's reserve remaining in the tanks?

12 If there is 27 USG on board and the average fuel consumption is 6.8 USG/hr, how far can you fly at a GS of 93 kt and still have 6 USG reserve remaining in the tanks?

Calculator-4

1 If you are off-track by 3 nm after travelling 20 nm, how far off-track will you be after travelling a total of 60 nm?

2 If you are off-track by 6 nm after travelling 30 nm, how far off-track will you be after having travelling a total of 45 nm, and a total of 60 nm?

3 If you are 2 nm off-track after 15 nm, what distance will you be off-track after travelling a total of 60 nm and what is your track error in degrees?

4 If you are 4 nm off-track after 20 nm, what distance off-track will you be after a total of 60 nm, and what is the track error (TE) in degrees?

Calculator-5

1 Convert a temperature of +38°C to °F.

2 Convert +32°F to C.

3 Convert +20°C to F.

Calculator-6

1 Convert 100 nm to statute miles and kilometres.

2 Convert 55 nm to kilometres.

3 Convert 1,000 km to nm.

4 Convert 50 kt to km/hr, metres/hour, metres/minute and metres/second.

Calculator-7

1 An older pilot refers to a particular runway as being 1,300 ft long. How long is this in metres?

2 A runway 1,213 metres long is how long in feet?

3 A visibility of 500 metres is how many feet?

4 A continental European topographical chart shows an obstruction with an elevation of 100 metres. How high is this in feet?

5 A French topographical chart shows an obstruction with an elevation of 375 metres. How high is this in feet? At what altitude in ft amsl would you fly to clear it by 1,000 ft?

Calculator-8

1 Convert 60 lb to kg.

2 Convert 631 lb to kg.

3 Convert 80 kg to lb.

4 Convert 845 kg to lb.

5 Convert 5,700 kg to lb.

Calculator-9

1 The specific gravity of 100 octane or greater Avgas is .... .

2 1 imperial gallon of Avgas weighs .... lb.

3 1 litre of Avgas weighs .... kg.

4 10 litres of Avgas weighs .... kg.

5 50 litres of Avgas weighs .... kg.

6 1 imperial gallon = ... US gallons.

7 5 imperial gallons = ... USG.

8 10 imperial gallons = ... USG = ... litres.

9 10 USG = ... litres.

10 1 USG = ... litres.

11 Your fuel gauges are graduated in USG. You wish to fuel up from 27 USG to 45 USG. How many litres of Avgas would you order from the fuel agent?

12 To refuel from 16 USG to 45 USG you should order .... litres.

13 If your fuel gauges initially read 12 USG and the refueller has added 86 litres, what should your gauges read approximately?

14 What is the weight in kg of 100 litres of Avgas?

15 What is the weight in kg of 53 litres of Avgas?

16 30 USG of Avgas = ... litres = ... kg.

17 37 USG of Avgas = ... litres = ... kg.

Assuming a SG of 0.71 for your fuel:

18 Convert 44 USG to kg.

19 Convert 27 USG to litres.

20 Convert 27 USG to kg.

21 Convert 91 USG to kg and litres.

22 Convert 48 USG to UK imperial gallons and calculate its weight given that, in this case, 1 imperial gallon of fuel weighs 7 lb.

Exercises 6

Vertical Navigation

Vertical Nav-1

1 The vertical distance of a point above mean sea level (amsl) is called its a........ .

2 The standard unit for altitude in the UK is the .... .

3 The altimeter provides the pilot with an (exact/approximate) altitude.

4 A pilot needs to know the altitude of the aeroplane for t...... clearance, t...... separation, and to calculate the aeroplane's p.......... capabilities.

5 Air pressure (decreases/increases) with an increase in height.

6 The altimeter is a p.......-sensitive instrument.

7 The International Civil Aviation Organisation (ICAO) Standard Atmosphere is abbreviated to ... .

8 The ISA is a theoretical standard atmosphere and is used as a m........ s..... .

9 Standard mean sea level pressure in the ISA is .... millibars/hectopascals.

10 Standard mean sea level temperature in the ISA is ....°C.

11 From ground level up to a pressure altitude of about 36,000 ft, the temperature in the ISA is assumed to fall at ....°C/1,000 ft.

12 The main purpose of the International Standard Atmosphere is to c........ a.......... .

13 The p....... a....... of a point is the height in the ISA above the 1013.2 mb pressure level at which the pressure equals that of the point under consideration.

14 As altitude increases, air pressure will ....

15 Up to about 5,000 ft amsl, atmospheric pressure drops by approximately 1 mb for each .... ft increase in altitude.

16 If the MSL pressure is 1013 mb, what is the pressure at 30 ft amsl?

17 If the MSL pressure is 1013 mb, what is the pressure at 60 ft amsl?

18 If the MSL pressure is 1013 mb, what is the pressure at 3,000 ft amsl?

19 If the MSL pressure is 1013 mb, at what pressure altitude would you expect the pressure to be 990 mb?

20 If the MSL pressure is 1013 mb, at what pressure altitude would you expect to find a pressure of 900 mb?

Vertical Nav-2

1 The standard mean sea level temperature in the International Standard Atmosphere (the ISA) is ...°C.

2 What is the ISA temperature at 1,000 ft pressure altitude?

3 What is the ISA temperature at 5,000 ft pressure altitude?

4 What is the ISA temperature at 10,000 ft pressure altitude?

5 Calculate the ISA values of temperature and pressure for a pressure altitude of 3,000 ft.

6 Calculate the ISA values of temperature and pressure for a pressure altitude of 600 ft.

7 Calculate the ISA values of temperature and pressure for a pressure altitude of −600 ft.

8 What is the pressure altitude of the 970 mb pressure surface?

9 What is the pressure altitude of the 1010 mb pressure surface?

10 What is the pressure altitude of the 1020 mb pressure surface?

Vertical Nav-3

1 With 1013 mb set on the altimeter subscale, the altimeter will read height above the ...... mb pressure level, which we call *pressure altitude* or *pressure height*.

2 The ISA MSL pressure is defined as 1013.2 mb(hPa). Does this mean the actual MSL pressure existing at all times in a real atmosphere is 1013.2 mb?

3 Does mean sea level pressure at a particular place vary from day to day?

4 The approximate value of the actual mean sea level pressure in millibars is called the Q...

5 Altitude is the height of an aeroplane (above mean sea level/above the 1013.2 mb pressure level).

6 To measure altitude, we should set (QNH/1013.2) on the altimeter's subscale.

7 If you are taxiing at an aerodrome, and QNH is set on the altimeter subscale, then the altimeter should indicate (aerodrome elevation amsl/pressure altitude/zero).

8 If you wind an extra 20 mb (say from 1013 to 1033 mb) onto the subscale, you would also wind the altimeter's pointer on to indicate .... ft higher, even though the actual height of the aeroplane has not changed.

9 QNH is m... s.. l.... pressure in millibars.

10 You enter your aeroplane which has been parked overnight at an aerodrome (elevation 1,545 ft). The altimeter reads 1,635 ft with 1011 mb set on the subscale. You wind the knob until 1,545 ft is indicated. What pressure value appears on the subscale and what is the current QNH?

11 The elevation of an aerodrome is 386 ft amsl. With QNH set on the subscale and the aeroplane on the runway, the altimeter should read approximately .... ft.

12 An aerodrome has an elevation of 1,334 ft amsl. On the ground with QNH set, the altimeter should read .... ft. Flying a circuit 1,000 ft above the aerodrome level, the altimeter should read .... ft.

Departing the circuit area in a north-easterly direction where the highest terrain is 3,669 ft amsl, to clear it by a minimum of 1,000 ft your altimeter, with QNH set, should indicate at least .... ft.

Vertical Nav-4

1 With QFE set on the subscale, the altimeter will measure height above the .... pressure datum, which is usually chosen to be the level of the a......... .

2 To simplify circuit procedures for a student flying at an aerodrome of elevation 1,334 ft, the instructor may set the altimeter on the ground so that it reads 0 ft. The setting on the subscale would be referred to as Q.., and flying around the circuit the altimeter would indicate the height (above aerodrome level/above mean sea level).

Vertical Nav-5

1 The UK is divided into a number of ASRs, or A........ S...... R....... .

2 Aircraft cruising at 3,000 ft amsl should have R....... QNH set on the altimeter subscale.

3 For take-off and landing, the pilot may set either Aerodrome ... or Aerodrome ... on the altimeter subscale.

4 When cruising below the transition altitude, the pilot should update the .... when crossing ASR boundaries or when it is amended by ATC.

5 For approach and landing, a pilot may set either Aerodrome ... or ... .

6 When flying beneath a Terminal Control Area (TMA) or Control Area (CTA), the pilot may have to set (1013 mb/QNH of a nearby aerodrome beneath the TMA or CTA).

7 When flying through a Military Aerodrome Traffic Zone (MATZ), the pilot may have to set (1013/Aerodrome QNH) and then, after having left the MATZ, return to .... QNH.

8 The transition altitude in the UK is usually .... ft amsl.

9 The transition level in the UK is usually FL..... .

10 To cruise at FL55, the pilot should set .... mb on the altimeter subscale as the aeroplane climbs through (transition altitude/5,000 ft/transition level).

11 If the QNH is 1013, the transition altitude is .... ft amsl, and the transition level is FL35, which will be .... ft amsl. *Do this by calculation and also by using the chart.*

12 If the QNH is 1003, the transition altitude is .... ft amsl, and the transition level is FL35, which will be .... ft amsl.

13 If the QNH is 1023, the transition altitude is ..... ft amsl, and the transition level is FL35, which will be .... ft amsl.

14 If the Manchester TMA in the area where you are flying extends from 2,500 ft ALT upwards, and the QNH is 1006, what is the maximum altitude at which you can fly and not penetrate controlled airspace? (Note that the lower level of controlled airspace is still outside controlled airspace.).

15 If the Daventry CTA in the area where you are flying extends from FL45 upwards, and the QNH is 1006, what is the maximum altitude at which you can fly and not penetrate controlled airspace?

16 If the Daventry CTA in the area where you are flying extends from FL45 upwards, and the QNH is 1018, what is the maximum altitude at which you can fly and not penetrate controlled airspace?

Vertical Nav-6

1 The highest obstacle within 5 nm of track is 1,536 ft amsl, and within 10 nm of track is 1,642 ft amsl. What minimum safe altitude would you nominate to achieve a safety clearance of:
  (i) 1,000 ft within 5 nm of track?
  (ii) 1,500 ft within 5 nm of track?
  (iii) 10% plus 1,500 ft within 5 nm of track?
  (iv) 1,000 ft within 10 nm of track?
  (v) 1,500 ft within 10 nm of track?
  (vi) 10% plus 1,500 ft within 10 nm of track?

Vertical Nav-7

1 For each deviation from ISA of 1°C, the density altitude increases by .... ft.

2 An aerodrome has elevation 1,334 ft, outside air temperature (OAT) +30°C, QNH 1013. What is its pressure altitude and density altitude?

Exercises 7

Time

Time-1

Express the following dates and times as a six-figure date/time group:

1 November 29th, 10:15 a.m.

2 July 19th, 3:17 p.m.

3 April 1st, 5 p.m.

4 Express the above dates and times as an eight-figure date/time group.

Time-2

Convert the following time intervals to arc units:

1 1 hour.

2 3 hours.

3 10 hours.

4 9 hours 30 minutes.

Convert the following arcs to time:

5 150°.

6 135°.

7 120°.

Time-3

1 Cardiff is 3° of longitude west of London. How much earlier or later will midday occur at Cardiff compared with midday in London?

2 Norwich is 1° of longitude east of London. How much earlier or later will midday occur in Norwich compared with midday in London?

3 Portsmouth is at 001°W longitude. Plymouth is at 004°W longitude. Which place is behind in Local Mean Time, and by how much?

Convert the following times from LMT to UTC:

4 151345 LMT at 003°W.

5 251732 LMT at 001°E.

6 090840 LMT at 002°30′W.

Convert the following times from UTC to LMT:

7 191000 UTC at longitude 004°W.

8 271234 UTC at longitude 150°E.

9 270434 UTC at 003°45′W.

Time-4

1 Travelling eastwards across the date-line from Hong Kong to Hawaii, you would expect to (lose/gain) 1 day.

2 British Standard Time is based on the ..... meridian of longitude.

3 German Time (MEZ) is based on the 015°E meridian of longitude, so is .... hour (ahead of/behind) UTC.

4 You depart Nottingham at 1018 UTC for a 3 hour 15 minute flight to Hamburg. The ETA at Hamburg is .... UTC, ... MEZ.

5 You depart Hamburg at 1540 MEZ for the 3 hour 30 minutes return flight to Nottingham. The ETA at Nottingham is .... UTC.

Time-5

1 Night, for the purposes of air navigation in the United Kingdom, commences at s..... plus .... minutes, at surface level.

2 Sunrise and sunset times (are/are not) available from ATS units and Met Forecast offices.

3 The official source of sunrise and sunset times is the A.. A......, a publication not required by a pilot.

4 High ground to the west of an aerodrome will cause the (earlier/later) onset of darkness.

5 Cloud cover will cause the (earlier/later) onset of darkness.

6 Heavy smog would cause the (earlier/later) onset of darkness.

7 Sunrise and sunset times vary with the l....... and the d.... .

8 British Summer Time (BST) applies from .... to ....

9 For British Summer Time, UK clocks are (advanced/retarded) by .... hour(s) from UTC.

10 Convert 1400 British Summer Time on July 28th to UTC.

11 Convert 1023 UTC on September 30th to British Summer Time.

Exercises 8

The Earth

1 The plane of a great circle on the earth (passes/does not pass) through the centre of the earth.

2 The centre of a great circle drawn on the earth's surface (is/is not) the centre of the earth.

3 The plane of a small circle drawn on the surface of the earth (passes/does not pass) through the centre of the earth.

4 The reference plane from which we measure latitude is the plane of the e......, from which we measure angular distance in degrees north or south.

5 The equator is latitude 0, and (is/is not) a great circle.

6 A parallel of latitude joins all points of the same latitude and is a (small/great) circle (except for the equator).

7 The circumference around a parallel of latitude becomes smaller the closer the particular parallel is to the (pole/equator).

8 Parallels of latitude (are/are not) parallel to the equator and to each other.

9 The basic reference for longitude is the p.... meridian that passes through the Gr....... observatory just outside London.

10 Meridians of longitude all pass through the north and south geographic poles and are (small/great) circles.

11 Longitude is angular position e... or w... of the prime meridian.

12 The length of one minute of arc of a great circle on the earth's surface is .... nm.

13 1 minute of latitude (is/is not) 1 nm in length.

14 1 degree of latitude is .... nm.

15 1 nm = ... metres.

16 It (is/is not) important for the map-maker to use a projection that preserves angular relationships when making aeronautical charts.

17 Scale is the ratio of c.... length to e.... distance.

18 A large-scale map can show (more/less) detail than a small-scale map.

19 What earth distance is represented by a chart length of 8 inches on a 1:250,000 chart?

20 What earth distance is represented by a chart length of 8 inches on a 1:500,000 chart?

21 What earth distance is represented by a chart length of 43 inches on a 1:500,000 chart?

22 8 inches on a 1:500,000 chart represents approximately 55 nm. How many kilometres does 8 inches represent on a 1:250,000 chart?

23 8 inches on a 1:500,000 chart represents approximately 55 nm. How many statute miles does 8 inches represent on a 1:250,000 chart?

24 3 inches on a chart represents approximately 10.3 nm. Is the scale of the chart 1:250,000, 1:500,000, or 1:1,000,000?

Exercises 9

Aeronautical Charts

1 The most commonly used charts for visual air navigation in the UK are the:
(a) 1:500,000 ICAO series.
(b) CAA 1:250,000 UK Topographical Air Charts.
(c) 1:1,000,000 ONC series.

2 The CAA 1:250,000 Topographical series (does/does not) show aeronautical information regarding controlled airspace whose base, i.e. lower limit, is below 5,000 ft amsl or FL55.

3 Water features (hydrographic features) are generally depicted in the colour ..... .

4 Contour lines join places of:
(a) equal magnetic variation.
(b) equal height above mean sea level.
(c) equal latitude.

5 Spot elevations (the greatest height in the immediate vicinity) are indicated on UK aeronautical charts by:
(a) a small arrow with the elevation stated.
(b) a small black dot with the elevation stated beside it in feet.
(c) a small black dot with the elevation stated beside it in metres.

6 If a spot height on an aeronautical chart is found to be in error, it can be amended by notification in ... .

7 Mount Snowdon has its elevation shown on the 1:500,000 chart in large print against a white background surrounded by a black border. Why?

8 A Restricted Area shown on a French aeronautical chart has a lower limit of 2,500 metres amsl. What is this altitude in feet?

9 Convert 3,300 metres to feet.

10 Convert 5,000 ft to metres.

Refer now to your copy of the 1:500,000 ICAO Chart, Sheet No 2171AB, for Northern England and Northern Ireland.

11 Military Aerodrome Traffic Zones (MATZ) extend from the surface to:
(a) 3,000 ft above mean sea level.
(b) 3,000 ft above aerodrome level.
(c) 5,000 ft above mean sea level.
(d) 5,000 ft above aerodrome level.

12 Military aerodromes are portrayed in:
(a) blue.
(b) magenta.
(c) black.

13 What is the magnetic variation at York (approximately 54°N, 001°W)?

14 What is the magnetic variation (correct to the nearest 1°) at Liverpool (approximately 53°26′N, 002°58′W)?

15 Aerodrome A is located at (54°14′N, 000°58′W). What aerodrome is it?

16 What is the elevation of Aerodrome A?

17 The position of Aerodrome B is (53°48′N, 000°11′W). What aerodrome is it?

18 What is the elevation of Aerodrome B?

19 What is the distance in nm from Aerodrome A to Aerodrome B?

20 What is the true rhumb line track from A to B (accurate to ±1°)?

21 What is the true rhumb line track from B to A?

22 What is the mean magnetic variation for the flight between A and B (to the nearest whole degree)?

23 What is the height of the highest obstruction within 10 nm of Aerodrome A, both *agl* and *amsl,* and what is its true bearing and distance from the aerodrome? Describe the obstruction.

24 Aerodrome A is in the Vale of York AIAA. What does AIAA mean and what are its vertical limits in this case?

25 Are there any Aerodrome Traffic Zones en route between A and B, and if so what must you do if you want to transit through the zone?

26 What do the letters ASR represent?

27 Within which Altimeter Setting Region(s) does the track between A and B lie?

28 What does the magenta circle centred on (54°11′N, 000°25′W) signify?

29 What radio frequency should be used to contact London Flight Information Service en route between A and B?

30 What radio frequency (or frequencies) should be used to contact the Lower Airspace Radar Service en route between A and B?

31 What is the highest obstacle within 10 nm of the two aerodromes and the track between A and B?

32 What is the highest maximum elevation figure en route between A and B?

33 What is the highest obstacle within 10 nm of the track between A and B, if you do not consider the high ground behind you when departing A?

34 If you wanted to clear all obstacles within 10 nm of the track between A and B by at least 1,000 ft, neglecting high obstacles behind Aerodrome A, at what minimum altitude would you fly?

35 What controlled airspace exists between A and B?

36 What controlled airspace exists in the vicinity of Aerodrome B and from what level?

37 Just northeast of Aerodrome B is an round-shaped area specially marked in magenta. What is it?

38 Some aerodrome names are printed in blue. What does this signify?

39 What activities occur at Leconfield aerodrome (10 nm north-west of Burton Constable)?

40 South and south-west of Liverpool are two small aerodromes, Hawarden and Lleweni Parc. Would a flight between these two aerodromes below 3,000 ft amsl pass through controlled airspace?

41 What is the classification and base of the controlled airspace above Hawarden?

42 How is the airspace described in which Lleweni Parc is situated, and what is its Class?

43 Describe the airspace that you would pass through on a flight from Huddersfield, Yorkshire to Newcastle at 3,000 ft.

44 The village of Grassington lies at (54°04′N, 002°00′W). According to the relief shown on the chart using colours, what is the maximum possible elevation of Grassington?

45 Just east of Macclesfield, which lies in the Manchester Control Zone, and south of the VRP at Buxton, is Danger Area 314. What are its vertical limits, and which NATSU can pass you information on it?

46 Interpret the aeronautical information printed on the chart within 5 nm of Bridlington aerodrome (54°03′N, 00°16′W).

47 Around the boundary of the Liverpool and Manchester Control Zones, the letters 'E/E' are shown in boxes with a name underneath. What does this display signify?

48 Part of the Daventry CTA, south-east of Manchester CTR, has vertical limits of FL45+. By flying at its lower limit, you will not penetrate the CTA. What is the maximum altitude (in ft amsl) at which you can fly without penetrating the CTA if the QNH is:
(i)   1013?
(ii)   1004?
(iii) 1024?

49 Latest aeronautical chart editions are notified to pilots in the AIP and by issue of an A.......... I.......... C......... .

50 Lines of equal magnetic variation are called i........ .

51 The 7½°W isogonal joins all places on the chart that experience a magnetic v........ of .... and is depicted by a dashed ....-coloured line.

52 Places of zero variation where true north and magnetic north are the same direction are joined by the a..... line.

53 The bearing of a rhumb line and great circle track between the same two places will be the same at the m..-m........ .

54 True direction is measured against (true/magnetic) north.

55 Meridians of longitude run (true/magnetic) north and south.

56 To convert from a true direction that you have measured on a chart to a magnetic direction for use when flying on a magnetic compass, you would need to apply m........ v......... .

57 "Variation west, magnetic ......!"

58 Distance on a chart can be measured against the graduated s.... l... shown on the chart somewhere, usually at the bottom.

59 Distance on any chart can be measured against the lat..... s.... down the side of that particular chart, because 1 minute of latitude = ... nm.

Flight Planning

Exercises 10
Introduction to Flight Planning

1 Planning a cross-country flight, you should study m............. forecasts for weather conditions, and N....s for other operational considerations.

2 It is recommended that, for a cross-country flight, the cloud ceiling be at least .... ft above all obstacles en route or within a reasonable distance either side of the planned route (say 5 nm or 10 nm).

3 For a flight outside controlled airspace flown below 3,000 ft amsl by a PPL holder with no IMC rating under the Visual Flight Rules in an aeroplane that cruises at or less than 140 kt:

(i) The aeroplane (must/need not) remain clear of cloud.

(ii) The aeroplane (must/need not) remain in sight of the surface.

(iii) Flight visibility must be at least .... kilometres.

4 VFR flight should occur only by day. (True/False)?

5 Flight time to the destination, where *night* commences at 1917 UTC, is 53 minutes. What is the latest estimated time of departure, ETD, if you wish to arrive at least 30 minutes before night commences?

6 Flight time to the destination, where night commences at 1917 UTC, is 53 minutes. The weather conditions at the destination are not all that good, so you carry sufficient fuel for a 23 minute flight to an alternate aerodrome where night commences at 1915 UTC. What is the latest ETD if you wish to arrive at least 30 minutes before night-time?

Exercises 11
Pre-Flight Briefing

1 A pilot (should/need not) obtain a meteorological forecast, if available, before embarking on a cross-country flight.

2 AIRMET information providing Area Forecasts is available via:

(a) aerodrome Briefing Offices using AFTN or Telex.

(b) the public telephone network and facsimile.

(c) the postal service.

3 The relevant contact telephone numbers for the AIRMET Telephone Recording Service can be found on the AIRMET Proforma chart published in the UK AIP GEN. (True/False)?

4 The cloud base on an Area Forecast is given as height:

(a) above mean sea level.

(b) above aerodrome level.

5 The cloud base on an Aerodrome Forecast is given as height:

(a) above mean sea level.

(b) above aerodrome level.

6 Define CAVOK.

7 New weather phenomena expected to become the prevailing conditions during a TAF period will be preceded with the abbreviation ..... .

8 A period expected to last for less than 60 minutes may be expressed as ....

9 Embedded thunderstorms will be indicated in a weather forecast or report by the abbreviation ....

10 8 oktas of cloud is shown in a forecast or report by the abbreviation ... .

11 The TAF for Cardiff reads as follows:

TAF EGFF 1221 20010KT 9999 BKN020 BECMG 1416 9999 SCT025 TEMPO 1720 5000 DZ OVC010=.

(i)   Is the visibility good throughout the whole period? If not, describe the visibility that is forecast.

(ii) What cloud conditions can you expect at 1630 UTC?

(iii) Is this cloud base in the TAF agl or amsl?

(iv) Do you foresee any problems landing at Cardiff at 1 p.m. British Standard Time?

(v)   Do you foresee any problems landing at Cardiff at 6 p.m. British Standard Time?

12 As well as a meteorological briefing you should have an operational briefing and study the appropriate N.... .

13 Interpret the following NOTAM:

AC D511 0830–1930 til 30 APR, 0830–2030 01 til 31 MAY, 2,500 ft, Active.

14 Interpret the following NOTAM:

RF 119 29 APR RAF Linton-on-Ouse 1215 to Heathrow 1325.

15 You are considering a flight to the Isle of Islay (55°41′N, 006°16′W) off the west coast of Scotland. (Refer to UK AIP AD.)

(i)   What are the landing distances available on Runway 08/26?

(ii) What surface is the runway?

(iii) What is the AFIS frequency and callsign?

Exercises 12

Route Selection and Chart Preparation

1 The shortest distance between two points on the earth's surface is the great circle track which, on most aeronautical charts including the ICAO 1:500,000 series, is a straight line. (True/False)?

2 If possible, it is advisable to avoid areas of high or rugged terrain, as well as areas where aerial activity such as parachuting and glider towing is concentrated, even if this involves a route slightly longer than the direct track. (True/False)?

3 To assist in the estimation of distance it is a good idea to have d....... markings along track; .... nm markings being very suitable.

4 The estimation of angles (such as track error or closing angle) on your aeronautical chart is aided by ruling in t.... g..... on the chart.

5 It is best to fold your chart so that you fly ('up'/'down') the chart.

6 A note is made on the 1:500,000 chart that it may become obsolete after approximately .... months.

Exercises 13

Compiling a Flight Log

1 Complete a flight log for a flight: from Elstree (51°39′N, 000°19′W); to overhead disused Ipswich aerodrome (52°02′N, 001°11′E); overhead Cambridge aerodrome (52°12′N, 000°11′E); returning to Elstree for a landing.

(i)   Calculate safety altitudes on a clearance of 1,500 ft above all obstacles within 10 nm of track.

(ii) Cruise at 3,000 ft if possible, where conditions are 090°T/25 kt, +12°C.

(iii) Cruise at IAS 120 kt, fuel consumption 8 USG/hr. Fixed reserve is to be 60 minutes, with a total of 22 USG on board.

2 Complete a series of flight logs for the following flights:

(i) From Leeds to Newcastle, via VRP Harrogate and Scotch Corner, (54°26.5′N, 001°40′W) carrying Teesside as an alternate.

(ii) From Newcastle to Teesside, via VRP Sedgefield Racecourse, with Newcastle as the alternate.

(iii) From Teesside to Leeds, via Scotch Corner and VRP Harrogate, with Sherburn-in-Elmet (SE of Leeds) as the alternate.

The wind is 300°T/20 kt, and you can plan on a TAS 90 kt with a fuel consumption of 24 litres per hour. Fixed reserve should be 45 minutes.

3 Complete a flight log for a flight from: Gloucester/Cheltenham (Staverton) (51°54′N, 002°10′W) to overhead Desborough (52°25′N, 000°50′W); to overhead Cranfield aerodrome (52°04′N, 000°37′W); then from Cranfield to overhead Oxford (Kidlington) aerodrome (51°51′N, 001°19′W) via the Beckley TV mast several miles southeast of the aerodrome; and then from Oxford back to Staverton for a landing.

(i) Calculate safety altitudes on the basis of the highest obstacle within 5 nm of track, plus 10%, plus 1,500 ft.

(ii) Cruise at 3,000 ft on the first leg, then at appropriate flight levels for the remaining legs.

(iii) The wind is 250°T/20 kt at 3,000 ft, and 260°T/25 kt at 4,000 ft and above.

(iv) Temperatures are: +12°C at 3,000 ft, +10°C at 4,000 ft.

(v) Cruising speed is RAS 90 kt.

(vi) Fuel consumption is 8.5 USG/hr; fixed reserve is to be 60 minutes at cruise rate; fuel on board is 40 USG.

4 You are planning a flight of 82 minutes' duration with 12 USG of flight fuel required. Cruise rate is 8.8 USG/hr. Taxi allowance is 1 USG. Total fuel capacity is 38 USG (usable). Fixed reserve is 45 minutes.

(i) What is the minimum required fuel to the nearest US gallon?

(ii) What endurance does this give?

(iii) If you carry full tanks, what endurance will you have?

(iv) If you carry 30 USG, what endurance will you have?

(v) Is 19 USG sufficient for the flight?

5 Repeat the above calculations for an aerodrome that is 40 minutes' flight time away.

6 Your aeroplane can carry 36 USG (usable) and has a fuel consumption of 6.5 USG/hr. Show the fuel calculations for a flight of 120 minutes' duration if you carry full tanks.

7 Repeat the above calculation for a flight of 65 minutes.

8 You are planning a flight of 53 minutes' duration with a flight fuel of 7 USG required. Cruise fuel consumption is 8 USG/hr. Taxi allowance is 1 USG.

(i) What is the minimum fuel that you require?

(ii) What endurance does this give?

(iii) If you carry 30 USG, what does your endurance become?

9 Repeat the above calculation if you decide to carry fuel for an alternate that is 20 minutes' flight time away.

10 Repeat the above calculation if you change your alternate aerodrome to one that is 35 minutes away from your destination.

Exercises 14

The Flight Plan

1 Complete a flight plan form for a private VFR flight with a pilot and two passengers in a Cessna 172, registered as G-BCDE, from Cardiff (EGFF) to Humberside (EGNJ), carrying Sturgate (EGCS) as an alternate, and tracking via Daventry (DTY) and Gamston (GAM).

Departure is expected to be at 1120 UTC, flight time 2 hours 30 minutes, and endurance 3 hours 45 minutes.

The aeroplane has *standard radio equipment,* a transponder with 4096 codes (Type A), and no survival equipment. The aeroplane is coloured blue and white, and the pilot's name is B. McInnes.

FLIGHT PLAN   **ATS COPY**

En Route Navigation

Exercises 15

En Route Navigation Techniques

En Route Nav Techniques-1

1 The angle between the HDG and the TMG is called ..... .

2 The angle between the desired track and the track made good is called the ....

3 A known position of an aeroplane at a given time is called a f.. or a p....... .

4 A fix is symbolised by a small ....

5 A DR (dead reckoning) position is symbolised by a small ....

6 Normal en route visual navigation should consist of flying accurate h....... and identifying l......... .

7 You cross a small town at 0325 UTC followed by a railway junction some 27 nm further on at 0340 UTC. What is your groundspeed?

En Route Nav Techniques-2

1 If you are 3 nm off-track to the right in 20 nm, what is your track error?

2 If you are 5 nm off-track to the right in 30 nm, your TE is ... .?

3 If you are 2 nm off-track to the left in 40 nm, TE is .. ....?

En Route Nav Techniques-3

1 You are 2 nm left of track after travelling 15 nm.
   (i) What is the track error?
   (ii) To regain track in another 15 nm, what is the closing angle?
   (iii) To regain track in another 30 nm, what is the closing angle?

2 You are 4 nm right of track after travelling 20 nm. By how many degrees should you change heading to regain track in another 40 nm?

3 You are on a long flight of 249 nm across featureless terrain. After flying a steady HDG for 96 nm you find yourself 13 nm right of track. By what amount should you alter your HDG to regain track:
   (i) at the destination?
   (ii) 50 nm before the destination?
   (iii) 20 nm before the destination?

4 At 0315 UTC you are on track, HDG 080M. At 0325 UTC you are 3 nm left of track, after travelling 20 nm. By what amount should you alter HDG to be back on track at 0335 UTC?

En Route Nav Techniques-4

1 You obtain a fix 5 nm left of planned track and make a HDG correction to regain track, but 20 nm further on you find that you are now 8 nm left of track.
   (i) What is the TE?
   (ii) What is the closing angle (CA) to regain track in another 60 nm?
   (iii) By how much should you alter HDG to do this?

2 You are 3 nm left of track and make a HDG change to regain track. 30 nm later you pinpoint your position as 3 nm right of track.
   (i) What is your TE?
   (ii) What is the CA to regain track in another 15 nm?
   (iii) If your HDG was 110°M, what will be your new HDG?

En Route Nav Techniques-5

1   Having maintained HDG 320°M, you fix your position 2 nm left of track after covering 15 nm and wish to regain track in another 30 nm.
    (i)   What is your TE?
    (ii) What is your CA?
    (iii) What should you alter HDG to initially?
    (iv) What should you alter HDG to on regaining track?

2   On HDG 293°M, you are 4 nm right of track after 34 nm.
    (i)   What is the TE?
    (ii) What is the CA to regain track in another 48 nm?
    (iii) What HDG should you take up to regain track?
    (iv) On track, what would you expect your HDG to be?

En Route Nav Techniques-6

1   You want to descend 3,500 ft at 500 ft/min. How long will this take?

2   At 300 ft/min, how long will it take to descend 2,700 ft?

3   To descend 4,500 ft in 11 minutes, what rate of descent is required?

4   You are 18 nm from the field and have a GS on descent of 100 kt. You wish to overfly the field (elevation 500 ft amsl) at 2,000 ft agl. If you are cruising at 6,000 ft, how many minutes from the field are you and what rate of descent do you require to arrive overhead the field as stated?

Exercises 16

Navigation in Remote Areas

1   Navigation in remote areas requires very careful p..-f..... planning.

2   When navigating in remote areas especially, you should maintain h....... accurately and keep an in-flight l.. .

Exercises 17

Entry/Exit Lanes and Low-Level Routes

1   Special Access Lane Exit/Entry points (are/are not) shown on 1:500,000 aeronautical charts and identified by a capital 'E/E' enclosed in a box with the name of the applicable aerodrome.

2   Entry/Exit Lanes are situated in close proximity to C...... Z..... .

3   Navigation in Entry/Exit Lanes and on Low-Level Routes should be accurate, and we achieve this by following normal VFR procedures of flying a........ h......s and backing up with frequent visual f.... .

4   Prior to entering an Entry/Exit Lane you should position your aeroplane accurately over a l....... and check that your h...... i........ is aligned with the magnetic compass to assist you in flying accurate headings.

Exercises

Climb Planning (Appendix 2)

1   Show the climb and cruise calculations for a Piper Warrior on a flight from a mean sea level aerodrome to a cruise altitude of 8,000 ft amsl under ISA conditions and nil wind. The first check point is 70 nm away.
    Compare the figures with those obtained without a climb allowance. CRZ TAS is 108 kt at 88 USG/hr.

2   Repeat the previous question for a Cessna 172 with a CRZ TAS of 112 kt at 74 USG/hr.

En Route Navigation with Radio Navaids

Exercises 19

Radar

1 The process of separating aircraft and positioning them by an ATC radar controller passing headings-to-steer is known as radar _____.

2 If a radar service is not available, then ATC will separate aircraft using procedures based on their estimated positions and known altitudes. This is known as:
(a) non-radar separation.
(b) procedural separation.
(c) standby separation.

3 Primary surveillance radar can detect signals from aircraft, even if they carry no radar equipment. Secondary surveillance radar (SSR) on the ground detects strong responding signals transmitted from aircraft equipped with a _____.

4 An approach to a runway under the guidance of a radar controller who passes tracking and descent advice is known as a _____.

5 What approximate RoD in ft/min is required to achieve a 3° glideslope, which is 300 ft per nm, if the ground-speed of the aeroplane is 60 kt?

6 What approximately RoD in ft/min is required to achieve a 3° glideslope, which is 300 ft per nm, if the ground-speed of the aeroplane is 90 kt?

7 The minimum visibility required for an SRA by an IMC-rated pilot is _____.

8 The decision height for an SRA carried out by an IMC-rated pilot will depend on the obstacle clearance height (plus additions), but in no case may be less than an absolute SRA minimum of _____ ft aal.

9 The approximate range of any VHF signals for an aeroplane at 6,000 ft above the level of a ground station is _____ nm.

10 The approximate range of any VHF signals for an aeroplane at 2,000 ft above the level of a ground station is _____ nm.

11 The approximate range of any VHF signals for an aeroplane at 2,500 ft above the level of a ground station is _____ nm.

12 Where in the UK AIP can you find the special-purpose codes used for secondary surveillance radar?

Exercises 20

DME

1 DME stands for _____.

2 DME measures:
(a) horizontal distance,
(b) vertical distance,
(c) slant distance.

3 The DME is selected on the _____ radio, usually along with a co-located VOR.

4 If an aircraft tracking directly towards a DME ground station is at 37 DME at time 0115, and at 27 DME at time 0120, what is its groundspeed?

5 If an aircraft tracking directly away from a DME ground station is at 22 DME at time 1223, and at 32 DME at time 1230, what is its groundspeed?

6 Tracking abeam a DME ground station, the DME readings change in the following manner as time passes: 25, 21, 17, 15, 14, 15, 17, 21. What was your abeam distance from the DME ground station?

7 A DME can provide a:
(a) circular position line.
(b) straight position line.

Exercises 21

The NDB and the ADF

1 NDB stands for _____ .

2 The NDB is (a ground-based transmitter/an airborne receiver).

3 NDBs transmit in either the _____ or _____ frequency bands.

4 ADF stands for _____ .

5 The ADF is (a ground-based transmitter/an airborne receiver).

6 A particular NDB may be identified by its _____ .

7 The Morse code is shown on many aeronautical charts. What is the Morse code ident of the Blackpool NDB, 'BPL'?

8 The three basic steps that a pilot should follow before using a particular NDB or locator beacon for navigation are _____.

9 QDM is the (magnetic/true) bearing (from/to) the ground station.

10 QDR is the (magnetic/true) bearing (from/to) the ground station.

11 RBI stands for _____ .

12 If an aircraft on heading 250°M has a reading of 030 on its relative bearing indicator, what is:
(i) the magnetic bearing of the NDB from the aircraft?
(ii) the magnetic bearing of the aircraft from the NDB?

13 If an aircraft on heading 250°M has a reading of 350 on its relative bearing indicator, calculate:
(i) the magnetic bearing of the NDB from the aircraft.
(ii) the magnetic bearing of the aircraft from the NDB.

14 Determine the range of the Chiltern NDB from UK AIP ENR 4-1.

15 An NDB used to locate the aircraft on an instrument approach is called a _____.

16 An NDB positioned so that it provides a fix for an aircraft during an instrument approach, and co-located with the outer marker for the approach, may be designated on the instrument approach chart with the letters _____.

17 Atmospheric conditions, such as electrical storms or the periods of sunrise and sunset, (may/will not) distort NDB signals, making ADF indications less reliable.

18 Mountains (may/will not) reflect and distort NDB signals, making ADF indications less reliable.

19 The range promulgated in the UK AIP for NDBs is based on a daytime protection ratio between wanted and unwanted signals that limits bearing errors to ± _____° or less.

20 Write down the Morse code in dots (·) and dashes (–) for all the letters of the alphabet.

Exercises 22

The Relative Bearing Indicator (RBI)

1 An aircraft has a heading of 035°M. Its RBI indicates 040. The magnetic variation in the area is 4°W. Calculate:
   (i) QDM;
   (ii) QDR;
   (iii) QTE.

2 An aircraft has a heading of 335°M. Its RBI indicates 355. The magnetic variation in the area is 4°W. Calculate:
   (i) QDM;
   (ii) QDR;
   (iii) QTE.

3 MH 080; RBI 000. Onto what heading should you turn to make a 90° intercept of a track of 040°M to the NDB? What will the RBI indicate at the point of intercept?

4 MH 080; RBI 000. Onto what heading should you turn to make a 60° intercept of a track of 040°M to the NDB? What will the RBI indicate at the point of intercept?

5 MH 070; RBI 010. Which way should you turn to intercept 075°M to the NDB?

6 MH 155, RBI 180. Which way should you turn to intercept a track of 140°M away from the NDB?

7 MH 155, RBI 180. Which way should you turn to intercept a track of 180°M away from the NDB?

8 When tracking towards an NDB, the ADF readings are:
   Time 1: MH 055, RBI 005;
   Time 2: MH 055, RBI 005.
   What track is the aircraft maintaining to the NDB?

9 When tracking towards an NDB, the ADF readings are:

Time 1: MH 055, RBI 005 and on track;
Time 2: MH 055, RBI 002.
Is the aircraft off track to the left or right?

10 To track towards an NDB on a track of 340°M, with an expected crosswind from the right causing 5° of drift, what magnetic heading should you steer, and what do you expect the RBI to indicate?

11 To track away from an NDB on a track of 120°M, with an expected crosswind from the right causing 8° of drift, what magnetic heading should you steer, and what do you expect the RBI to indicate?

12 You wish to track 360°M in nil-wind conditions. What magnetic heading should you steer? What will the RBI indicate as you pass abeam an NDB which is 10 nm to the right of track, i.e. when the NDB is on a bearing of 90° to the track?

13 You wish to track 360°M and you expect 10° of drift caused by a wind from the east. What magnetic heading should you steer? What will the RBI indicate as you pass abeam an NDB which is 10 nm to the right of track?

14 You wish to track 030°M in nil-wind conditions. What magnetic heading should you steer? What will the RBI indicate as you pass abeam an NDB which is 10 nm to the right of track?

15 You are heading 030°M in nil-wind conditions. What is your track? What will the RBI indicate as you pass abeam an NDB which is 10 nm to the left of track?

16 You wish to track 030°M and expect 7° left drift. What magnetic heading should you steer? What will the RBI indicate as you pass abeam an NDB which is 10 nm to the left of track?

17 You are tracking 278°M with 6° of port drift. You can determine your position abeam an NDB which is to the right of track by waiting until the RBI indicates ____ .

18 You are tracking 278°M with 6° of port drift. You can determine your position abeam an NDB which is to the left of track by waiting until the RBI indicates ____ .

19 You are tracking 278°M with 5° of starboard drift. You can determine your position abeam an NDB which is to the left of track by waiting until the RBI indicates ____ .

Exercises 23

The Radio Magnetic Indicator (RMI)

1 An aircraft has a heading of 035°M. Its RMI indicates 075. The magnetic variation in the area is 4°W. Calculate:

(i) QDM;

(ii) QDR;

(iii) QTE.

2 An aircraft has a heading of 335°M. Its RMI indicates 330. The magnetic variation in the area is 4°W. Calculate:

(i) QDM;

(ii) QDR;

(iii) QTE.

3 MH 080; RMI 080. Onto what heading should you turn to make a 90° intercept of a track of 040°M to the NDB? What will the RMI indicate at the point of intercept?

4 MH 080; RMI 080. Onto what heading should you turn to make a 60° intercept of a track of 040°M to the NDB? What will the RMI indicate at the point of intercept?

5 MH 070, RMI 080. Which way should you turn to intercept 075°M to the NDB? What will the RMI indicate at the point of intercept?

6 MH 155, RMI 330. Which way should you turn to intercept a track of 140°M away from the NDB? What will the RMI indicate at the point of intercept? What will the tail of the RMI pointer indicate?

7 MH 155, RMI 130. Which way should you turn to intercept a track of 090°M away from the NDB? What will the RMI indicate at the point of intercept? What will the RMI tail indicate?

8 When tracking towards an NDB, the ADF readings are:

Time 1: MH 055, RMI 060;

Time 2: MH 055, RMI 060.

What track is the aircraft maintaining to the NDB?

9 When tracking towards an NDB, the ADF readings are:

Time 1: MH 055, RMI 060 and on track; Time 2: MH 055, RMI 057.

Is the aircraft left or right of track?

10 To track towards an NDB on a track of 340°M, with an expected crosswind from the right causing 5° of drift, what magnetic heading should you steer, and what will you expect the RMI to indicate?

11 To track away from the an NDB on a track of 120°M, with an expected crosswind from the right causing 8° of drift, what magnetic heading should you steer, and what do you expect the RMI to indicate?

12 You wish to track 360°M in nil-wind conditions. What magnetic heading should you steer? What will the RMI indicate as you pass abeam an NDB which is 10 nm to the right of track?

13 You wish to track 360°M and expect 10° of drift caused by a wind from the east. What magnetic heading should you steer? What will the RMI indicate as you pass abeam an NDB which is 10 nm to the right of track?

14 You wish to track 030°M in nil-wind conditions. What magnetic heading should you steer? What will the RMI indicate as you pass abeam an NDB which is 10 nm to the right of track?

15 You are heading 030°M in nil-wind conditions. What is your track? What will the RMI indicate as you pass abeam an NDB which is 10 nm to the left of track?

16 You wish to track 030°M and expect 7° left drift. What magnetic heading should you steer? What will the RMI indicate as you pass abeam an NDB which is 10 nm to the left of track?

17 You are flying on a magnetic track of 239° with 7° of port drift. At a position directly abeam an NDB which is to the left of track, the RMI will read ____.

Exercises 24

The VOR

1 The VOR is a (VHF/LF/MF) radio navigation aid.

2 Many VORs in the UK are coupled with (ILS/DME/NDB/VDF).

3 An aeroplane at 3,000 ft amsl should be able to receive a VOR situated at sea level out to a range of approximately ____ nm.

4 A radial is the (magnetic/true) bearing (to/away from) a VOR ground station.

5 Radial is expressed in the Q-code as ____.

6 You are instructed to track outbound on the 070 radial from a VOR. The more suitable heading is (070/250).

7 You are instructed to track inbound on the 050 radial. The more suitable heading is (050/230).

8 A particular VOR may be identified by its ____.

9 A VOR ground station should transmit to an accuracy of at least ±____°.

10 VOR stands for ____.

11 The radio set in the cockpit used to select a VOR is the (VHF-COM/VHF-NAV/ADF).

12 The needle in the VOR cockpit display is known as the CDI (____).

13 Any one of 360 tracks may be selected in the VOR cockpit display using the OBS (____), with the selected track displayed on the ____.

14 A 1-dot deviation of the CDI on the VOR cockpit display indicates a displacement of ____° from the selected track.

15 A 2-dot deviation of the CDI on the VOR cockpit display indicates a displacement of ____° from the selected track.

16 A 3-dot deviation of the CDI on the VOR cockpit display indicates a displacement of ____° from the selected track.

17 A 4-dot deviation of the CDI on the VOR cockpit display indicates a displacement of ____° from the selected track.

18 A 5-dot deviation of the CDI on the VOR cockpit display indicates a displacement of ____° from the selected track.

19 If the CDI is centred with 090 selected on the OBI, and the FROM flag showing, what radial is the aircraft on?

20 If the CDI is centred with 090 selected, and the TO flag showing, what radial is the aircraft on?

21 If the CDI is 2 dots right with 090 selected, and the TO flag showing, what radial is the aircraft on?

22 If the CDI is 1dot left with 090 selected on the OBI, and the FROM flag showing, what radial is the aircraft on?

23 Check an aeronautical chart and determine the frequency of the Cranfield VOR (some 40 nm NW of London) and its Morse code ident.

24 What radial from the Cranfield VOR would keep you just to the north of D206?

25 Check an aeronautical chart and determine the frequency of the Newcastle VOR and its Morse code ident.

26 What NEW radial would you track on to the Dean Cross VOR (DCS)?

27 What DCS radial would you be tracking in on from NEW?

28 On the reciprocal track, from DCS to NEW, you would track on the ____ DCS radial and the ____ NEW radial.

29 Specify three means of fixing your position in IMC somewhere along the DCS to NEW track.

30 You depart over DCS at 1427 UTC and pass abeam 'CL' NDB at 1438 UTC. At what time do you estimate NEW?

31 What is the specified designated operational coverage (DOC) of the Dean Cross VOR?

32 You are flying MH 080, with the OBI selected to 080, CDI needle showing 2 dots right, and the FROM flag showing. Your desired track is the 080 radial outbound. Is this track to your left or your right?

33 You are flying MH 300, with the OBI selected to 300, the CDI needle showing 3 dots left, and the TO flag showing. Your desired track is 300°M to the VOR. Is this track out to your left or right?

34 You are flying MH 300, with the OBI selected to 300, the CDI needle showing 3 dots left, and the TO flag showing. If the aircraft is now turned onto the reciprocal heading of MH 120, would the indications in the VOR cockpit display change in any way, assuming the OBI is left unaltered?

35 Specify which of the aircraft illustrated in Figure 5 could have the VOR indications depicted in instruments (i), (ii) and (iii).

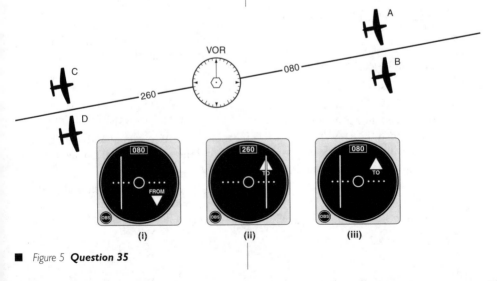

■ Figure 5 Question 35

Exercises 25

VHF Direction Finding (VDF)

1 VDF stands for _____ .

2 Another abbreviation for VDF is _____.

3 The airborne radio used for VDF is the (ADF/VHF-NAV/VHF-COM).

4 QDM is defined as _____.

5 QDR is defined as _____.

6 A Class B VDF bearing is accurate to ±_____°.

7 When tracking towards a ground station using the QDMs passed by ATC, the pilot (should/should not) allow a wind correction angle to counter any crosswind effect.

8 When tracking towards a ground station, the QDMs gradually increase: QDMs 340, 342, 345. The aircraft is moving to the (left/right) of track and should turn (left/right).

9 When tracking towards a ground station, the QDMs gradually decrease: QDMs 340, 336, 330. The aircraft is moving to the (left/right) of track and should turn (left/right).

10 When tracking away from a ground station, the QDMs gradually increase: QDMs 360, 006, 010. The aircraft is moving to the (left/right) of track and should turn (left/right).

11 When tracking away from a ground station, the QDMs gradually decrease: QDMs 360, 355, 350. The aircraft is moving to the (left/right) of track and should turn (left/right).

12 The difference between a VDF approach, in which a pilot requests QDMs from an ATSU, and a QGH approach is _____.

Exercises 26

Introduction to RNAV and GPS

1 A pseudo-VOR/DME is a (real/phantom) VOR/DME.

2 A pseudo-VOR/DME can be created (anywhere/anywhere within signal coverage).

3 A pseudo-VOR/DME is created by electronically adding a _____ to the position of the real VOR/DME.

4 The CDI, when being used as part of an RNAV system, displays (angular deviation/crosstrack error).

5 The fixes along an off-airways route are known as _____.

6 LORAN-C uses time-difference measurement from widely separated LORAN stations to fix position using (parabolic/hyperbolic/straight/circular) position lines.

7 Approved GPS aircraft systems (may/may not) be used for VFR navigation.

8 Approved GPS aircraft systems (may/may not) be used for IFR navigation.

9 For positional information, at least (one, two, or three) satellites are needed in order to determine aircraft position.

Air Navigation

Answers 1

The Pilot/Navigator

1 watch or clock
2 sound preparation
3 distance
4 nautical miles
5 ground nautical mile
6 air nautical mile
7 nm
8 gnm
9 anm
10 1 knot is 1 nautical mile per hour
11 metre
12 foot
13 great circle
14 360 degrees, 60 minutes
15 longitude
16 latitude and longitude
17 do
18 one
19 feet, metres
20 1 nm = 1,852 metres
21 clockwise
22 east
23 south
24 west
25 true airspeed, TAS
26 heading and true airspeed
27 single-headed arrow
28 wind
29 from
30 from
31 from
32 track
33 groundspeed
34 heading
35 track
36 wind effect
37 drift
38 drift angle
39 left drift
40 track error
41 track error
42 right
43 A: HDG/TAS, B: TR/GS, D: drift
44 (b) GS exceeds TAS

Answers 2

Speed

Speed-1

1 true airspeed
2 groundspeed
3 wind
4 airspeed indicator, abbreviated to ASI
5 indicated airspeed – IAS
6 indicated airspeed
7 true airspeed
8 knots
9 rectified airspeed, calibrated airspeed
10 indicated airspeed and rectified (calibrated) airspeed
11 (a) indicated airspeed

Speed-2

NOTE Airspeeds should be accurate to ±1 knot.

1 decrease
2 temperature and pressure
3 International Standard Atmosphere mean sea level conditions
4 greater than
5 8%
6 108 kt
7 216 kt
8 130 kt
9 17%
10 117 kt
11 234 kt
12 139 kt

Speed-3

1   138, 139, 135, 141, 146; (within ±1 kt is acceptable)
2   (b) 176
3   OAT = +10°C, TAS = 107 kt
4   OAT = −3°C, TAS = 195 kt
5   Pressure altitude is 8,920 ft, say 9,000 ft, where ISA = −3°C, and therefore ISA−5 = −8°C; IAS(RAS) = 131 kt
6   Pressure altitude = 7,990, say 8,000 ft. OAT = −8°C; RAS = 134 kt

Answers 3

Direction

1   360
2   east
3   south
4   west
5   true north, true south
6   true north–south
7   north magnetic pole, south magnetic pole
8   magnetic north, magnetic south
9   variation
10   east
11   west
12   isogonals
13   Variation east, magnetic least. Variation west, magnetic best.
14   097M, 280M, 006M, 012M, 161M, 265T, 087T, 359T
15   compass north
16   deviation
17   compass deviation
18   022C, 280C, 197M and 198C, 292M and 294C, 6W and 103C, 271T and 278M (Note: answers calculated using interpolation of deviation card between cardinal points.)
19   heading is 337°M, 339°C
20   track is 105°C, 104°M, 099°T
21   track is 002°C, 004°M, 357°T
22   track is 353°C, 355°M, 349°T
23   is not
24   (b)
25   (f)
26   (e)
27   (a)

28   (b)
29   (c)
30   (c)
31   (b)
32   (a)
33   (b)
34   (b)
35   (a)
36   (c)
37   (a)
38   (c)
39   (e)
40   (b)
41   (a)
42   (a)
43   (c)
44   every 10 or 15 minutes
45   should not
46   easier
47   relative bearing
48   060 REL
49   280 REL
50   050 REL and 085M
51   265M

Answers 4

Wind Side of the Navigation Computer

Wind Side-1

1   A: HDG/TAS, B: TR/GS
2   heading to track
3   desired track
4   calculate heading and groundspeed
5   HDG 322°T, GS 75 kt
6   HDG 261°T, GS 66 kt
7   HDG 100°T, GS 133 kt
8   HDG 062°T, GS 127 kt
9   HDG 061°T, TAS 90 kt
10   HDG 166°T, TAS 82 kt
11   077°T, 084°M, 88 kt
    055°T, 062°M, 84 kt
    111°T, 117°M, 157 kt
    308°T, 314°M, 120 kt
    (The last two tracks are reciprocals, but note that the headings are not reciprocals;

this is because you must point the nose of the aeroplane into wind to allow for drift.)

12 HDG 061°T, TAS 90 kt

13 HDG 166°T, TAS 82 kt, RAS 75 kt

14 TAS 119 kt, HDG 296°T and 302°M, GS 95 kt

15 092°M, 062°M/36, 085°M, 88 kt
062°M, 062°M/36, 062°M, 84 kt
126°M, 356°M/30, 117°M, 157 kt
306°M, 356°M/30, 314°M, 120 kt
(The last two tracks are reciprocals, but note that the headings are not reciprocals; this is because you must point the nose of the aeroplane into wind to allow for drift.)

Wind Side-2

1 140T/24

2 318T/17

3 290T/25

4 300T/17

Wind Side-3

1

TAS	Wind(T)	HDG(T)	TR(T)	GS
120	055/36	076°	085°	87
140	350/30	110°	120°	158
140	350/30	310°	300°	119
120	055/36	104°	120°	100
120	055/36	014°	360°	96
120	055/36	055°	055°	84

2 HDG 339°T, drift 5° right,
TR 344°T, GS130 kt

Wind Side-4

1 headwind 11 kt, crosswind 28 kt

2 no

3 RWY 03 has only 10 kt of crosswind, and 28 kt of headwind and therefore is OK. RWY 21, the reciprocal runway, has a 10 kt crosswind, but has a 28 kt tailwind, therefore is unsuitable. (Note: We do not advise taking off downwind normally, even though a 10 kt maximum tailwind component is specified for many aircraft. Our reasons are discussed in Vol. 4 of *The Air Pilot's Manual,* especially in the chapters on performance and windshear.)

Answers 5

Calculator Side of the Navigation Computer

Calculator-1

1 27 nm

2 52 nm

3 20 nm

Calculator-2

1 153 kt

2 93 kt

3 180 kt

4 180 kt

5 150 kt, 12 minutes

6 GS 132 kt, ETI 33 minutes

7 15 minutes

8 12 minutes

9 13 minutes

10 57 minutes

11 GS 115 for 45 nm = ETI 23.5 minutes, say 24 minutes, therefore ETA 1306 UTC

12 GS 147 for 28 nm = ETI 11.4 minutes, say 11 minutes, therefore ETA 0827 UTC

Calculator-3

1 13.3, say 14 litres (always round fuel figures upwards)

2 3.7, say 4 litres

3 26.4, say 27 litres/hour (notice again how we always round-up the fuel figure for safety reasons)

4 7.5, say 8 USG/hr

5 30 litres/hr, 34 minutes

6 40 USG of flight fuel, 300 minutes or 5 hours

7 20.5 USG of flight fuel, 224 minutes or 3 hours 44 minutes

8 45 minutes = 5.6 USG, therefore 30.4 USG of flight fuel, 243 minutes or 4 hours 3 minutes

9 ETI 150 minutes, flight fuel 18.2 USG, reserve 7.3 USG, total fuel 25.5 USG, say 26 USG

10 ETI 80 minutes, flight fuel 8.7 USG, reserve 6.5 USG, total fuel 15.2 USG, say 16 USG. (Note: always round fuel up, i.e. carry at least the bare minimum.)

11 Flight fuel 20.2 USG, safe flight endurance 178 minutes at GS 93 kt, 276 nm

12 Flight fuel 21 USG, safe flight endurance 185 minutes at GS 93 kt, 287 nm

Calculator-4

1   9 nm

2   9 nm, 12 nm

3   8 nm, 8°

4   12 nm, 12°

Calculator-5

1   +100°F

2   0°C

3   +68°F

Calculator-6

1   115 sm, 185 km

2   102 km

3   538 nm

4   92.5 km/hr, 92,500 metres/hr, 1,540 metres/minute, 25.7 metres/sec

Calculator-7

1   395 m

2   3,980 ft

3   1,640 ft

4   328 ft

5   Obstruction elevation 1,230 ft, so fly at an altitude of at least 2,230 ft. (If you think 123 ft, then obstacle clearance 1,000 ft above this is **not** guaranteed!)

Calculator-8

1   27.2, say 28 kg

2   287 kg

3   176 lb

4   1,860 lb (to a reasonable accuracy)

5   12,540 lb

Calculator-9

1   0.71

2   7.1 lb

3   0.71 kg

4   7.1 kg

5   35.5, say 36 kg

6   1 IG = 1.20 USG

7   5 IG = 6 USG

8   10 IG = 12 USG = 45.3, say 46 litres

9   10 USG = 37.8, say 38 litres

10   1 USG = 3.78, say 4 litres

11   18 USG = 68 litres

12   29 USG = 110 litres

13   86 litres = 22.6 USG, so the gauges should read 34.6 USG. Working on the conservative side we would say we had only 34 USG on board.

14   1 litre weighs 0.71 kg, therefore 100 litres = 71 kg

15   37.7 kg

16   114 litres, 81 kg

17   141 l, 100 kg

18   118 kg

19   102 litres

20   72 kg

21   244 kg, 344 litres

22   40 IG, 280 lb

Answers 6

Vertical Navigation

Vertical Nav-1

1   altitude

2   foot

3   approximate

4   terrain clearance, traffic separation, performance capabilities

5   decreases

6   pressure

7   ISA

8   measuring stick

9   1013.25 mb(hPa)

10   +15°C

11   −2°C/1,000 ft

12   calibrate altimeters

13   pressure altitude

14   decrease

15   30 ft

16   1012 mb

17   1011 mb

18   913 mb

19   690 ft

20   3,390 ft

Vertical Nav-2

1   +15°C

2 +13°C

3 +5°C

4 −5°C

5 +9°C, 913 mb

6 +14°C, 993 mb

7 +16°C, 1033 mb

8 1,290 ft

9 90 ft

10 minus 210 ft (−210)

Vertical Nav-3

1 1013.2

2 no

3 yes

4 QNH

5 altitude is height amsl

6 QNH

7 aerodrome elevation amsl

8 600 ft

9 mean sea level

10 1008 mb on subscale, and QNH 1008

11 386 ft

12 on ground 1,334 ft, in circuit 2,334 ft, for terrain clearance 4,669 ft

Vertical Nav-4

1 QFE pressure datum, aerodrome

2 QFE, above aerodrome level (aal)

Vertical Nav-5

1 Altimeter Setting Regions

2 Regional QNH

3 Aerodrome QFE or QNH

4 Regional pressure setting or Regional QNH

5 QFE (normal in UK), or QNH

6 QNH of an aerodrome beneath the TMA or CTA

7 Aerodrome QNH, Regional QNH

8 3,000 ft amsl

9 FL35

10 1013 mb, transition altitude

11 3,000 ft amsl, 3,500 ft amsl

12 3,000 ft amsl, 3,200 ft amsl

13 3,000 ft amsl, 3,800 ft amsl

14 2,500 ft amsl

15 4,290 ft amsl

16 4,650 ft amsl

Vertical Nav-6

1 (i) 2,536 ft (ii) 3,036 ft (iii) 3,190 ft (iv) 2,642 ft (v) 3,142 ft (vi) 3,307 ft

Vertical Nav-7

1 120 ft

2 pressure altitude 1,334 ft, say 1,500 ft where ISA = +12°C; therefore OAT +30°C = ISA+18; 18 × 120 = 2,160 ft; therefore density altitude = 1,334 + 2,160 = 3,494 ft, say 3,500 ft

Answers 7

Time

Time-1

1 291015

2 191517

3 011700

4 11291015; 07191517; 04011700

Time-2

1 15°

2 45°

3 150°

4 142.5°, (i.e. 142°30′)

5 10 hours

6 9 hours

7 8 hours

Time-3

1 12 minutes later in Cardiff

2 4 minutes earlier in Norwich

3 Plymouth LMT is 12 minutes behind Portsmouth LMT

4 151357 UTC

5 251728 UTC

6 090850 UTC

7 190944 LMT

8 272234 LMT

9 270419 LMT

Time-4

1 lose

2 prime (or Greenwich) meridian

3 1 hour ahead

4 1333 UTC, 1433 MEZ

5 1810 UTC

Time-5

1 sunset plus 30 minutes

2 are

3 Air Almanac

4 earlier

5 earlier

6 earlier

7 latitude and date

8 usually the 4th Sunday in March to the 4th Sunday in October, unless otherwise specified

9 advanced by 1 hour

10 1300 UTC

11 1123 BST

Answers 8

The Earth

1 passes

2 is

3 does not pass

4 equator

5 is

6 small circle

7 pole

8 are parallel

9 prime, Greenwich

10 meridians of long are all GCs

11 east or west

12 1 minute of GC arc = 1 nm

13 is

14 60 nm

15 1,852 metres

16 **very important** because the pilot will relate angular relationships on the chart to angular relationships on the earth

17 chart length to earth distance

18 more detail

19 27.4 nm

20 54.9 nm

21 295 nm

22 51 km

23 31.7 sm

24 1:250,000

Answers 9

Aeronautical Charts

1 (a)

2 does

3 blue

4 (b)

5 (b)

6 AIP, AIC and NOTAM

7 it is the highest point on that chart

8 8,200 ft (±50 ft)

9 10,830 ft (±50 ft)

10 1,525 metres (±10 m)

11 (b)

12 (b)

13 4°W (±½°)

14 5°W (±½°)

15 Wombleton

16 120 ft amsl

17 Burton Constable

18 60 ft amsl

19 38 nm (±1 nm)

20 134°T (±1°)

21 314°T

22 4°W (±½°)

23 1,050 ft agl, 2,297 ft amsl, 322°T, 10 nm, lighted mast

24 Area of Intense Aerial Activity, from the surface to FL200

25 yes, at Beverly; contact the responsible ATS unit for permission to fly within the zone

26 Altimeter Setting Region

27 Barnsley ASR

28 A High Intensity Radio Transmission Area (HIRTA)

29 125.475 MHz – see legend

30 Leeming LARS on 127.75 MHz; Linton LARS on 129.15 MHz

31 2,297 ft amsl

32 1,800 ft amsl

33 807 ft amsl

34 1,807 amsl

35 none

36 Airway B1, from FL75 upwards (to at least FL245, maximum coverage of chart)

37 Danger Area up to 5000 ft amsl (D306) covered by bylaws which prevent penetration when active.

38 civil aerodromes

39 helicopter operations

40 no

41 Class A, 3,000 ft amsl

42 Class G

43 Leeds Bradford CTA (Class D), Leeds Bradford CTR (also Class D), Class G, Newcastle CTR (Class D)

44 1,000 ft amsl

45 0–2,900 ft amsl, Manchester Approach 119.4 MHz (Legend)

46 disused aerodrome; intense free-fall parachuting; single unlit obstruction 508 ft amsl, 300 ft agl; boundary of Barnsley and Humber ASRs, foot-launched hang-gliding east of Bridlington town

47 Special Access Lane Entry/Exit to the nominated aerodrome

48 (i) 4,500 ft amsl (ii) 4,230 ft amsl (iii) 4,830 ft amsl

49 AIP MAP, Aeronautical Information Circulars (Green)

50 isogonals

51 variation 7½°W, blue

52 agonic line

53 mid-meridian

54 true north

55 true north and south

56 magnetic variation

57 best

58 scale line

59 latitude scale, 1 nm

Flight Planning

Answers 10

Introduction to Flight Planning

1   meteorological forecasts, NOTAMs
2   1,000 ft
3   (i) must (ii) must (iii) 3 km
4   true
5   ETD 1754 UTC
6   ETD 1729 UTC

Answers 11

Pre-Flight Briefing

1   should
2   (a) and (b)
3   true
4   (a)
5   (b)
6   visibility 10 km or greater; no cloud below 5,000 ft amsl or below the highest minimum sector altitude, whichever is the higher, and no significant weather phenomena at or in the vicinity of the aerodrome
7   BECMG
8   TEMPO
9   EMBD TS

10 OVC
11 (i) no; visibility is reduced to 5,000 metres in drizzle for temporary periods (less than 60 minutes) between 1700–2000 UTC
    (ii) 3–4 oktas of cloud at base 2,500 ft agl
    (iii) agl (iv) no (v) yes; temporary periods of reduced visibility, low cloud and drizzle
12 NOTAMs
13 In the Scottish FIR, Danger Area 511 will be active between the hours of 0830–1930 UTC until April 30th, then 0830–2030 UTC between May 1st–31st, up to 2,500 ft
14 A Royal Flight departing Linton-on-Ouse at 1215 UTC and proceeding to Heathrow, arriving at 1325 UTC, on April 29th
15 (i) 635 m and 575 m (ii) asphalt (iii) 123.15 MHz, "Islay Information"

Answers 12

Route Selection and Chart Preparation

1   true
2   true
3   distance markings, 10 nm
4   track guides
5   fly *up* the chart
6   12 months

Answers 13 Compiling a Flight Log

1

From/To	Safety ALT	ALT	Temp	RAS	TAS	W/V	TR °T	Drift	HDG °T	Var	HDG °M	GS	Dist	Time	ETA
Elstree															
	2420	3000	+12	120	126	090/25	069	4°L	073	3°W	076	102	60	36	
Ipswich															
	2272	3000	+12	120	126	090/25	286	3°L	289	3°W	292	150	40	16	
Cambridge															
	2420	3000	+12	120	126	090/25	208	10°S	198	3°W	201	136	38	17	
Elstree															

Consumption rate   8.5 USG/hr

	min	US gal
Destination	100	14.2
Alternate	–	–
Flight fuel	100	14.2
Reserve	60	8.5
Taxi	–	–
Fuel required	160	22.7
Margin	124	17.3
Total fuel	284	40.0

Total 138 69

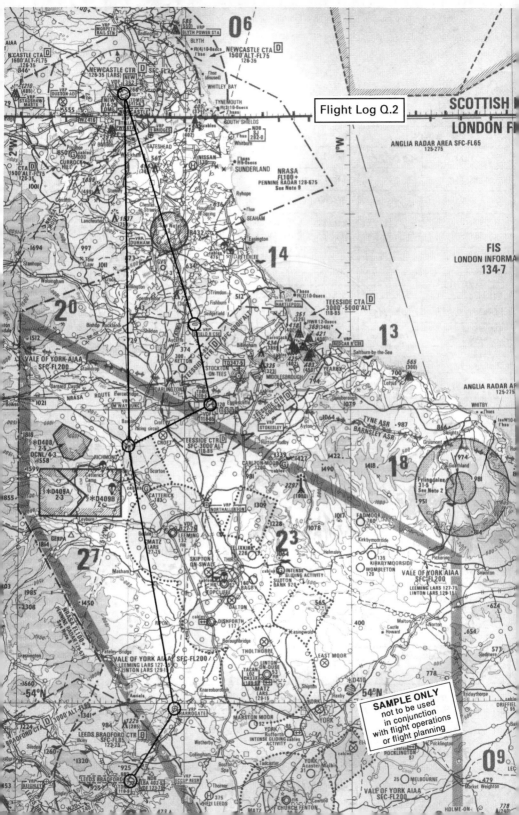

Flight Log Q.2

2 Flight log for Question 2 *(continued)*

LEEDS — NEWCASTLE

WINDS		RUNWAY							
2000	300/20	QNH							
5000		QFE							
T.A.S.	90	WIND							

STAGE	MSA	TR (T)	HDG (T)	VAR	HDG (M)	DIST	GS	TIME	ETA	ATA
TAKE OFF									→	
SET COURSE									→	
HARROGATE	1500	034	021	4°W	025	9	90	6		
SCOTCH CORNER	1500	349	339	4°W	343	28	76	22		
NEWCASTLE ZONE BDY	2000	358	347	4°W	351	30	78	23		
NEWCASTLE	1500	358	347	4°W	351	6	78	5		
ALTERNATE TEESSIDE	(SEE	NEWCASTLE	— TEESSIDE	SHEET	TIME,	20				
LANDED									→	

LEEMING RADAR 127.75
TEESSIDE TWR 119.8
        APP 118.85
NEWCASTLE TWR 119.7
        APP 126.35

FUEL REQUIRED
Fuel on Board = 98 Lt
Consumption   = 24

	Time	Fuel
Route	56	23
Alternate	20	8
Reserve (45 min)	—	18
TOTAL		49

	TWR	APP	RAD	
LEEDS	120.30	123.75	121.05	**DISTRESS 121.50**

Flight log for Question 2 *(continued)*

NEWCASTLE — TEESSIDE

WINDS			**RUNWAY**								
2000	300/20		QNH								
5000			QFE								
T.A.S.	90		WIND								
STAGE	**MSA**	**TR (T)**	**HDG (T)**	**VAR**	**HDG (M)**	**DIST**	**GS**	**TIME**	**ETA**	**ATA**
TAKE OFF									→	
SET COURSE									→	
VRP SEDGEFIELD	2000	165	174	4°w	178	25	103	15		
TEESSIDE	1500	165	174	4°w	178	8	103	5		
ALTERNATE NEWCASTLE		345	335	4°w	339	33	75	26		
LANDED									→	

NEWCASTLE   TWR 119.7
            APP 126.35
TEESSIDE   TWR 119.8
            APP 118.85

FUEL REQUIRED
Fuel on Board =
Consumption   = .24

	Time	Fuel
Route	20	8
Alternate	26	11
Reserve (45 min)	–	18
TOTAL		37

	TWR	APP	RAD	
LEEDS	120.30	123.75	121.05	**DISTRESS 121.50**

Flight log for Question 2 *(continued)*

TEESSIDE — LEEDS

WINDS		RUNWAY							
2000	300/20	QNH							
5000		QFE							
T.A.S.	90	WIND							

STAGE	MSA	TR (T)	HDG (T)	VAR	HDG (M)	DIST	GS	TIME	ETA	ATA
TAKE OFF								→		
SET COURSE								→		
SCOTCH CORNER	1500	244	254	4°w	258	10	77	8		
VRP HARROGATE	1500	169	179	4°w	183	28	101	17		
LEEDS	1500	214	227	4°w	231	9	86	6		
ALTERNATE SHERBURN		108	106	4°w	110	16	109	10		
LANDED								→		

TEESSIDE TWR 119.8
             APP 118.85

LEEMING RADAR 127.75

SHERBURN 122.6

FUEL REQUIRED
Fuel on Board =
Consumption = 24

	Time	Fuel
Route	31	13
Alternate	10	4
Reserve (45 min)	−	18
TOTAL		35

	TWR	APP	RAD	
LEEDS	120.30	123.75	121.05	**DISTRESS 121.50**

3 Flight log:

From/To	Safety ALT	ALT / Temp	RAS	TAS	W/V	TR °T	Drift	HDG °T	Var	HDG °M	GS	Dist	Time	ETA	HDG °C
Staverton															
	2770	3000 +12	90	95	250/20	056	−3	053	4°W	057	114	59	31		
Desborough															
	2070	FL35 +11	90	96	250/20	161	+12	173	4°W	177	93	24	16		
Cranfield															
	2570	FL40 +10	90	96	260/25	231	+7	238	3°W	241	73	27	22		
Beckley															
	2570	FL45 +10	90	97	260/25	299	−9	290	4°W	294	76	6	5		
Kidlington															
	2690	FL45 +10	90	97	260/25	276	−4	272	4°W	276	72	31	26		
Staverton															

Consumption rate 8 USG/hr — **Total 147 100**

	min	US gal
Destination	69	9.2
Alternate	–	–
Flight fuel	69	9.2
Reserve	60	8.0
Taxi	–	–
Fuel required	129	17.2
Margin	36	4.8
Total fuel	165	22.0

4 (i) 20 USG (ii) 127 minutes (iii) 250 minutes (iv) 195 minutes (v) no

5 (i) 14 USG (ii) 85 minutes (iii) 249 minutes (iv) 194 minutes (v) yes

6

	min	US gal
Destination	120	13
Alternate	–	–
Flight fuel	120	13
Reserve	45	5
Taxi	–	–
Fuel required	165	18
Margin	166	18
Total fuel	331	36

7

	min	US gal
Destination	65	7
Alternate	–	–
Flight fuel	65	7
Reserve	45	5
Taxi	–	–
Fuel required	110	12
Margin	221	24
Total fuel	331	36

8 (i) 14 USG (ii) 98 minutes
(iii) 218 minutes

	min	US gal
Destination	53	7
Alternate	–	–
Flight fuel	53	7
Reserve	45	6
Taxi	–	1
Fuel required	98	14
Margin	120	16
Total fuel	218	30

9

	min	US gal
Destination	53	7
Alternate	20	2.7
Flight fuel	73	10
Reserve	45	6
Taxi	–	1
Fuel required	118	17
Margin	98	13
Total fuel	216	30

10

	min	US gal
Destination	53	7
Alternate	35	4.7
Flight fuel	88	12
Reserve	45	6
Taxi	–	1
Fuel required	133	19
Margin	82	11
Total fuel	215	30

Answers 14 **The Flight Plan**

1

FLIGHT PLAN   ATS COPY

PRIORITY   ADDRESSEE(S)

<< ≡ FF →

     << ≡

FILING TIME   ORIGINATOR

→   << ≡

SPECIFIC IDENTIFICATION ADDRESSEE(S) AND/OR ORIGINATOR

---

3 MESSAGE TYPE   7 AIRCRAFT IDENTIFICATION   8 FLIGHT RULES   TYPE OF FLIGHT

<< ≡ (FPL   − G,B,C,D,E,   − V   G << ≡

9 NUMBER   TYPE OF AIRCRAFT   WAKE TURBULENCE CAT.   10 EQUIPMENT

−   C,1,7,2   / L   − S /A << ≡

13 DEPARTURE AERODROME   TIME

− E,G,F,F   1,1,2,0 << ≡

15 CRUISING SPEED   LEVEL   ROUTE

− N,0,1,2,0   A,0,2,5, → DTY GAM

     << ≡

TOTAL EET

16 DESTINATION AERODROME   HR MIN   ALTN AERODROME   2ND ALTN AERODROME

− E,G,N,J   0,2,3,0   → E,G,C,S   →   << ≡

18 OTHER INFORMATION

− 0

) << ≡

SUPPLEMENTARY INFORMATION (NOT TO BE TRANSMITTED IN FPL MESSAGES)

19 ENDURANCE   EMERGENCY RADIO

HR MIN   PERSONS ON BOARD   UHF   VHF   ELBA

−E/ 0,3,4,5   → P/ 0,0,3   → R/ ☒ ☒ ☒

SURVIVAL EQUIPMENT   POLAR   DESERT   MARITIME   JUNGLE   JACKETS   LIGHT   FLUORES   UHF   VHF

→ ☒ / ☒   ☒   ☒   ☒   → ☒ / ☒   ☒   ☒   ☒

DINGHIES

NUMBER   CAPACITY   COVER   COLOUR

→ ☒ /   →   → ☒ →   << ≡

AIRCRAFT COLOUR AND MARKINGS

A/ BLUE & WHITE

REMARKS

→ ☒ /   << ≡

PILOT IN COMMAND

C/ B. McINNES   ) << ≡

FILED BY

SPACE RESERVED FOR ADDITIONAL REQUIREMENTS

En Route Navigation

Answers 15

En Route Navigation Techniques

En Route Nav Techniques-1
1 drift
2 track error
3 fix or pinpoint
4 circle
5 triangle
6 flying accurate headings and identifying landmarks
7 108 kt

En Route Nav Techniques-2
1 9° right
2 10° right
3 3° left

En Route Nav Techniques-3
1 (i) 8° left
  (ii) 8°
  (iii) 4°
2 TE = 12°, CA = 6°, so change heading by 18° left
3 (i) 13° left
  (ii) 16° left
  (iii) 14° left
  (see diagrams below)

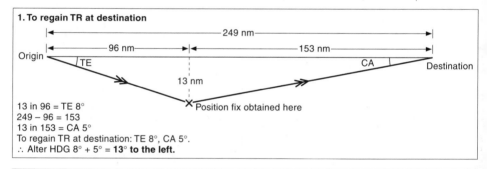

1. To regain TR at destination

13 in 96 = TE 8°
249 − 96 = 153
13 in 153 = CA 5°
To regain TR at destination: TE 8°, CA 5°.
∴ Alter HDG 8° + 5° = **13° to the left.**

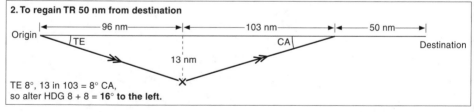

2. To regain TR 50 nm from destination

TE 8°, 13 in 103 = 8° CA,
so alter HDG 8 + 8 = **16° to the left.**

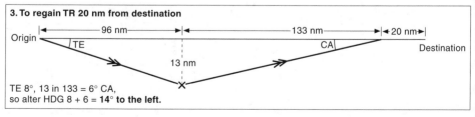

3. To regain TR 20 nm from destination

TE 8°, 13 in 133 = 6° CA,
so alter HDG 8 + 6 = **14° to the left.**

4   TE = 3 in 20 = 9° left
    We assume that in the following 10
    minutes you will travel the same distance as
    in the previous 10 minutes, i.e. 20 nm;
    therefore CA = 3 in 20 = 9°. Alter HDG
    by 18° to the right, i.e. to HDG 098°M

En Route Nav Techniques-4

1   (i)   TE = 3 in 20 = 9°
    (ii) CA = 8 in 60 = 8°
    (iii) Alter HDG 17° to the right
2   (i)   TE = 6 in 30 = 12°
    (ii) CA = 3 in 15 = 12°
    (iii) Alter HDG by 24° to the left, i.e. to
          HDG 086°M

En Route Nav Techniques-5

1   (i)   TE = 2 in 15 = 8°
    (ii) CA = 2 in 30 = 4°
    (iii) Alter HDG by TE + CA = 12° to the
          right, i.e. to HDG 332°M
    (iv) Remove the CA by turning 4° left
          onto HDG 328°M
2   (i)   TE = 4 in 34 = 7 in 60 = 7°
          (by computer)
    (ii) CA = 4 in 48 = 1 in 12 = 5 in 60 = 5°
    (iii) HDG 281°M
    (iv) HDG 286°M

En Route Nav Techniques-6

1   7 minutes
2   9 minutes
3   410 ft/min
4   18 nm at GS 100 = 11 minutes to descend
    from 6,000 to 2,500 ft amsl, i.e. 3,500 ft in
    11 minutes = 320 ft/min

Answers 16

Navigation in Remote Areas

1   careful pre-flight planning
2   fly accurate headings (HDGs) and keep an
    in-flight log

Answers 17

Entry/Exit Lanes and Low-Level Routes

1   are
2   Control Zones
3   accurate headings (HDGs) and frequent
    visual fixes
4   position yourself over a landmark, and
    check that the heading indicator is aligned
    with the magnetic compass

En Route Navigation with Radio Navaids

Answers 19

Radar

1 vectoring
2 (b) procedural separation
3 transponder
4 surveillance radar approach
5 300 ft/min
6 450 ft/min
7 1,800 m
8 600 ft aal
9 95 nm
10 55 nm
11 61 nm
12 UK AIP ENR 1-6-2-1

Answers 20

DME

1 distance-measuring equipment
2 (c) slant distance
3 VHF-NAV
4 10 nm in 5 min = GS 120 kt
5 10 nm in 7 min = GS 86 kt
6 14 nm
7 (a) circular position line

Answers 21

The NDB and the ADF

1 non-directional beacon
2 ground-based transmitter
3 low frequency or medium frequency bands (LF/MF)
4 automatic direction finding
5 airborne receiver
6 its Morse code ident
7 "dah-dit-dit-dit dit-dah-dah-dit dit-dah-dit-dit"
8 Select the ADF frequency, identify the NDB or locator, and check that the needle is indeed 'ADFing'.
9 magnetic bearing to the ground station
10 magnetic bearing from the ground station
11 relative bearing indicator

12 (i) QDM 280°M (ii) QDR 100°M
13 (i) QDM 240°M (ii) QDR 060°M
14 25 nm
15 locator
16 LOM (locator outer marker)
17 may
18 may
19 ±5°
20 refer to a CAA 1:500,000 chart

Answers 22

The Relative Bearing Indicator (RBI)

1 (i) QDM 075, (ii) QDR 255, (iii) QTE 251
2 (i) QDM 330, (ii) QDR 150, (iii) QTE 146
3 right turn onto MH 130, RBI 270
4 right turn onto MH 100, RBI 300
5 right
6 left
7 right
8 060°M
9 right
10 MH 345, RBI 355
11 MH 128, RBI 172
12 MH 360, RBI 090
13 MH 010, RBI 080
14 MH 030, RBI 090
15 030°M, RBI 270
16 MH 037, RBI 263
17 RBI 084
18 RBI 264
19 RBI 275

Answers 23

The Radio Magnetic Indicator (RMI)

1 (i) QDM 075, (ii) QDR 255, (iii) QTE 251
2 (i) QDM 330, (ii) QDR 150, (iii) QTE 146
3 right turn onto MH 130, RMI 040
4 right turn onto MH 100, RMI 040
5 right, RMI 075
6 left, RMI 320, RMI tail on 140
7 left, RMI 270, RMI tail on 090
8 060°M

9   right
10 MH 345, RMI 340
11 MH 128, RMI 300, RMI tail 120
12 MH 360, RMI 090
13 MH 010, RMI 090
14 MH 030, RMI 120
15 030°M, RMI 300
16 MH 037, RMI 300
17 RMI 149

Answers 24

The VOR

1   VHF
2   DME
3   67 nm
4   a radial is a magnetic bearing *from* a VOR ground station
5   QDR
6   MH 070
7   MH 230
8   Morse code ident
9   ±2° accuracy
10 VHF omni-directional radio range
11 VHF-NAV
12 course deviation indicator
13 omni bearing selector, omni bearing indicator
14 2°
15 4°
16 6°
17 8°
18 10° or more
19 090 radial
20 270 radial
21 274 radial (094-TO)
22 092 radial
23 CFD, 116.5 Mhz *"dah-dit-dah-dit dit-dit-dah-dit dah-dit-dit"*
24 CDF 070 radial
25 NEW, 114.25 Mhz, *"dah-dit- dit dit-dah-dah"*
26 258 NEW radial
27 078 DCS radial
28 outbound from DCS on the 078 DCS radial, and inbound to NEW on the 258 NEW radial

29 (i) using the DCS VOR/DME combination to provide a radial and a distance;
(ii) using NEW VOR/DME;
(iii) using one of the VORs and an abeam position off the Carlisle NDB
30 22 nm in 11 min = GS 120, 38 nm will take 19 min, ETA 1457
31 DOC 60 nm/50,000 ft; 100 nm in the sector 270°–360°T (UK AIP ENR 4-1)
32 desired track is out to the right
33 desired track is out to the left
34 no, the VOR cockpit display is not heading sensitive.
35 (i) aircraft B (ii) aircraft B (iii) aircraft D

Answers 25

VHF Direction Finding (VDF)

1   VHF direction finding
2   VHF D/F
3   VHF-COM
4   magnetic bearing to the station
5   magnetic bearing from the station
6   ±5°
7   should
8   left of track, turn right
9   right of track, turn left
10 right of track, turn left
11 left of track, turn right
12 In a VDF approach, the pilot initiates his own heading corrections based on the QDMs given to him, and initiates his own descent. In a QGH approach, ATC gives the pilot heading and descent instructions.

Answers 26

Introduction to RNAV and GPS

1   phantom
2   anywhere within signal coverage
3   vector
4   crosstrack error
5   waypoints
6   hyperbolic
7   may
8   may
9   three

Index